Surfin' the Internet:
Practical Ideas from A to Z

Written by
Annette Lamb
Nancy Smith
Larry Johnson

Dedicated to

Family Internet Surfing Teams Everywhere

Edited by Annette Lamb, Nancy Smith, Larry Johnson, and William L. Smith.

First Printing: June 1996

Copyright © 1996 by Annette Lamb.

All rights reserved. No part of this book may be reproduced or transmitted in any form or by any means now known or to be invented, electronic or mechanical, including photocopying, recording, or by any information storage or retrieval system without written permission from the authors or publisher, except for the brief inclusion of quotations in a review.

Permission is given for individual classroom teachers, computer coordinators, and library/media specialists to reproduce pages for classroom use. Contact the publisher for other types of copyright permissions.

The information and resources contained in this book are true, complete, and accurate to the best of our knowledge. All recommendations and suggestions are made without any guarantees on the part of the author or publishing company.

Printed in the United States of America.

ISBN 0-9641581-2-4

For additional information or to place an order:

    Vision to Action
    10732 E. Sunset Drive
    Evansville, Indiana 47712

Table of Contents

Preface iii

Section 1: Findin' the Beach: Introductory Activities 1
    Silly Surfin' Sites 5
    Lists of Lists 12
    Collections Capers 14
    Sports Shorts 20
    Pen Pals: First Steps 24
    Kids On the Web 34
    Show & Tell 37
    Clip Art Fun 42
    Animal Antics 44
    Zany Zoos 51
    Pets 54
    Dinosaur Expo 56
    My Favorite Thing 59

Section 2: Lookin' for Waves: Information Exploration Ideas 63
Part 1: Information Process 67
Part 2: Social Issues Topics 93

Section 3: Ridin' the Surf: Subject Area Activities 115
The Arts 118
Mathematics 129
Science 132
Social Studies 167
Literacy 206
Health and Fitness 229

Section 4: Hangin' Ten: Interdisciplinary Thematic Units 235
Our Global Community 237
Our Environment 261
Exploration and Development 278
Imagine, Investigate, Invent 295

References 305

Index 307

Acknowledgements

We would like to thank the following people for their contributions:

Web developers everywhere who have created a whole new world for educators over the past couple years. Web names and URLs are provided with each example.

Preface

I know how to use the Internet, now what do I do with it in my classroom?

It seems like all my Internet activities take forever, I need some ideas for simple projects.

I'd really like to integrate Internet rather than use it as a "extra" in the classroom.

These are typical responses by teachers who have started using Internet in the classroom. On the surface, it seems like a fun, easy technology to use. However, like all technologies it requires carefully planned learning environments to be effective. This book will help you design practical classroom activities that make use of the communication and informational resources of the Internet. Rather than focusing on "how to use" Internet, we'll be focusing on "how to integrate" Internet. If you need basic skills in using the Internet, try our book titled **Cruisin' the Information Highway: Internet in the K-12 Classroom.**

Overview of the Book

Practical ideas are the key words for this book. *Practical* is the most important key because you can use the materials in your classroom today if you have access to the Internet. *Ideas* is the second key because the book provides suggestions. You need to fit the ideas into activities that will work with your individual classroom, grade level, content area, and students.

The book is sequenced to provide increasingly complex, integrated activities. Start with projects from the first section to get your students involved with Internet before jumping into a full-blow project.

Findin' the Beach. The first section will help you and your students "find the beach." It will give students an opportunity to explore a variety of information resources in popular topic areas and try some simple email activities. These activities could be linked to almost any academic area. We suggest that you focus on literacy activities that involve reading, analyzing, interpreting, and communicating ideas and information.

Lookin' for Information Waves. After becoming comfortable with the tools of Internet, students will begin looking for waves of information in section two. They'll explore specific health, nutrition, science, or social issues of interest. Again, these activities can easily cross content areas. This chapter will ask students to identify and answer research questions and use Internet resources along with other materials to address important issues, problems, and questions.

Ridin' the Surf. The third section of the book focuses on subject area activities. Students begin riding the waves of technology by integrating Internet into the traditional content area projects from Art to Zoology.

Hangin' Ten. Interdisciplinary thematic units are highlighted in the final section. Rather than emphasizing a particular subject area, broad areas of interest that cross disciplines will provide the basis for a variety of activities. We'll focus on providing learning environments to meet the multiple intelligences of your students.

Words to the Wise

This is a "doing" book, not a "reading" book. Some activities will fit with your needs, while others will not. Pick those activities and projects that meet the needs of your individual students and class. Use the following guidelines as you work through the book.

Use a variety of resources. In addition to Internet, you'll also want to use other traditional and emerging technologies including fiction and nonfiction books, maps, globes, filmstrips, videos, CD-ROMs, laserdiscs, and other informational and instructional materials. We've provided a short list of selected materials with each activity. These are not intended to be the "best" resources, but ones we've found useful in working with the subject area. You'll want to expand the list for your particular group of students.

Preface

This book is for all ages. Although we've provided age or grade level guidance on some of the supplemental materials, as a whole we avoid the age issue. Most of the activities can be revised for use with any grade level. You'll find that most of the resources on the Internet are written at the middle school reading level or above. However much of the general information, pictures, and graphics can be used at all levels. In addition, you may wish to direct student attention to particular areas of a document that are easy to understand.

Internet changes constantly. Each activity provides sample Internet addresses. We've tried to provide popular sites that contain links to other examples. These represent only a few of the many sites available. The resources we've listed may or may not be available when you try them in your classroom. The addresses may have changed or may be gone entirely. Many times when an Internet address is changed, you'll see a "forwarding" page that will take you to the updated address. If the address doesn't work at all, it may be that particular pages in the site have been renamed. In this case, you may still be able to get to the site by removing part of the address. For example, if the following address doesn't work (http://magic.usi.edu/treehouse/intro.html), then try (http://magic.usi.edu/treehouse) or just (http://magic.usi.edu).

In some activities, we've provided "search words" in case the sites we've identified don't work. Try the suggested words in one of the many Internet search tools such as **InfoSeek** or **WebCrawler** to create your own list of Internet sites. Use these sites and words to demonstrate how to use Internet for the particular activity. Encourage students to explore other sites and add them to the class resource list.

Do it yourself. Before assigning any of the activities in this book, you'll want to check them yourself. Internet sites change frequently. In developing the hands-on activities that relate to specific sites, we've tried to create generic assignments that will work even if the site has been updated. As such, we haven't included any "answer" because in most cases the results will vary from student to student. You need to work with the sites and develop a means of evaluating student assignments based on the needs of your classroom.

Another reason for checking the sites relates to age appropriateness. Some materials may be inappropriate for your particular class. Although you can't preview everything, at least check the main links for the site you'll be using. You may find that some of the "fun" sites contain inappropriate language or terminology. You never know what "Beavis and Butthead" might say. You'll have to be the judge of whether to integrate a particular site or not.

Get help. You can't be everywhere at once! Many adults are interested in learning about the Internet. Get parent or community volunteers to work with your students. Develop collaborations across grade levels. Many of the Internet resources contain content that may be above the reading level of primary students, but just right for older students. Try the each one teach one approach. In other words, work with a small group of children and let these students teach to others in the class.

You can also use Internet resources for support. For example, use the bookmark feature of Netscape to organize bookmarks for each unit. You could create a bookmark folder for each content area or unit topic. You could also place Internet addresses and activities on laminated notecards.

Consider creating your own home page containing links to specific sites. Or, access our home page at one of the following two addresses. We'll be updating addresses and adding activities.

http://alamb.usi.edu
http://magic.usi.edu

Let's Get Surfin'!

This book will only scratch the surface when it comes to the uses for Internet resources in your classroom. Think of the project ideas as stepping stones for getting started with Internet. Often the hardest part of using a new technology is "getting started." We've provided some resources that will help you design both small and large scale projects that integrate Internet into your active learning environment.

We hope you enjoy using this book as much as we have identifying the resources. Happy surfin'!

Annette Lamb, Nancy Smith, and Larry Johnson
Spring, 1996

Section 1

Findin' the Beach
Introductory Activities

I want to get beyond "pen pals" with email. Where do I go next?

How can I blend fun activities with Internet sites that will still be relevant in my classroom?

I want to start with something fun, what's a good beginning project?

We've found that new technologies require "playtime." Rather than jumping into a heavy project such as a social issues assignment or science experiment, we suggest that you begin with a series of lighter activities that will help students get the hang of the technology without worrying about new, complex content. As a result, we've designed a series of projects centering on popular topics such as hobbies, sports, authors, movies, and animals.

Don't think of these beginning activities are "low-level" thinking activities. Encourage students to apply the information they locate. Try to think of creative and motivating ways to involve students with the Internet. If you have difficulty developing specific objectives for Internet projects, consider the verbs on the next page. These words can sometimes expand your thinking about student outcomes (see Figure 1-1). In addition, it's easy to get bogged down in traditional paper and pencil products. Rather than activities that involve copying paragraphs or printing articles move toward more creative projects that require students to apply the information in new and exciting ways. Students could create a poster, debate a topic, write a story, or formulate a solution to a problem (see Figure 1-2).

This section examines a topic, then provides sample activity sheets. If you don't find an activity sheet at your grade level interest, try some of the suggested Web sites and create your own! The Topics and Activity Pages for this section are listed in Figure 1-3.

Action Words for Objectives

add	demonstrate	justify	remove
alphabetize	derive	label	reorganize
analyze	describe	list	restate
animate	design	locate	retell-in-
apply	designate	make	your-own-
appraise	determine	manipulate	words
arrange	develop	match	revise
assemble	diagnose	measure	rewrite
brainstorm	diagram	memorize	select
browse	differentiate	modify	share
build	discuss	multiply	show
carve	dissect	name	sketch
categorize	distinguish	operate	solve
choose	document	order	sort
classify	draw	organize	speak
cluster	estimate	outline	specify
color	evaluate	paint	spell
compare	examine	paraphrase	square
compile	explain	plan	state
complete	explore	plot	subtract
compose	extrapolate	position	suggest
compute	find out	predict	summarize
conclude	fit	prepare	support
conduct	formulate	present	swing
connect	generate	pretend	synthesize
construct	give-an-example	prioritize	tabulate
contrast	graph	produce	tell
convert	hit	pronounce	throw
correct	hold	put-in-order	time
create	identify	rank	trace
cut	illustrate	rate	translate
debate	indicate	read	type
decide	infer	rearrange	use
deduce	install	recall	verbalize
deduct	interpret	reconstruct	verify
defend	invent	reduce	weigh
define	judge	relate	write

Figure 1-1. Action words for objectives.

Findin' the Beach: Introductory Activities

Sample Student Products

Action Plan	Invention	Radio Show
Advertising Campaign	Invitation	Recipe
Animation	Graphs	Research Paper
Anecdotes	Graphic	Riddle
Articles	Greeting Card	Role Playing
Bibliography	Jigsaw Puzzle	Rubbings
Board Game	Journal	Samples
Book	Letter	Scavenger Hunt
Brochure	Light Show	Scrapbook
Bumper Sticker	Limerick	Sculpture
Card Game	Magazine	Seek & Find
Cassette Recording	Map	Simulation
Chart	Mini-Center	Short Story
Collage	Mobiles	Skit
Collection	Models	Slide Show
Comic/Cartoon	Multimedia	Songs
Contest	Mural	Specimens
Costume	Museum Exhibit	Spread sheets
Cubes	Musical Composition	Surveys
Dance	Musical Instrument	Tape Recordings
Database	Newscast	Terrarium
Debate	Newsletter	Time line
Demonstration	Newspaper	Tour
Diagram	Oral Report	Transparencies
Diary	Pamphlet	Travel Poster
Dictionary	Panel Discussion	Travelogue
Diorama	Paper folding	Television Show
Display	Patterns	Word Processing
Documentary	Photos	Word Search
Essay	Play	Video
Experiment	Poem	
Flowchart	Portfolio	
Futuristic model	Posters	
Hidden picture	Presentation	
Illustration	Puppets Quilt	
Interview	Quiz Bowl	

Figure 1-2. Sample Student Activities

Findin' The Beach Topics and Activities

Silly Surfin' Sites
    Mr. Edible Starchy Tuber Head
    Bureau of Missing Socks
    Laugh Link Page
    Wacky Tales

Lists of Lists
    Kathy Schrock's Site

Collections Capers
    Warner Brothers Collectibles
    Plastic Princess Site
    Hobby News
    The All Magic Guide

Sports Shorts
    ESPNET SportZone
    Mountain Biking Site

Pen Pals: First Steps
    CyberKids Interactive
    KidsCom
    International Kid Space
    Net Contacts
    Intercultural Email Classroom
        Connections

Kids On the Web

Show & Tell
    Online Magazines for Students
    KidNews
    International Kids Space
    Global Show-n-Tell Museum

Clip Art Fun
    Clip Art Server

Animal Antics
    World Wide Raccoon Web
    Net Full of Animals
    Birds
    World Center for Birds of Prey

Zany Zoos
    ZooNet Links!
    Sea World!

Pets
    CyberPet Web!

Dinosaur Expo
    The Dinosaur Expo!

My Favorite Thing
    Internet Movie Database!
    Future Place Site!

Figure 1-3. List of Topics and Activities.

Findin' the Beach: Introductory Activities

Silly Surfin' Sites

Do you ever just feel like goofing off? Let's have some fun. There are many sites that will lead you to silly sites that will let you color pictures, do a puzzle, play a game, create a riddle, or make a Mr. Potatohead. The Surfer Starters below contain lots of silly links.

Surfer Starters
Fun and Games
   http://www.weblust.com/NS/BuildPadPage/Fun_Games
Spider's Picks
   http://gagme.wwa.com/~boba/pick.html
Classroom Connect's Fun Links
   http://www.wentworth.com/classroom/fun.htm
Useless Pages
   http://www.primus.com/staff/paulp/useless.html

To get started, you may want to explore some simple activities. Most of the sites listed are intended for elementary and middle school age children. Students can play games, create puzzles, read stories, or develop projects. You may wish to create a chart featuring the areas that students have explored or completed.

Surfer Starters
ABC Educational Games
   http://www.klsc.com/children/
Aha
   http://www.aha-kids.com/
Bright Ideas
   http://intranet.on.ca:80/~dlemire/sb_kids.html
Carlos' Coloring Page
   http://www.ravenna.com/coloring/
Crayola Site
   http://www.crayola.com/crayola/home.html
CyberKids
   http://www.woodwind.com:80/cyberkids/
CyberSeas Treasure Hunt
   http://www.cyberjacques.com/
Flags
   http://www.adfa.oz.au/CS/flg/col/index.html

http://www.crayola.com/crayola/home.html

Fun and Games
   http://www.nova.edu/Inter-Links/fun_games.html
Holidays
   http://www.capecod.net/Wixon/holidays.htm
I Spy
   http://www.lexmark.com/data/spy/spy.html
International Kids Space
   http://plaza.interport.net/kids_space/
Jackson's Page for Five Year Olds
   http://www2.islandnet.com/~bedford/jackson.html
KidsCom
   http://www.kidscom.com/
Kid's Corner
   http://www.ot.com/kids/
Kid's Crambo Games
   http://www.primenet.com/~hodges/kids_crambo.html
Kid's Net
   http://www.PonyShow.com/KidsNet/website.htm
Lite Brite Online
   http://www.galcit.caltech.edu/~ta/cgi-bin/lb-ta?new+3
Nikolai's Web Site
   http://www.h-plus-a.com/nikolai/
Puppets Page
   http://fox.nstn.ca/~puppets/activity.html
Crossword Puzzles by Grolier
   http://www.grolier.com/crossword/
Splash Kids
   http://www.splash.com/
WWW Spirograph
   http://juniper.tc.cornell.edu:8000/spiro/spiro.html

http://www.lexmark.com/data/spy/spy.html

Wave Words

Fun	Games	Humor
Jokes	Riddles	Puzzles
Coloring	Kids	

Findin' the Beach: Introductory Activities

Powerful Projects

If you were going to add a silly project to the Internet what would it be? Build it in a word processor or graphics package.

Learn to use a silly site and share it with a friend.

Create a silly site based on your silly interests. Visit the Bureau of Missing Socks for ideas.

Adult Alert

You may find some humor that is inappropriate for schools. Let your teacher know.

Super Surfer: Wave Rider File
• •

Put your favorite web activity on a Wave Rider Card.
    What's your name and grade?
    What's the name and URL address of the site?
    What kind of information and activity is found there?
    What age student would like this site?
    How many waves does it get?
    1 = okay   2 = good   3 = cool   4 = the best
    Why do you think it's a good place to surf?
Keep these in a Wave Rider file box and share them with your friends.

Visit the Mr. Edible Starchy Tuber Head!
http://winnie.acsu.buffalo.edu/potatoe/

Explore the Mr. Edible Starchy Tuber Head and try the following activities. Use the words in bold to help you find the information you need for each activity.

Start by playing Mr. Edible Starchy Tuber Head game. What did you think of the game? Is playing the computer game as much fun as using the real Mr. Potatohead? Why or why not? What would make the computer game more fun?

Did you know that Mr. Potatohead has gone **Hollywood**? Explore **The Toy Story** site to learn more about his role in the film. Who played the voice of Mr. Potatohead? When and where was Mr. Potatohead born? When was Baby Potatohead born? Create a timeline of important Potatohead information. Watch and listen to the animated examples from the movie. Which are your favorites? Why?

Explore the other examples of Mr. Potatohead in movies and on television. These were made up by the author. Create your own silly Mr. Potatohead appearance. Draw a picture of Mr. Potatohead on a TV show that you watch or in a book you've read.

Compare the Mr. Edible Starchy Tuber Head game with **Chris Rywalt's game**. Which do you like better? Why?

Create your own Mr. Potatohead with a real potato.

Invent a toy based on another vegetable. What would it look like and act like? What would it be called? Do you think people would buy it? Why or why not? Write a short song to go with your new character.

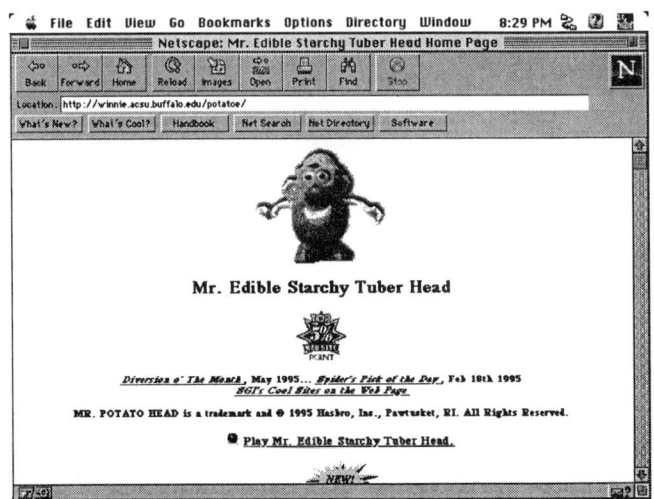

Findin' the Beach: Introductory Activities

Visit the Bureau of Missing Socks!
http://www.jagat.com/joel/socks.html

Explore the Bureau of Missing Socks and try the following activities. Use the words in bold to help you find the information you need for each activity.

Create a silly sock advertisement to add to their **commercial page.**

News! News! News! Write a funny news story for the SOCK NEWS section. Remember to include the Who, What, When, Where, Why, and Hows of the story.

Which of the **historical or weird socks** do you think is the silliest? Can you do any better? Scan or draw a picture of a sock and write a silly historical account to go with it. Who wore it? When? Why? What is its historical significance? Use actual information about an important historical figure. If your account is "historical" or "hysterical" enough, it might get into the Smithsonian Museum or at least the Bureau of Missing Socks site. Be sure to include the name, value, and location along with the story.

Fill out the sock **survey**, just for fun!

Are you interested in becoming a **Sock Investigator**? Don't forget to complete the careers section. Write a resume and job application letter that might be used by a sock investigator.

What do you think happens to socks that get lost in the laundry? This web site provides lots of ideas, but I bet you can think of a different story. Send it to the web master and see if he'll add it to his page!

Visit the Laugh Link Page!
http://longwood.cs.ucf.edu:80/~MidLink/laughlink.home.html

Explore the Laugh Link Page!

Read the jokes and riddles.
Write your own riddle and send it in.

Other Fun Things To Do:

Write a joke or riddle that relates to something you're doing in science, math, or social studies.

Read a book that contains lots of jokes and riddles. Choose your top three. Make a class joke book and vote on the top three jokes in the room. Send your top three to Laugh Link along with some drawings.

What makes a joke funny? Create a list of things to include in a good joke. Write a paragraph about the steps involved with creating a humorous joke or riddle.

Some jokes and riddles are funny and some are just cruel and mean. Can you think of types of jokes that are not funny? For example, they might make fun of a particular type of person.

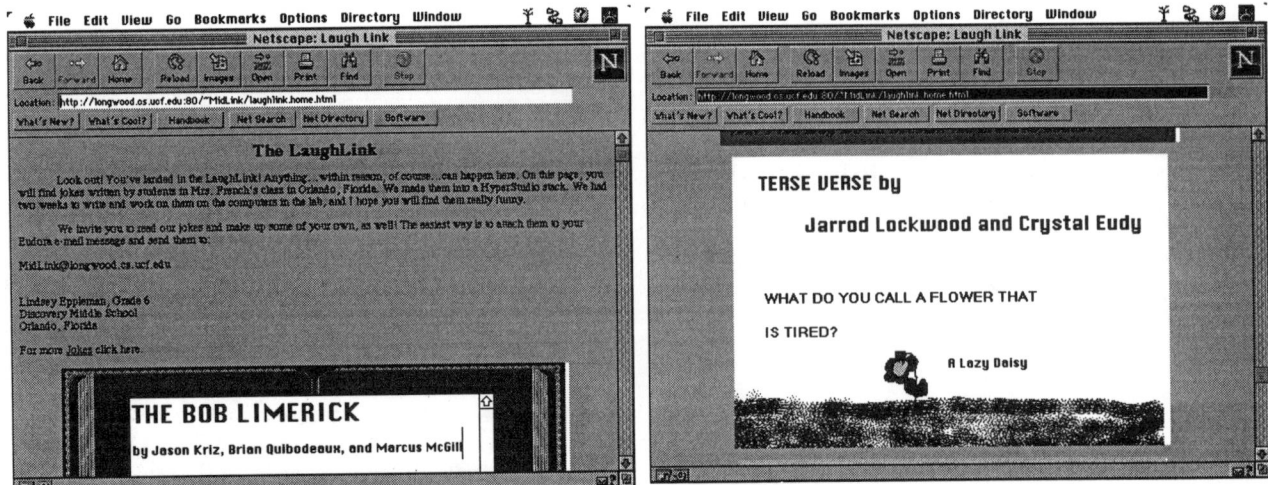

http://longwood.cs.ucf.edu:80/~MidLink/laughlink.home.html

Findin' the Beach: Introductory Activities

Visit the Wacky Web Tales Site!
http://www.hmco.com/hmco/school/tales/

Explore the Wacky Web Tales Site!

Choose your favorite story title.
Review the parts of speech you need and enter your words.
Ask a teacher to check your words.
Create the story.
Print out the story and draw a picture to go with the story.
Post your story on the Wacky Tales Bulletin Board!

Other Fun Things To Do:

Try the same story again. Make the story totally different by just changing the words.

Create an empty story in a word processor and submit it to the Wacky Tales Site. Ask a classmate to list words that might fit the empty spaces and add them to your story.

Create a wacky picture with empty spaces for someone to fill in.

Write a wacky report with some important facts missing. Ask a friend to see if they can find the missing facts!

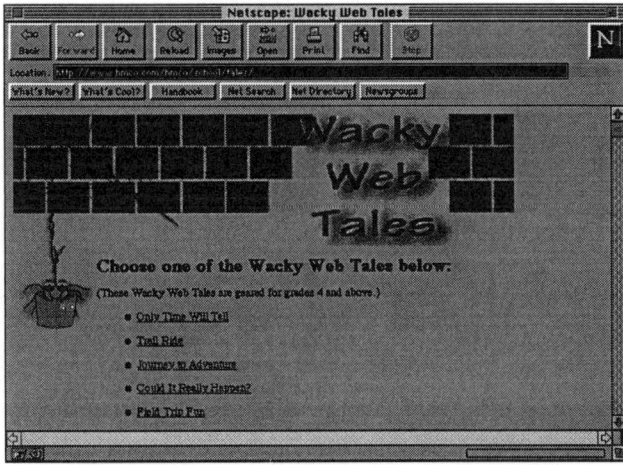
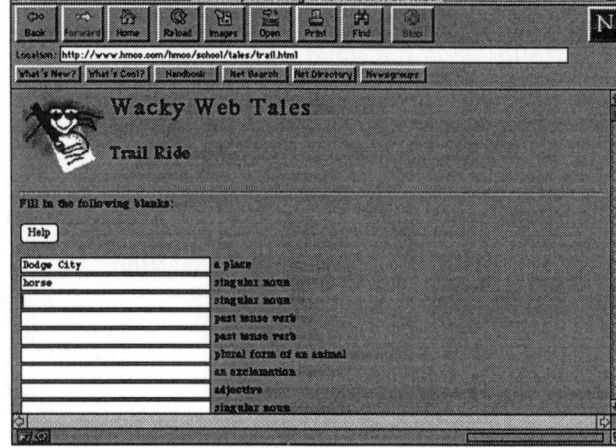

http://www.hmco.com/hmco/school/tales/

Lists of Lists

One of the easiest ways to start exploring Internet is through finding a really good list of lists. In other words, you need to find some places that contain links to things of interest to you. A really good list can have endless possibilities for projects. Explore some K-12 lists of lists. Then brainstorm a list of places you'd like to visit.

Surfer Starters
Canadian SchoolNet
   http://schoolnet2.carleton.ca/
Family Surfboard
   http://www.familysurf.com/
HomeWork Page
   http://www.tpoint.net/Users/jewels//homework.html
Kathy Schrock's
   http://www.capecod.net/Wixon/wixon.htm
Kidscom
   http://www.spectracom.com/kidscom/index1.html?
Kid's Page
   http://nucleus.com/kids.html
KidsWeb
   http://www.npac.syr.edu/textbook/kidsweb/
Middle School Students & Sites
   http://longwood.cs.ucf.edu:80/~MidLink/surf.hp.html
   http://longwood.cs.ucf.edu:80/~MidLink/web.sites.html
Schoolhouse Project
   http://www.nwrel.org/school_house/
Tessa's Cool Links for Kids
   http://www2.islandnet.com/~bedford/tessa.html
The Kids on the Web
   http://www.zen.org/~brendan/kids.html
Uncle Bob's Kid's Page
   http://miso.wwa.com/~boba/kidsi.html
Yahooligans
   HTTP://www.yahooligans.com

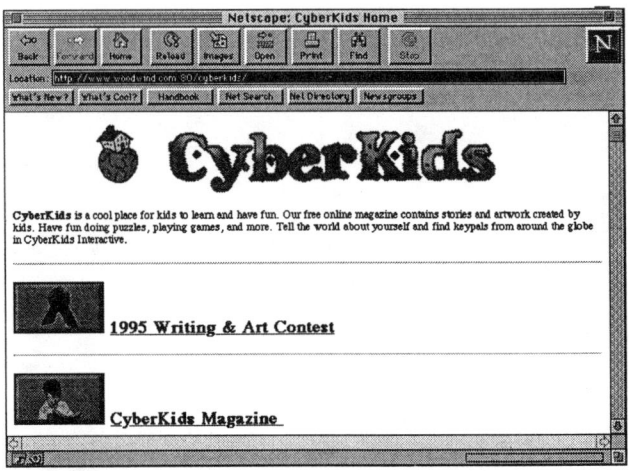

http://www.woodwind.com:80/cyberkids/

Visit Kathy Schrock's Site!
http://www.capecod.net/Wixon/wixon.htm

Explore Kathy Schrock's Guide for Educators! She has lots of ideas for exploring the Internet.

Kathy Schrock changes her red school house depending on the time of year. The picture below was taken in the Spring. What does Kathy have on the door today? Why? If you were going to create your own web page, what kind of introduction picture would you use? Why?

Start by using one of the **Search Tools** to search for information on a topic you'd like to study. Use one of the following search tools: AltaVista, Inktomi, Excite, Lycos Infoseek, WebCrawler

Choose a site from the **Kids' Stuff** section. Did Kathy do a good job selecting fun sites for kids? As a class, rate each site and email Kathy your reviews.

Find a math activity in the **Mathematics** section.

Explore the **Newspapers & Magazines** section. Read about a current event. Write a news story for your class newspaper.

Explore the **Entertainment & Travel** section. Pick an event or place you'd like to visit. Why is this important to you? What time of year would you be going? Why? Do you think anyone else in the class would like to go with you? Create a poster advertising your event or place.

Select the **Holidays** Section and find out about a holiday.

Use the **Weather** Section to find out about the current weather in three places in the world. Where would you like to be right now? Why?

Print out the **Critical Evaluation** form for your grade level. Select and evaluate a site using this form.

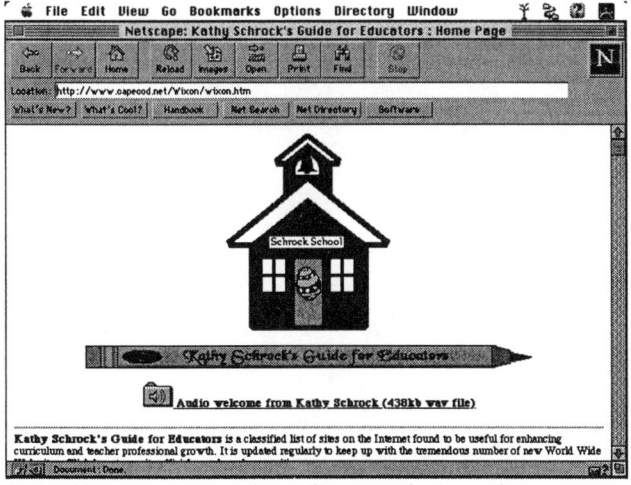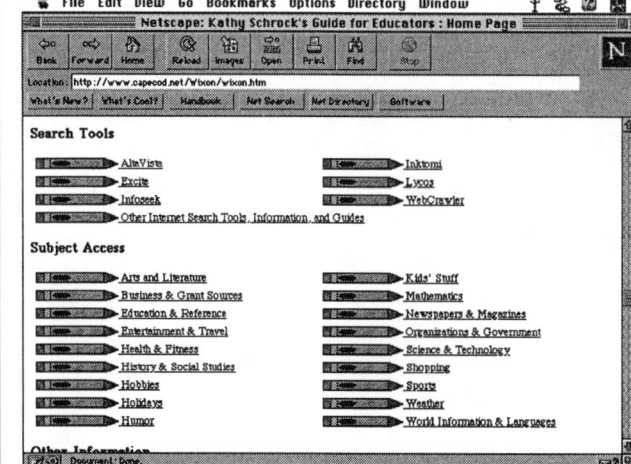

http://www.capecod.net/Wixon/wixon.htm

Collections Capers

Let's explore collections. You may already have a collection or you might want to start one. A collection is a group of things you've gathered. It could be baseball cards, teddy bears, pencils, or matchbooks. Explore an interest and learn about some of the things people collect.

Surf Starters

Collections
   http://www.wwcd.com/index.html
Muppets
   http://www-leland.stanford.edu/~rosesage/Muppet.html
Baseball Cards
   http://www.wwcd.com/scdealer.htmlc_toons.htmlcards.sites/carvlib.html
   Ford, Jerry (1992) **Grand Slam Collection: Have Fun Collecting Baseball Cards.** Lerner.
   Owens, Thomas S. (1993) **Collecting Baseball Cards.** Millbrook.
Dolls
   http://deeptht.armory.com/~zenugirl/barbie.html
   http://www.cascade.net/dolls/alexander.html
   Young, Robert (1992) **Dolls.** Dillon
Hot Wheels
   http://www.paccon.com/hotwhl/hotwheel.htm
Teddy Bears
   http://www.rhein.de/Mailing-Lists/teddy-bears/
   Young, Robert (1992) **Teddy Bears.** Dillon.
   Bond, Michael (1992) **Michael Bond's Book Of Bears.** Aladdin/Macmillan.

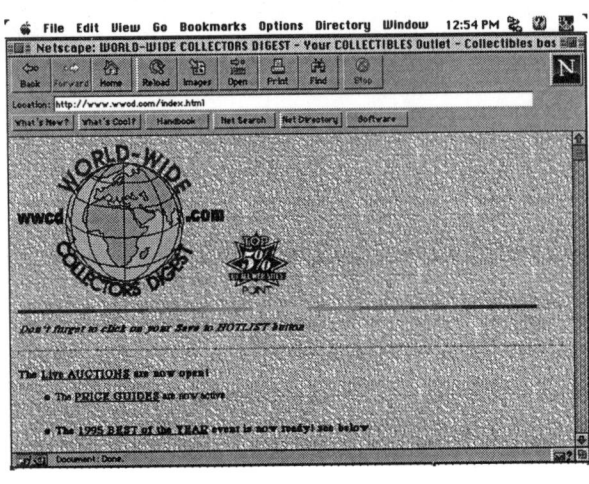

Visit the Warner Brothers Collectibles Web!
http://www.studiostores.warnerbros.com/

Some people like to collect things from particular companies. For example, you might like Disney or Star Trek collectibles. Explore the Warner Brothers site and try the following activities. Use the words in bold to help you find the information you need for each activity.

- You have $500 to spend on yourself. What would you buy? Write down the name of the item and the cost. How much money do you have left?

  If there's a 25% discount, how much would you be spending? How much would you have left? What would you buy with the extra money?

- You have $100 to spend on a member of your family. What will you buy? Why?

- If you were buying something for a person your age who is going to be in the hospital for an extended time, what would you buy? Why? You've got $100 to spend and they will give you a 30% discount on everything you buy.

- What's missing from the Warner Collectibles page? Create a product including a description, colors, sizes, and mottos available, and the price.

- Part of collecting is knowing what will be valuable in the future. Select an item and write about what you think it might be worth in the future and why.

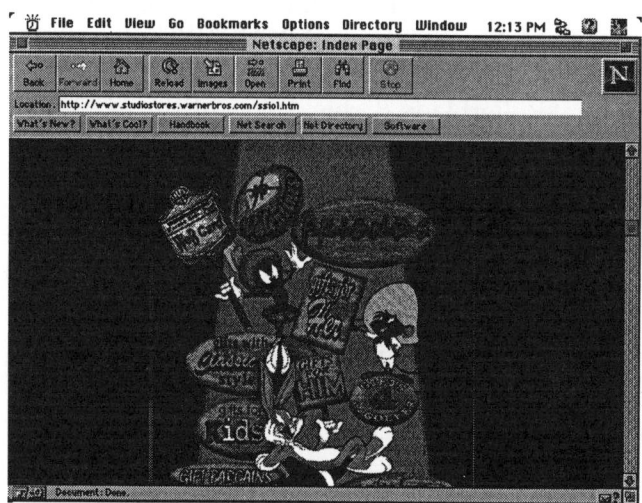

Visit the Plastic Princess Site!
http://deeptht.armory.com/~zenugirl/barbie.html

Explore the Barbie Site and try the following activities. Use the words in bold to help you find the information you need for each activity.

The **introduction** talks about doll collecting. What's the least expensive type of doll collection? Do you like any of the doll themes? Which ones? Why?

Go to the **Frequently Asked Questions** about Barbie Collecting.
Let's say I have three dolls. During what years were they probably produced?
Doll #1: The earrings are plastic and they are removeable.
Doll #2: The swivel plate with no prongs.
Doll #3: Her hair goes past her waist.

Go to the **Glossary of terms**. Doll collecting has its own language. Use the glossary and try to interpret the following sentences.
My Barbie has ballerina arms and is HTF. It's wearing an o/f with o/t.
My doll is MIP. It's titian and comes from the DOTW collection.
My Ken is in nearly mint condition and is worth a lot of USD.

Go to the **Sewing and Crafting** section. Read about the ways you can create Barbie clothes. Design a barbie outfit.

Go to the **Price Guide**. Let's say you've started collecting dolls. You have the following dolls in your collection. How much is your collection worth?
Evening Enchantment Barbie (1989, MIB)
Teacher Barbie (white) (1995 , NRFB)
Malibu Skipper (1971, M/NP)
Air Force Barbie (1991, M/NP)
Rollerblade Barbie (1992 , MIB)
Wedding Day Ken (1991, MIB)

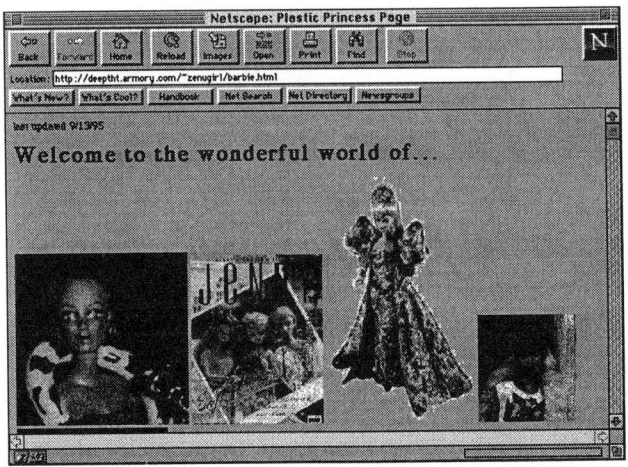

You have $200. You want to buy the following items. Do you have enough money? How much more money do you need?
35thAniversary Barbie blonde(1994,NRFB)
TRU Fire Fighter (1995 , MIB)
International Japanese (1985, MIB)

Hobby News

Hobbies are things that people like to do in their spare time. People of all ages are interested in hobbies.

Site Starters
Kathy Schrock's Hobby List
　　http://www.capecod.net/Wixon/hobbies.htm
Aunt Annie's Craft Page
　　http://www.coax.net/annie/
Computer Games
　　http://longwood.cs.ucf.edu:80/~MidLink/report.html
Lego
　　http://legowww.homepages.com/
Bicycles
　　http://www.cis.ohio-state.edu/hypertext/faq/usenet/bicycles-faq/part1/faq-doc-1.html
　　http://xenon.stanford.edu/~rsf/mtn-bike.html
　　http://nimitz.mcs.kent.edu/~bkonarsk/
　Lafferty, Peter (1990) **Pedal Power: The History Of Bicycles**. Watts.
　Lord, Trevor (1992) **Amazing Bikes**. Knopf.
Camping
　　http://www.barint.on.ca/cybermal/ponderosa/barnes4.html
　Evans, Jeremy (1992) **Camping & Survival**. Crestwood House.
　Hines, Fritz (1994) **Introduction To Family Camping**. Boy Scouts Of America.
Model Trains
　　http://www.mcs.net/~dsdawdy/NMRA/nmralink.html
Origami
　　http://www.cs.ubc.ca/spider/jwu/origami.html
　　http://kiku.stanford.edu:80/KIDS/origami/kids_origami_crane1.html
String Figures
　　http://www.iquest.net/~webweavers/isfa.htm
　　http://www.ece.ucdavis.edu/~darsie/string.html

Wave Words

Fishing	Hunting	Gardening
Backpacking	Ballooning	Bird watching
Camping	Cards	Crafts
Cooking	Crocheting	Kites
Models	Needlecrafts	Wood working
Pets	Photography	Pottery
Quilting	Puzzles	Sewing
Spelunking	Weaving	Chess

Powerful Projects

Read a book about a hobby. Use some of the words you find to search for more information on the Internet.

Find the email address of someone sharing your interest in a hobby. Email them a question you have about the hobby.

Interview someone with a particular hobby. Create a hobby newsletter that contains information about your hobby.

Have a hobby fair. Create a table display showing information about your hobby.

Create a list of sites related to your hobby. Create a hobby page for the Web.

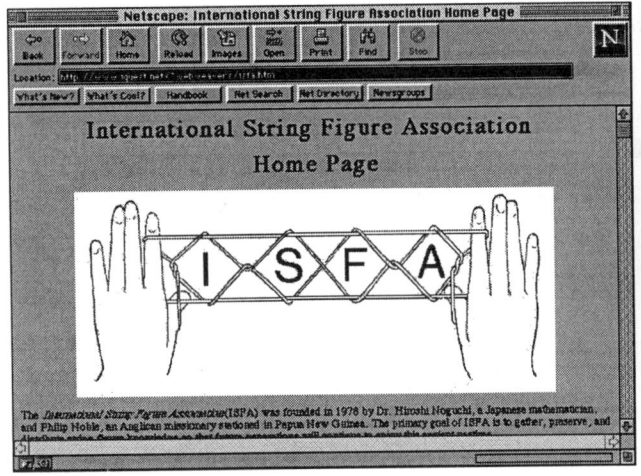
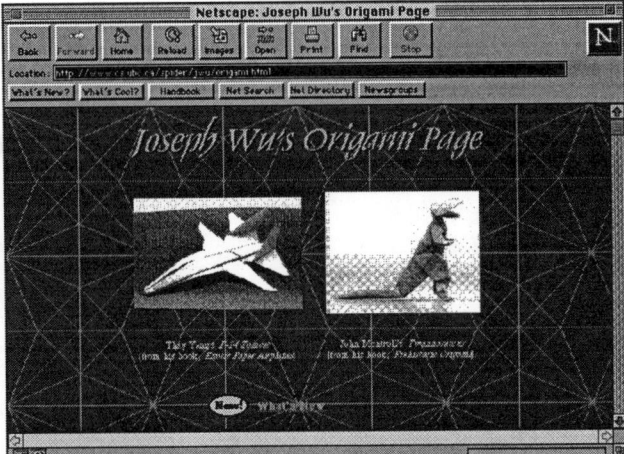

Findin' the Beach: Introductory Activities   19

Visit The All Magic Guide Site!
http://www.uelectric.com/allmagicguide.html

■ ■

Explore The All Magic Guide Site! This site has lots of neat examples of magic as well as links to other great magic resources.

Click on **Magic Show's Basically Amazing** and you'll go to a page with neat activities.

Select **Richard Robinson's Stage Magic**. What does it take to be a great illusionist? Do you have what it takes?

Select **Meir Yedid**. Try some of Scott Kim's inversions. Try creating your own inversion! Share it with a friend.

Read the **Review**. Write your own book review of a magic book you've read.

Choose the **Magic Show News**. Choose something you'd be interested in exploring. Read more about it!

Go to **Ask Mr. Magic**. Read the questions and answers. Ask a magic question!

Click on **Basically Amazing**. Try this magic trick!

Go to the **Magician Lecture Network**. Create a map showing where one of these magicians will be during the next few months. How many miles will they be traveling?

Read about the **Tricks of the Trade**. Which are you most interested in? Why?

Check out the **Magic Movie**. Use it in a HyperStudio stack on magic. Explain how the trick works along with some of your other favorite tricks.

Explore some of the other magic sites listed in All Magic Guide.

Learn about a famous magician. How did he or she get started? What are your favorite magic tricks?

Create a magic trick book of your own.

Go to a magic dealer. Make a price list of some magic tricks you'd like to buy. How much money do you need all together? If you could earn $5 per hour, how long would it take to make enough money to buy these magic tricks?

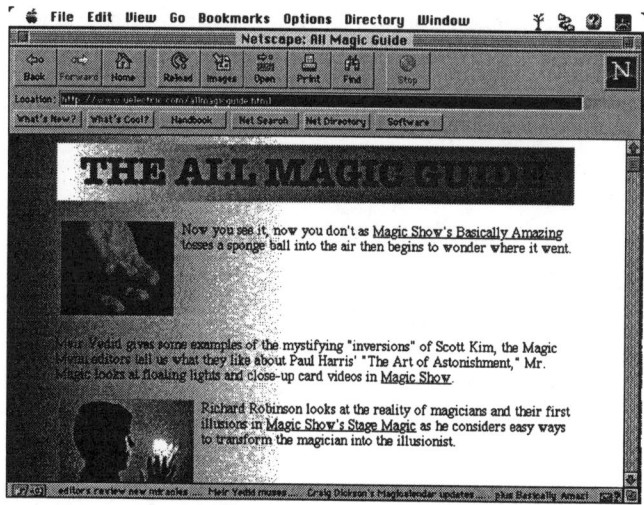

Sports Shorts

A sport is any physical, recreational activity. Some people like indoor sports and others prefer outdoor sports.

Surf Starters
Sport Launchpad
  http://www.weblust.com/NS/BuildPadPage/Sports
Bass Fishing
  http://wmi.cais.com/bassfish/index.html
Baseball Rules
  http://www2.pcy.mci.net/mlb/rules/
Bowling
  http://www.rpi.edu/~miller3/bowling.html
Figure Skating
  http://www.cs.yale.edu/HTML/YALE/CS/HyPlans/loosemore-sandra/skate.html#general
Indy Car Racing
  http://www.yahoo.com/Recreation/Sports/Auto_Racing/Indy_Car_Racing/
  http://www.icr.com/indy/icr/default.htm
  Andretti, Michael (1992) **Michael Andretti At Indianapolis**. Simon & Schuster.
  Sullivan, George (1992) **Racing Indy Cars**. Cobblehill/Dutton.
Karate
  http://cswww2.essex.ac.uk/Web/karate/CyberDojo/faq.html
  http://www.yahoo.com/Recreation/Sports/Martial_Arts/Karate/
  Neff, Fred (1980) **Karate Is For Me**. Lerner.
  Queen, J. Allen (1989) **Fighting Karate**. Sterling.
Motorcycles
  http://www.yahoo.com/Recreation/Motorcycles/
  Lafferty, Peter (1990) **Superbikes: The History Of Motorcycles**. Watts.
  Jaspersohn William (1984) **Motorcycle: The Making Of A Harley-Davidson**.
    Little Brown.
Rodeo
  http://electricstores.com/pikes-peak/prhm/prhhe16.htm
Unicycling
  http://www.unicycling.org/

Findin' the Beach: Introductory Activities

21

Wave Words

Auto racing	Baseball	Basketball
Bowling	Boxing/Wrestling	Football
Golf	Gymnastics	Hockey
Horse/Dog racing	Skiing	Soccer
Surfing	Swimming	Tennis
Track and Field	Hang Gliding	Karate
Ice Skating	Roller-blading	Rock Climbing
Scuba diving	Snorkeling	

Super Surfers

Email a person who participates in your sport. Ask them how they got started and how they prepare for the sport. Are there certain things they eat or drink? Do they do particular exercises? Ask about special skills and training required of the sport.

Create a math story problem that uses Internet information. For example, you might create a statistics problem from ESPN's site.

Explore the science of sports. Why does the ball fly so far when it's hit by a bat? What determines how far a kicked football sails?

Trace the history of a sport. How did it get started? Have the rules always been the same?

Persuade someone that they should get involved with your sport. You'll need to include information about the sport and a convincing argument. Include lots of examples from real sporting events.

http://www.atlanta.olympic.org/index.html

http://www.flyshop.com/

Visit the ESPNET SportZone!
http://espnet.sportszone.com/

Explore the ESPNet SportZone and try the following activities.

Explore the Frequently Asked Questions. Ask your own question.

Create a news article on one of your favorite athletes.

Write a news article reviewing the playing season of a favorite sports team.

Create a new sports team complete with league, logo, motto, and colors. What athletes would you like to recruit for your new team?

Sign up for one of their contests.

Learn more about a sport that isn't as popular as baseball, basketball, football, or golf. You can find them under Other Sports. Find a book about the sport to learn more. Then write a sport article that could be used to promote the sport. Some of these sports include arena football, bowling, cricket, figure skating, lacrosse, rodeo and sled dog racing.

Create a set of math story problems that relate to your favorite area of ESPNet.

Create a map showing the locations of your favorite teams. Color code each league or sport. Make sure to create a key.

Visit the Mountain Biking Site!
http://xenon.stanford.edu/~rsf/mtn-bike.html

Explore the Mountain Biking Site and try the following activities. Use the words in bold to help you find the information you need for each activity.

- Go to **Previous Featured Areas**. Select an area where you might like to mountain bike. After reading about the trail, do you still think it would be fun? Why or why not? How long do you think it would take to bike the trail?

- Go to **USA** and examine the links. Find a site you'd like to share with others interested in mountain biking. Write the address on a card along with a description.

- Visit a bike site anywhere in the world. For example, check out the New Zealand Mountain Bike Web (http://www.wcc.govt.nz/extern/kennett/homepage.htm).

- Use the information about accidents to write an article about bike safety.

- What does food have to do with biking? What do bikers eat? Why?

- What equipment do you need to take on a bike trip? Draw a diagram and explain the purpose of each item.

- Design a bike trail. Would your trail be flat, bumpy, steep, or rolling? Why? What kind of surface? Rocks, sand, or concrete? What kind of environment? Plants? Animals?

- If you could build a bike path in your neighborhood. Where would you put it? How long would it be? Create a map showing the path.

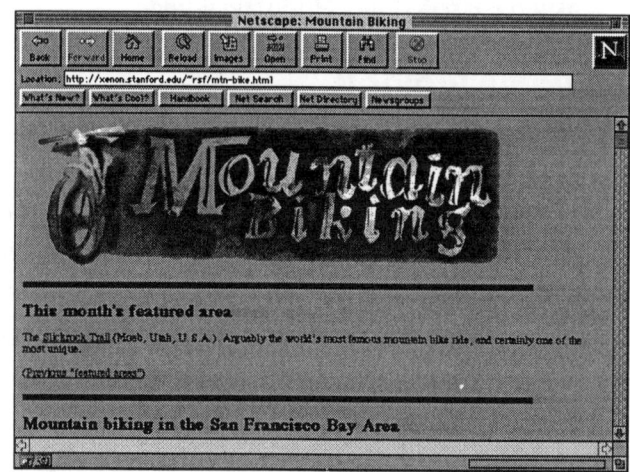

Pen Pals: First Steps

Pen pals are a great way to make friends with other students all over the world. How do you get a pen pal? Before you jump in, explore some of the Surfer Starters. For example, CyberKids has a place where you can make comments and interact with other students without making a long term commitment to a pen pal. The Surfer Starters are divided into projects initiated by students and those led by teachers.

Surfer Starters
Contacts made by students
CyberKids Interactive
   http://www.cyberkids.com/cyberkids/Interactive/Interactive.html
International E. Club
   http://www.nptn.org/cyber.serv/AOneP/academy_one/student/menu.eclub.html
Kid's Page Mail Office - International Kids Space
   http://plaza.interport.net/kids_space/mail/mail.html
The Kid's Place
   http://wwww2.islandnet.com/~bedford/kids.html
Pen Pal Connections
   http://www.start.com/start/ppmenu.html
KidsCom
   http://www.kidscom.com/adults.html
Contacts made with teacher help
Net Contacts
   http://gnn.com/gnn/meta/edu/dept/contacts/contacts.html
Intercultural Email Classroom Connections
   http://www.stolaf.edu/network/iecc/

Powerful Projects

Be creative! If you don't have enough connections for everyone, get involved in teacher led activities. For example, two teachers could share their students' projects. Each child could write a poem in a word processing document. The file could be emailed to the other teacher who could print out the poems and distribute them to the class on paper.

You could also try small group activities. Each week a different member of the group would send and retrieve the mail for the group.

Pen pals don't have to just write each other. Younger children can attach picture files such as KidPix pictures or QuickTake pictures. Older children may share HyperStudio projects.

Findin' the Beach: Introductory Activities

Visit CyberKids Interactive!
http://www.cyberkids.com/cyberkids/Interactive/Interactive.html

Go to CyberKids Interactive and try the following activities.

Read through the list of people looking for pen pals. Select a person and write down their email address. Send them a message asking them questions and introducing yourself. You might include the following information:
- Name
- School, City, Country
- Your Family Life
- Your Interests: hobbies, sports, collections
- Your Favorites: TV and movies, foods, things to do, school subjects
- A Typical Day at School
- Weather

Write a poem, riddle, or short story. Post it on CyberKids Interactive. Make sure you ask for other people's comments.

Write a story starter for CyberKids Interactive. Ask people to add to the story.

Ask a trivia question and see if anyone knows the answer.

Ask for comments on an important issue. For example, ask people if they recycle paper or plastic in their area.

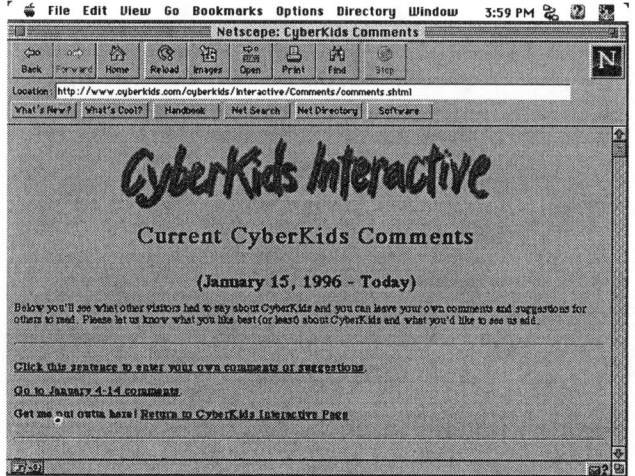
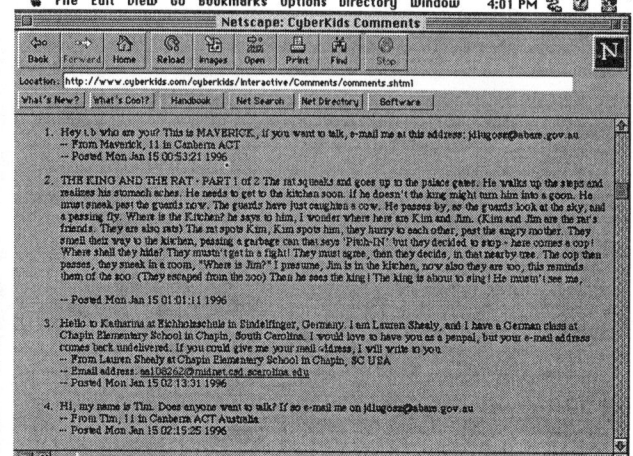

http://www.cyberkids.com/cyberkids/Interactive/Interactive.html

Visit KidsCom!
http://www.kidscom.com/

KidsCom is a great place for kids to interact as well as explore.

Fill out the **Registration Form**.

Find a Key Pal and write to a new friend.

Use the **Graffiti Wall** to post a favorite quote.

Ask **Tobie Wan Kenobi** an Internet question.

Play the **Geography Game**.

Talk about your favorite thing in **What Do Ya Think?**

Try some **KidsKash Questions** and collect KidsKash points.

Check out the **Pet Arena** to learn about the pets of people from around the world.

Explore **Write Me A Story** and write a story.

Don't forget to explore **New Stuff For Kids.**

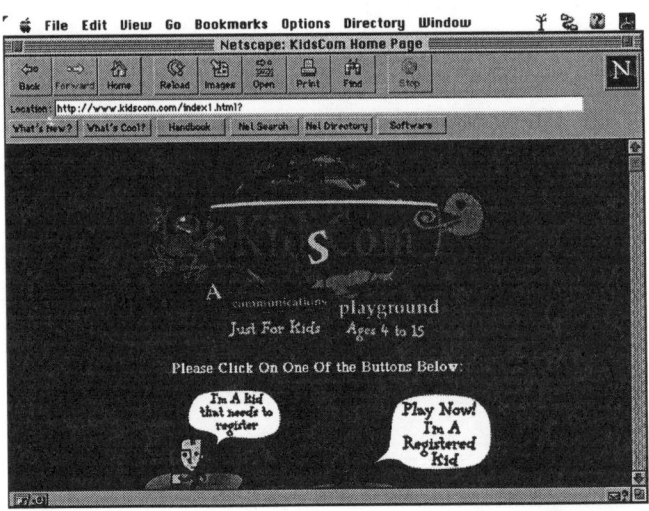

Visit International Kid Space!
http://plaza.interport.net/kids_space/mail/mail.html

Go to International Kid Space and identify pen pals. Try some of the following communications projects.

Getting to Know You

Help students get to know each other by encouraging them to share information about themselves. They can also ask questions of their pen pal. Here are some ideas:

What time do you get up?   Do you ride a bus to school?
What do you wear to school?   What time do you go to school?
What do you eat for breakfast?   What's the weather like in December?
What's your favorite ...?   What do you like to read ...?

Mix and Match

Try mixing different types of people together to share life experiences. For example, develop a cross generational project that matches young people with senior citizens. Have students living in the rural south compare their life with those living in rural Canada. Mix city kids with country kids. Ask students from affluent schools to compare life in disadvantaged schools. Autobiographies, short stories, and poetry are a good start. Consider having students interview each other. Compare statistical information about the areas where people live.

Experiments, Polls, and Surveys

Polls and surveys may be more effective when they cover large geographic areas. Students can conduct experiments at their school and compare results. An environmental survey might include the following questions:
Where do you live?
What is the major cause of water pollution in your area?
How do you dispose of garbage?
Do you have a recycling project going in your town?

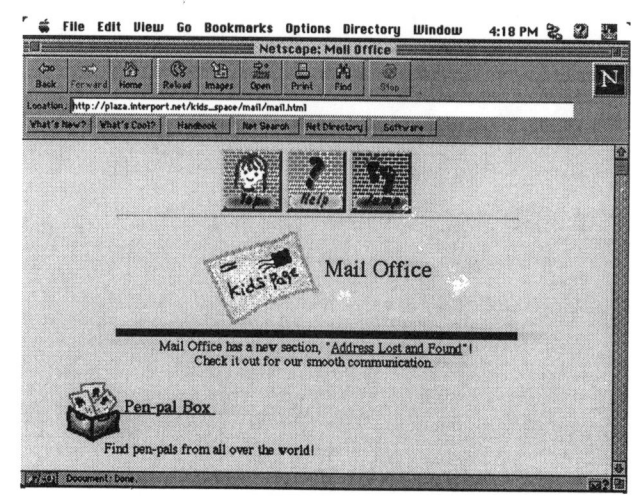

Visit Net Contacts!
http://gnn.com/gnn/meta/edu/dept/contacts/contacts.html

Net Contacts is designed to help teachers make connections with other teachers. You might develop collaborative pen pal projects, off-computer activities, or share professional interests.

Collaborate
Unlike mix and match which focuses on sharing projects by comparing and contrasting, collaboration projects deal with working together toward a single goal. Students could work together on writing projects, or build a large database of information. Children up and down the Pacific coast could build a travel guide.

Skill Sharing
When students learn a new skill, they need many opportunities to share and practice. Foreign language is one of the best example of this need. Students need opportunities to interact with native speakers. This is also a great time to cross disciplines. Students can work on projects in the language, plan trips, or share creative writing. Many other content areas can use skill sharing activities. For example, students may create practical math problems for students at another site to solve. Geography is another interesting concept to study while working online.

Electronic Field Trips
Through electronic mail, students will explore many exciting places worldwide. Electronic expeditions will take students to Alaska, Africa, or Australia. Students on the trip to an actual location describe their adventures, while the online students follow along with the maps and email throughout the world.

Mentorships
Helping others is one of the best ways to learn. Establish a mentoring program. Ask older students to tutor younger students or adults to help middle school students. High school students can be great mentors for older people just getting started with technology. Electronic homework hotlines are a great example of how this idea can work.

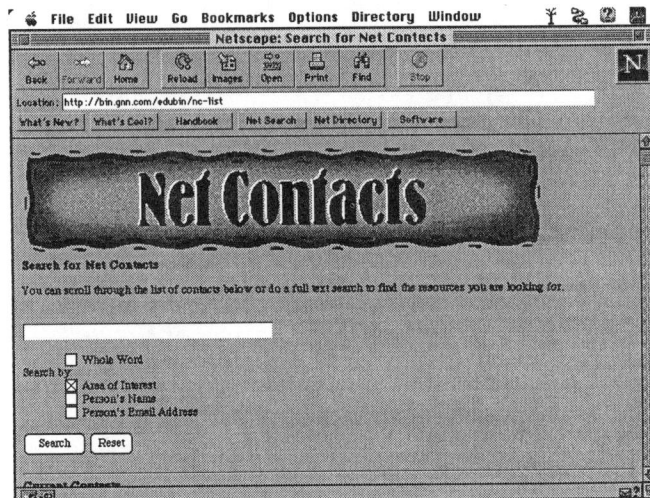

Visit Intercultural Email Classroom Connections!
http://www.stolaf.edu/network/iecc/

Intercultural Email Classroom Connections contains listing of many sites that promote intercultural exchange.

Put Out a "Call for Projects"
If you have a great project idea, you may want to put out your own "Call for Projects" on the Internet. When placing a "Call for Projects" make certain you include all the information needed for a teacher to decide if they might be interested in your activity. Get students involved by asking them about the type of exchange they envision!

Designing a "Call for Projects"

Topic and subject of the project. What is the general theme, topic, or areas covered by the project?

Overview. How will the project work? What are the roles of teachers and students? How will the initial instruction, practice, sharing, and evaluation take place? What kinds of sites are needed (i.e., rural/urban, rich/poor, international, north/south, by language, gender, race, or ethnic group)?

Objectives. What educational outcomes will students achieve during the project?

Grade level. Does the project focus on a particular grade or age level?

Level of participation requested. Will students be paired across sites? Will the project incorporate individual, small group, or large group interaction? Will sharing occur daily, weekly, or monthly? Will there be lots of interaction or specific activities? How many sites will be participating?

Timeline. What is the duration of the project? When does it begin and end?

Name, school, snail mail, email, phone mail. Who is the project administrator and how can I contact this person directly?

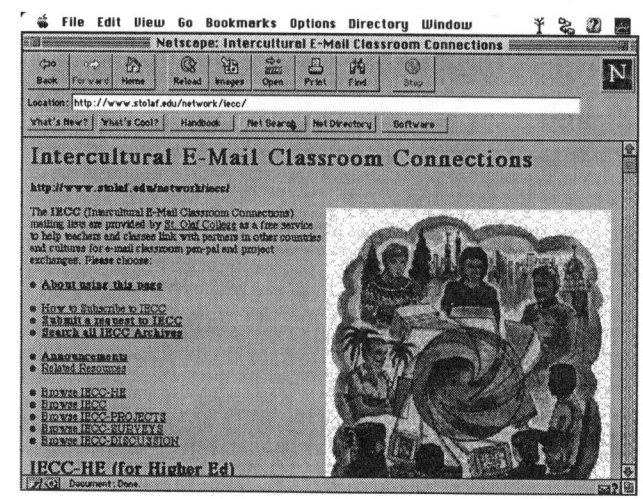

Email Tips for All Ages

Use Smilies!

Use smilies to express emotions:

:-)	Smiley
;-)	Winkey Smiley
:->	Devilish grin
:-(	Frowny Smiley
8-)	User wears glasses
%-)	User's gone goofy
(-:	Left handed Smiley
:-{)	User has a mustache
:-[	User is a vampire
:-E	User is bucktoothed vampire
|-I	User is asleep
[:-)	User is wearing a walkman
*<:-)	It's Santa Claus
=|:-)=	It's Abe Lincoln
+<:-)	User is a nun
@:-)	User wears a turban
:-D	User is laughing
:-\	User is skeptical
:-x	User is disappointed
:-@	User is screaming
:v	User has broken nose
:<)	User is a snob
:-&	User is tongue tied
o :-)	User is an angel
(8-o	Uh Oh, It's Mr. Bill
:-9	User is licking his/her lips

Important Keyboard Symbols

You'll use some of the following symbols in email addresses:

.	period or dot
@	at sign
-	dash
_	underscore
~	tilde

Use Abbreviations!

Advanced email users use abbreviations to avoid lengthy phrases. Some of the most common abbreviations and phrases are listed below:

IMHO:	In My Honest Opinion
FWIW:	For What It's Worth
FYI:	For Your Information
BTW:	By The Way
Flame:	Criticism
PMJI:	Pardon My Jumping In
RTM:	Read the Manual
TPTB:	The Powers That Be

Building an Email Address

An email address is the place where your email is stored. Let's look at the parts of an email address:

alamb@aol.com

alamb	personal mailbox
@	separates personal/group
aol	America OnLine
.com	commercial group

Other email endings include:

.com	commercial organizations
.edu	educational organizations
.gov	governmental organizations
.mil	military
.org	other organizations
.net	network resources

Email Tips for All Ages

Netiquette Basics

Netiquette is the word we use to describe good manners on the Internet. Remember that your message is a reflection of yourself. The person reading your message can't see you. All their positive or negative impressions will come from your writing. Incomplete sentences, poor grammar, and misspelled words will make you look bad. Although the Internet is more "laid back" than the rest of the world, you still need to consider appearances.

Match the level of message formality to the situation. The tone, formatting, words, and style of a quick note to your best friend will be much different than a serious message to a congressman.

Message Size

Keep your messages short.

If you're sending a long message, divide it into paragraphs with good topic sentences or headings.

Most of what we read is a mixture of upper and lowercase lettering. Notes that are written in all capital letters are difficult to read. In "email" talk, using capitalization is like YELLING AT YOUR READER! Only use capitalization for emphasis.

Add Fun to Your Messages

When you talk to someone on the telephone, your voice tells a person if you're happy or sad. When you see someone in person, the way they sit, stand, or smile tells you about their feelings. Email misses your sound and sight senses. You need to build these into your message. For example, you may write (tee hee) after a joke to make certain the reader understands your humor. You can use smilies to convey your feelings including :-) happy faces and :-(sad faces. If you're writing a business email message, but wish to add a personal note, consider a PS at the end of the message. PS stands for post script or after the message.

Use Subjects

When you write a message, use the SUBJECT line to introduce the topic of your message to the reader. This is important because it lets the reader know what to expect.

When you receive a message, you often want to reply immediately. If your message contained the subject Sports, then the subject of your reply will be RE: SPORTS. This way the reader will know what the letter is about.

List Other Email Reminders

Email Tips for All Ages

Living in an Email World

Don't assume that people receive and read your email. Not everyone reads their email every day. If you want to make certain a person receives and understands your message, ask the receiver for a confirmation.

The meeting will be held on Tuesday March 28 at 9AM in the library. Please let me know if you can or cannot come.

You're asking them to reply regardless of whether they can or cannot come. If you don't get a response, the person may not have read the message. Remember to include the date, not just the day of the week.

Replying to Messages

If you are responding to a series of questions, you may want to copy their email, relate answers to numbered questions, or provide a short review of the question. If people are busy, it may take several days to get back to your message. The answers "maybe, no, Monday, and red," won't mean anything without the original questions.

Examine the address closely when you are responding to a message. Make certain you are responding to an individual and not a group.

Forwarding Messages

Often you'll get mail that might be of interest to a friend. For example, my sister gets David Letterman's Top Ten list every morning and forwards the funny ones to me. I sometimes get information about new books or videos that might be of interest to my friends. I can forward the notice to them.

Jokes are a great example of how email can get out of hand. We've received jokes that have been forwarded throughout the world. Often people fail to remove the address information from previous viewers, as a result the joke can get lost in the "postmarks." Copy only that portion of the message that is relevant, unless you're interested in "tracing" the origin of the message. For example, it might be fun to see how many places in the world a joke could be forwarded.

Make certain the message is relevant and will be meaningful to the receiver. For example, sometimes people will forward notices of meetings to you. These can be confusing. "You're invited to a meeting next Friday." Am I invited to the meeting or is the person who originally received the notice invited? Add a brief note to the message indicating the purpose of forwarding the note. Also, don't forward messages that contain personal references. Do you want your personal "hugs and kisses" or "I think Brooke is cute." to be forwarded?

Rules of the Information Highway

Each computer user is responsible for his/her actions in accessing network systems. Each system has its own set of policies and procedures. It is the user's responsibility to abide by the policies and procedures of these other networks/systems.

Use of the network is a privilege, not a right, which may be revoked at any time for abusive conduct such as:
- placing unlawful info on the system.
- use of abusive or objectionable language in public or private messages.
- sending messages that are likely to result in loss of recipients work.
- sending "chain" letters or broadcast messages to lists to cause congestion.

EMail and File User Responsibility

Check email daily.
Delete unwanted messages.
Keep stored messages to a minimum.
Never assume that your email can be read by no one except yourself.
Only send things that you would not mind seeing in the newspaper.
Keep files to a minimum. Download files to your microcomputer.
Don't assume that your files are private.

Telnet Protocol/File Transfer Protocol

Follow instructions for uploading and downloading files.
Be courteous to other users seeking info.
Remain on the system only long enough to get information.
Download after normal business hours.
If you're not sure about copyright, don't copy it!

Electronic Communications

Keep paragraphs and messages short and to the point.
Focus on one subject per message.
Be professional and careful what you say about others.
Cite all quotes, references, sources.
Limit line length.
Include your signature at the bottom of messages.
Signatures include: name, position, affiliation, address, phone, email address.
Capitalize words only to highlight an important point. Use *asterisks* to surround words of importance.
Use discretion when forwarding mail addressed to groups.
It is rude to forward personal mail without the author's permission.
Be careful when using sarcasm and humor. Without face to face communications your joke may be viewed as criticism.
Respect copyright/license agreements.
When quoting, edit out what isn't directly relevant.

Listserv and Mailing Lists

Get to know the list before contributing.
Keep your questions/comment relevant.
Resist the temptation to "flame" others.
Remember, discussions are public and meant for constructive exchanges.
When posting a question, request that responses be directed to you personally.
When replying to a message, check the address to be certain it's going to the intended location.
Save subscription information.
Turn off the list if you're going on vacation.
Be tolerant of new users.

Kids On the Web

There are students all over the world using the Interent to share projects and post information. Explore some of the School and Individual Web Pages.

Surfer Starters

Tools for Finding School Pages
Web66 - School Pages
   http://web66.coled.umn.edu/schools.html
Classroom Connect - ClassroomWeb
   http://www.wentworth.com/classweb/
Launchpad - School Pages
   http://www.weblust.com/NS/BuildPadPage/Schools
Middle Schools
   http://longwood.cs.ucf.edu:80/~MidLink/middle.home.html
K-12 CyberTrail
   http://www.wmht.org/trail/trail.htm

Sample School Sites
Coyote Elementary School
   http://www.greywolf.com/coyote/index.html
Wangaratta Primary School
   http://www.ozemail.com.au/~ctech/acts.htm
Arbor Heights School
   http://www.halcyon.com/arborhts/arborhts.html
Hoffer School
   http://cmp1.ucr.edu/exhibitions/hoffer/hoffer.homepage.html
Armadillo: Texas
   http://chico.rice.edu/armadillo/
Hillsdale School
   http://hillside.coled.umn.edu/
Fairbanks Alaska School
   http://www2.northstar.k12.ak.us/schools/upk/upk.home.html
Japanese Middle School
   http://www.nptn.org/cyber.serv/AOneP/schools/ukima/home.html

Findin' the Beach: Introductory Activities

Children's Home Pages
Berit's Best Sites for Kids: Students and Family Home Pages
   http://www.cochran.com/theosite/Ksites_part2.html#family
Children's Home Pages
   http://www.comlab.ox.ac.uk/oucl/users/jonathan.bowen/children/alice.html
   http://niikaan.fdl.cc.mn.us/~isk/kidpage.html
   http://www.isd77.k12.mn.us/schools/kennedy/openhouse/artgallery.html
Kids Space - Kid's Village
   http://plaza.interport.net/kids_space/

Powerful Projects

Find a site that's similar to one you'd like to create. Write email to the developer (Webmaster) and ask how they got started.

Create a list of things that you'd like to put in your school, class, and personal home page.

Evaluate a home page. List the strengths and weakness. What do you think is missing? What would you add?

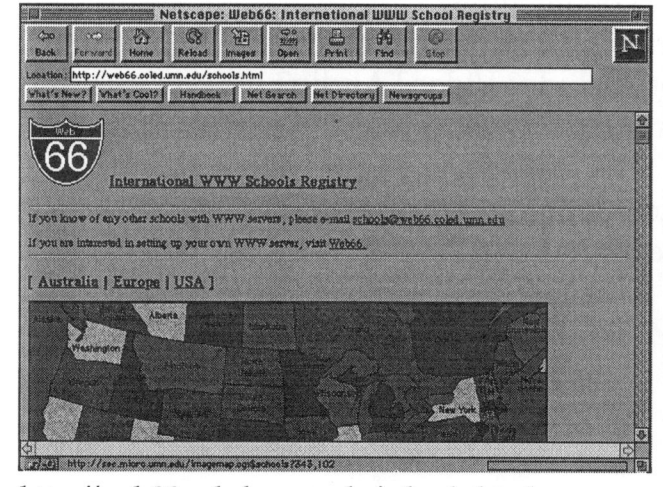

http://web66.coled.umn.edu/schools.html

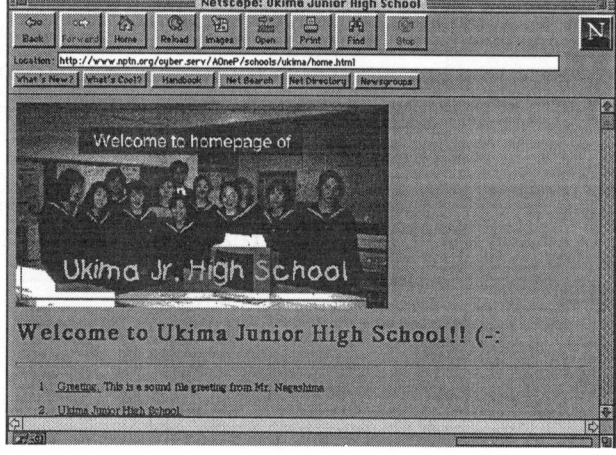

http://www.nptn.org/cyber.serv/AOneP/schools/ukima/home.html

Super Surfer: Virtual Friends
• •

Explore student home pages and find a person you think would make a good friend.

What's the name and address of the site and student?
What do you find interesting about the student?
What do you have in common with the student?
In what ways are you different from this student?
What would you like to ask this student?

Email the student or school and make a new friend!

Super Surfer: Be a Web Weaver!
• •

Explore student home pages. Write to students and find out how they created their pages. Design your Web page.
What information would you include?
(Likes, dislikes, projects, family/friends)
What pictures would you include? Video? Audio?
What color would you make the background/text?

Create your own home page! If you can't post it on the web, create a word processing or Hyperstudio file.

Findin' the Beach: Introductory Activities

Show & Tell

Students all over the world are showing and telling about themselves. Students are creating their own pages on the Internet to share personal information, stories, science projects, and interests. Use **Project Watch** for upcoming activities.

Surfer Starters

CyberKids - Elementary Students
    http://www.cyberkids.com/cyberkids/
MidLink Magazine - Middle School Students
    http://longwood.cs.ucf.edu:80/~MidLink/
LinkUp - Secondary Students
    http://wacky.ccit.arizona.edu/~susd/linkup.html
React - Secondary
    http://www.react.com
Yahooligans Guide to Newspaper and Publications for Kids
    http://www.yahooligans.com/School_Bell/Newspapers_and_Publications/
Academy One
    http://www.nptn.org/cyber.serv/AOneP/
Classroom Projects
    http://www.wentworth.com/notebook/
Global Show & Tell
    http://emma.manymedia.com:80/show-n-tell/
Kid News
    http://www.vsa.cape.com/~powens/Kidnews3.html
KidPub
    http://en-garde.com/kidpub/intro.html
Hotlist
    http://sln.fi.edu/tfi/hotlists/kids.html
HyperStudio Projects to Download
    http://www.ladue.k12.mo.us/Wildwatch/hyper/project.html
Peace in Pictures
    http://www.macom.co.il/peace/index.html
Press Return
    http://www.scholastic.com/public/Network/PressReturn/Press-Return.html
Project Watch
    http://gnn.com/gnn/meta/edu/dept/project/project.html
The Computer Clubhouse
    http://www.tcm.org/clubhouse/index.html
Vid Page
    http://cmp1.ucr.edu/exhibitions/cmp_ed_prog.html

Visit Online Magazines for Students!
http://www.cyberkids.com/cyberkids/

CyberKids - Elementary
   http://www.cyberkids.com/cyberkids/
MidLink Magazine - Middle School
   http://longwood.cs.ucf.edu:80/~MidLink/
LinkUp - Secondary
   http://wacky.ccit.arizona.edu/~susd/linkup.html
React - Secondary
   http://www.react.com

Read a back issue. Write a review of the magazine. What do you like and dislike about the magazine? What do they need to add? Email your ideas to the Webmaster.

Read the current issue. Does it deal with an issue of interest to you? What was the best article? Can you do better? Write an article for a future issue.

Design a project or contest that you think this magazine should sponsor. Send it in.

Read an article from a back or current issue. Surf the Internet for additional information that might be added to the article including facts, pictures, and other elements that might be added. Revise the article.

Explore a project posted in the magazine. Write a paragraph trying to convince your teacher that your class should participate in the project. As a class, vote on a project to work on as a group.

Explore other online magazines. Compare this magazine to another. Which would you recommend? Why?

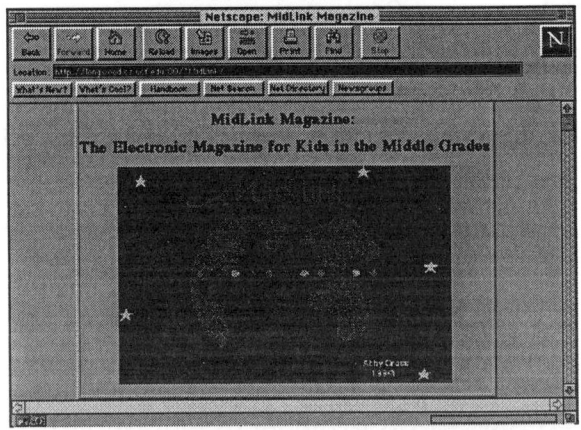

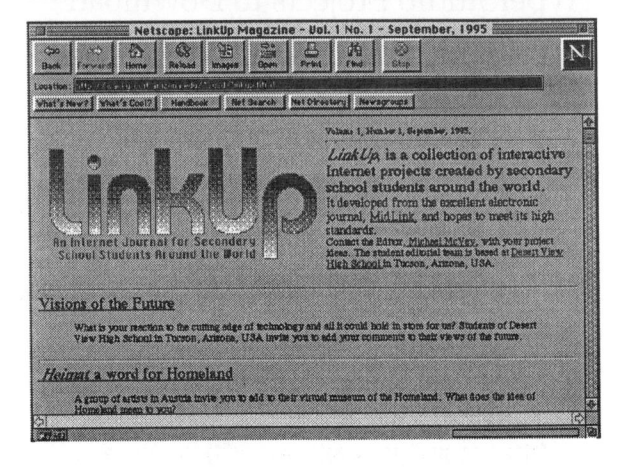

Findin' the Beach: Introductory Activities

Visit the KidNews Site!
http://www.vsa.cape.com/~powens/Kidnews3.html

Go to KidsNews and find out how you can add your own projects.

Explore the **News** Section. Write a news story about your family, neighborhood, class, school, community, or the world.

Explore the **Features** Section. Write a story about nature, school projects, travel, adventures, difficult challenges, things that fascinate you, or things you can teach others.

Explore the **Profiles** Section. Write a short paragraph about yourself and submit it to profiles. This is a great way to find a new friend!

Explore the **Creative Writing** Section. Draw a picture to go with one of the writing projects you find. Write your own story. Write about a day in your life, the history of your town, or your favorite thing.

Explore the **Goodies** Section. Find something you'd like to see, do, or read about. Share it with another member of the class. Write the author and tell them how much you liked their information or resource. Add your own goodies from something you've been doing in a class. What can you do that you'd like to share?

Explore the **Reviews** Section. Books, movies, TV shows, and Internet sites are all things you could review.

Explore the **Sports** Section. Write about a sports event you've watched or attended recently.

Remember to submit your great work! They'll post it thanks to the people at KidNews!

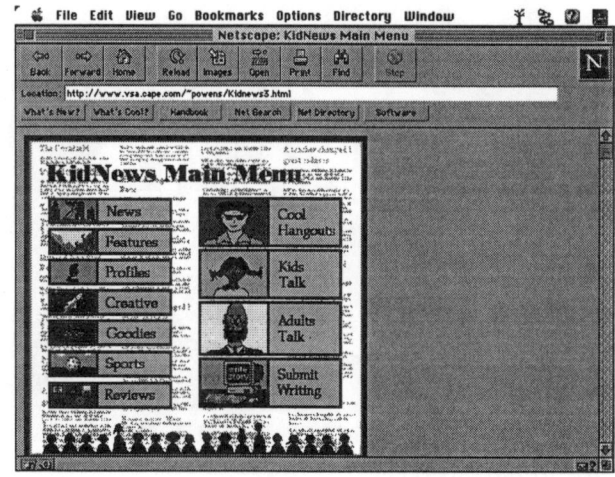

Visit International Kids Space!
http://plaza.interport.net/kids_space/

Visit International Kids Space! There are tons of fun things to do in KidsSpace!

Start at the **Kids' Gallery** and explore student projects.
- Submit a picture.
- Illustrate a story.
- Write a story to go with a picture.

Explore the **Story Book**. Read a story by someone who lives in a different country. Learn about this country. Email the student and tell him or her what you thought of their story. Also ask the person a question about their country.

Go to the **On Air Concert**. Record your voice singing a song, playing an instrument, or reading a poem! Record your sound in Real Audio and send it in!

Explore the **Beanstalk**. Add something to the Beanstalk!

Don't forget to go to the **Mail Room** and find a pen pal!

The **Web Kids' Village** has kids home pages you don't want to miss! Add your page to the Art village, Computer village, Literature village, Nature village, Science village, or Sports village.

Go **Outside** and explore some Kids Space favorite links. Which do you like best? Create a card for your favorite.

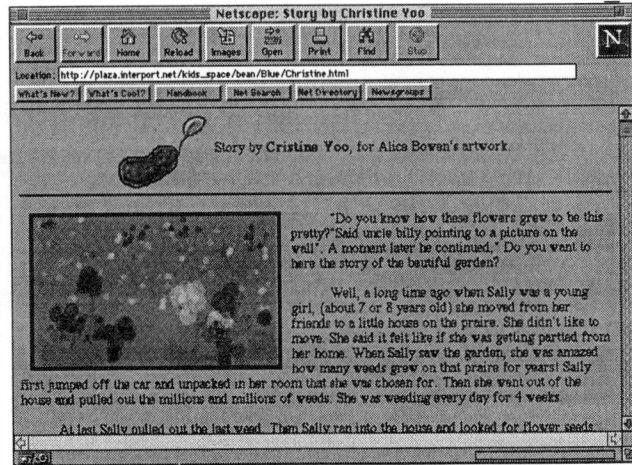

http://plaza.interport.net/kids_space/

Findin' the Beach: Introductory Activities

Visit Global Show-n-Tell Museum!
http://emma.manymedia.com:80/show-n-tell/

Go to the Global Show-n-Tell Museum.

Explore the projects at your age level. You're either an Egg, Hawaii Creeper, Red-Spectacled Parrot, California Condor, or Bald Eagle.

Design a project that includes both text and graphics. Send it to Global Show-n-Tell. You can even link to your home page.

Select another student's project you really like. Email them a message telling them how much you like their project.

Find a picture or a story created by another student. Add to the project and then email your ideas to the student.

Create a fictional story and pictures. Then create links to sites that have information that might go with the topic. Use the Parrot or Eagle sections on Global Show-n-Tell for ideas.

Create a project based on a social studies or science project you did recently. Draw a picture about the project and describe what you did in class.

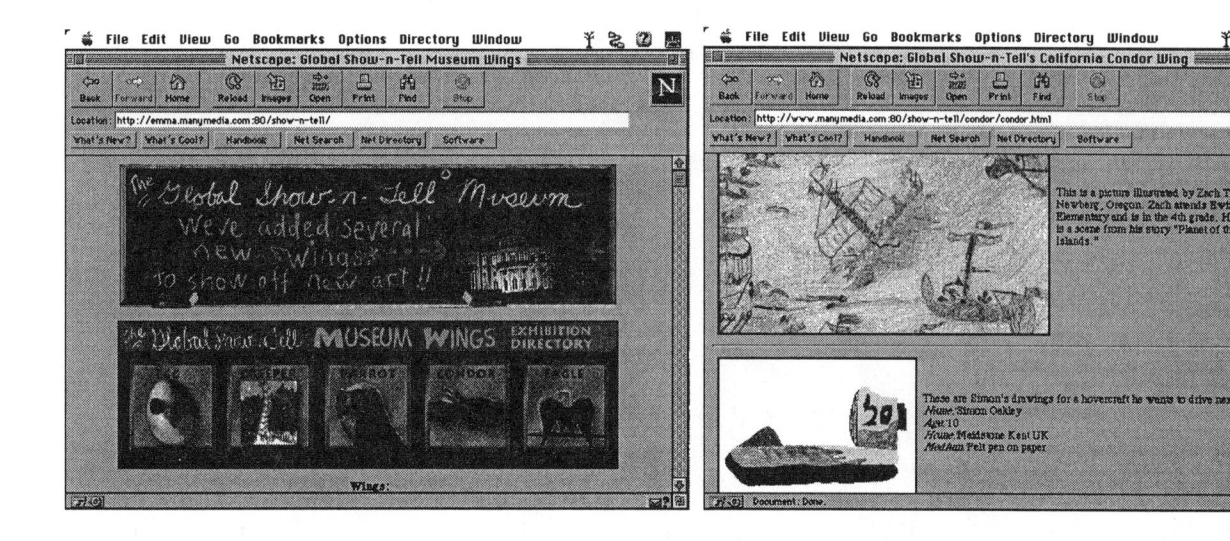

Clip Art Fun

Add clip art to your project. The Internet has tons of clip art waiting for you.

Surf Starters

Clip Art Server
  http://www.n-vision.com/panda/c/
The Clip Art Collection
  http://www.n-vision.com/panda/c/
Caboodles of Clip Art
  http://www.toltbbs.com/~jhudson/clipart.htm
Barry's Clip Art
  http://www4.clever.net/graphics/clip_art/clipart.html
Yahoo Clip Art
  http://www.yahoo.com/Computers_and_Internet/Multimedia/Pictures/Clip_Art/
Zia's Clip Art Sites
  http://www.zia.com/kclip.htm

Powerful Projects

In Netscape you can copy or save most pictures easily. You click on the picture and up pops a list of choices. You can also use software such as **Capture** to grab the picture. Once you've got the picture, you can put it in almost any document. The one below will be used as a logo for a summer school newsletter. Make sure you create a citation for where you found the picture even if it comes from clip art.

Use clip art to illustrate book reports, stories, poetry, report covers, signs, multimedia projects, banners, papers, and homework assignments.

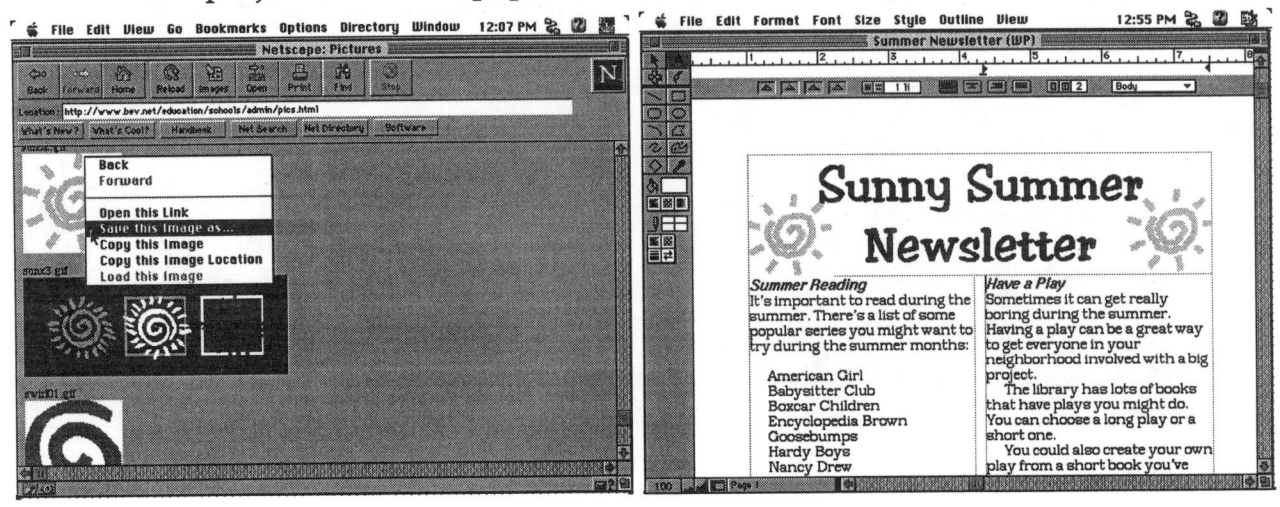

Findin' the Beach: Introductory Activities

Visit the Clip Art Server!
http://www.n-vision.com/panda/c/

Explore the Clip Art Server and try the following activities. Use the words in bold to help you find the information you need for each activity.

Write a poem or short story and use the clip art to illustrate your poem.

Create a sign for a special event. Use clip art to draw interest into your event.

Modify some clip art. For example, find a butterfly picture and turn it into a moth. Find a picture of a student and change the characteristics so it looks more like you.

Select your ten favorite pictures and put them into a Scrapbook or graphics file to use later.

Create a set of pictures related to the same topic such as Sports, Holidays, Business, Weather, Maps, or other topics. If each person in your class chooses a different topic, you'll end up with a great set of clip art files.

Find your favorite humor clip art. Write your own captions. Create a book of humor to send to a local hospital or classmate that might be sick.

The **Alt.binaries.clip-art** archive has lots of health and medical clip art. Create a brochure including information on one of the following topics: basic first aid, preparing to go to the hospital, what to expect at the hospital, or preventing injuries.

The **Alt.binaries.clip-art** archive contains pictures of people in various settings. Create a story character from one of the pictures. Describe the person including their name, background, where they live, what they do, what they like, and other information that might be used in a short story containing this character.

Select **Music-related clip art**. Learn more about an artist, composer, or instrument. Use the graphics to illustrate your project. Incorporate your writing into a flier to be distributed during a music program at your school.

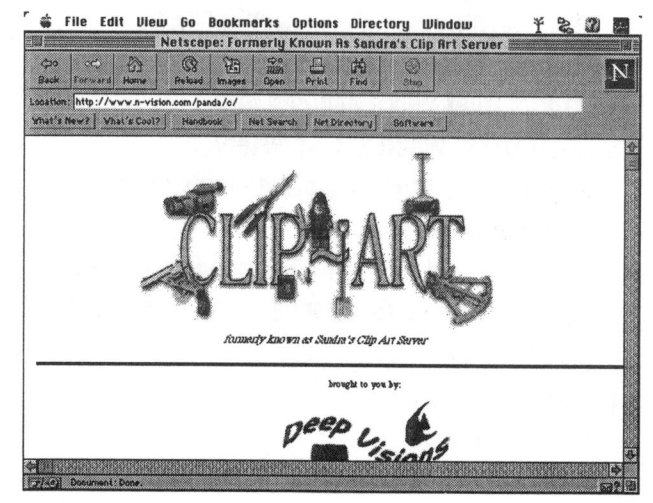

Animal Antics

Animals are always interesting to explore. Whether you're interested in animals as pets, farm animals, or endangered animals you can find lots of information on the Internet.

Surfer Starters
General Animals Links
Alaskan Animals
   http://www.alaska.net/~steel/animals/animals.html
National Wildlife Federation
   http://www.igc.apc.org/nwf/
Nature Links
   http://mh.osd.wednet.edu/
Sea World
   http://www.bev.net/education/SeaWorld/homepage.html
Teacher Resources: Wildlife Curriculum
   http://gnn.com/gnn/meta/edu/curr/rdg/gen_act/animal/index.html
US Fish and Wildlife
   http://www.fws.gov/
ZooNet Animal Links
   http://www.mindspring.com/~zoonet/anilinks.html
ZooNet Animal Pictures
   http://www.mindspring.com/~zoonet/gallery.html
Animals
   http://sln.fi.edu/tfi/hotlists/animals.html
   http://www.zoo.org/science/animal_index.html
   http://www.yahoo.com/Entertainment/Animals_Insects_and_Pets/
   http://netvet.wustl.edu/org.htm
   http://www.wolfe.net/~critter/
   http://sln.fi.edu/tfi/hotlists/animals.html
   http://www.yahoo.com/Business_and_Economy/Companies/Animals/
   http://www.cs.city.ac.uk/archive/image/lists/animals.html
Specific Animals
Animal Sounds
   http://www.ics.uci.edu/~pazzani/4H/Sounds.html

Findin' the Beach: Introductory Activities

Armadillo
   http://www.quadralay.com/www/Austin/Dillo/index.html
LlamaWeb
   http://www.webcom.com:80/~degraham/
Reptiles
   http://www.seanet.com/Vendors/billnye/nyeverse/shows/e212.html
Wolves
   http://informns.k12.mn.us/wolf.html
   http://wwwmncc.scs.unr.edu/wolves/desertm.html
Net Full of Animal Activities
   http://www.familysurf.com/act2.htm

Other Information Resources
Books
   Alden, Peter (1987) **Peterson First Guide To Mammals of North America.** Houghton.
   Boorer, Michael (1984) **Animals.** Silver.
   Bramwell, Martyn, (1989) **Mammals: The Small Plant-Eaters.** Facts On File.
   Crump, Donald J. ed. (1984) **How Animals Behave: A New Look At Wildlife.** National Geographic.
   Davidson, Margaret (1980) **Wild Animal Families.** Hastings.
   Minelli, Guiseppe (1988) **Mammals.** Facts On File.
   O'Toole, Christopher & Stidworthy, John (1989) **Mammals: The Hunters.** Facts On File.
   Selsam, Millicent (1987) **Strange Creatures That Really Lived.** Scholastic.
   Whitaker, John O. Jr. (1980) **The Audubon Society Field Guide to North American Mammals.** Knopf.

Computer Software
   Zurk's Learning Safari, Soleil
   How Animals Move CD, Discovery Channel
   Davidson's Zoo Keeper, Davidson.
   Zootopia CD, Lawrence Productions
   Explorapedia: World of Nature CD, Microsoft
   The Animals 2.0 CD, Mindscape
   Dangerous Creatures, Microsoft

Wave Words
Mammals: platypus, anteater, kangaroo, koala, opossum, wallaby, wombat, armadillo, hedgehog, bat, ape, monkey, gorilla, gibbon, orangutan, wolf, fox, lion, tiger, bear, badger, cheetah, cougar, coyote, leopard, panda, polar bear, hyena, jaguar,

otter, raccoon, skunk, seal, sea lion, whale, dolphin, manatee, elephant, donkey, horse, rhinoceros, zebra, aardvark, sheep, camel, goat, buffalo, caribou, deer, cattle, elk, giraffe, antelope, llama, moose, wildebeest, yak, chipmunk, rat, beaver, mouse, squirrel, gopher, rabbit.
Birds: oriole, blackbird, bluebird, bluejay, robin, thrasher, thrush, canary, catbird, sparrow, cowbird, finch, kingbird, magpie, meadowlark, raven, redbird, starling, dove, swallow, warbler, titmouse, wren, hummingbird, eagle, hawk, owl, buzzard, condor, falcon, emu, woodpecker, lory, macaw, parrot, quail, toucan, vulture, albatross, goose, duck, gull, loon, mallard, pelican, puffin, teal, egret, flamingo, heron.
Reptiles & Amphibians: snake, alligator, lizard, turtle, chameleon, crocodile, dragon, Gila monster, toad, iguana, frog.
Others: fish, arachnids, insects, crustaceans, mollusks, worms.

Powerful Projects

Compare the behavior of a particular animal to that of humans.
Describe the way an animal protects itself.
Select one of the animals listed above and write about a day in their life.
Compare the social organization of two different types of animals.
How do migrating birds navigate?
How do animals communicate? Study one animal and it's method of communication.
Many people say that dolphins are very intelligent. Do you agree? Why or Why not?

Super Surfer: Animal Antics
• •

Find a web site with animal information. Use the site and other resources to answer the following questions:
  What does the animal eat?
  Where does the animal live?
  Who are the animal's friends and enemies?
  Would this animal make a good pet? Why or why not?
  What is the life cycle of the animal? What about babies? How long does it live?
Create your own web page that answers these and other questions.

Findin' the Beach: Introductory Activities

47

Visit the World Wide Raccoon Web!
http://www.loomcom.com/raccoons/

Explore the World Wide Raccoon Web and try the following activities. Use the words in bold to help you find the information you need for each activity.

- Read the story **The Raccoon and the Bee-Tree**.
    - What three birds cried out in warning? Why?
    - When the raccoon stuck his hand in the tree, what covered his hand?
    - Why do you think the raccoon ran around so strangely?
    - What would you have done if you were the raccoon?
    - When the raccoon ran up the tree, whose tail did he pull?
    - What other kind of animal might curl up like the raccoon did at the end of the story? Have you ever seen an animal do this?
    - Create your own story about a raccoon in the woods.

- Copy a picture from the **image gallery** and paste it into a word processor. Write a story about what the raccoon might be doing.

- Write down the author and title of a book from the **bibliography** that you might want to check out from the library.

- Explore the **Raccoon Namesakes**. Select three favorites. Describe why you think they are descriptive of a raccoon.

- Create a poster showing the proper way to feed wild raccoons. Use the information in the **Raccoon Feeding** section.

- Visit **another raccoon site**. If you were looking for help on whether raccoons make good pets, would this be a good resource? Why or why not?

- Post a message on the **Wildlife Worker's Cafe** before you leave.

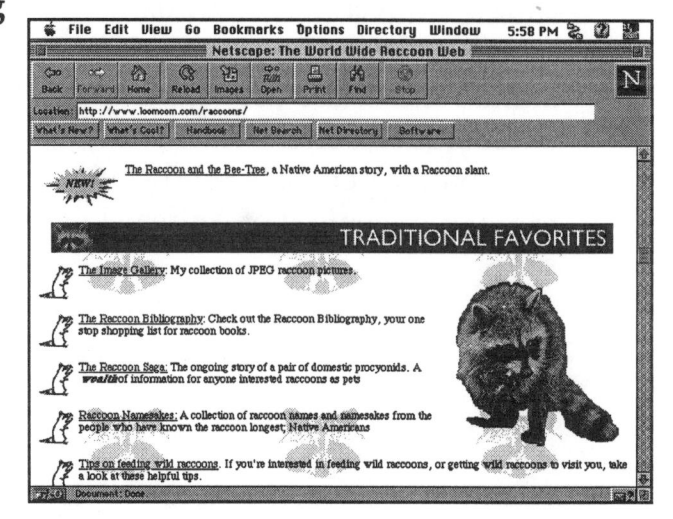

Visit a Net Full of Animals!
http://www.familysurf.com/act2.htm

Explore A Net Full of Animals. This site has lots of fun activities and sites about animals.

Visit the **EE-Link: Endangered Species** page. Select an endangered animals and create a web page that explains how we can save this animal.

Leap over to the **LlamaWeb** page. Would you like to have a llama as a pet? Would you rather have a llama or a horse? Why?

Visit the **Southern Australia Whale Centre**. If you were a whale, would you be worried about humans? Why or why not? How big is a whale? Compare it's weight to something you've weighed. 1 whale = how many things?

Explore the **Carl Hayden Bee Research Center**. Where do bees live? Why? How do bees spend most of their time? Create a list of questions and see if you can answer them at the Bee Research Center.

Take a trip to the **Tampa Bay Aquarium** and **Sea World Busch Gardens**. Create a wall mural of a coral reef. Write a report about one of the sea creatures. Put the report on the back of the animal you draw. Put your animal in the correct place on the coral reef.

Explore the web for other animal sites. Create your own trivia questions that might go with the animal site. Share your ideas with other students in the class and your online pen pals. Send your ideas to A Net Full of Animals! site.

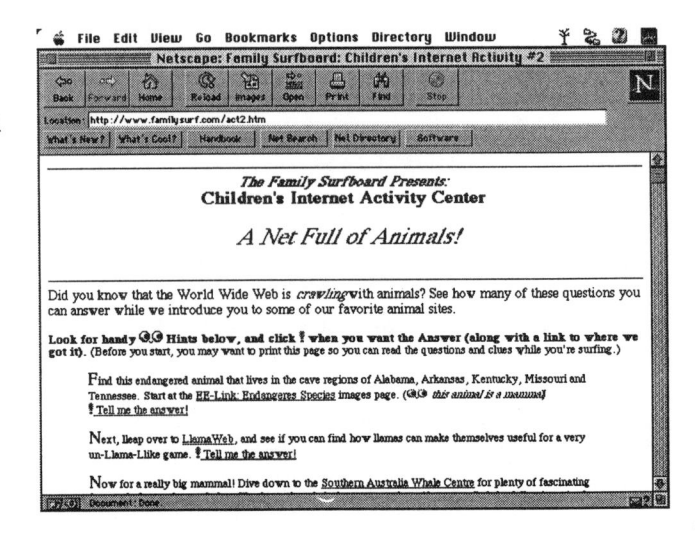

Findin' the Beach: Introductory Activities

Birds

You'll find lots of information on all kinds of birds. Some birds are endangered and some are pets. There are different types of birds found throughout the world. Explore the world of birds!

Surfer Starters

Bird Site
   http://mgfx.com/bird/
Birds
   http://www.si.edu/organiza/museums/zoo/homepage/zooview/smbc/smbchome.htm
   http://www.raptor.cvm.umn.edu/raptor/more.html
   http://www.bev.net/education/SeaWorld/birds/bird.html
   http://www.nceet.snre.umich.edu/Curriculum/birdfacts.html
   http://ice.ucdavis.edu/US_National_Park_Service/NPS_birds.html
Bald Eagle Pictures & Description
   http://www.fws.gov/bio-eagl.html
Parrots
   http://www.ub.tu-clausthal.de/PAhtml/aratingidae/a_pretrei.html
   http://www.mecca.org/~rporter/PARROTS/wptproj.html

Other Information Resources

Ehrlich, P., David S., & Wheye, D. (1988) **The Birders Handbook A Field Guide To The Natural History of North American Birds**. Simon & Schuster.

Brooks, Bruce (1989) **On The Wing.** Charles Scribner's Sons N.Y.

Burn, Barbara, (1984) **North American Birds National Audubon Society Collection Nature Series**. Crown Publishers Inc.

Burton, Robert (1985) **Bird Behavior**. Alfred A. Knopf New York.

Page, Jake & Martin, Eugene S. (1989) **Lords of The Air: Smithsonian Book of Birds**. Orion.

Proctor, Noble (1988) **Song Birds How To Attract Them & Identify Their Songs**. Rodale Press.

Powerful Project

Explore a particular kind of bird. Find out: Name, Size, Color, Habitat, Nutrition, Life Cycle.

Visit the World Center for Birds of Prey!
http://www.peregrinefund.org/

Explore the World Center for Birds of Prey and try the following activities.

Visit the **The Peregrine Fund Section**. Do you think this is an important group? Why?

Explore the **Conservation Projects**. Visit two sites around the world. How are their missions similiar and different? Which do you think is the most important project? Why? Is there anything you could do to help?

Visit the **Bald Eagle Project**? Why is the project important to the people of the United States? What does the bald eagle mean for Americans?

What does **Biological Diversity** mean? Why is it important?

What is **captive breeding**? Explore some of the projects. Which ones use captive breeding? Why?

There are two different kinds of **release programs**. Give examples of each type of release program. Create a chart with an example of each.

Read one of their **news releases**. Write a news release about a bird that lives in your area.

Create your own bird page focusing on one of the endangered birds in the Peregrine Program.

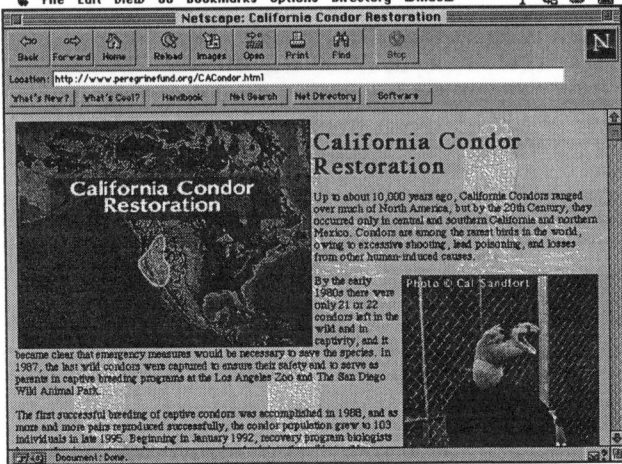

Findin' the Beach: Introductory Activities

Zany Zoos

Use the computer to visit zoos all over the world. Start at ZooNet. There are hundreds of zoos, so it's easiest to choose one right from ZooNet's Zoo Links.

Surfer Starters
General Zoo Links
ZooNet Zoo Links
   http://www.mindspring.com/~zoonet/zoolinks.htm
World Wide Web Virtual Zoo - Lists of Online Zoos
   http://www.mindspring.com/~zoonet/www_virtual_lib/zoos.html
Yahoo Zoo List
   http://www.yahoo.com/Science/Museums_and_Exhibits/Zoos/

Zoos to Visit
Birmingham Zoo - Good for primary grades
   http://www.bhm.tis.net/zoo/
Canadian National Zoo
   http://www.si.edu/organiza/museums/zoo/homepage/nzphome.htm
Metro Washington Park Zoo
   http://www.caboose.com/a1topics/portland_zoo/MAINGATE/
Sea World
   http://www.bev.net/education/SeaWorld/homepage.html
Woodland Park Zoo
   http://www.zoo.org/
ZooNet
   http://www.mindspring.com/~zoonet/
Zoological Email Directory
   http://www.indyzoo.com/zed/

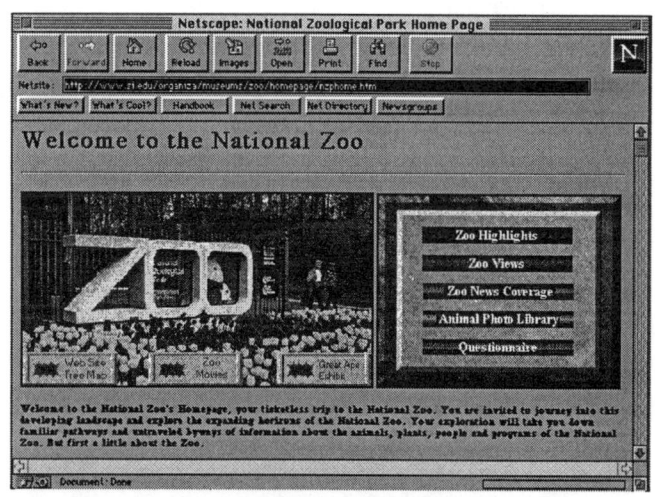

http://www.si.edu/organiza/museums/zoo/homepage/nzphome.htm

Visit ZooNet Links!
http://www.mindspring.com/~zoonet/zoolinks.htm

Explore ZooNet Links. This page will take you to lots of zoos all over the world.

Visit a virtual zoo. Compare the zoo that you visited on-line with a real zoo. What are the advantages and disadvantages of the computer zoo? What about the real zoo? Which do you like better, why? Compare the animals at your local zoo with the animals on the computer zoo. How are they alike and different?

Compare and contrast two on-line zoos. Compare the resources available, maps provided, information about the zoo and its animals, history, personnel, and other information.

Create a checklist for evaluating on-line zoos. What's most important to have in an online zoo? What's least important?

Plan a zoo. What animals would you want in your zoo? Why?

Plan your own online zoo that would link to your favorite animals.

Use the Zoological Email Directory to locate a person who works with a particular type of animal or another job at a zoo. Email the person and ask about their job.

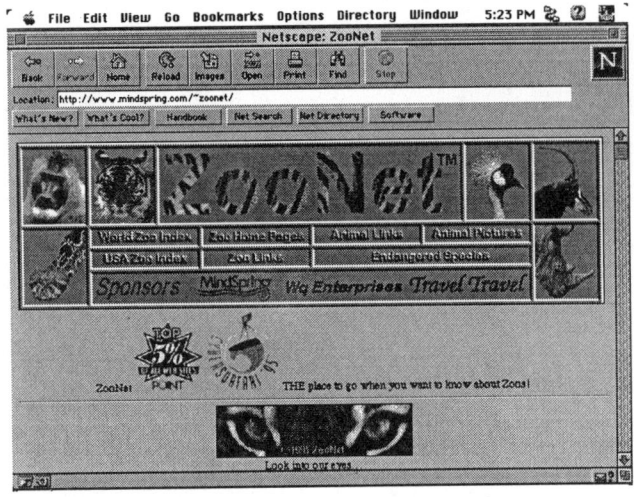

http://www.mindspring.com/~zoonet/ *http://netvet.wustl.edu/e-zoo.htm*

Visit the Sea World site!
http://www.bev.net/education/SeaWorld/homepage.html

Explore the Sea World site and try the following activities.

Go to the **Animal Bytes** and select an animal. Copy a picture into a word processor and write a paragraph advertising your animal. Include its most interesting features.

Try one of the **Animal Quizzes**. What question did you think was most interesting? Create your own animal quiz for one of the animals at Sea World.

Learn how to set up an **aquarium**. Create a sign that might be used at a pet store explaining the most important things to know about aquariums.

Who are **Klondike and Snow** and why would anyone want to visit them? Create a travel brochure advertising this neat new attraction.

Would you be interested in a career as a **marine mammal scientist**? Why or why not? Support your stand with information you find at this site. Besides marine mammal scientist, there are other careers associated with Sea World. Describe one.

Read a **lesson** from the Curriculum Guide that is at your grade level. Try it!

Read about the **Pledge and Promise** awards. What kind of project could you do at your school to win this award?

The **Conservation partners** play an important role at Sea World. Create a timeline showing the history of the Izaak Walton League. Create a chart showing how money is spent by the National Fish and Wildlife Foundation.

Pets

Pets are some of our favorite animals. Regardless of whether you have a pet or wish you had a pet, you'll enjoy exploring pets on the Internet.

Surfer Starters

General Pet Sites

Pet Paths - Pets Starting Point
   http://pathfinder.com/@@9DcxziLX3gEAQDio/twep/petpath/

Pets
   http://www.yahoo.com/Recreation/Animals__Insects__and_Pets/
   http://www.yahoo.com/Entertainment/Animals_Insects_and.Pets/
   http://www.dynamo.net/dynamo/pets/pets.html
   http://www.zmall.com/pet_talk/dog-faqs/homepage.html
   http://netvet.wustl.edu/e-zoo.htm

CyberPet
   http://www.cyberpet.com/cgibin/var/cyberpet/index1.htm

Student Activities on Pets
   http://longwood.cs.ucf.edu:80/~MidLink/dogs.html

Live Food for Pets
   http://www.cco.caltech.edu/~aquaria/Faq/live-food.html

Specific Pets

Cats
   http://www.zmall.com/pet_talk/cat-faqs/homepage.html

Ferrets
   http://www.optics.rochester.edu:8080/users/pgreene/central.html

Frogs
   http://www.cs.yale.edu/HTML/YALE/CS/HyPlans/loosemore-sandra/froggy.html

Rabbits
   http://www.psg.lcs.mit.edu/~carl/paige/HRS-home.html

Findin' the Beach: Introductory Activities

Visit the CyberPet Web!
http://www.cyberpet.com/cgibin/var/cyberpet/index1.htm

Explore the CyberPet Web and try the following activities.
Go to **Cyberdog** and the **Featured Articles**:

Read **A Puppy Buyer's Poem**. What kind of puppy does this person need?

Write your own puppy poem and submit it to Cyberdog!

Read about the **Responsibility of Canine** ownership. Create a list of four considerations when owning a dog. Would you make a good dog owner? Why or why not?

Read about **Choosing a Breed**. What kind of dog breed would be best for you and your family? Why? Use information from the article to support your ideas.

Read the article **People Prefer Pets**. What do you think of their survey results? Create a survey that contains some of the same questions they asked. Ask your class members to answer the questions. Were your results the same or different from their findings?

Read about the **dangers of Halloween** for a pet. Create a list of tips for pet owners around the holidays.

Select **Breeder's Showcase** from the **CyberDog** menu. Select a breed of dog. Create a map of the world that locates breeders of that type of dog. If you find less than five, try adding another breed of dog in a different color to your map.

Explore some of the other features of CyberPet!

Write suggestions for CyberCat!

Dinosaur Expo

Dinosaurs are exciting creatures to explore. Unlike zoo animals and pets, dinosaurs lived long ago. There are many museums around that world that have information about dinosaurs.

Surfer Starters

General Dinosaur Information
- http://www/yahoo.com/Science/Geology_and_Geophysics/Paleontogy/
- http://www.hcc.hawaii.edu/dinos/dinos.1.html
- http://www.tyrrell.com/
- http://ucmp1.berkeley.edu/expo/dinoexpo.html
- http://www.injersey.com/Media/lenSci/features/dino/dino.html
- http://www.bvis.uic.edu/museum/exhibits/Exhibits.html
- http://rs6000.bvis.uic.edu:80/museum/exhibits/Exhibits.html
- http://www.cuug.ab.ca:8001/VT/tyrrell/
- http://www.unm.edu/~greywolf/test/nmfp.html

Prehistoric Sharks
- http://turnpike.net/emporium/C/celestial/epsm.htm

Great Teacher Resources with Books & Activities
- http://www.bvis.uic.edu/museum/education/LOTguide1.html

Other Information Resources

Czerkas, Sylvia & Olson, Everett (Editors) (1987) **Dinosaurs Past & Present V.2**. Natural History Museum of L.A. Co. with Univ. of Washington Press.

Cohen, Daniel (1983) **Monster Dinosaur**. Harper.

Lambert, D. & Currant, A. (1986) **The World Before Man**. Facts On File.

Lambert, David (1978) **Dinosaurs**. Crown Publishers, Inc. N.Y..

Lampton, Christopher (1983) **Dinosaurs & The Age Of Reptiles**. Watts.

Lauber, Patricia (1987) **Dinsosaurs Walked Here & Other Stories Fossils Tell**. Bradbury Press.

Lauber, Patricia (1989) **The New About Dinosaurs**. Bradbury.

Pringle, Laurence (1978) **Dinosaurs & People: Fossils Facts & Fantasies**. Harcourt.

Sattler, Helen Roney (1981) **Dinosaurs of North America**. Lathrop, Lee & Shepard Books/New York.

Sattler, Helen R. (1989) **Tyrannosaurus Rex & It's Kin: The Mesozoic Monsters**. Lothrop.

Zallinger, Peter (1986) **Dinosaurs & Other Archosaurs**. Random.

Findin' the Beach: Introductory Activities   57

CD-ROM Resources
Compton's 1995
Encarta 1995
HyperStudio
Microsoft Dinosaurs
Prehistoria

Super Surfer: Dino Expo
•••••••••••••••••••••••••••••••••

Explore the Dinosaur Sites. Think about how you would organize information for a Dinosaur Web page. Some ideas are below:

Periods: Triassic, Jurassic, Cretaceous
Saurischaian: theropods, sauropods
Ornithischian: stegosaurs, ceratopsians, ornithopods, ankylosaurs

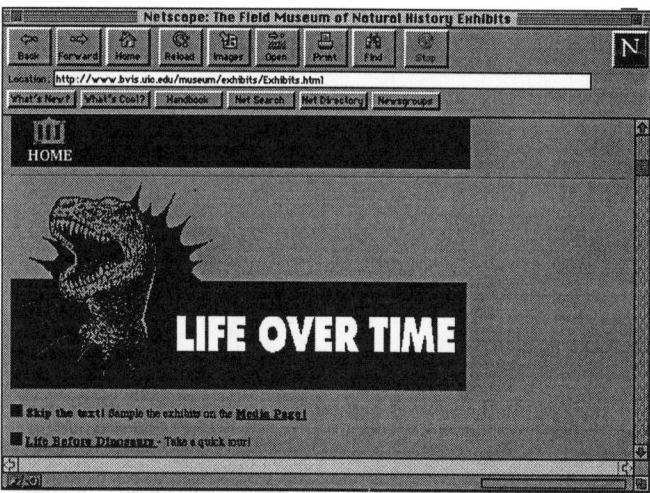

---

http://www.bvis.uic.edu/museum/exhibits/Exhibits.html

Visit the The Dinosaur Expo!
http://ucmp1.berkeley.edu/expo/dinoexpo.html

Explore the dinosaur page and try the following activities. Use the words in bold to help you find the information you need for each activity. This web site contains lots of graphics, so it may be slow.

- Go to **Early Dinosaur Discoveries**. Create a map of North America that shows the locations and dates of important events in the discovery of dinosaurs.

- Select a dinosaur. Create a chart showing the characteristics of the dinosaur including when it lived, where it lived, what it looked like, where remains were found, and its friends and enemies. You may only be able to find part of the information at this site. For more information try some other dinosaur sites. Dinosaur Hall - **http://www.tyrrell.com/tour/dinohall.html**

- Go to another section and explore. Create a card containing the name of the section and questions for someone else in the class to answer.

- Check out some virtual reality trilobites at **http://www.nhm.ac.uk/museum/tempexhib/VRML/pictures.html**.

- Create a HyperStudio stack to share dinosaur information such as herbivore, carnivore, and omnivores.

- Compare the sizes, weights, and lengths of different dinosaurs.

- Create your own version of Jurassic Park. Which dinosaurs would you bring to life? Why? What would be in your dinosaur park?

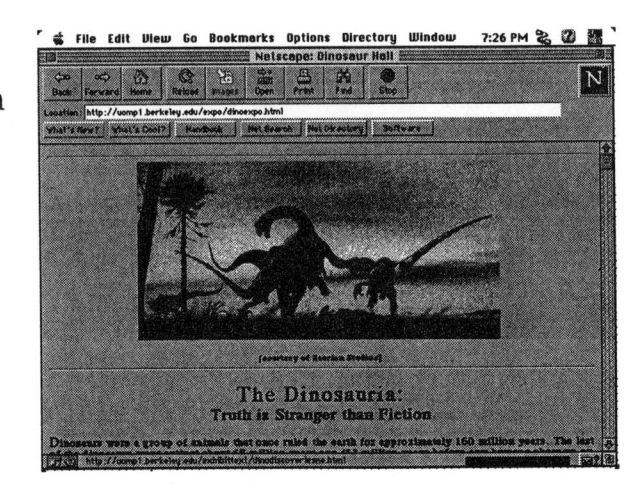

My Favorite Thing

Listen to the song **My Favorite Thing** from the movie **The Sound of Music**. What's your favorite thing? Use one of the following search tools: AltaVista, Inktomi, Excite, Lycos Infoseek, WebCrawler to find information about your topic. You could also go to the sites listed in **List of Lists** for ideas.

Surfer Starters

CyberKidsCyberTeens - LaunchPad
    http://www.woodwind.com/mtlake/CyberKids/Launchpad/Testpad.html
Kathy Schrock's Kid's Stuff
    http://www.capecod.net/Wixon/kidstuff.htm
Berit's Best Sites for Kids
    http://www.cochran.com/theosite/KSites.html

Powerful Projects

Try one of the following activities:
- Draw a picture that represents your favorite thing. Add three facts you already knew about the topic and three new facts.
- Select your "favorite" site on your "favorite" topics. Explain why these are your favorites.
- If you were going to create your own Internet site, what would you include?
- Create a display containing real items that are related to your favorite thing.
- Write a paragraph trying to convince other members of your class that your favorite thing should become their favorite thing.
- Describe someone, someplace else in the world that shares your interest in your favorite topic.
- Describe a place in the world you'd like to visit and do "your favorite thing." Why would you go there?
- Create a Top Ten List of reasons why you like your favorite thing.
- Create a trivia sheet answering popular questions about your topic.

Surfin' the Internet: Project Ideas from A to Z

Examples of favorite things sites.

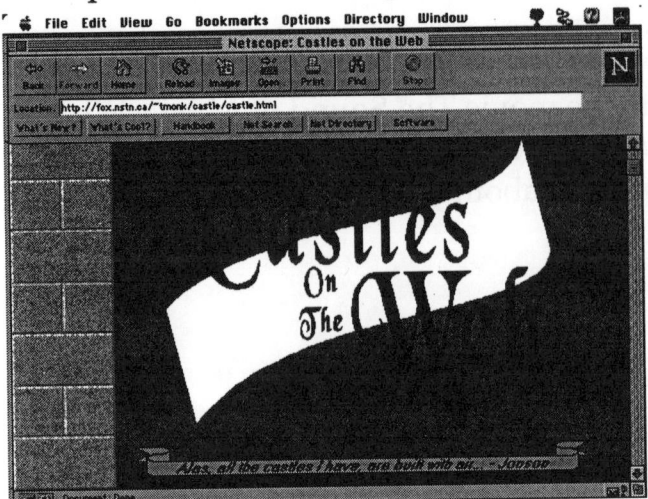

http://fox.nstn.ca/~tmonk/castle/castle.html

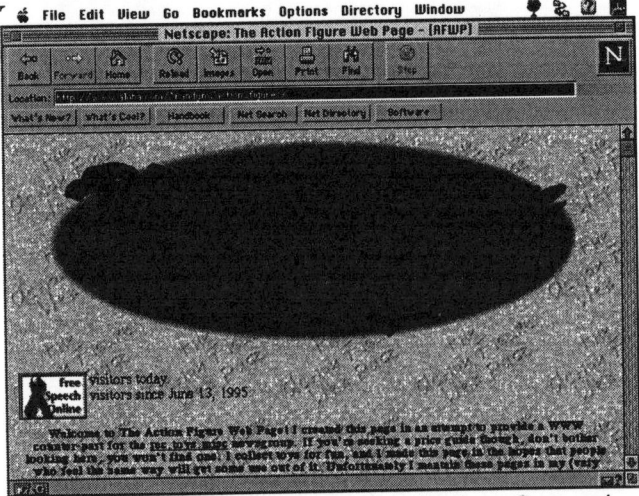

http://www.aloha.com/~randym/action_figures/

http://gagme.wwa.com/~boba/mj1.html

Findin' the Beach: Introductory Activities

Visit the Internet Movie Database!
http://www.msstate.edu/Movies/

Visit the Internet Movie Database. Everyone loves the movies. Let's explore your favorites.

Find a movie that's based on a popular book such as James and the Giant Peach.

Choose a favorite actor and create a timeline showing his or her work over time.

Choose a favorite movie and create a set of trivia questions about it. Create a review of the movie using information from the movie site.

Compare an official and unofficial movie site. How are they alike and how are they different?

Compare and contrast two of your favorite movies. How are they alike and different?

Choose a movie set in another time period. Do you think they did a good job showing life during that time period? Why or why not? Give examples.

Many people work on films. Pick a career to explore related to the film industry. Learn about a person who has worked in one of your favorite movies.

Create a movie page for a movie you'd like to produce. Include pictures and information about the actors you'd like to hire.

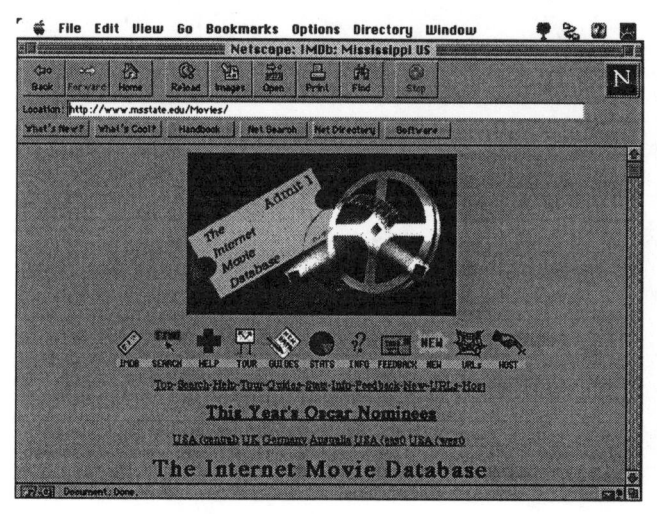

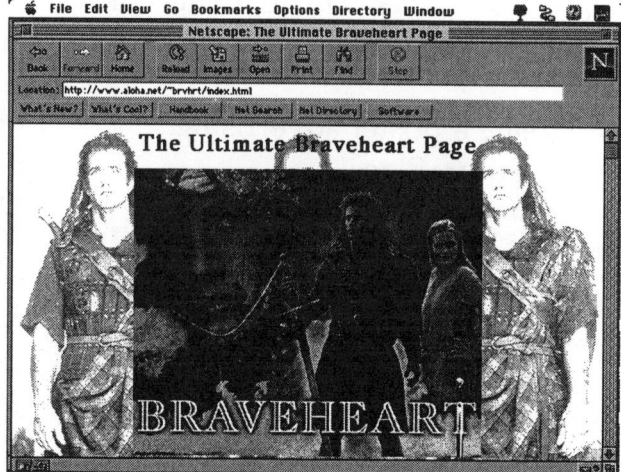

Visit the Future Place Site!

http://www.itp.tsoa.nyu.edu/~alumni/dlasday/xx/intro.chall.html

Explore the Future Place Site! Have you always wanted to create your own theme park? Here's your chance!

Explore some of the designs already submitted. As a small group, design an attraction for one of the following areas:
Ride
Pavilion
Exhibit
Game
Demonstration

Remember to include a statement of purpose, graphics, construction, and design process information. See the guidelines at the site. Although the final designs were due November of 1995, you can still send them.

Explore Internet Sites for real theme parks such as Sea World, Universal, DisneyWorld, DisneyLand, and Cedar Point. Write about one of their attractions.

Search the Web for information about roller coasters. How do they work? Why? What are the biggest, fastest, highest, and oldest coasters? What park has the most roller coasters? Where are the best roller coaster?

As a class, lay out an entire theme park. Then, create models of each attraction.

Create a poster advertising FuturePlace!

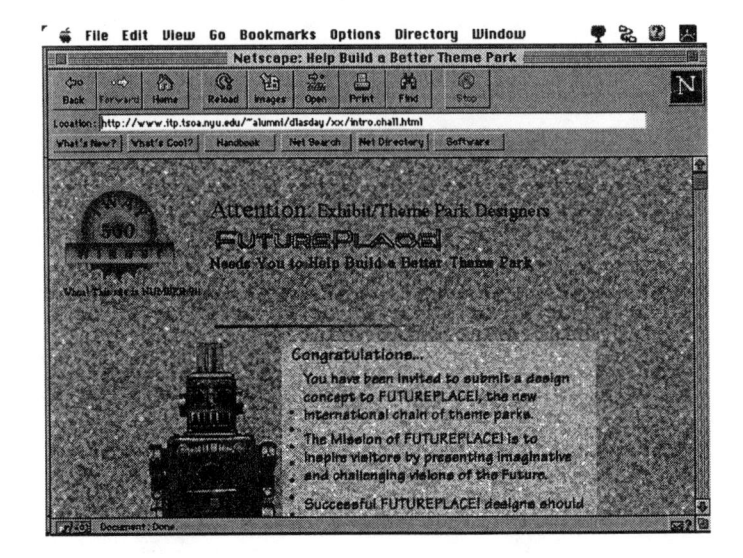

Section 2

Lookin' For Waves:
Information Exploration Ideas

How do I get my students started with an Internet-based project?

My students have trouble organizing information, how can I help them deal with information overload?

How can my students go beyond copying and develop truly creative projects?

Children don't just "do" information, technology, and Internet. A project-based learning environment involves wondering about a topic, wiggling through information, and weaving elements together. Each child learns and expresses themselves in a unique way. This section will explore the process of wondering, wiggling, and weaving.

Project-based learning blends traditional subject-matter goals and objectives with authentic learning environments. This section focuses on projects that require students to explore information, select issues and problems, and apply information processing skills to the development of a meaningful project. While designing learning environments for children, it's important to consider individual needs and interests along with technology options. Howard Gardner's multiple intelligences provide an excellent framework for "constructing strategies for student success (Armstrong, 1994)." There are many ways to design technology environments to address the specific needs of students in the linguistic, logical-mathematical, spatial, musical, bodily-kinesthetic, interpersonal, and intrapersonal areas. By focusing on specific attributes of technology such as text, sound, still images, and motion images we can assist students in selecting channels of communication that are most effective for accessing resources, synthesizing information, and communicating ideas.

For example, the interactivity and immediacy of Internet technologies are useful for particular types of learners and their projects. As we explore the possibilities for technology it's important to explore all the possibilities from traditional resources (i.e., print, projected, display) to CD-ROM materials, multimedia tools, and Internet resources.

This section focuses on the development of learner-centered, information-rich, problem-based projects: The New 8W's (see Figure 2-2). This approach focuses on the process students experience in developing projects. **Watching** requires students to become observers of their environment. It asks students to become more in tune to the world around them from family needs to global concerns. **Wondering** focuses on the exploration of ideas. Brainstorming, discussing, and reflecting on questions, concerns, and ideas are all part of the wondering phase. **Webbing** directs students to begin locating information and connecting ideas. One piece of information may lead to new questions and areas of interest. Students select those resources that are relevant and organize them into meaningful clusters. **Wiggling** is often the toughest phase for students. They're often uncertain about what they've found and where they're going with a project. Wiggling involves twisting and turning information looking for clues, ideas, and perspectives. **Weaving** requires the highest levels of thinking. It focuses on the application and synthesis of information. Students begin to originate new ideas, create models, and formulate plans. **Wrapping** involves packaging the ideas, solutions, and communications. Why is this important? Who needs to know about this? How can I effectively communicate my ideas to others? **Waving** is the publishing aspect of the project. Students share their ideas, try out new approaches, and ask for feedback. Finally, **wishing** is the reflection point in the project. Students begin thinking about how the project went and consider possibilities for the future.

This information processing model is similar to the work of others in the field such as Kuhlthau, Pappas and Tepe. The implementation of this model is innovative. It focuses on changing roles of the media specialist, teacher, students, and technology. This section will work through each aspect of this model.

We've found that new technologies require "playtime." Rather than jumping into a heavy project such as a social issues assignment or science experiment, we suggest that you begin with a series of lighter activities (like those discussed in the first section) that will help students get the hang of the technology without worrying about new, complex content. This section examines a topic, then provides sample activity sheets. If you don't find an activity sheet at your grade level interest, try some of the suggested Web sites and create your own! The Topics and Activity Pages for this section are listed in Figure 2-3.

Learner-Centered, Information-Rich, Problem-Based Projects:
The New Eight Ws

Watching
Wondering
Webbing
Wiggling
Weaving
Wrapping
Waving
Wishing

Figure 2-2. Information model

Lookin' For Waves Topics and Activities

This section is divided into two parts. First, we focus on the steps in the information exploration process. A description of popular social issues topics, Internet resources, and project ideas is found in the second part.

Part 1: Information Process
Watching
Wondering
    Topicing
    Metacognition Map
    5Ws & H
    Internet Search Sites
Webbing
    Theme Development/Webbing
    Classifying Information
    Gallup Poll Site
Wiggling
    Ask-An-Expert Site
    Global Youth Dialog Site
    Kathy Schrock's Evaluation
Weaving
    Compare/Contrast
    What Ifing
    Writing Resources
Wrapping
    Nonprofit Prophets Site
    Web Page Development Sites
Waving
    Online Magazine Sites
    The Vocal Point Site
Wishing
    Info Zone Site

Part 2: Social Issues Topics
General Social Issues
Abuse: Physical & Emotional
Aging
AIDS
Cancer
Crime, Conflict, & Resolution
Death & Dying
Diabetes
Eating Disorders
Families and Relationships
Homelessness, Hunger, & Poverty
Smoking
Substance Abuse
Suicide
Teen Pregnancy, Abortion, & Adoption
Women's Issues

Figure 2-2. List of Topics and Activities.

Lookin' For Waves: Information Exploration Ideas

Watching

Watching requires students to become observers of their environment. According to Webster's dictionary, watching is a state of alert and continuous attention, close observation. A person who is watching is looking for action and change. The watching phase of information exploration asks students to become more in tune to the world around them from family needs to global concerns.

Activities for Students

Observe

Begin with observation. Take a couple days to really explore the world around you. Keep a journal of what you see, hear, say, touch, and taste. Describe how you feel physically and emotionally.

Explore each aspect of your life including your family, community, work, play, and school. Watch the interaction among family members. Observe your friends and their actions. Explore the environment where you live. If aliens were examining you and your community, what would they think?

Reach out to the world through the newspaper, radio, television, and Internet. What do you see and hear? What are the current issues of interest and concern? What problems need solutions? Which of these issues impact your life directly or indirectly?

Consider the future. How will the world around you change over time? How will you change? What will you be doing in 10, 25, 50, or 75 years?

Write

Explore the Journal Writing Page.
http://www.spies.com/~diane/journals.html

Incorporate some ideas from the Journal Writing Page in your own writing.

Discuss

Share your journal with a friend. Pick out your favorite parts to share. Ask their ideas and opinions. Make a list of topics of greatest concern.

Wondering

Wondering focuses on the exploration of ideas. According to Webster's dictionary wondering includes many different emotions including surprise, curiosity, and doubt. Brainstorming, discussing, and reflecting on questions, concerns, and ideas are all part of the wondering phase. The challenge of the wondering phase is keeping an open mind. Students need to explore all the possibilities before focusing on a specific topic or issue. As students narrow their topic help them focus on particular issues, concerns, problems, or questions related to the topic. Don't let them get bogged down with "the topic." Instead, help them focus on ideas and perspectives they'd like to explore.

Activities for Students

Brainstorm
  Before jumping into a project, brainstorm possible ideas. Read the following pages to learn how to brainstorm.
    gopher://gopher.utexas.edu:3003/00/pub/uwc/Handouts/brainsto.txt
    http://www.demon.co.uk/mindtool/brainstm.html
  Use your journal for ideas. Ask your family and friends for suggestions. Complete some of the following sentences:
    I wonder ...
    I like ...
    I dislike ...
    I am in favor of ...
    I am opposed to ...
    I wish I could convince people that ...
  Examine your responses. Create a list of topics. Brainstorm a list of words or ideas associated with each of the topics.
  Select one of the topic areas. Use the **Topicing** worksheet to brainstorm words that are more broad, more narrow, and related to your topic. Also consider synonyms and alternative forms of the same word. These words will be helpful in searching for information on this topic.
  Create a **Metacognitive** map or "What I Know" chart of your topic. Use the worksheet to list: What I know, What I need to know, and What I want to know. Later you can go back and answer the last two questions: What I learned, and What I still wonder about.
  Develop a **5Ws and H** chart for your topic.
  Use a variety of **Internet search tools** including search engines to locate information on your topic.

Lookin' For Waves: Information Exploration Ideas

Topicing

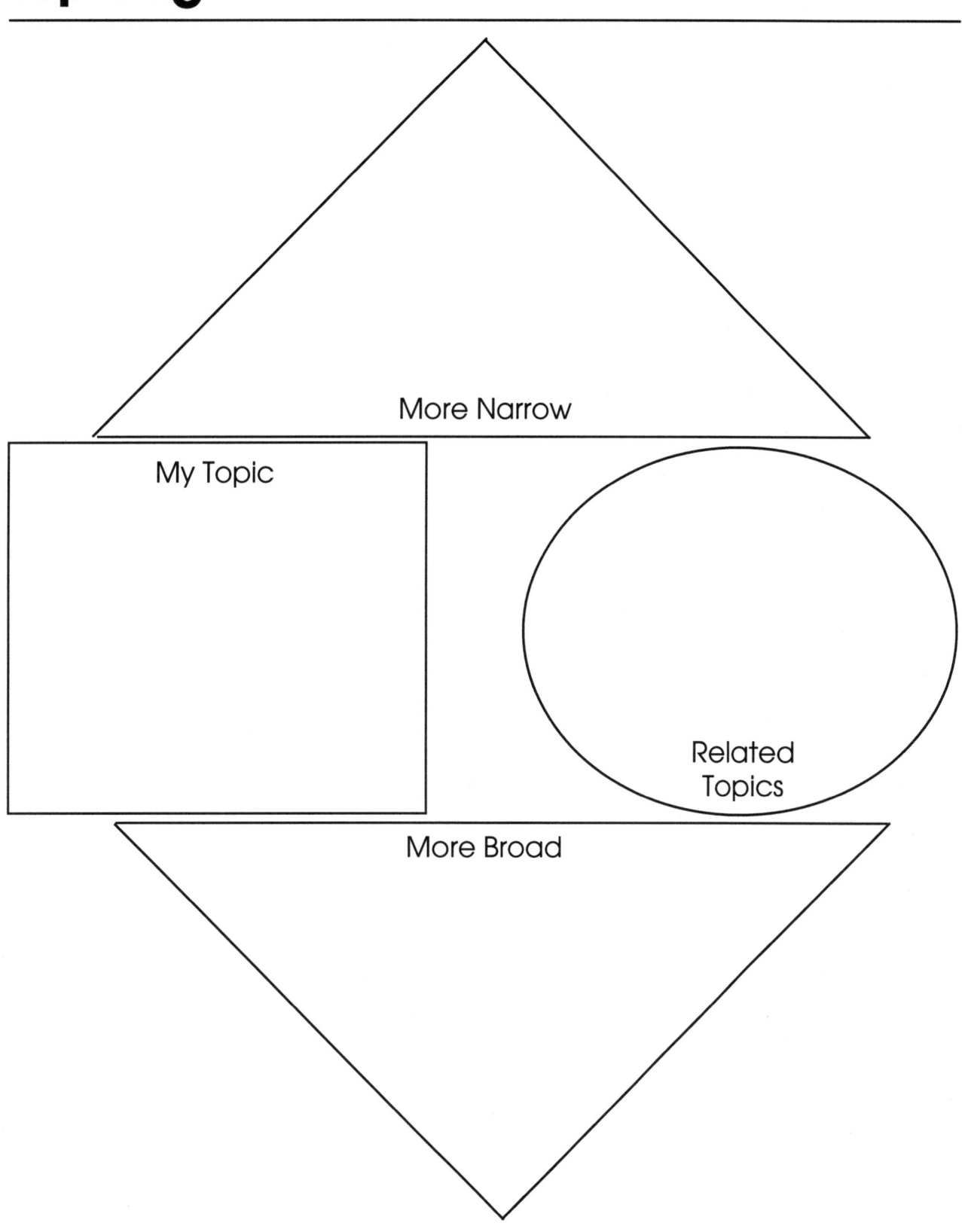

More Narrow

My Topic

Related Topics

More Broad

Metacognition Map

Topic

What I know
What I need to know
What I want to know
What I learned
What I still wonder about

Lookin' For Waves: Information Exploration Ideas

5W&H

Question	Answer	Details
Who?		
What?		
Where?		
When?		
Why?		
How?		

Visit Internet Search Sites!
http://arlo.wilsonhs.pps.k12.or.us/construct.html

Use a variety of search tools when exploring information on your topic. Read about the steps in conducting an effective search at Constructing an Internet Search (http://arlo.wilsonhs.pps.k12.or.us/construct.html).

Search Engines to Explore
- All-In-One
  - http://www.albany.net/allinone/
- Alta Vista
  - http://altavista.digital.com/
- Boba World Searcher
  - http://gagme.wwa.com/~boba/search.html
- Hometown Free Press
  - http://emporium.turnpike.net/~walk/hometown/globe.htm
- Internet Sleuth
  - http://www.intbc.com/sleuth/
- WebCrawler
  - http://metacrawler.cs.washington.edu:8080"/
- Yahooligans
  - HTTP://www.yahooligans.com

Lists of Lists to Explore
- HomeWork Page
  - http://www.tpoint.net/Users/jewels//homework.html
- Kathy Schrock's
  - http://www.capecod.net/Wixon/wixon.htm
- Schoolhouse Project
  - http://www.nwrel.org/school_house/
- Tessa's Cool Links for Kids
  - http://wwww2.islandnet.com/~bedford/tessa.html
- Uncle Bob's Kid's Page
  - http://miso.wwa.com/~boba/kidsi.html
- Reference/Research/Library Research Materials
  - http://www.classroom.net/classroom/gradesref.html

Lookin' For Waves: Information Exploration Ideas

Webbing

Webbing directs students to begin locating information and connecting ideas. According to Webster's dictionary, a web is a woven network. For example, one piece of information may lead to new questions and areas of interest. Students select those resources that are relevant and organize them into meaningful clusters.

Students use a variety of information resources. General resources such as a dictionary and encyclopedia can provide useful background information. Use national resources such as the Gallup Poll Site to find data and statistics. Nonfiction books, videos, and Internet sites can provide more specific information. Treat all forms of communication equally. Consider different channels of communication such as words, pictures, motion images, and sounds. Try seeking information in all the following areas:

Audio	Books	Charts, graphs, tables
Computer Software	Internet resources	Interview People
Laserdiscs	Magazines	Maps and Globes
Multimedia	Newspapers	Realia (real objects)
Reference materials	Still Pictures	Video

Activities for Students

Theme Development/Webbing
Create a web of information related to your topic or theme. Use the **Theme Development/Webbing** worksheet as a model. Place the key word or idea in the middle, then weave a network of information around the center. Start with information you already know about the topic. Next, go to the dictionary and encyclopedia for general information that might be helpful.

Classifying Information
With some topics it's helpful to cluster information into categories. Use the **Classifying Information** worksheet for ideas.

Public Opinion
Explore **public opinion** related to your topic. Use information from public opinion polls. Compare the results with your own survey of people in your area.

Theme Development/Webbing

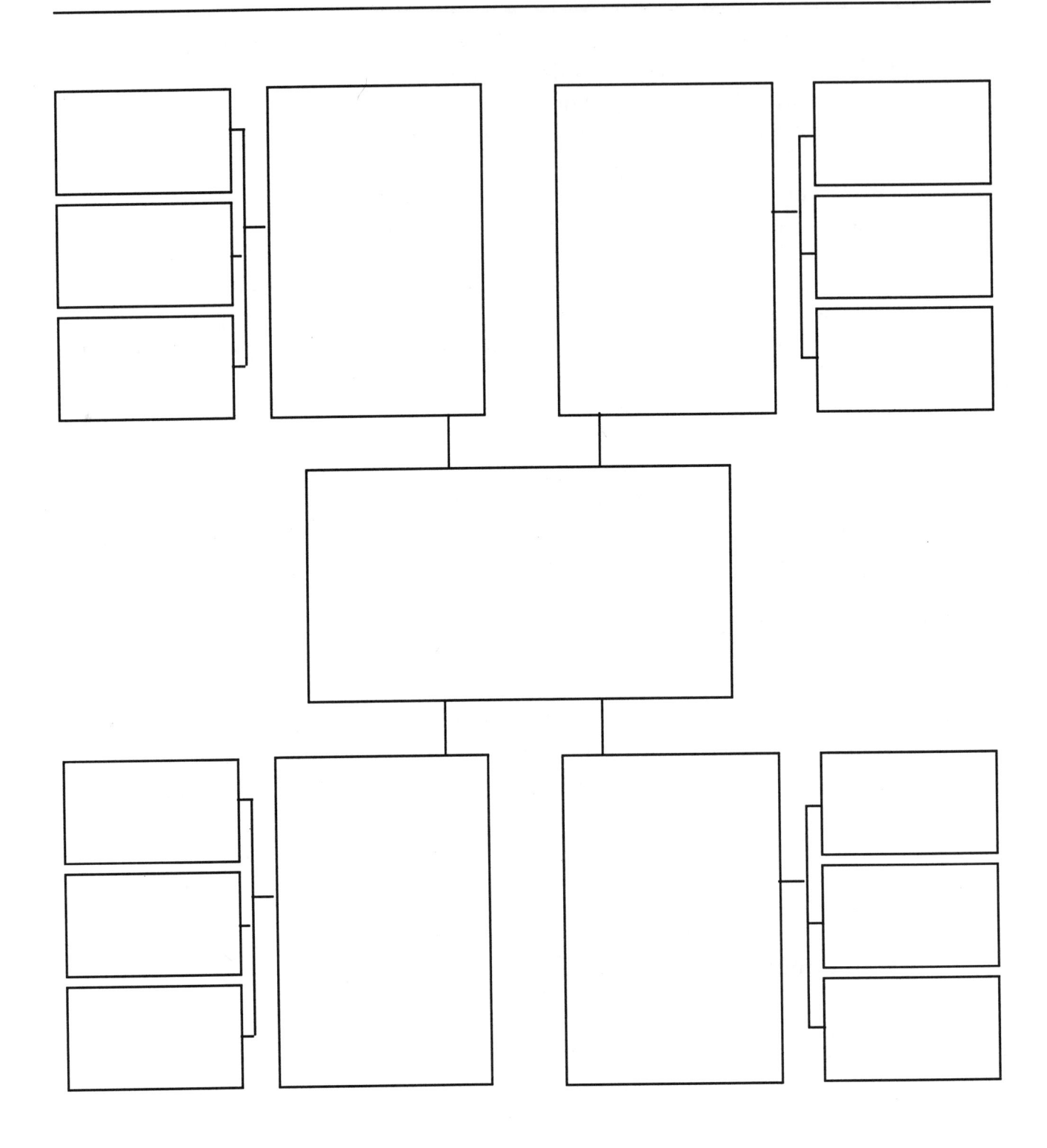

Lookin' For Waves: Information Exploration Ideas

Classifying Information

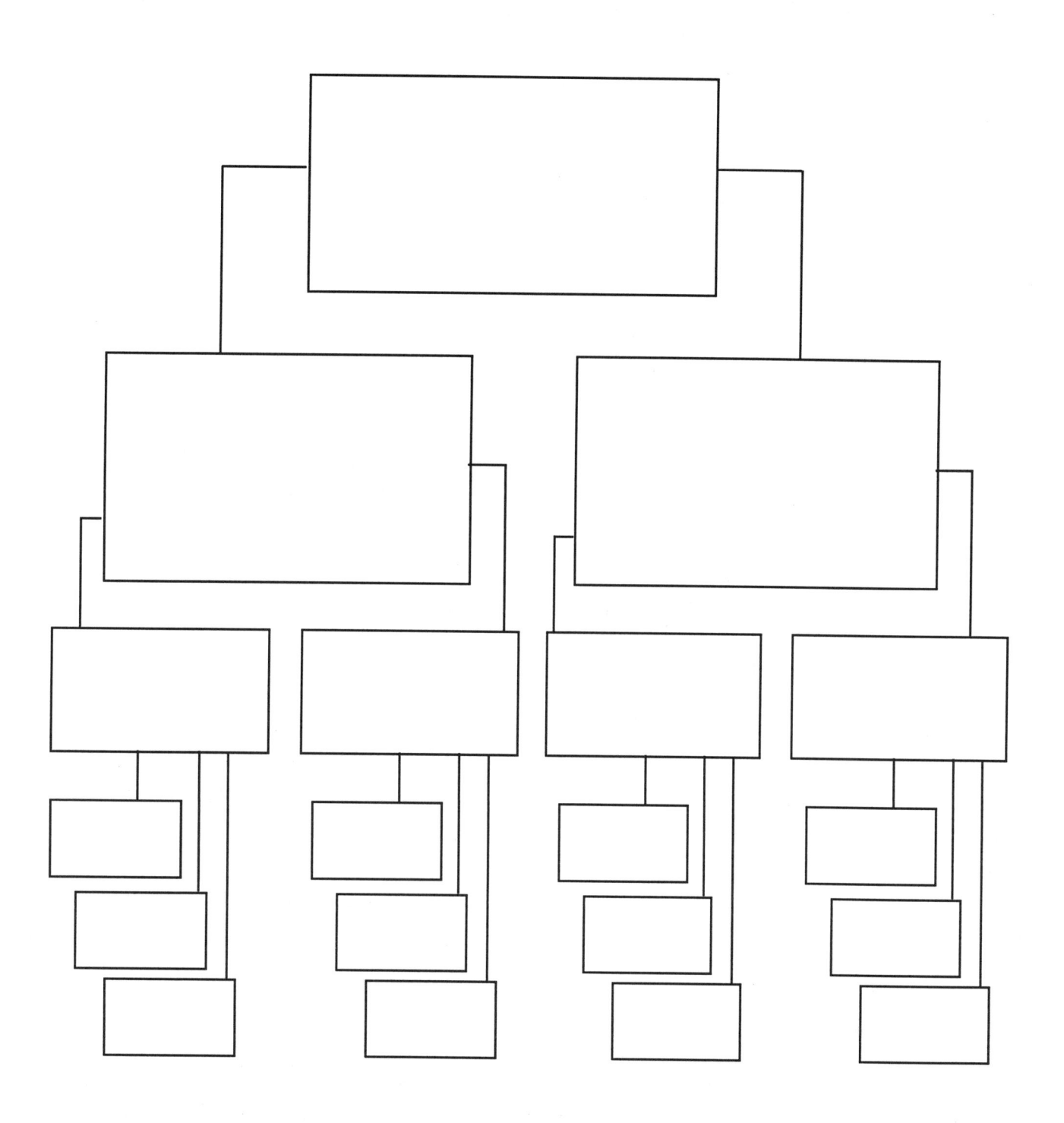

Visit the Gallup Poll Site!
http://www.gallup.com/

Public opinion polls are useful in tracing people's views on many important social issues. Explore the Gallup Poll Site.

Use the **Search Gallup Web Site** to identify information on a social issue or concern.

Trace the history of public opinion related to your issue. Create a timeline showing changes in opinion over time. Identify key turning points in public opinion. Speculate on reasons for these changes.

Develop and conduct a public opinion poll in your school on this issue. Compare these results to national and global polls. How are they alike and different? Why?

Create a list of questions you'd like the Gallup Poll people to explore. Email them to the web site.

Select a political campaign from recent history. Trace changes in public opinion in the year prior to the election. What conclusions can you draw? How could you use this information if you were developing a political campaign?

Take A Gallup Poll.

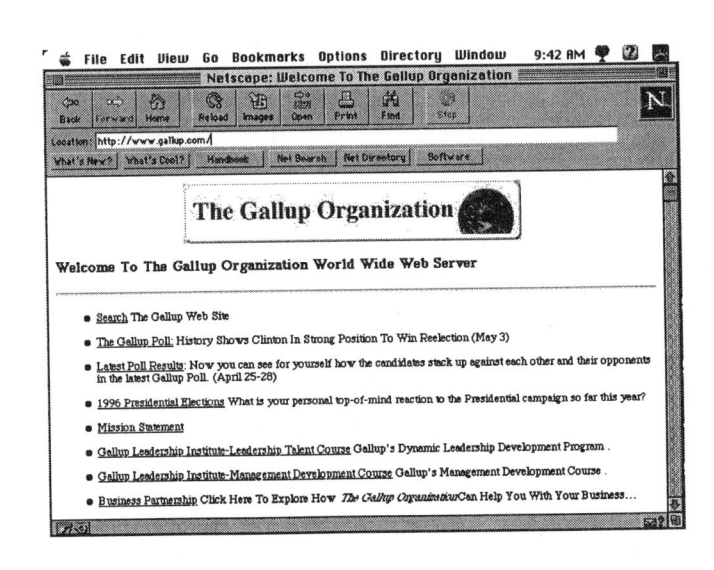

Wiggling

Wiggling is often the toughest phase for students. They're often uncertain about what they've found and where they're going with a project. According to Webster's dictionary, wiggling involves moving to and fro. In the wiggling phase, students twist and turn information looking for clues, ideas, and perspectives. Students working in small groups on a collaborate project can turn to the each other for support. However students working independently may need the support of friends, family, and teachers. Encourage students to use online support systems such as Ask the Expert sites or online pen pals and discussion groups.

Students need to learn to evaluate the quality of information. Encourage them to compare and contrast different information resources. Consider the following ideas:

Authority: Who says? Know the author. Is he or she stating fact or opinion? What knowledge or skills do they have in the area? Who created this information and why?

Objectivity: Is the information biased? Think about perspective. Is the information subjective or objective? Is it full of fact or opinion? Does it reflect bias? How?

Reliability: Is this information accurate? Consider the origin of the information. Does the information come from a school, business, or company site? What's their motive? Are they trying to inform or sell? Does this matter?

Relevance: Is the information helpful? Consider the currentness and timeliness of the information. Do the facts contribute something new or add to your knowledge of the subject? Will this information be useful to your project?

Activities for Students

Ask-the-Expert
Use **Ask-the-Expert** Pages to expand your project and answer important questions about your topic.

Share and Collaborate
Use Internet as a communication tool to discuss your project with other people who are interested in your topic. For example, use **Global Youth Dialog** to discuss your topic with other students.

Web Page Evaluation
Use **Kathy Schrock's Evaluation** page to evaluate web pages for your topic. Explore other sites that contain valuable information about evaluation.

Visit the Ask-An-Expert Site!
HTTP://njnie.dl.stevens-tech.edu/curriculum/aska.html

There are many places you can go to explore issues related to your topic. Find an expert in the area you're studying and ask a question. Start with the Ask-An-Expert Site (HTTP://njnie.dl.stevens-tech.edu/curriculum/aska.html). This will lead you to lots of other "ask" sites.

Go Ask Alice: Medical
   http://www.columbia.edu/cu/healthwise/
Ask the Mad Scientists
   http://pharmdec.wustl.edu/YSP/MAD.SCI/MAD.SCI.html
Ask Betty - The Cockroach Lady
   http://www.nj.com/yucky/betty/index.html#question
Ask-An Earth Scientist
   http://www.soest.hawaii.edu/GG/ASK/askanerd.html
Ask-A-Geologist
   http://walrus.wr.usgs.gov/docs/ask-a-ge.html
Ask-The-Curator (History Questions)
   http://earlyamerica.com/earlyamerica/curator.html
Ask-The-Folklore Folk
   http://www.islandnet.com/~shall/folklore/askfolk.htm
Ask-an-Astronomer
   http://www-hpcc.astro.washington.edu/k12/ask.html

Wouldn't it be fun to follow an architect on the design of a building or assist an astronomer in calculating some data? Many professionals welcome the opportunity to interact with young people. Try an "Ask the Expert" project where students contact a professional such as an engineer or physician through email. At the low end, ask questions about their career. At the high end, become involved with a rainforest protest, a NASA mission, or an archeological dig online!

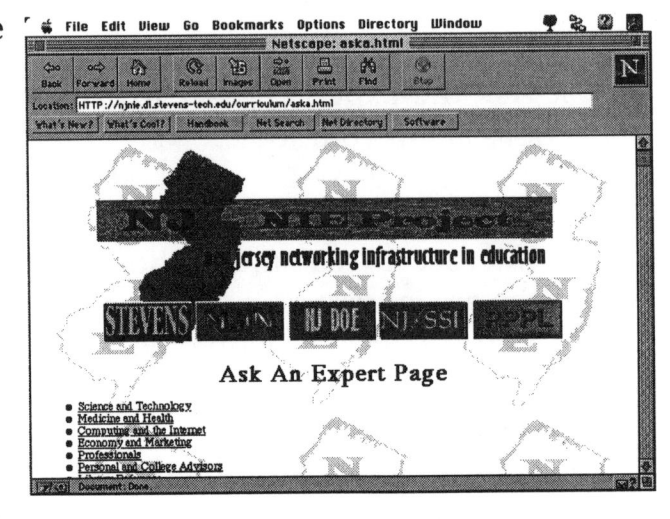

Lookin' For Waves: Information Exploration Ideas

Visit the Global Youth Dialog Site!
http://www.kidlink.org/home-std.html

Use the Internet to connect with other students who are interested in your topic.

Use **Global Youth Dialog** page in Kidlink to find out how you can discuss your topic with other students. Try using different forms of communication such as Web interaction, email, and chat.

Communicate with a student in another country about your topic. How is their perspective like and unlike yours?

You don't have to have an ask-the-expert site to contact a professional in your area of interest. Email the Webmaster of a site in your topic area. You can usually find the address of the Webmaster on the bottom of the Home page of the site. They may be able to put in you contact with a professional in your field of study.

Visit Kathy Schrock's Evaluation Page!
http://www.capecod.net/Wixon/eval.htm

Explore Kathy Schrock's Critical Evaluation Surveys.

Read the article titled **Thinking Critically about World Wide Web Resources** by Esther Grassian.

Read the article titled **Library Selection Criteria for WWW Resources** by Carolyn Caywood.

Select a survey and evaluate the Web sites you're using in your project.

Create a rating system for the Web sites in your content area. Rate each Web site included in your bibliography.

Write an article that reviews all the Web sites in your content area. Submit this article for publication on one of the sites.

Create your own web survey that focuses on evaluating web sites in your content area. Be sure to include items in each of the following areas:

Layout
Information Organization
Technical Aspects: Speed, Complete Links
Content Quality and Accuracy
Typography
Graphics
Navigation
Links within site
Links outside site
Contact information
Interaction

For other ideas about evaluating all types of information, try the following sites:

http://arlo.wilsonhs.pps.k12.or.us/evaluate.html

http://urislib.library.cornell.edu/skill20.html

http://urislib.library.cornell.edu/skill26.htm

http://library.uwaterloo.ca/howto/howto28.html

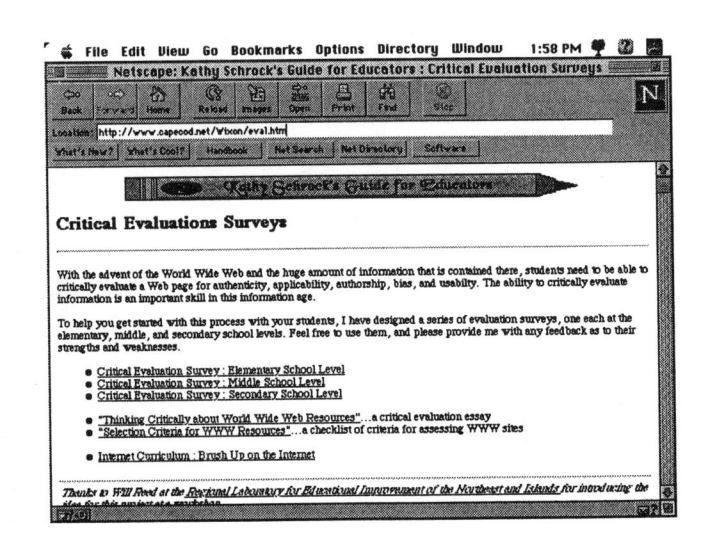

Lookin' For Waves: Information Exploration Ideas

Weaving

Weaving requires the highest levels of thinking. According to Webster's dictionary, weaving involves forming a product by interlacing strands. Elements are elaborately combined to produce a coherent whole. In this case, weaving focuses on the application and synthesis of information. Students originate new ideas, create models, and formulate plans. New questions emerge as the ideas are woven together: Can the problem be resolved? How? Who would need to be involved? Is it realistic? What can I do? Weaving ideas together is an important information skill. As students develop their projects, they should:

Compare. How is the information from different resources alike and different? Why? Compare and contrast sources and types of information.

Select. What information is useful? Eliminate extra information and keep the most powerful ideas. Be sure to cite your sources.

Organize. What's the best way to arrange the information? Identify key ideas. Cluster information together into categories. Determine a logical order of presentation.

Express. What's the best way to communicate your ideas to others? Synthesize the information into new words, develop a picture, create a chart, design a timeline, or make a video.

Activities for Students

Comparisons
Use the **Comparisons** worksheet to help organize and analyze information on topics where there are two or more sides. For example, you might compare and contrast two views on public smoking. Or, you could compare fur and anti-fur industry perspectives.

What-Ifs
Use the **What-Ifs** worksheet to examine the possibilities related to an issue. For example, what would happen if UFOs landed? What would happen if we eliminated the current welfare system? What would happen if we tried an alternative form of punishment for particular crimes?

Write It Up
Explore the writing process through the article **Quilt Analogy** (http://curry.edschool.virginia.edu/~ybf2u/metaphor/quilt.html).

Use a **Mind Map** (http://world.std.com/~emagic/mindmap.html) to help you organize ideas regarding your topic.

Organize your thoughts in writing. There are lots of web resources to help. Use the **Writing Resources** activity.

Compare/Contrast

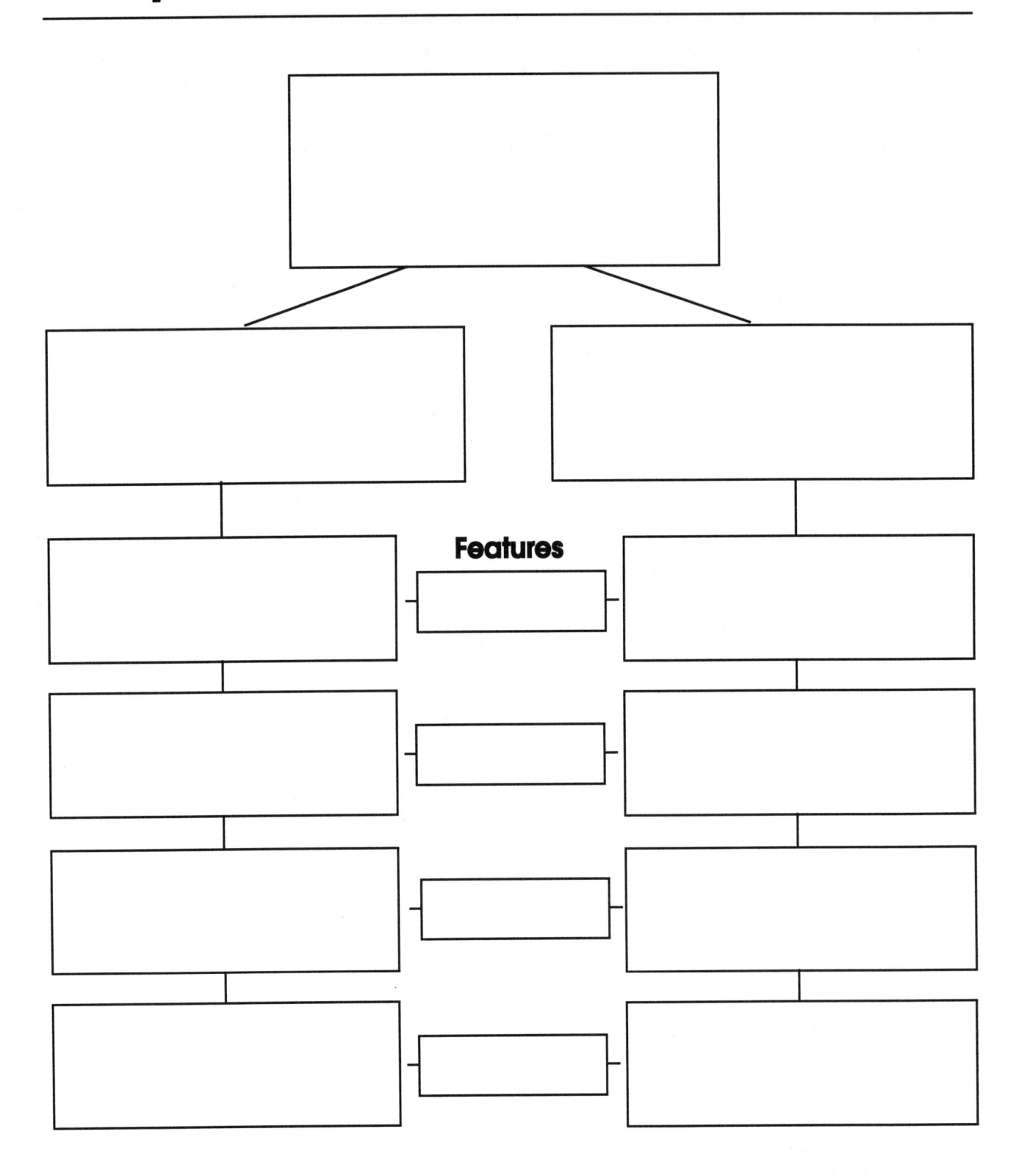

Features

Lookin' For Waves: Information Exploration Ideas 83

What Ifing

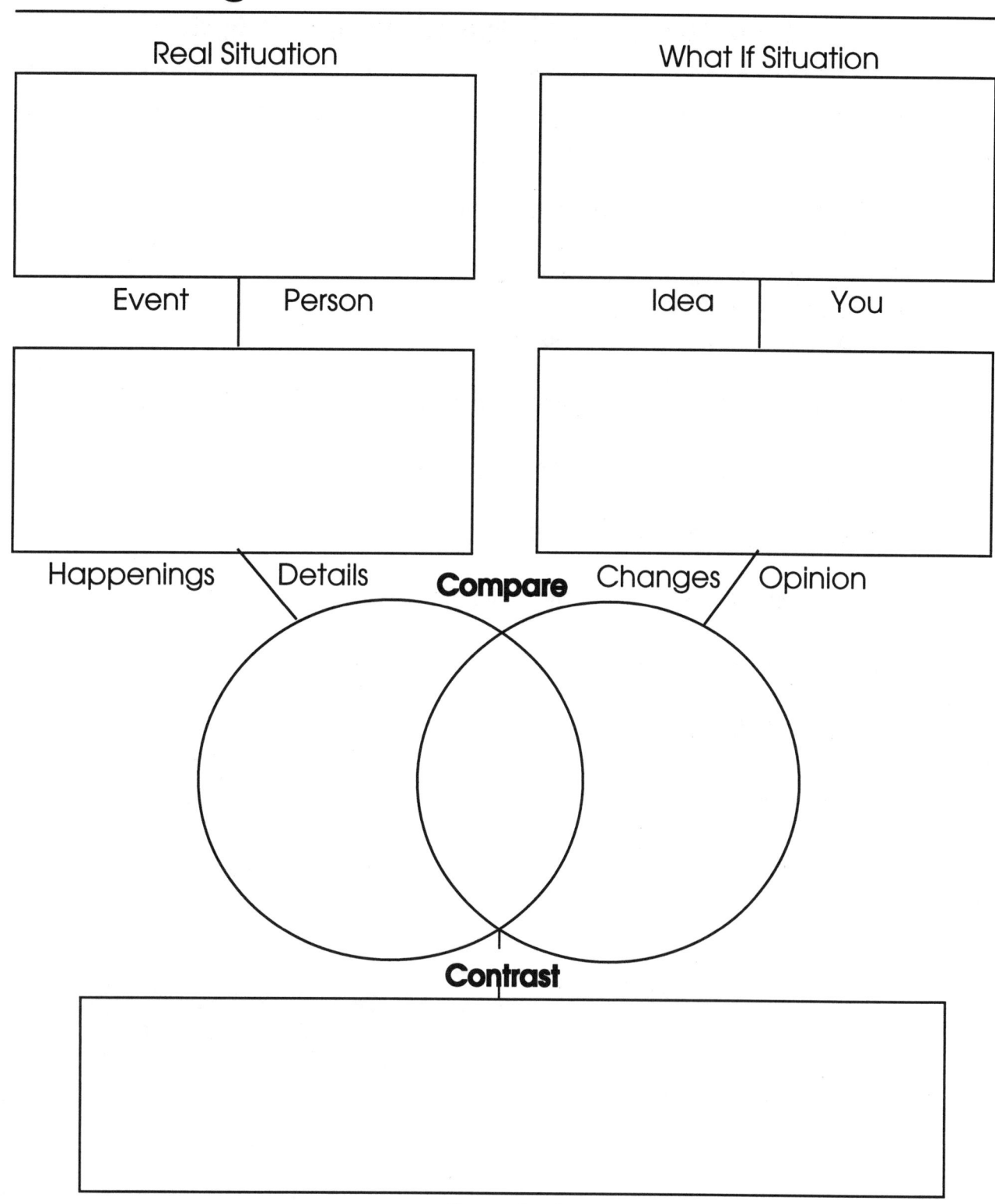

Real Situation

What If Situation

Event | Person

Idea | You

Happenings | Details

Changes | Opinion

Compare

Contrast

Conclude

Based on Moss Pointe, MS What If Model.

Visit Writing Resources Site!
http://www.missouri.edu/~wleric/writehelp.html

Explore thinking and writing resources. Use the resources below:

MindTools
http://www.demon.co.uk/mindtool/brainstm.html
Writing Resources
http://www.missouri.edu/~wleric/writehelp.html
Tools for Reading and Writing
http://garnet.berkeley.edu:4255/rnctools.html
Study, Research, & Writing Tools
http://www.uark.edu/depts/comminfo/www/study.html
Writing Tools
gopher://gopher.uiuc.edu:70/11/Libraries/writers/techniq
The Online Writery: Share Your Ideas
http://www.missouri.edu/~wleric/writery.html
Basic Prose Style and Mechanics
http://www.rpi.edu/dept/llc/writecenter/web/text/proseman.html
CyberCitations
http://kalama.doe.hawaii.edu/hern95/rt007/
Guide for Citing Electronic Information
http://www.wilpaterson.edu/wpcpages/library/citing.htm
Bibliographic Citations
http://www.uvm.edu/~xli/reference/estyles.html
Internet Citations
**gopher://h-net.msu.edu:70/00/lists/
H-AFRICA/internet-cit**
MLA Style Guide
**http://www.hcc.hawaii.edu:80/
education/hcc/library/mlahcc.html**
Copyright Information
gopher://marvel.loc.gov/11/copyright

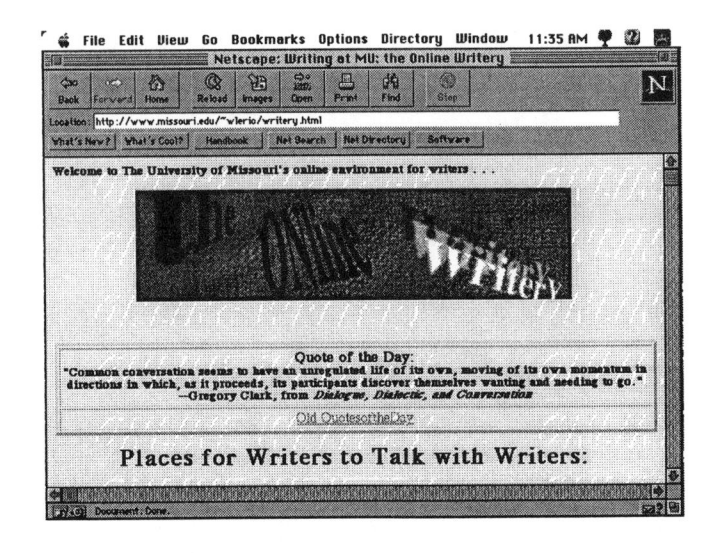

Wrapping

Wrapping involves packaging your ideas, solutions, and communications. Why is this issue important? Who needs to know about this? How can you effectively communicate your ideas to others? According to Webster's dictionary, wrapping involves winding, folding, surrounding, or embracing a product for transportation or storage. Students need to consider how they will communicate their vision to others.

Activities for Students

Develop a Product
Select a product to develop. Some ideas are listed below:

Action Plan	Advertising Campaign	Animation
Board Game	Brochure	Bumper Sticker
Cassette Recording	Chart	Collage
Debate	Demonstration	Diagram
Diorama	Display	Documentary
Essay	Interview	Invention
Letter	Magazine	Map
Mobile	Model	Multimedia Project
Mural	Musical Composition	Newscast
Newsletter	Newspaper	Oral Report
Pamphlet	Panel Discussion	Photo Essay
Play	Poem	Portfolio
Posters	Presentation	Quilt
Quiz Bowl	Radio Show	Research Paper
Role Playing	Simulation	Short Story
Skit	Slide Show	Survey Results
Transparencies	Web Page	Video

Find even more ideas at **Info Zone** (http://portal.mbnet.mb.ca/~mstimson/text/Producing.html).

Build a Web Page
There are lots of Internet resources that will help you build a web page. The **Nonprofit Prophet** does a great job exploring ways to communicate social issue ideas through web pages. The **Web Development** activity provides lots of tools and advice on developing web pages.

Visit the Nonprofit Prophets Site!
http://www.kn.pacbell.com/wired/prophets/prophets.html

Explore the Nonprofit Prophets site. Use their guidelines to create a web page.
Teams of students work together to select a local or global problem that they want to understand, serve, and solve. In partnership with a nonprofit organization, students develop a Web site that focuses on providing information and solutions to local problems. Investigate and write about a social issue.

Overview/Introduction
What are the main issues / controversies about your topic?

Causes of the Problem
What are the factors contributing to the problem you'd like to solve?

Fact or Fiction?
What are the realities and/or the stereotypes about your topic?

Profiles
What are specific examples of people or places affected by your topic?
Describe the lives of real people who confront the problem you're studying
Interview someone involved in your topic
Analyze a specific place and how it is affected by your topic

Comparison
What is a similar problem to the one you're studying?

Future Impact
What is a current action/trend/event and the likely future outcomes if it is not addressed now?

Solutions
What is a possible solution to your problem? Would it work in the real world?

Call to Action
What is a specific, local problem related to your topic? Create one possible way people could be called into action to make a change for the better.

Questionnaire / Statistics
What are the numbers related to your topic? Draw conclusions.

Quiz
What do people need to know after exploring your team's Web site?

Book Review
What is your analysis of an important book related to your topic?

Visit the Web Page Development Sites!
HTTP://www.wmht.org/trail/tender11.htm

Explore sites that will help you build your own web page.

Start at CyberTrail and learn about the HTML language.
HTTP://www.wmht.org/trail/tender11.htm

Then, try the following HTML guides.

HTML Crash Course for Educators
http://k12.cnidr.org:90/htmlintro.html

The Beginner's Guide to HTML
http://www.ncsa.uiuc.edu/General/Internet/WWW/HTMLPrimer.html

Use the Web Developer's Virtual Library - Style as a guide to lots of web development resources.
http://WWW.Stars.com/Vlib/Providers/Style.html

Explore Guidelines for Web Page Development

HTML Writer's Guide
http://www.synet.net/hwg/

Making the Most of the Web
http://www.gsfc.nasa.gov/documents/making_most_www.html

Web Wonk: Tips for Web Writers
http://www.dsiegel.com/tips/tips_home.html

On Design
http://128.95.12.62:1030/essays/design.html

Composing Good HTML
http://www.cs.cmu.edu/afs/cs.cmu.edu/Web/People/tilt/cgh/

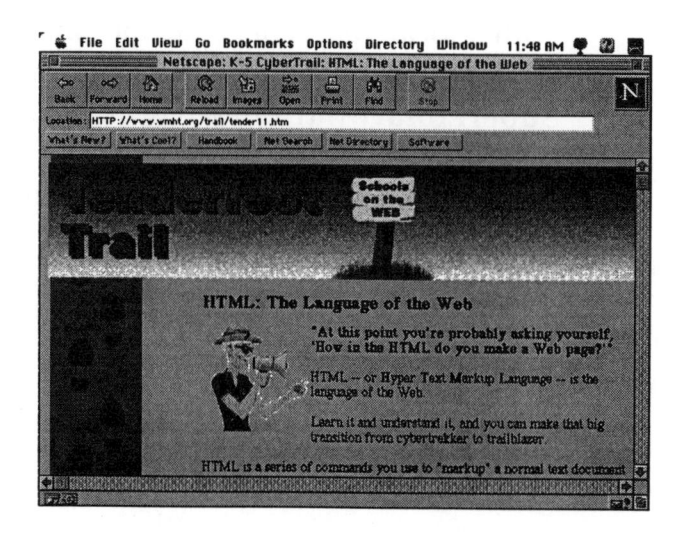

Waving

Waving is the publishing aspect of the project. Students share their ideas, try out new approaches, and ask for feedback. According to Webster's dictionary, waving is a gesture or signal. Students need to develop waves to gain the attention of their audience.

Waving a flag, volunteering at a soup kitchen, marching for a cause, presenting to a county board, publishing in an ezine, and sending a video to a nonprofit organization are all effective ways to draw attention and convey ideas. Some students may contact local, state, national, or international agencies to share their ideas directly with organizations that can initial change. Others may publish their projects in print or online form for other students.

Activities for Students

Identify an Audience
You've carefully explored issues, identified problems, and developed solutions. Who needs to hear, see, or read about your ideas? How can you have an impact? Explore ways to communicate your ideas to others.
Explore the **Act Locally** (http://www.igc.apc.org/igc/act.locally.html) page to learn how you can have an impact in your community.
Explore the **Social Activism** web pages (http://www.excite.com/Subject/Personal_Home_Pages/Activism/Social_Activists/s-index.msn.html).

Publish for the Audience
Explore ways to gain the attention of your audience. You may share your ideas with a local, regional, state, national, or international nonprofit agency, government organization, business, or industry. Use the **Information SuperLibrary** (http://www.mcp.com/) to locate information about organizations. For example, try the World Wide Web Yellow Pages (http://www.mcp.com/137135001568875/nrp/wwwyp/index.html) for organization and web sites.

Publish on the Web
Explore **ezines** and **kid pages** where you might publish your written communications.

Visit Online Magazine/Ezine Sites!
http://www.hmco.com/hmco/school/kids/links/kids_4.html

Many ezines publish student articles. Many of these are serious publications that even pay young authors for their work!

Sources for Student Online Magazines
Yahooligans Guide to Newspaper and Publications for Kids
    http://www.yahooligans.com/School_Bell/Newspapers_and_Publications/
Online Magazines for Kids
    http://www.hmco.com/hmco/school/kids/links/kids_4.html
Electronic Newsstand
    http://www.enews.com/

Student Ezines
CyberKids
    http://www.cyberkids.com/
Edge
    http://www.jayi.com/jayi/Fishnet/Edge/
Flash
    http://freezone.com/flash/flash.html
KidzMagazine
    http://www.thetemple.com:80/KidzMagazine/
Midlink
    http://longwood.cs.ucf.edu:80/~MidLink/
React
    http://www.react.com/
YesMag
    http://www.islandnet.com/~yesmag/
Zeen
    http://www.mtlake.com/cyberteens/ezine/Issues.html

Learn more about writing for these ezines by exploring the editorial guidelines.
Edge
    http://www.jayi.com/Fishnet/Edge/contrib.html

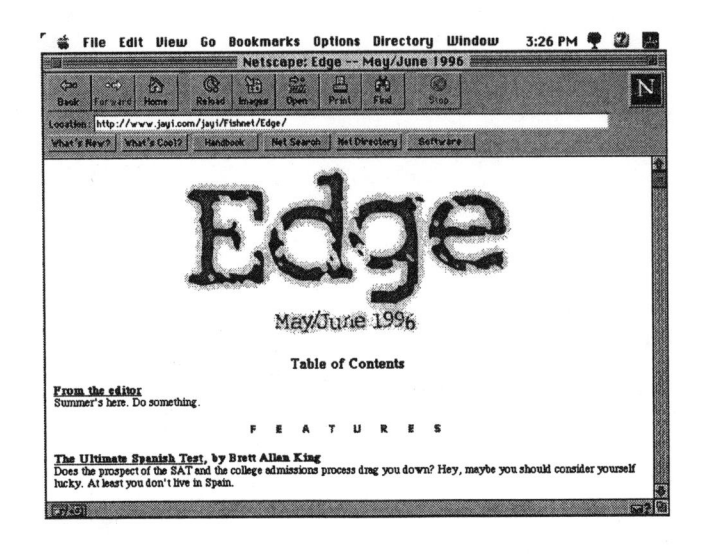

Visit The Vocal Point Site!
http://bvsd.k12.co.us/schools/cent/Newspaper/Newspaper.html

Many sites publish student work. The Vocal Point (http://bvsd.k12.co.us/schools/cent/Newspaper/Newspaper.html) is a student newspaper that focuses on important issues such as Animal Rights, Poverty, and the Environment. Check the upcoming issue and see if they will be addressing your topic.

Many other sites also post student work. They may publish pictures, paragraphs or articles. Explore some of these sites.

Hotlist: Kids Did This!
   http://sln.fi.edu/tfi/hotlists/kids.html
Global Show & Tell
   http://emma.manymedia.com:80/show-n-tell/
Kid News
   http://www.vsa.cape.com/~powens/Kidnews3.html
KidPub
   http://en-garde.com/kidpub/intro.html
International Kids Space
   http://plaza.interport.net/kids_space/
Kidopedia
   http://rdz.stjohns.edu/kidopedia/
Press Return
   http://www.scholastic.com/public/Network/PressReturn/Press-Return.html

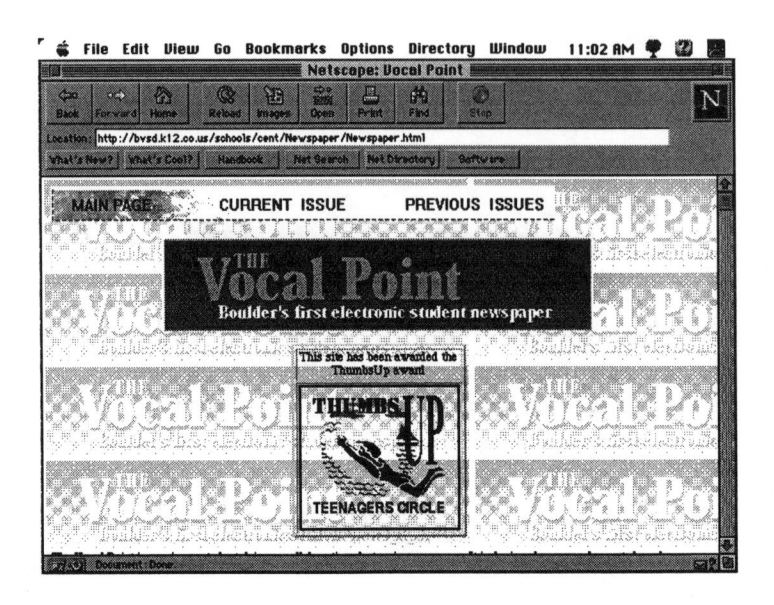

Wishing

Wishing is the reflection point in the project. Students begin thinking about how the project went and consider possibilities for the future. Students have the opportunity to reflect on their project and express their desires for the future. Looking back: What were the strengths and weaknesses of the project? What would I do differently? What would I change? How could I approach the problem from an alternative perspective?

Try the following easy self-evaluation tool:
   The strengths of this project are ...
   The weaknesses of this project are ...
   Next time I'll ...

It's helpful to explore the project from multiple perspectives. Teachers, friends, peers, parents, and other may be able to provide useful insights for future projects. For example, your art, computer, and English teachers would each be able to provide different views on your project.

Activities for Students

Evaluate Your Project
   Use the **Information Skills Rating System** to evaluate your project (http://www.pacificrim.net/~mckenzie/libskill.html).
   Use **Keating's Peer Evaluation** page (http://eee.oac.uci.edu/classes/wr139wi/doc/handouts.html#peer).

Explore Future Projects
   Explore online projects you might join in the future such as **Kidlink** (http://www.kidlink.org/KIDPROJ/).

Review the Process
   Review the entire information exploration process through **Info Zone** (http://portal.mbnet.mb.ca/~mstimson/).

Visit the Info Zone Site!
http://portal.mbnet.mb.ca/~mstimson/

- -

Explore the Info Zone. It will review the entire information skills process. It's very similar to our Ws. Explore each of the following areas:

Wondering about something

Seeking information

Choosing information

Connecting useful information you have found

Producing information of your own in a new form

Judging the entire process and your product

Explore other sites that might be helpful in research.

BeforeNet and AfterNet
http://www.pacificrim.net/~mckenzie/aforenet.html
Seven Effective Steps to Library Research
http://urislib.library.cornell.edu/tutorial.html
Study Skills
http://coos.dartmouth.edu:80/~gmz/asctr.html#study
Searching the Net
http://arlo.wilsonhs.pps.k12.or.us/search.html
Using Search Engines
http://dune.srhs.k12.nj.us/WWW/SEARCH1.HTML

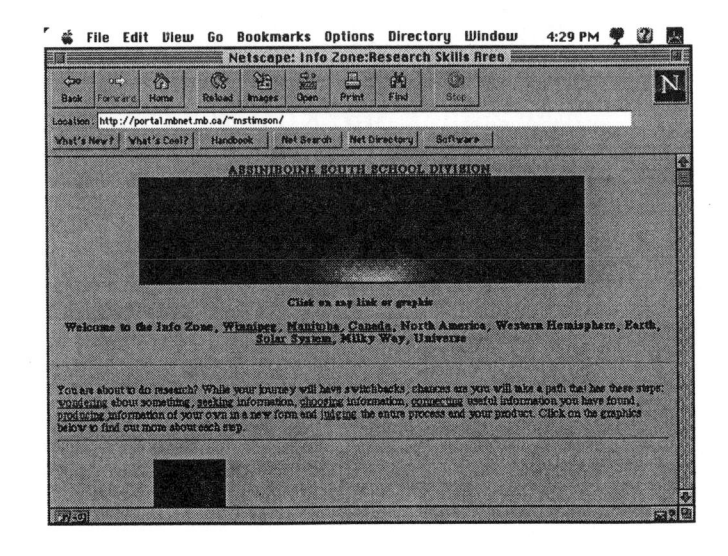

General Social Issues

The second part of this section provides suggestions for projects related to social issues. Internet is full of opinion. People love to share their ideas about every topic imaginable. Explore what people are talking about on the Internet and add your perspective!

Surfer Starters

Life Education Network
   http://www.lec.org/
Human Rights Page
   http://www.traveller.com/~hrweb/hrweb.html
Social Services for Teens
   http://ipl.sils.umich.edu/teen/socser/
Loss of Innocence in Literature
   http://www.computek.net/public/barr/good.html
Abuse of Power in Literature
   http://www.computek.net/public/barr/utopia.html
Self Help and Psychology
   http://www.well.com/user/selfhelp/
PeaceNet
   http://www.igc.apc.org/peacenet/pn_issues.html
Health
   http://www.cdc.gov/cdc.html
   http://www-sci.lib.uci.edu/HSG/Ref.html
Achoo
   http://www.achoo.com/
Mental Health Net
   http://www.cmhcsys.com/
General Psychology Resources
   http://rdz.stjohns.edu/~warren/psych.html

CD-ROM

ADAMS Essentials, Broderbund
BodyPark, Virtual Entertainment
BodyWorks 4.0, Softkey
Mayo Clinic, IVI Publishing
Ultimate Human Body, Dorling Kindersley

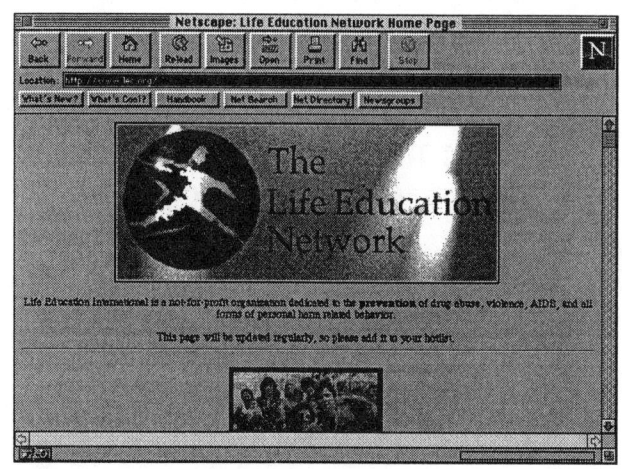

http://www.lec.org/

Abuse: Physical & Emotional

Physical and emotional abuse is a worldwide problem. Has it had an impact on your life? What can you do to prevent abuse?

Surfer Starters
   http://www.ai.mit.edu/people/ellens/NCRA/ncra.html
   http://www.med.umich.edu/aacap/child.abuse.html
Domestic Violence
   http://www.abanet.org/textonly/domviol/home.html
Safety Net
   http://www.cybergrrl.com/dv.html
Family Violence Prevention Fund
   http://www.igc.apc.org/fund/
Silent Witness
   http://www.cybergrrl.com/dv/orgs/sw.html
Abuse Survivor's Page
   http://www.tezcat.com/~tina/psych.shtml

Other Information Resources
Anderson, Deborah (1986) **Liza's Story: Neglect & The Police**. Dillon Press.
Anderson, Deborah (1986) **Michael's Story: Emotional Abuse & Working With A Counselor**. Dillon Press.
Anderson, Deborah (1986) **Robin's Story: Physical Abuse & Seeing the Doctor**. Dillon Press.
Hyde, Margaret (1992) **Know About Abuse**. Walker.
Mufson, Susan (1991) **Straight Talk About Child Abuse**. Facts On File.
Stark, Evan (1989) **Everything You Need To Know About Family Violence**. Rosen Pub. Group.

Powerful Projects
Explore the **Family Violence Prevention Fund.**
Get the Facts first! Then, create a Violence Prevention poster using a quote from a celebrity.
Take the Domestic Violence Quiz.
Explore some aspect of Violence Prevention such as Global, Personal, Workplace.

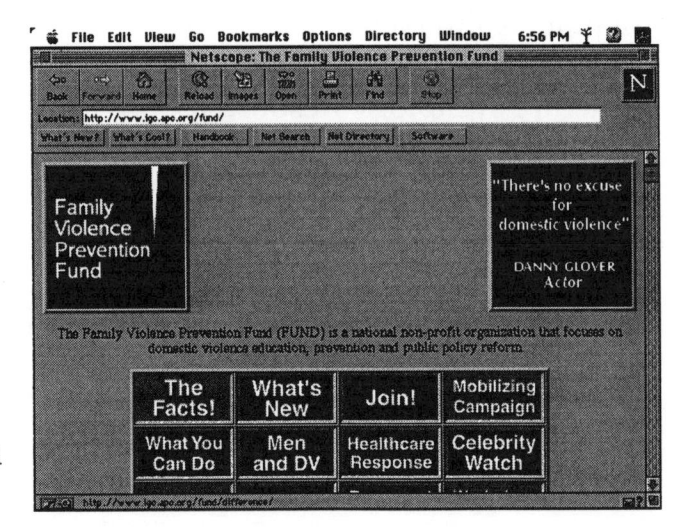

Aging

Aging is a natural part of life, but for many people it is filled with concerns about loneliness and medical problems. Learn about the concerns of the elderly including diseases such as Alzheimer's and osteoporosis.

Surfer Starters
    http://www.pitt.edu/HOME/GHNet/GHWomen.html#Aging
    http://www.service.com/answers/cover.html
    gopher://cuhsla.cpmc.columbia.edu/h/health.sci/dental.toc/Dental_Ed
Health Care for Elderly
    http://www.hslib.washington.edu:80/your_health/elderly.html
Alzheimer's Disease
    http://www.cais.com/adear/
    http://werple.mira.net.au/~dhs/ad.html
    http://teri.bio.uci.edu/
Alzheimer's Association
    http://www.alz.org/
Administration on Aging
    http://www.AoA.DHHS.GOV/aoa/pages/info.html
National Osteoporosis Foundation
    http://www.nof.org/
Aging Resource Center
    http://www.hookup.net/mall/aging/agesit59.html
Centre for Studies of Aging
    http://library.utoronto.ca/www/aging/depthome.html
Elder Care Web
    http://www.ice.net/~kstevens/AGING.HTM

Other Information Resources
Comfort, Alex (1990) **Say Yes To Old Age: Developing A Postive Attitude Toward Aging**. Crown.
Farber, Norma (1979) **How Does It Feel To be Old?** Dutton.
Frank, Julia (1985) **Alzheimers Disease The Silent Epidemic.** Lerner Publications Co. Minneapolis.
Klein, Leonore (1983) **Old, Older, Oldest.** Hastings House.
Guthrie, Donna (1986) **Grandpa Doesn't Know It's Me**. Human Sciences Press.
Heston, Leonard L. (1991) **The Vanishing Mind: A Practical Guide To Alzheimer's Disease and Other Dementias**. W.H. Freeman.

Landau, Elaine (1987) **Alzheimer's Disease**. Watts.
Langone, John (1991) **Growing Older: What Young People Should Know About Aging**. Little Brown.
Leshan, Eda J. (1984) **Grandparents: A Special Kind of Love**. Macmillan.
Raymond, Florian (1994) **Surviving Alzheimer's: A Guide For Families**. Elder Books.
Reisberg, Barry (1983) **A Guide To Alzheimer's Disease**. Free Press.
Silverstein, Alvin (1979) **Aging**. Watts.
Taira, Frances (1983) **Aging: A Guide for The Family**. Technomic Pub Co.
Vierck, Elizabeth (1990) **Fact Book On Aging**. ABC-CLio.

Wave Words

aging   Alzheimer's   Elderhostel   AARP
retirement medicare   elderly

Powerful Projects

Explore the **Administration on Aging**. Address one of the following questions:

What are the key issues of concern for the Aging? Develop a debate about one of the following age-related issues: compulsory retirement, early retirement, medicare, or illness.

What are the major issues in determining longevity? What can you do to extend your life? If you could extend your life through genetic engineering, would you do it? Why or why not?

Where would you want a terminally ill family member to live? Compare and contrast living at home, in the hospital, or in a hospice. Which one would you suggest? Why?

Why is Alzheimer's disease called the silent epidemic? What are the symptoms of Alzheimer's disease?

What is meant by the statement, "you're only as old as you feel"? Some people say that age is a mental state, not a physical state? What do they mean by that statement? Give some examples.

What's AARP? How has AARP become such a large lobbying group? How is AARP having an impact on legislative issues?

What's the Elderhostel program? Why is it a popular program?

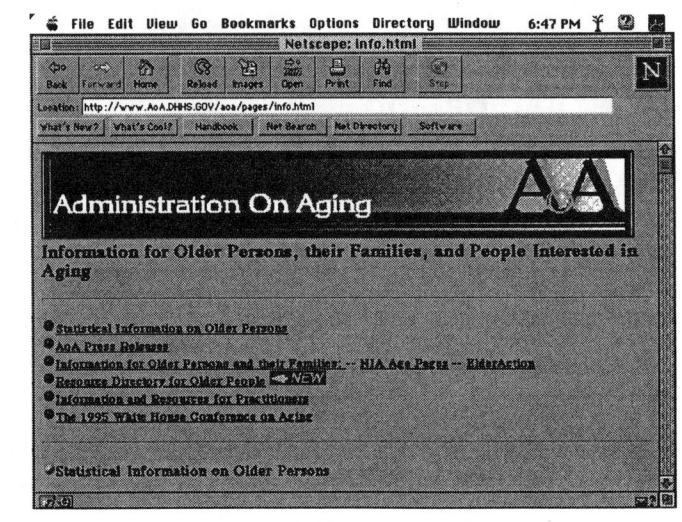

AIDS

AIDS is a disease of this generation. What causes AIDS? How can it prevented? How can you help? Explore issues related to AIDS and AIDS awareness.

Surfer Starters

Achoo Aids Index
   http://www.achoo.com/human/diseases/immunity/aids_hiv.htm
General Resources
   http://www.hslib.washington.edu:80/your_health/aids.html
   http://www.nnlm.nlm.nih.gov/pnr/etc/aidspath.html
   http://bianca.comm/lolla/politics/aids/
   http://www.med.umich.edu/aacap/child.adol.aids.html
How is AIDS Transmitted?
   http://www.cmpharm.ucsf.edu/~troyer/safesex/howisaidstransmitted.html
Condoms and Safe Sex
   http://www.cmpharm.ucsf.edu/~troyer/safesex/condomuse.html
AIDS Information
   http://www.aidsnyc.org/index.html
CDC National AIDS Clearinghouse
   http://www.cdcnac.org/
Names Project: Quilts Memorial
   http://www.aidsquilt.org/

Other Information Resources

Hyde, Margaret O. & Forsyth, Elizabeth (1992) **Know About Aids**. Walker & Company.

Silverstein, Alvin & Virginia (1991) **Aids Deadly Threat**. Enslow Publishers Inc.

Colman Warren (1988) **Understanding & Preventing AIDS**. Childrens.

Hawkes, Negel (1987) **AIDS**. Gloucester.

Hausherr, Rosmarie (1989) **Children & the AIDS Virus**. Ticknor.

Powerful Projects

Watch QuickTime videos at the **CDC National AIDS Clearinghouse**.

Some people have said that fear and ignorance is an important part of the battle against AIDS. What is meant by this statement? How would you suggest we deal with fear and ignorance?

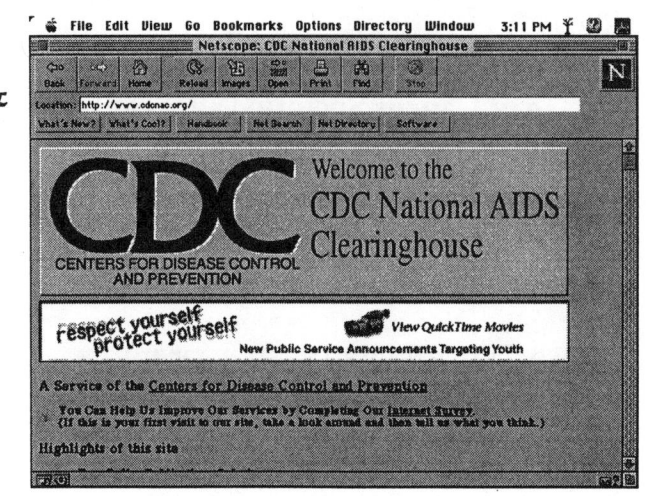

Cancer

Cancer is a leading cause of death. There are many types of cancer with many treatments. Explore a specific type of cancer and its prevention.

Surfer Starters
General Cancer Resources
   http://www.yahoo.com/Health/Medicine/Cancer/
   http://www.hslib.washington.edu:80/your_health/cancer.html
   http://mlink.hh.lib.umich.edu/health/health-disease-cancer-web.html
American Cancer Society
   http://www.cancer.org/
Cancer Guide
   http://asa.ugl.lib.umich.edu/chdocs/cancer/CANCERGUIDE.HTML
CancerNet
   http://icicc.nci.nih.gov/clinpdq/canet.html

Other Information Resources
Burns, Sheila (1982) **Cancer: Understanding It & Fighting It**. Messner.
Fine, Judylaine (1986) **Afraid To Ask: A Book For Families To Share About Cancer**. Lothrop, Lee, & Shepard Books.
Fradin, Dennis B. (1988) **Cancer**. Childrens.
Herda, D. J. (1989) **Cancer**. F. Watts.
Silverstein, Alvin (1987) **Cancer: Can It Be Stopped?** Harper Collins.
Terkel, Susan Neiburg (1993) **Understanding Cancer**. F. Watts.
Yount, Lisa (1991) **Cancer**. Lucent.

Powerful Projects
Explore the resources at the **American Cancer Society**. What can you do to prevent cancer?

Find general cancer information at **Cancer Guide**.

Use **CancerNet** to search for information about a particular type of cancer.

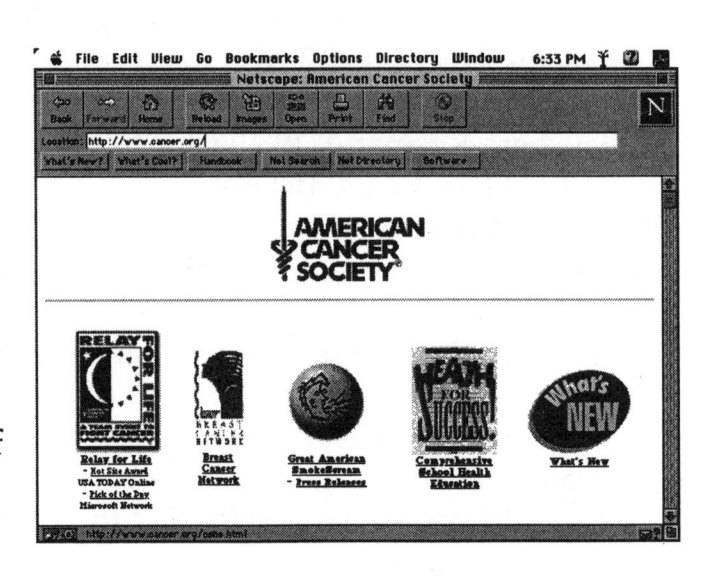

Lookin' For Waves: Information Exploration Ideas

Crime, Conflict, & Resolution

Crime, gangs, and violence is an increasing problem. What can we do to fight back? Explore Internet resources that explore conflict and resolution.

Surfer Starters

Bureau of Justice Statistics
   http://www.ojp.usdoj.gov/bjs/
Criminal Justice
   http://www.stpt.usf.edu/~greek/cj.html
   http://www.usc.edu/users/help/flick/Reference/la_main.html
Death Penalty
   http://sun.soci.niu.edu/~critcrim/dp/dp.html
Federal Bureau of Investigation
   http://www.fbi.gov/
Gun Control
   http://www.med.umich.edu/aacap/child.firearms.html
Juvenile Justice
   http://www.ncjrs.org/jjhome.htm
Justice Information
   http://www.ncjrs.org/homepage.htm
Sexual Assault
   http://www.cs.utk.edu/~bartley/saInfoPage.html
Peacenet
   http://www.peacenet.apc.org/peacenet
Nonviolence Resources
   http://www.igc.apc.org/nonviolence/
Conflictnet
   http://www.igc.apc.org/conflictnet/

Other Information Resources

Bernards, Neal (1991) **Gun Control**. Lucent Books.
Davidson, Osha Gray (1993) **Under Fire: The NRA & The Battle For Gun Control**. H. Holt.
Goldstein, Arnold P. (1991) **Delinquent Gangs: A Psychological Perspective**. Research Press.
Greenberg, Keith Elliot (1992) **Out Of The Gang**. Lerner.
Haskins, James (1977) **Street Gangs: Yesterday & Today**. Hastings.
Hjelmeland, Any (1992) **Kids In Jail**. Lerner.

Johnson, D. (1992) **This Thing Called Gangs: A Guide To Recognizing the Danger Signs**. Lone Tree Publishing Co.

Larson, Erik (1994) **Lethal Passage: How the travels of a single handgun expose the roots of America's crisis**. Crown Publishers.

La Pierre, Wayne (1994) **Guns, Crime, & Freedom (NRA)** Regnery Gateway.

Meltzer, Milton (1993) **Crime In America**. Morrow.

Nisbet, Lee (1990) **The Gun Control Debate: You Decide**. Prometheus Books.

Osman, Karen (1992) **Gangs**. Lucent Books.

Weinberg, Tom (Videorecording) (1992) **The 90's Guns & Violence. Fund For Innovative TV**. Subtle Communications.

Powerful Projects

Choose an issue related to violence such as gangs, gun control, or capital punishment. Trace the history of the issue. How have things changed over the past 30 years?

Explore the **Bureau of Justice Statistics** (http://www.ojp.usdoj.gov/bjs/). Create a chart showing statistics in one of the following areas: Drugs and crime or Criminal offenders. Then, explore one of the following areas and relate it to the issue you traced over 30 years: law enforcement, prosecution, courts and sentencing, corrections, expenditure and employment, or criminal record systems. Use the "What Ifing" planning sheet to speculate on the future of one of these areas.

Explore one of the **FBI** (http://www.fbi.gov/) ongoing investigations.

Find **Peacenet** (http://www.peacenet.apc.org/peacenet/). Select an activity of an organization working for peace. Do you think their approach will or will not be effective? What would you suggest? Find out how you can have an impact in your local area (http://www.peacenet.apc.org/igc/act.locally.html). Create a peace plan for your community.

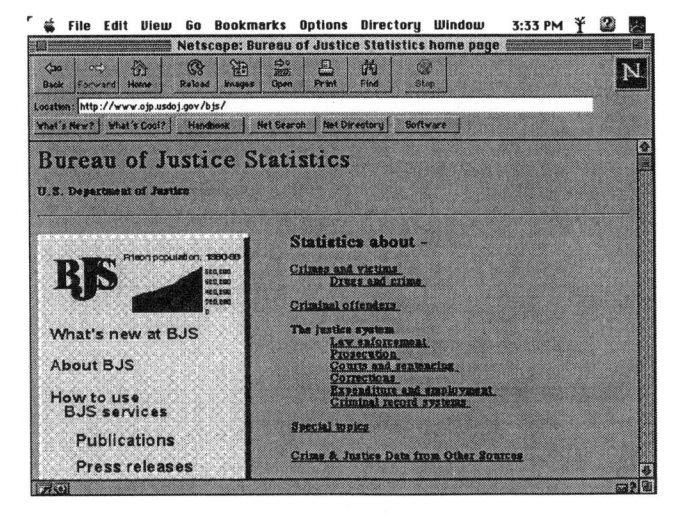

Death & Dying

At one time or another we all must deal with issues related to death and dying. Whether it's a friend, grandparent, or pet, it's an emotional process. What do you need to know to help yourself or a friend?

Surfer Starters

Emotional Support Guide
   http://asa.ugl.lib.umich.edu/chdocs/support/emotion.html
Death, Dying, and Grief Resources
   http://www.cyberspy.com/~webster/death.html
GriefNet
   http://www.griefnet.org.uk/
Grief and Loss
   gopher://gopher.uiuc.edu:70/00/UI/CSF/Coun/SHB/grief
   http://www.med.umich.edu/aacap/children.grief.html
Project on Death in America
   http://www.soros.org/death.html
Raindrop
   http://iul.com/raindrop/
Crisis, Grief, and Healing
   http://www2.dgsys.com/~tgolden/

Other Information Resources

   Bratman, Fred (1992) **Everything You Need To Know When A Parent Dies**. Rosen.
   Hyde, Margaret (1989) **Meeting Death.** Walker.
   Krementz, Jill (1981) **How It Feels When A Parent Dies.** Knopf.
   Holden, Dwight (1989) **Gran-Gran's Best Trick**. Magination Press.
   Rafes, Eric E. (1985) **Kids Book About Death & Dying.** Little Brown.
   Saying Goodbye (Videocassette) (1993) Sunburst.

Powerful Projects

   Read the poem and story called **Raindrop** (http://iul.com/raindrop/). How does it relate to life and death? Create your own story to illustrate your perspective.

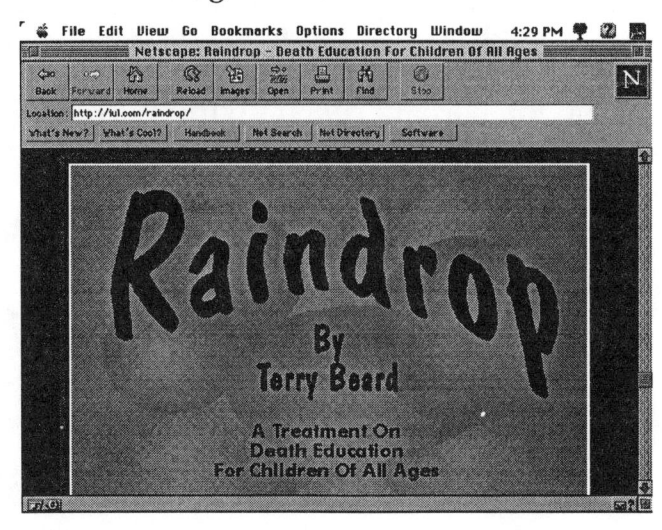

Diabetes

Diabetes is a very misunderstood disease. Children, young adults, and the elderly are all targets of diabetes. About 10% of Americans have been diagnosed with diabetes. It affects the way your body uses food. Although these is no cure, treatment is available.

Surfer Starters
American Diabetes Association
   http://www.diabetes.org/
Diabetes Index
   http://www.hslib.washington.edu:80/your_health/diabetes.html
General Resources
   http://www.niddk.nih.gov/overview/overview.html
   http://www.versa.com/adahome.html
What is Diabetes?
   http://www.diabetes.org/ada/c20.html
Diabetes Self-Management
   http://www.enews.com/magazines/diabetes/

Other Information Resources
Kipnis, Lynne & Adler, Susan (1979) **Diabetes**. Triad Scientific.
Kipnis, Lynne (1979) **You Can't Catch Diabetes From A Friend**.
Bergman, Thomas (1992) **Meeting The Challenge: Children Living With Diabetes**. Gareth Stevens.
Pirner, Connie White (1991) **Even Little Kids Get Diabetes**. Whitmore.
Silverstein, Alvin (1979) **Diabetes: The Sugar Disease**. Harper.
Silverstein, Alvin (1984) **Runaway sugar; All About Diabetes**. Lippincott.
Taylor, Barbara (1989) **Living With Diabetes**. Watts.
Tiger, Steven (1987) **Diabetes**. Messner.

Powerful Projects
Start at the **American Diabetes Assocation** for an overview of issues related to diabetes.
Take the diabetes test.
Explore state information.

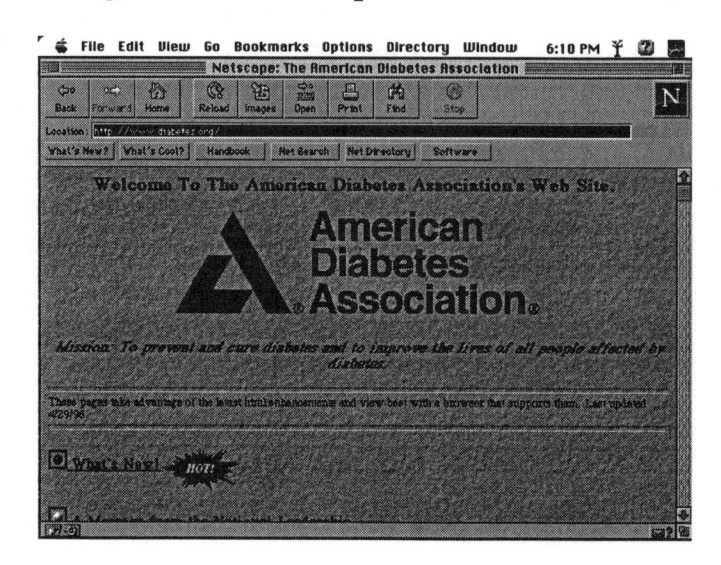

Eating Disorders

Eating disorders such as anorexia nervosa and bullimia are more common than you might think. You probably even have a friend that shows some of the signs of an eating disorder. Learn how you could save a life by helping a friend with an eating disorder.

Surfer Starters

Eating Disorders
   http://www.pb.net/usrwww/w_fishy/ed.htm
   http://www.med.umich.edu/aacap/teenage.eating.html
Ask the Dietitian
   http://www.hoptechno.com/rdindex.htm
Eating Disorders
   http://www.fda.gov:80/opacom/catalog/eatdis.html
Anorexia Nervosa: A Definition
   http://www.coil.com/~grohol/sx2.htm
Bullimia Nervosa: A Definition
   http://www.coil.com/~grohol/sx3.htm

Other Information Resources

Claypool, Jane & Nielsen, Cheryl D. (1983) **Foods Trips & Traps: Coping With Eating Disorders**. Watts.

Epstein, Rachel (1990) **Eating Habits & Disorders**. Chelsea House.

Erlanger, Ellen (1988) **Eating Disorders: A Question & Answer Book About Anorexia Nervosa & Bulimia Nervosa**. Lerner.

Hautzig, Deborah (1981) **Second Star To The Right**. Greenwillow.

Landau, Elaine (1983) **Why Are They Starving Themselves? Understanding Anorexia Nervosa & Bulimia**. Messner.

Ruckman, Ivy (1983) **The Hunger Scream** (Novel) Walker.

Willey, Margaret (1983) **The Bigger Book of Lydia** (Story) Harper.

Wolhart, Dayna (1988) **Anorexia & Bulimia**. Crestwood.

Powerful Projects

Explore **Eating Disorders**. Do you have a friend with an eating disorder? Check out the signs and symptons. What are the physical dangers? What would you do to help a friend?

Families and Relationships

Families are changing. You may live with parents, grandparents, guardians, or siblings. Your world also includes other kinds of relationships such as friends, peers, and mentors. Explore relationships through the Internet.

Surfer Starters

Marriage and Family
http://WWW.Trinity.Edu/~mkearl/family.html
Family Relationships
http://www.med.umich.edu/aacap/children.divorce.html
http://www.med.umich.edu/aacap/stepfamily.problems.html
The Divorce Page
http://www.primenet.com/~dean/
Divorce Statistics
http://www.cdc.gov/nchswww/releases/fs_439s.htm
Family.com
http://www.family.com/
Family Page
http://web.gc.cuny.edu/dept/socio/resource/family/index.htm
Welfare and Families
http://epn.org/idea/welfare.html

Other Information Resources

Booker, Dianna Daniels (1982) **Making Friends With Yourself & Other Strangers**. Messner.

Brown, Lairene Krasny (1986) **Dinosaurs Divorce: A Guide for Changing Families**. Atlantic Monthly Press.

Fassler, David (1988) **Changing Families: A Guide for Kids & Grown-Ups**. Waterfront Books.

Gilbert, Sara (1982) **How To Live With A Single Parent.** Lothrop.

Kid's Guide To Divorce (Sound Filmstrip) (1988) Learning Tree.

Leshan, Eda J. (1990) **When Kids Drive Kids Crazy: How To Get Along With Your Friends & Enemies.** Dial.

McGuire, Paula (1987) **Putting It Together: A Teenagers Talk About Family Breakup**. Delacare Press.

Morris, Ann (1990) **Loving**. Lothrop, Lee, & Shepard.

Prokop, Michael S. (1986) **Divorce Happens To The Nicest Kids: A Self Help Book for Kids & Adults**. Alegra House.

Robins, Arthur (1988) **Why Are We Getting A Divorce?** Harmony Books.
Rogers, Fred (1987) **Making Friends**. Putnam.
Rogers, Fred (1987) **Mister Rogers Talks with Families About Divorce**. Berkley Books.
Schneider, Meg F. (1985) **Two In A Crowd: How To Find Romance Without Losing Your Friends**.
Schroeder, Ted (1985) **Art Of Playing Second Fiddle: Encouraging Teens Who Never Place First**. Concordia Paper.
Stinson, Kathy (1984) **Mom & Dad Don't Live Together Anymore**. Annick Press.
Watson, Jane Werner (1988) **Sometimes a Family Has To Split Up**. Crown Publishers.

Powerful Projects

Explore the Marriage and Family Page (http://WWW.Trinity.Edu/~mkearl/family.html).
Select one of the following areas to explore:
   Families Across Culture and Time
   Family Structure: gender, age, sexuality
   Violent Families
   Life-Cycle & Family Relationships:
   Courtship and Pairing
   Marriage
   Parenting
   The Father
   The Mother
   Single Parenting
   Adoption and Foster Parenting
   Children
   Multiple Generation Families
   Divorce
   Child Custody
   Death

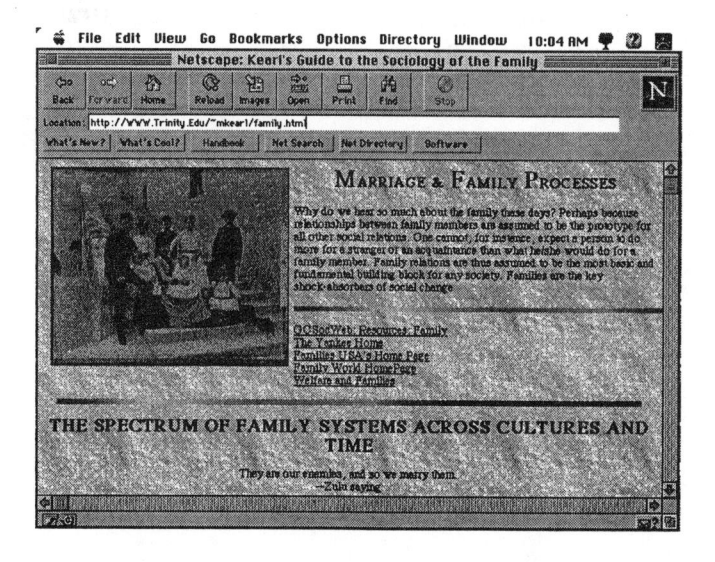

Homelessness, Hunger, & Poverty

Homelessness, hunger, and poverty are found everywhere. How can you help?

Surfer Starters

http://www.iia.org/~deckerj/
Coalition for Homelessness
http://www2.ari.net/home/nch/
54 Ways to Help the Homeless
http://ecosys.drdr.virginia.edu/ways/54.html
One Family's Path to Homelessness
http://nch.ari.net/sjoblom1.html
National Center for Children in Poverty
http://cpmcnet.columbia.edu:80/dept/nccp/

Other Information Resources

Atavsky, Lois (1992) **The Place I Call Home: Voices & Faces Of Homeless Teens**. Spapolsky Publishers.

Burt, Martha R. (1989) **America's Homeless: Numbers, Characteristics, & Programs That Serve Them**. Urban Institute Press.

Down & Out In America (Videorecording) (1987) MPI Home Video

Greenberg, Keith Elliott (1992) **Erik Is Homeless**. Lerner.

Hyde, Margaret O. (1989) **Homeless: Profiling The Problems**. Enslow.

Kenyon, Thomas L. (1991) **What You Can Do To Help The Homeless**. Simon & Schuster.

Kozol, Jonathan (1988) **Rachel & Her Children: Homeless Families in America.** Crown Publishers.

O'Conner, Karen (1989) **Homeless Children**. Lucent Books.

Resener, Carl R. (1988) **Crisis In The Streets**. Broadman Press.

Powerful Projects

Read about the homeless at **Homeless Profiles** (http://www.iia.org/~deckerj/). Identify the specific problems on one of the four homeless profiles. Provide suggestions that might be used by the community or government to address their concerns and needs.

Read **54 Ways to Help the Homeless**.

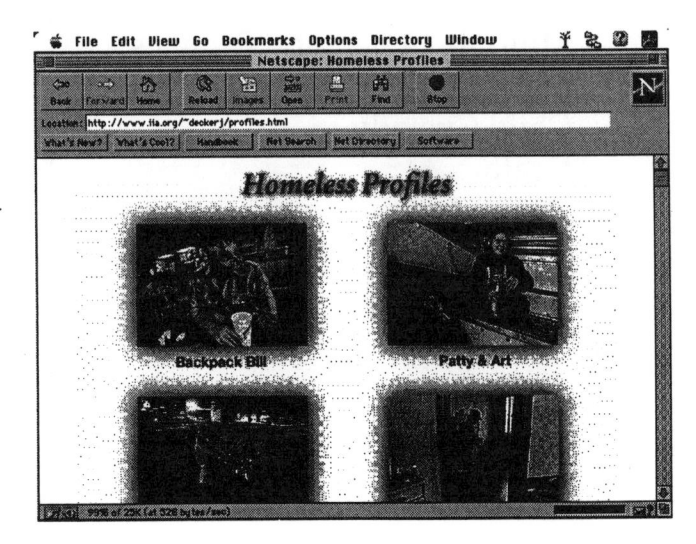

Smoking

Smoking kills. What does smoking do to the body? Why do people smoke? What can people do to quit smoking? Is smoking a right? What about smoking in public places? Join the debate!

Surfer Starters

Master Anti-Smoking Site
   http://www.autonomy.com/smoke.htm
General Smoking
   http://www.setine.com/ash/papers.html
   http://sunsite.unc.edu/boutell/infact/health.html
   http://sunsite.unc.edu/boutell/infact/exposed.html
Tobacco BBS
   http://www.dx.com/tobacco/
Smoking From All Sides
   http://www.cs.brown.edu/people/lsh/smoking.html
Great American Smoke Scream
   http://www.tx.cancer.org/scream/

Other Information Resources

Hyde, Margaret (1990) **Know About Smoking**. Walker.
Marr, John S. (1971) **Breath Of Air & A Breath of Smoke**. Evans.
Seixas, Judith S. (1981) **Tobacco-What it is, What It Does**. Greenwillow.
Stepney, Rob (1987) **Tobacco**. Watts.
Smoking: A Research Undate (Sound Filmstrip) (1984) Pleasantville Media/Sunburst.
Up In Smoke How Smoking Affects Your Health (Videocassette) Guidance Associates.

Powerful Projects

Explore the Great American Smoke Scream (http://www.tx.cancer.org/scream/). Play clungs. Write Ikeman a smoking-related question. Read their top ten list and then create your own.

Use the **Compare and Contrast** chart to explore two perspectives on smoking.

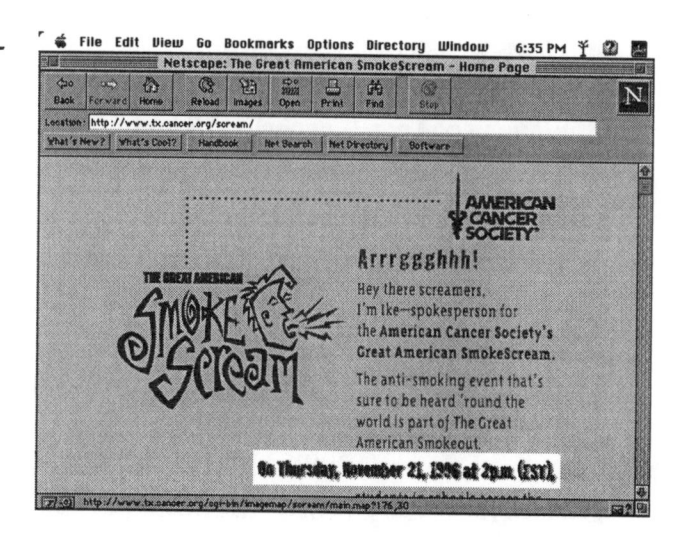

Substance Abuse

Substance Abuse is a serious problem whether it's drugs, alcohol, or abuse of any other substance including glue, gasoline, and spray cans. How are families affected by substance abuse? What are the side effects of substance abuse? What can you do to help someone who has a substance abuse problem?

Surfer Starters

Al-anon
   http://solar.rtd.utk.edu/~al-anon/
National Clearinghouse For Drug and Alcohol Abuse
   http://www.health.org/
National Institute on Drug Abuse
   http://www.nida.nih.gov/
General Resources
   http://www.med.umich.edu/aacap/teen.drugs.html
   http://www.med.umich.edu/aacap/children.of.alcoholics.html
   http://cpmcnet.columbia.edu/health.sci/.gcps/gcps052.html
Binge Drinking
   http://www.health.org/pubs/primer/binge.htm
Blood Alcohol Concentration
   http://www.health.org/pubs/primer/blood.htm
Canadian Centre on Substance Abuse
   http://www.ccsa.ca/
National Institute on Alchol Abuse and Alcoholism
   http://www.niaaa.nih.gov/
Web of Addictions
   http://www.well.com/user/woa/
Substance Abuse Definition
   http://www.coil.com/~grohol/sx15.htm

Other Information Resources

Alcohol: What Do You Know About It? (Sound Filmstrip) (1984) Sunburst.
Amerikaner, Susan (1986) **How To Way No: It's OK To Say No To Drugs**. Simon & Schuster.
Brainstorm The Truth About Your Brain On Drugs. (Videorecording) Children's Television Workshop (1994).
Claypool, Jane (1988) **Alcohol & You.** Watts.
D.A.R.E. To Say No! (Videodisc) (1992) Disney Educational Productions.

Lookin' For Waves: Information Exploration Ideas

Dolmetsch, Paul (1987) **Teens Talk About Alcohol & Alcoholism**. Doubleday Paper.
Friedman, David (1990) **Focus On Drugs & The Brain**. Twenty-First Century.
Hyde, Margaret O. (1990) **Know About Drugs**. Walker.
Hyde, Margaret O. (1988) **Alcohol, Uses & Abuses**. Enslow Publishers.
Lee, Mary Price (1994) **Drugs & The Media**. Rosen Pub. Group.
Madison, Arnold (1990) **Drugs & You**. Messner.
Seixas, Judith S. (1977) **Alcohol-What It Is, What It Does**. Greenwillow.
Seixas, Judith S. (1987) **Drugs—What They Are, What They Do**. Greenwillow Books.
Seixas, Judith S. (1979) **Living With A Parent Who Drinks Too Much**. Greenwillow.
Seymour, Richard B. (1987) **Drugfree: A Unique, Postive Approach To Staying Off Alcohol & other Drugs**. Facts On File Publications.
Snyder, Anne (1977) **Kids & Drinking**. Comp Care.
Stepney, Rob (1987) **Alcohol**. Watts.

Wave Words

Alcohol abuse   Drug Abuse   Substance Abuse

Powerful Projects

Read the **definition of substance abuse** (http://www.coil.com/~grohol/sx15.htm).

Explore **Al-anon** (http://solar.rtd.utk.edu/~al-anon/). Take the questionnaire.

Select a particular type of substance abuse to explore:
  Alcohol
  Cocaine
  Heroine
  Marijuana
  Methamphetamine
  PCP
  LSD
  Prescription
  Over-the-Counter
  Glue
  Gasoline

Suicide

Suicide is a serious problem among teens. What leads some people to suicide? How can it be prevented?

Surfer Starters

General Suicide Resources
  http://www.med.umich.edu/aacap/teen.Suicide.html
  http://www.yahoo.com/Society_and_Culture/Death/Suicide/
Suicide Awareness
  http://www.save.org/
Suicide Prevention
  http://web.idirect.com/~casp/
Suicide Essay
  http://members.aol.com/alhinil/suicide.htm

Other Information Resources

Frances, Dorothy B. (1989) **Suicide: A Preventable Tragedy**. Lodestar.

Hermes, Patricia (1987) **A Time To Listen: Preventing Youth Suicide**. Harcourt.

Hyde, Margaret O. & Forsyth, Elizabeth H. (1986) **Suicide: The Hidden Epidemic**. Watts.

Klagsbrun, Francine (1984) **Too Young to Die: Youth & Suicide**. Pocket.

Kolehmainen, Janet & Handwerk, Sandra (1986) **Teen Suicide: A Book For Friends, Family, & Classmates**. Lerner.

Langone, John (1986) **Dead End: A Book About Suicide**. Little.

Schleifer, Jay (1988) **Everything You Need To Know About Teen Suicide**. Rosen.

Stewart, Gail (1988) **Teen suicide**. Crestwood.

Powerful Projects

Explore the **Suicide Awareness Page**. Write a short story or skit that includes a character that exhibits symptoms of depression. Include characters who demonstrate common misconceptions about suicide. How will you end the skit?

Teen Pregnancy, Abortion, and Adoption

Teen pregnancy is a common concern. Although some teens choose abortion or adoption, many teens are choosing to raise their children on their own. Some pregnant teens live with their parents or grandparents, while others choose marriage or single parenthood. Explore the controversy and concerns regarding teen pregnancy.

Surfer Starters

Abortion Rights Activist
  http://www.cais.com/agm/frames/index.html
Adoption
  http://www.med.umich.edu/aacap/adopted.child.html
Atlanta Reproductive Health Center
  http://www.ivf.com/index.html
Planned Parenthood Online
  http://www.ppca.org/
Pregnancy & Childbirth
  http://www.ivf.com/preg.html
  http://vh.radiology.uiowa.edu/Patients/IowaHealthBook/OBGyn/OBGyn.html
Voices on Adoption
  http://www.best.com./~savage/adoption.html

Other Information Resources

Banish, Roslyn (1992) **Forever Family**. Harper Collins.
DuPrau, Jeanne (1990) **Adoption: The Facts, Feelings, & Issues of a Double Heritage**. Messner.
Gay, Kathlyn (1990) **Adoption & Foster Care**. Enslow.
Girard, Linda Walvoord (1989) **We Adopted You, Benjamin Koo**. Albert Whitman.
Krementz, Jill (1982) **How It Feels To Be Adopted**. Knopf.
Powledge, Fred (1982) **So You're Adopted**. Macmillan.
Rosenberg, Maxine B. (1989) **Growing Up Adopted**. Bradbury.
Sobol, H. L. (1984) **We Don't Look Like Our Mom & Dad**. Coward-McCann/Putnam.

Powerful Projects

Explore **Planned Parenthood Online**. Select an area to explore: Birth Control, STD's, Abortion, Women's Health, Health Centers, or Public Affairs.

Create an informational brochure focusing on an issue of interest to teens.

Compare and contrast different methods of birth control including abstinence. Which would you recommend? Why?

Write a short story about a person your age who becomes pregnant. Include factual information about the process in your story.

Explore **Voices on Adoption** (http://www.best.com./~savage/adoption.html) to learn about adoption. Read the stories of adoptees. How do you feel about some adoptee's search for their biological parents?

Interview a young mother. How is this person like and unlike you? Do you think you would have made the same or different choices? Why?

Explore the teen pregnancy statistics in your school. How do they compare to the national statistics. Why do you think your school is above or below the national average?

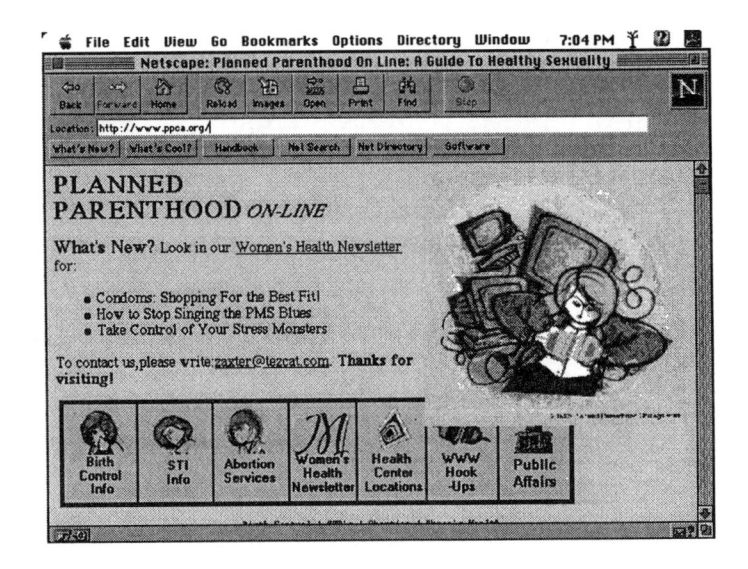

Women's Issues

Men and women share many common concerns. However, there are some concerns that are specific to a particular gender. Explore some of these issues.

Surfer Starters
Women Studies through Literature
   http://www.computek.net/public/barr/women.html
Women Writers
   http://www.cs.cmu.edu/Web/People/mmbt/women/celebration.html
Beijing 95
   http://www.igc.apc.org/womensnet/beijing/beijing.html
Followup to Beijing Conference
   http://www.igc.apc.org/womensnet/beijing/
Women's Net
   http://www.igc.apc.org/womensnet/
Women Pioneers
   http://pathfinder.com/photo/essay/women/pg1.htm

Other Information Resources
Alter, Judy (1989) **Women of the Old West.** Watts.
Ash, Maureen (1989) **Story of the Women's Movement.** Childrens Press.
De Pauw, Linda Grant (1982) **Seafaring Women.** Houghton Mifflin.
Fox, Mary Virginia (1988) **Women Astronauts Aboard The Shuttle.** Messner.
Rappaport, D. (1990) **American Women: Their Lives In their Words: A Documentary History.** Crowell/Harper Collins.
Smith, Betsy Covington (1989) **Women Win The Vote.** Silver Burdett.

Powerful Projects
Explore the **Beijing '95 conference** (http://www.igc.apc.org/womensnet/beijing/beijing.html).
Why is gender an issue? Why are there conferences that focus on "women's issues"?

Section 3

Ridin' the Surf: Subject Area Activities

Many of the sites in the area of science are designed for adults, are there quality resources for K-12 students?

Can students find information about their favorite author using the Web?

Are there sites that will really get students exciting about their subject area?

Yes, yes, yes! Although most of the subject area sites are designed by and for university, business, and industry level people, many sites are designed specifically for the K-12 audience. There's information on almost any people, place, or thing you can imagine in your subject area. Internet is a great way to get your students interested in real world applications of your content.

In this section of the book we'll focus on subject area activities. Students begin riding the waves of technology by integrating Internet into the traditional content area projects including Art/Music, Math/Science, and Social Studies. The scope and sequence of content varies by grade level and school, but you'll find lots of ways to get started. Many of the books and CD-ROM resources listed are aimed at the middle school level but can be used by both younger and older students. A majority of Internet sites are not grade level specific.

Ridin' the Surf Topics and Activities

The Arts - Art
Student Art Projects
Cartoons
WebMuseum

The Arts - Performance Arts
Music
Rock and Roll
Theatre

Mathematics
Math

Science - General Resources
Science TV Programs

Earth/Space Science
US Geological Survey
Rockhounds

Earth/Space Science - Air
Stratosphere Ozone

Earth/Space Science - Archaeology
ArchNet

Earth/Space Science - Astronomy
Views of the Solar System

Earth/Space Science - Water
Hydrology

Earth/Space Science - Weather
Snow

Life Science - Anatomy & Biology
Cells Alive

Life Science - Genetics
Fruit Flies

Life Science - Insects
Cockroach World
Butterfly World

Life Science - Plant Life
Seeds of Life
Missouri Botanical Garden!

Physical Science
Physical Science

Social Studies - Continents & Countries
Exploring Australia
Wangaratta Australia

Social Studies - Cities of the World
Cities Around the World
Paris
City Projects for Kids

Social Studies - US States
State Pages
CyberWest

Social Studies - US History
Oregon Trail Information Cente
Presidents of the US
Revolution to Reconstruction

Social Studies - Colonial America
   Colonial Williamsburg

Social Studies - Civil War
   American Civil War

World History
   French & Indian War
   World War II

Anthropology

People of the World - Native Americans
   Native American Indian Stories

Law, Political Science, and Goverment
   Thomas Site

Economics

Psychology

Literacy - Authors
   Ask the Author
   Early Childhood
   Elementary Authors
   Series Lovers
   Middle School Authors
   Secondary Authors
   Tales of Wonder
   Poetry
   Mark Twain
   Mythology and Folklore

Reading Comes Alive!
   Parents and Children Together
   Storyhour
   World of Reading
   Teen Ezines
   Resources for Young Writers
   Bartleby Library
   Writing Help Pages
   Fun English Sites
   Banned Book Sites

Health and Fitness
   First Aid
   Nutrition
   Health and Fitness

The Arts - Art

Under the category of "The Arts" you'll find information on art, music, theatre, and many other creative forms of expression.

Surfer Starters
Art Sites
African Art
   http://www.lib.virginia.edu/dic/African.html
Andy Warhol
   http://www.warhol.org/warhol
Ansel Adams Collection
   http://bookweb.cwis.uci.edu:8042/AdamsHome.html
Art Gallery Pointers
   http://www.comlab.ox.ac.uk/archive/other/museums/galleries.html
Art of China
   http://pasture.ecn.purdue.edu/~agenhtml/agenmc/china/china.html
Arts & Art Education
   http://www.artsusa.org/
ArtSource
   http://www.uky.edu/ArtSource/artsourcehome.html
Asian Arts
   http://www.webart.com/asianart/index.html
The Bayeux Tapestry, an 11th century French embroidery
   http://blah.bsuvc.bsu.edu/bt
The Book of Kells, a Medieval Irish illuminated manuscript
   http://www.honors.indiana.edu/~atrium/kells.html
Crayon Site: History, activities, contests
   http://www.crayola.com/crayola/home.html
Francisco Goya
   http://www.primenet.com/~image1/goya/goya.html
French Painting
   http://dmf.culture.fr/files/imaginary_exhibition.html
Impressionist Art - Student Project
   http://longwood.cs.ucf.edu:80/~MidLink/Impress.html
Krannert Art Museum
   http://www.art.uiuc.edu/kam/
Les Tres Riches Heures of the Duc de Berry, a 14th century illuminated manuscript
   http://www.honors.indiana.edu/~atrium/berry.html

National Museum of American Art
   http://www.nmaa.si.edu
Online Art Gallery
   http://www.tcm.org/clubhouse/projects/gallery/index.html
   http://www.ai.mit.edu/~spraxlo/rune/Rune.html
   http://heiwww.unige.ch/art/
Paintings of Vermeer
   http://www.ccsf.caltech.edu/~roy/vermeer/thumb.html
The Sistine Chapel
   http://www.christusrex.org/www1/sistine/0-Tour.html
Tibetan Mandala Archive
   http://www.nets.com/site/ian/mandalaimages.html
WebMuseum
   http://sunsite.unc.edu/louvre/
Wildlife Art
   http://www.ottawa.net./~sjhewer/
World Art Treasures
   http://sgwww.epfl.ch/BERGER/intro.html
Young Children's Art Projects
   http://plaza.interport.net/kids_space/gallery/gallery.html

Cartooning
Lesson in cartooning
   http://www.sara-jordan.com/edu-mart/cartoon/lesson1.html
Different cartoon sites
   http://pages.prodigy.com/UT/cartoon/factory.html
   http://www.phlab.missouri.edu/~c617145/comix.html
   http://www.yahoo.com/Entertainment/Comics/

Other Information Resources
American Art And Architecture (Videocassette) (1991) Clarion.
Brown, Laurene Krasny (1986) **Visiting The Art Museum**. Dutton.
Cumming, Robert (1982) **Just Image: Ideas In Painting**. Macmillan.
Goffstein, M. B. (1980) **An Artist**. Harper.
Keightley, Moy (1984) **Investigating Art A Practical Guide For Young People**. Facts On File.
Looking At Art (Videocassette) (1992) American School Publishers.
National Gallery of Art, laserdisc.
Silverman, Ronald H. (1982) **Learning About Art: A Practical Approach**. Romar Arts.
Ventura, Piero (1984) **Great Painters**. Putnam.

Wilton Art Appreciation Program Series 200 (Sound Filmstrip) (1980) Reading & O'Reilly Associates.

Woolf, Felicity (1993) **Picture This Century: An Introduction To Twentieth-Century Art**. Doubleday.

Yenawine, Philip (1991) **How To Look at Modern Art.** H.N. Abrams.

CD-ROM Resources

Art Gallery, Microsoft
Digital Chisel, Pierian Spring
Famous Artists Series, Queue
Fine Artist, Microsoft
HyperStudio, Roger Wagner
Kid Pix, Kid Pix Studio, Broderbund
Kid Works Deluxe, Davidson
Multimedia Workshop, Davidson
Opening Night, MECC
Print Shop, Broderbund

Powerful Projects

Some people call it junk and other people call it art. What do you think? Explore some of the following areas:

    Compare and contrast different artists.
    Explore an object or animal in art.
    Compare different mediums of art.
    Provide examples of how current events impact art.
    Describe how a particular art reflects it's origins.
    Trace the history of photography or computer art.
    Select a piece of art that you like. Learn about the artist. Why do you think this person selected this particular technique or art form?
    Trace the history of a particular decorative art such as weaving, spinning, pottery, jewelry, wood carving, paper crafts, or embroidery.
    Describe the science of an art such as the fibers used in weaving or the dyes in fabric work.

http://www.nmaa.si.edu

Ridin' the Surf: Subject Area Activities 121

Visit Student Art Projects!
http://www.tcm.org/clubhouse/projects/gallery/index.html

Children around the world are sharing their art work on the Internet!

Explore some student art projects. Create a story to go with one of the projects.

Select your top three projects and ask another student if they agree or disagree. Discuss how your ideas are alike and different.

Select three very different pieces of art and describe the techniques and tools that were used to create them.

http://www.isd77.k12.mn.us/schools/kennedy/ openhouse/artgallery.html

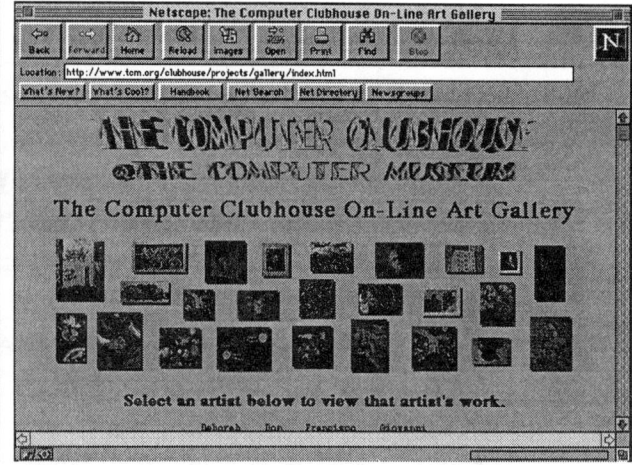

http://www.tcm.org/clubhouse/projects/ gallery/index.html

Explore an artist or a medium and write a report. Think about how your report might link to other Internet sites. Create a web page and submit it to Midlink like the project on the right.

Develop your own art project and submit it to be published online.

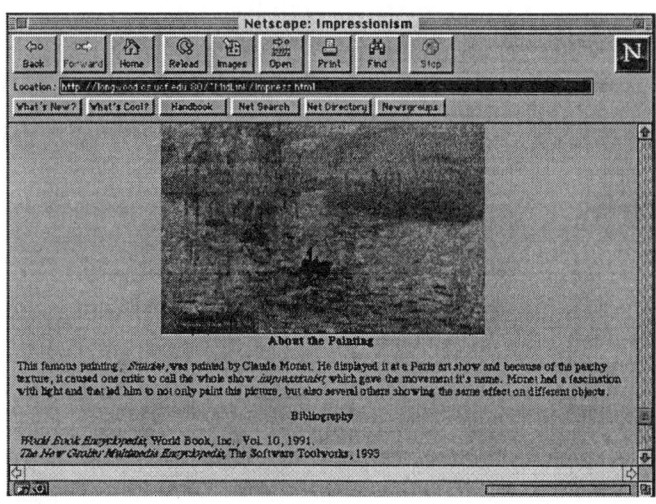

http://longwood.cs.ucf.edu:80/~MidLink/Impress.html

Visit Cartoon Sites!
http://www.sara-jordan.com/edu-mart/cartoon/lesson1.html

Explore the wonderful world of cartoons.

Start by reading books about cartooning. Here are some ideas.

Lightfoot, Marge (1993) **Cartooning For Kids**. Owl.
Weiss, Harvey (1990) **Cartoons & Cartooning**. Houghton Mifflin.

Explore a couple cartoon sites and find your favorite cartoon and cartoonist. Try some of the sites below.

http://pages.prodigy.com/UT/cartoon/factory.html
http://www.phlab.missouri.edu/~c617145/comix.html
http://www.yahoo.com/Entertainment/Comics/

Try making your own cartoons. Use the lessons in the following site to learn the basics of cartooning.

http://www.sara-jordan.com/edu-mart/cartoon/lesson1.html

Print out your cartoon and see how other people like it! Create your own school cartoon magazine.

Select your favorite cartoon and send it to one of the online kid project publishers we explored in the first section!

Try creating a political cartoon or one related to a subject you're studying.

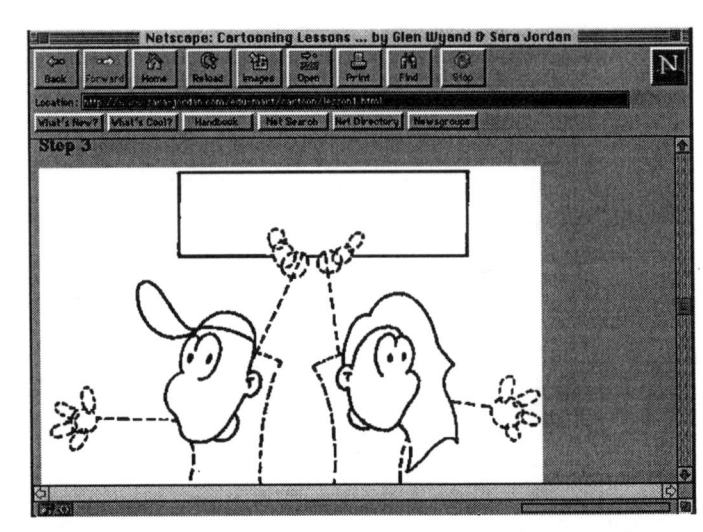

http://www.sara-jordan.com/edu-mart/cartoon/

Ridin' the Surf: Subject Area Activities

Visit the WebMuseum!
http://sunsite.unc.edu/louvre/

Visit the WebMuseum at The Louvre.
Select one of the following styles and create a web page that highlights it.

What makes the style interesting and unique?
How can you identify works of this style?
How and where did the style originate?
Explore three examples of the style.

Baroque	Classicism
Cubism	Dada
Expressionism	Fauvism
Futurism	Impressionism
Realism	Renaissance
Romanticism	Surrealism

Select one of the following artists. Create a timeline showing key events.

Select your favorite piece of work by this artist and describe how it reflects the person and style. Compare your artist with another artist.

Cézanne, Paul	Eakins, Thomas
Goya, Francisco de	Greco, El
Kandinsky, Wassily	Leonardo da Vinci
Matisse, Henri	Michelangelo
Monet, Claude	Pollock, Jackson
Renoir, Pierre-Auguste	Rembrandt
Rossetti, Dante Gabriel	Rubens, Peter Paul
Sargent, John Singer	Gogh, Vincent van
Whistler, James Abbott	

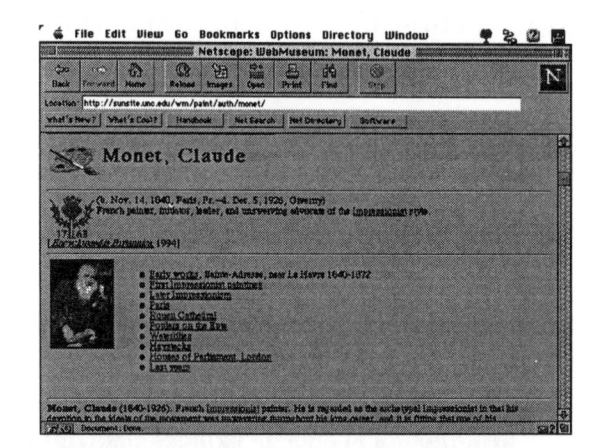

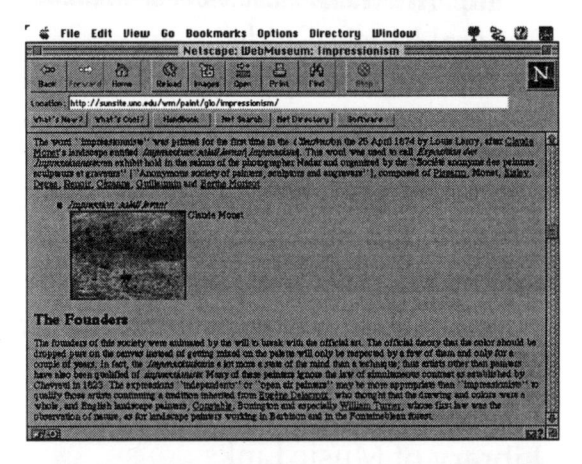

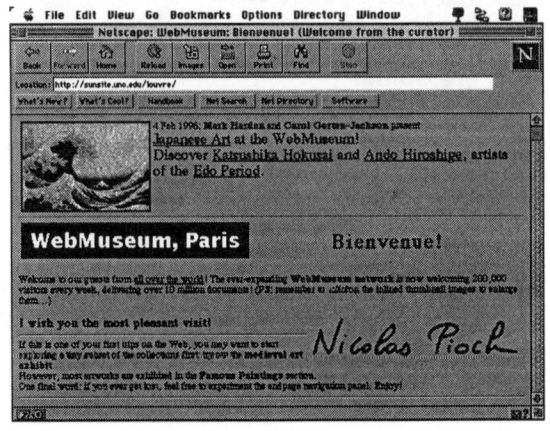

The Arts – Performance Art

Performance art includes music, theatre, and creative movement. You'll find lots of sites that contain information about performances around the world. Many universities and schools contain information about their programs and performances. You'll also find lots of examples of music on the Web including "sheet" music, music sound clips and information about types of music. The Music Launchpad is a good place to start for information about music for K-12 students.

Surfer Starters

Music Launchpad
   http://www.weblust.com/NS/BuildPadPage/Music
Blues
   http://www.portal.com/~mojohand/delta_snake.html
Composer Information
   http://classicalmus.com/bmgclassics/comp-index/index.html
   http://www.cl.cam.ac.uk/users/mn200/music/composers.html
General Music Guide
   http://www.music.indiana.edu/misc/music_resources.html
Grooves Online Music Magazine
   http://pathfinder.com/grooves
History of Rock and Roll
   http://www.hollywood.com/rocknroll/
Web Wide World of Music
   http://www.galcit.caltech.edu~ta/music/index.html
Internet Underground Music Archive
   http://www.iuma.com/
Library of Music Links
   http://www-scf.usc.edu/~jrush/music/index.html
Music
   http://www.hollywood.com/rocknroll/index.html
   http://www.portal.com/~mojohand/delta_snake.html
Music Teachers
   http://www.cstp.umkc.edu/users/bhugh/musici.html
   http://riceinfo.rice.edu:80/armadillo/Projects/Music/

http://www.peabody.jhu.edu/

Traditional Folk Song Database
   http://web2.xerox.com/digitrad
Warner Brothers Jazzspace
   http://www.jazzonln.com:80/LABELS/WBSPACE/menu.htm

Other Information Resources

Berger, Melvin (1989) **The Science of Music**. Thomas Y. Crowell, New York.

Headington, Christopher (1981) **The Performing World of the Musician**. Silver Burdett Company.

McLeish, Kenneth & Val (1992) **The Oxford First Companion to Music**. Oxford University Press New york, Melbourne.

Haas, Karl (1984) **Inside Music**. Doubleday & Company Inc. Garden City, N.Y.

Sommer, Elyse (1992) **The Kids World Almanac of Music**. Pharos Books.

Walter, Tom (1981) **Make Mine Music**. Little, Brown & Co. Boston Toronto.

Zorn, Jay D. (1988) **The Music Listeners Companion**. Prentice Hall Englewood Cliffs, New Jersey.

CD-ROM Resources

Making Music, Voyager

Julliard's Music Adventure, Theatrix

Microsoft Music Central, Microsoft

Microsoft Musical Instruments, Microsoft

Dr. T's Sing-A-Long Around the World, Scholastic

Powerful Projects

Trace the history of a type of music such as barbershop quartets, gospel, or folk music. Create a wall chart timeline.

Compare and contrast two types of music such as folk and country. Select specific songs to illustrate the differences and similarities.

Explore a musical instrument. Compare two very different types of music that might be played on the same instrument. For example, a trumpet in jazz versus classical music. Record examples and create a web page of your work.

Find out about the unique musical instruments of a particular culture such as China, Japan, or Africa. Create a Hyperstudio stack containing pictures of the country, a description of the instrument, and sample sounds.

Trace the history of the American Musical. What's your favorite musical and why? How did American Musicals evolve?

Explore the lyrics of a popular song such as American Pie. Compare your ideas with other people by sharing on listservs or newsgroups.

Explore how music therapy is used with patients having particular mental or emotional problems. Do you think it works? Why or why not?

Find out how babies react to different types of music. Did you know some mothers play music to their unborn infants? Find out why. Would you do this?

Visit Music Sites!

http://classicalmus.com/bmgclassics/comp-index/index.html

Explore Music Sites on the Web.

Explore the Classic Composers.

http://classicalmus.com/bmgclassics/comp-index/index.html

Select one of the following periods:
Medieval   Renaissance
Baroque   Classical
Romantic   Twentieth Century
Contemporary

Select two composers from the same period. Compare their lives.

Explore information about your favorite composer from history. Why do you think the music of this composer has remained popular?

Explore Grooves magazine.

http://pathfinder.com/grooves

Write an article about your favorite music artist or music type and submit it to the magazine.

Write a review of your favorite CD.

Write an article about a classic composer and pretend that it is being published during a time when he or she is alive.

Visit the Rock & Roll Hall of Fame & Museum!
http://www.rockhall.com/index.html

Explore the Rock & Roll Hall of Fame and Museum.

Compare and contrast two music groups. Create a HyperStudio project that incorporates sound clips into the project.

Compare and contrast the lives and musical talents of two individuals.

Create a speech that you would use if you were going to introduce the group at an awards ceremony.

Do you know the 500 songs that shaped rock and roll? As a class, pick your top ten. In pairs create a HyperStudio card for your favorite song and artist.

Explore the Hall of Fame through the QuickTime VR clips. Do you want to make a real visit now? Find out how many miles you'd need to drive to get to the museum. What else would you visit as long as you're in Cleveland? Create a schedule and estimate costs.

Go shopping! How much will your purchases cost? What if I give you a $10 coupon? What's your total if I take 20% off? Let's say that shirts are "buy 1, get 1 half off." How would that change your total?

Create a birthday card for your favorite rock 'n roller. Include the date and interesting information about the person.

Use the archives to create a set of trivia questions for your friends and family to play. Put each question on a separate card. You might want a different color card for categories like lyrics, music, artists, bands, awards, etc. Create a "Rock and Roll" board game that uses the trivia.

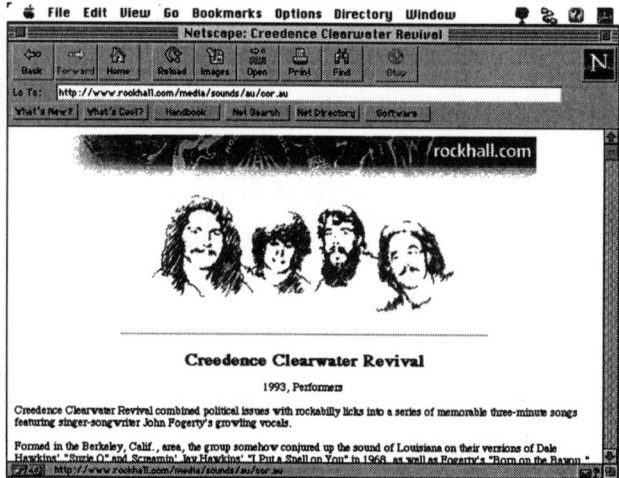

Visit Theatre Sites!
http://www.theatre-central.com/

Visit Theatre Central.

Explore the **Performers**. The Directory of Theatre Professionals on 'Net is a central resource for contacting and communicating with theatre professionals across the world with specific interests or background information. Use the directory to find an actor or other person in the theatre field. Conduct an online interview. What are the pros and cons of this field? What are the most important skills? How much money can you make? How much money is typical?

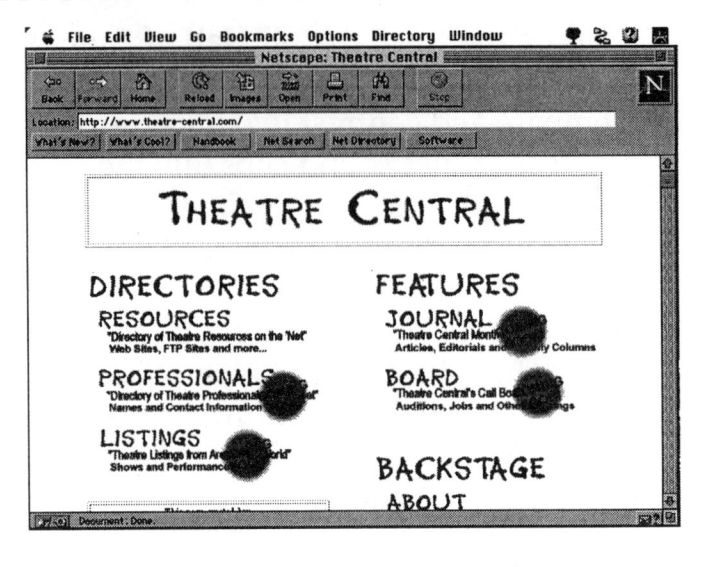

Explore **The Journal**, Theatre Central's monthly publication. Write a short article about some aspect of theatre you find appealing.

Explore the **theatre links**. Find a play that you've read that is being performed. What aspects of the play would you want to review if you could see it?

Explore a particular **type of theatre**. For example, explore the world of dinner theatre and compare this type of theatre to traditional stage productions.

Visit the Children's Theatre site.
http://pubweb.acns.nwu.edu/~vjs291/children.html

Learn about the history of Children's Theatre.
Write a short play of your own!
Select a Theatre production you'd like to do.

Read some Reader's Theatre Scripts
http://www.ucalgary.ca/~dkbrown/readers.html

Mathematics

There are lots of math sites. Many of these provide information about real world math applications, history of math, and math projects.

Surfer Starters

Algebra For Everyone Home Page
http://sands.psy.cmu.edu/ACT/awpt/algebra-home.html

Calculus graphic
http://www.math.psu.edu/dna/graphics

Cool Stat/Math Sites
http://www.indiana.edu/~statmath/moresites.html

Data Powers of Ten
http://www.ccsf.caltech.edu/~roy/dataquan/Fun Math Games
http://www.uni.uiuc.edu/departments/math/glazer/fun_math.html

Explorer Home Page
http://unite2.tisl.ukans.edu/

FUTURES II: Teacher's Guide
http://www.pbs.org/learning/k12/resources/futures/futurestg.html

Geography Forum
http://forum.swarthmore.edu/mathmagic/

History of Mathematics
http://www-groups.dcs.st-and.ac.uk/~history/index.html

Kid's Web - Math
http://www.npac.syr.edu/textbook/kidsweb/math.html

Lessons and Appetizers for Math
http://www.cam.org/~aselby/lesson.html

Math
http://acorn.educ.nottingham.ac.uk/ShellCent/
Math Magic Projects

Math Dictionary
http://www.mathpro.com/math/glossary/glossary.html

Math History
http://www.maths.tcd.ie/pub/HistMath/HistMath.html

Math Problems
http://plainfield.bypass.com/bypass/users/union/problems.html

Mathematicians
http://aleph0.clarku.edu/~djoyce/mathhist/mathhist.html

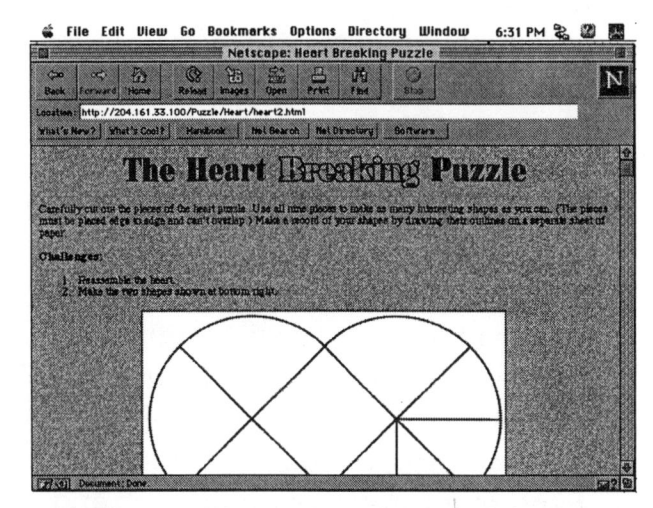

http://204.161.33.100/Puzzle/Heart/heart2.html

Mathematics
   http://hub.terc.edu:70/hub/math
Mathematics Archives Sites
   http://archives.math.utk.edu/k12.html
Mathematics Education
   http://www.halcyon.com/cairns/math.html
MATHMOL --K-12 Mathematics
   http://www.nyu.edu/pages/mathmol/
Mega-Math
   http://www.cam.org/~aselby/lesson.html
Money - Australia
   http://www.pegasus.oz.au/~gorokep12/curcomp1.html
MSTE List of Web Sites in Math ED
   http://www.mste.uiuc.edu/mathed/mathedlinks.html
Place for Math Resources
   http://gnn.com/gnn/meta/edu/curr/math/res/links/index.html
Reed Interactive's Subject Guide
   http://www.ozemail.com.au/~reed/subject/maths.html
Schoolhouse Rock - Math
   http://hera.life.uiuc.edu/multiplication.html
Spirograph
   http://juniper.tc.cornell.edu:8000/spiro/spiro.html
Thomas Banchoff's Project List
   http://www.geom.umn.edu/~banchoff/projects.html
Transitional Maths Project
   http://othello.ma.ic.ac.uk/
Yahoo Math Sites
   http://www.yahoo.com/Science/Mathematics/

Powerful Projects

Use the Math sites to identify math puzzles and projects to post on the board in class as challenge activities.

Explore a famous mathematician. Create a biographical Hyperstudio stack about the person's life and his or her impact on math.

Explore a math theory. Where did it come from? Why is it important?

Email a famous person or someone in a career you'd like to explore. Ask about how they use math in their profession. Ask them for specific examples. Create a stack called Math in the Real World that contains comments and examples from these people.

Explore information on the web and ask students to create story problems for other students. For example, sports sites have statistics, insurance agencies have prices, and online shopping has pricing.

Ridin' the Surf: Subject Area Activities 131

Visit Math Sites!
http://www.pegasus.oz.au/~gorokep12/curcomp1.html

Visit math sites around the world and join their projects.

Explore an Australian project that examines currency and prices around the world.

http://www.pegasus.oz.au/~gorokep12/curcomp1.html

Try some math magic problems from the following site.

http://forum.swarthmore.edu/mathmagic/

Try the math problems at the following site in Vermont! Create your own math problems at the end of each unit and post them on the Web for another class.

http://plainfield.bypass.com/bypass/users/union/problems.html

Try **Spirograph**. How does it work? Why does it work? What does it do?

http://juniper.tc.cornell.edu:8000/spiro/spiro.html

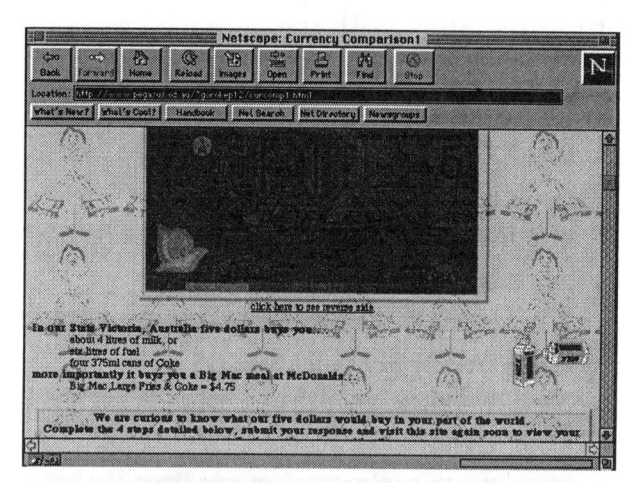

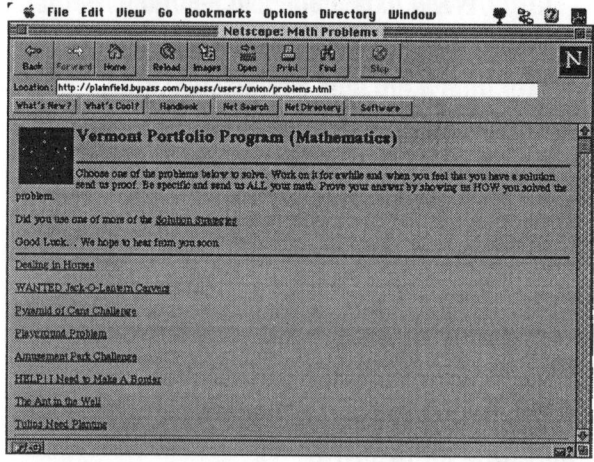

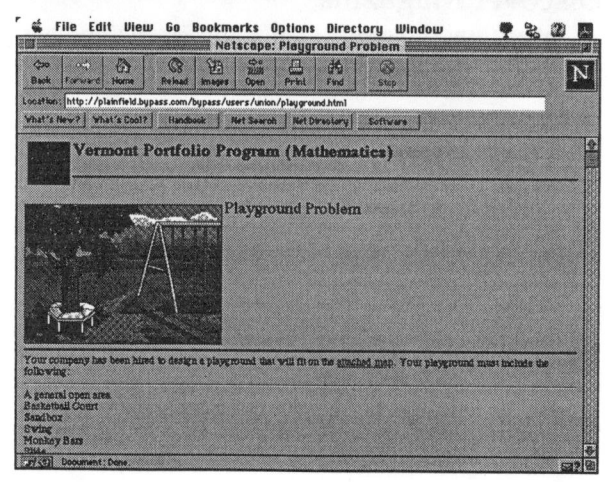

Science - General Resources

There are endless possibilities for using Internet in the Science classroom. We've listed lots of general science sites to get you started. Science museums, government agencies, and university-sponsored projects often contain information for K-12 students. Start with the Science Launchpad or go directly to the sites listed below.

Surfer Starters
Science Lists of Links
Science Launchpad
   http://www.weblust.com/NS/BuildPadPage/Science
Science Links
   http://www.nhm.ac.uk/index/life-sciences.html
   http://www.yahoo.com/Science/
   http://www.ed.gov/pubs/parents/Science/index.html
   http://www-sci.lib.uci.edu/HSG/Ref.html
   http://www.exploratorium.edu/floor/Hotlist.html
Schoolhouse Rock - Science Rock
   http://hera.life.uiuc.edu/science.html

Great General Science Sites
"Bad science" Site
   http://www.ems.psu.edu/~fraser/BadScience.html
Beakman's World
   http://www.nbn.com:80/youcan/beakworld/beakTV.html
Bill Nye the Science Guy
   http://www.seanet.com/Vendors/billnye/nyelabs.html
Discover Magazine
   http://www.enews.com/magazines/discover/
Exploratorium Learning Studio:
     Experiments and teacher activities
   http://www.exploratorium.edu/
   learning_studio/
ENC (Eisenhower)
   http://www.enc.org
EPA
   http://www.epa.gov
HUB Math/Science
   http://hub.terc.edu

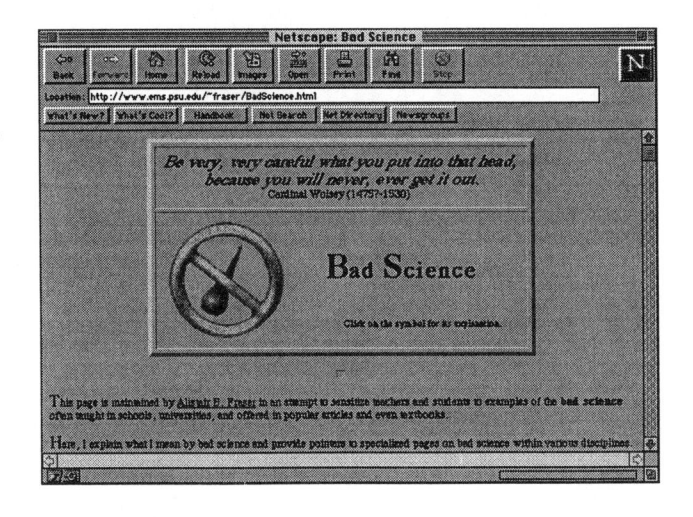

Icon Science
    http://www.injersey.com/Media/IonSci/
National Science Foundation
    http://www.nsf.gov/
Newton's Apple
    http://ericir.syr.edu/Newton/welcome.html
Ontario Science Museum
    http://www.osc.on.ca/
SciEd: Science/Math Ed
    http://www.halcyon.com/cairns/science.html
Science Learning Network
    http://sln.fi.edu
Science - General Sites
    http://turnpike.net/metro/adorn/science.html
    http://www.si.edu/
    http://www.eskimo.com/~billb/
Science Projects for Kids
    http://www.ed.gov/pubs/parents/Science/index.html
Science Magazine Online
    http://science-mag.aaas.org/science/
Teacher activities
    http://www.gene.com:80/ae/

Other Information Resources

Ardley, Neil et al. (1984) **Why Things Are.** Messner.
Martin, Paul D. (1985) **Science: It's Changing Your World.** National Geographic.
Stein, Sara Bonnett (1980) **The Science Book.** Wortman.
Sutton, Caroline (1981) **How Do They Do That? Wonders Of The Modern World.** Morrow.
Walpole, Brenda (1989) **Science.** Warwick.
Why on Earth? (1988) National Geographic.

CD-ROM Resources

Eyewitness Encyclopedia of Science, DK
Sammy's Science House, Edmark
Way Things Work, DK
What's My Secret, 3M Learning

Laserdisc Resources
Optical Data Windows on Science Series
Video Discovery Science Series
Systems Impact Science Series

Powerful Projects
Bring science alive by exploring everyday questions. Use **What's My Secret** CD-ROM as the focal point for your activities. Use the Internet resources to find information based on questions found in **What's My Secret** and brainstormed in class.

Create your own **What's My Secret** multimedia stack using **HyperStudio**. Create short stories that incorporate "science in the real world" ideas from the CD.

Hold a "real world" science fair. Share results of science experiments with other schools through the Internet.

Explore hands-on, Internet-based science experiments like those at Exploratorium Learning Studio.

http://www.exploratorium.edu/learning_studio/

Ridin' the Surf: Subject Area Activities

Visit Science TV Program Sites!
http://www.seanet.com/Vendors/billnye/nyelabs.html

Do you watch Beakman's World or Bill Nye, the Science Guy? Do you like the Discovery Channel? You can find them on TV, but you can also explore their resources on the Internet!

Choose a science TV site to explore.
Beakman's World
http://www.nbn.com:80/youcan/ beakworld/beakTV.html
Bill Nye the Science Guy
http://www.seanet.com/Vendors/billnye/ nyelabs.html
Discovery Channel
http://www.discovery.com/DCO/doc/1012/ online.html
Newton's Apple
http://ericir.syr.edu/Newton/welcome.html

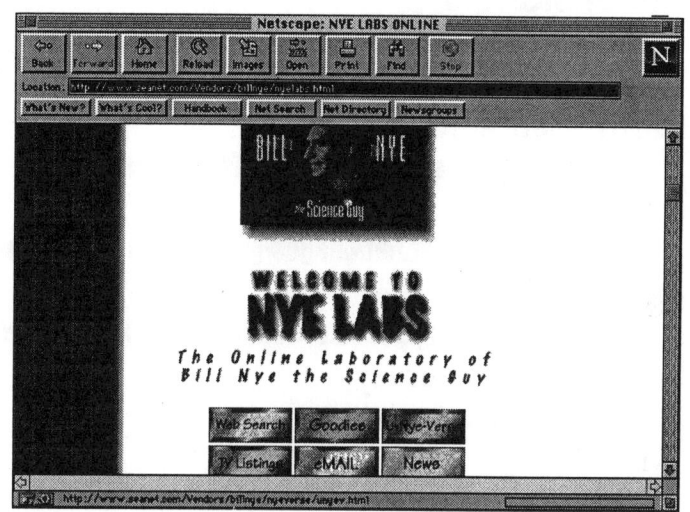

Find the information and activities that go with a program that you've already seen. Try one of the activities and email the Web page about how you liked the activity.

Explore information about a topic of interest. Would you like to see the program that goes with it? Why or why not?

Do you have an idea for a topic for one of these programs that hasn't been covered before? Write a little about the topic and why you think it would be a good program for the show. What kinds of skits or experiments would you include in your program?

Create your own science TV program and web site. What would you include? Write a script for a skit from your new science show.

Earth/Space Science

The Earth is an exciting place to live. It's diverse and always changing. Use the Internet to learn how the earth was formed, how the earth survives, and how humans impact the earth.

Surfer Starters
Color Landfoms Atlas
   http://fermi.jhuapl.edu/states/states.html
Earth Science Resources
   http://www.ems.psu.edu/RelatedWebSites.html
Gems
   http://galaxy.einet.net/images/gems/gems-icons.html
Rock Hounds
   http://www.perspective.com/infodyn/rockhounds/rockhounds.html
US Geological Survey
   http://www.usgs.gov/
Nine Planets: Earth
   http://Seds.lpl.arizona.edu/nineplanets/nineplanets/earth.html
Desert Project
   http://snunit.huji.ac.il/desert/desert.htm

Other Information Resources
Berger, Melvin (1980) **The New Earth Book: Our Changing Planet**. Harper.
Bramwell, Martyn (1987) **Planet Earth**. F. Watts.
Cole, Joanna (1987) **The Magic School Bus: Inside The Earth**. Scholastic.
Jaspersohn, William. **How Life On Earth Began**. Watts.
Lye, Keith (1984) **The Earth**. Silver.
Gallant, Roy A. (1986) **Our Restless Earth**. Watts.
Gamlin, Linda (1988) **Life On Earth**. Gloucester.
Gans, Roma (1984) **Rock Collecting**. Harper.
Hiscock, Bruce. (1988) **The Big Rock**. Atheneum.
Horenstein, Sidney S. (1993) **Rocks Tell Stories**. Millbrook Press.
Markie, Sandra (1987) **Digging Deeper: Investigations Into Rocks, Shocks, Quakes, and Other Earthy Matters**. Lothrop, Lee & Shepard Books.
Pettigrew, Mark (1987) **Planet Earth**. Gloucester Press.
Scarry, Huck (1984) **Our Earth**. Messner.
Simon, Seymour (1984) **Earth: Our Planet in Space**.

Ridin' the Surf: Subject Area Activities

Powerful Projects

Create a travel packet on the planet earth. If people from another universe could access the Internet, what would you want to tell them about the earth? Would it be a place they could live and thrive? Create a web page that highlights the features of our planet.

What's the recipe of the earth? Create a list of ingredients and create a recipe for someone who might want to make a planet like earth. Would it work? Why or why not?

If you were looking for gems and minerals, where would you go? Why?

If you were planting a garden, what elements would you want in your soil?

Describe the role that weather, earthquakes, volcanoes, and other events have on the earth.

What are fossil fuels? How are they made? Where are they found? Who cares?

Explore deserts. What's a desert and why do we have them? How is life in the desert different from life in another area? Would you like to live in a desert? Why or why not?

Visit the US Geological Survey!
http://www.usgs.gov/education/living/index.html

The US Geological Survey contains useful information about our world.

Explore the section that discusses issues related to living on earth. It's called the Learning Web. In small groups, select a question to investigate.

- Where does your household water come from?

- What is radon gas and how can you test your home for radon?

- How does weather affect streams in your state?

- How do you prepare for volcanic eruptions?

Each question is important. Do you have more questions about the topic? Select three other questions to explore.

Organize all the information and report to the class about your findings.

As a class, decide who else needs to know this information. How could you share this information with the people who need it most?

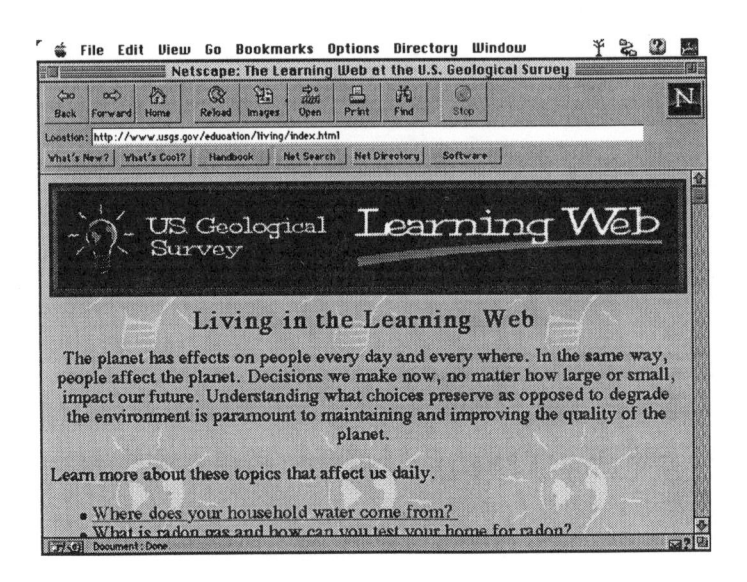

Ridin' the Surf: Subject Area Activities

Visit the Rockhounds Information Page
http://www.perspective.com/infodyn/rockhounds/rockhounds.html

The Rockhounds Information Page is a great place to start an exploration of rocks and minerals!

- Start by learning to be a good rock hound through **Grolier Online** (http://www.grolier.com/e-pub/rockstry.html). Create a chart showing the steps in identifying rocks. Go to **Dave's Story** (http://www.grolier.com/e-pub/rockmain.html) and help him identify his rock.

- Visit a **rockshop** or gallery. Would you like to really visit this site? Why or why not? What item did you find most interesting? Compare and contrast the prices at two or more of these galleries.

- Visit rockshops and galleries that contain fossils such as the **Stone Company** (http://www.stonecompany.com/ency.html). What's a fossil? Select a fossil to write about such as a trilobite, ammonites, dino egg, dino bone, or fish fossil. Copy the picture into your report. What was the creature who left the fossil like? What kind of habitat did it live in? Compare the fossils you find on the Web with the fossils in your classroom.

- Go to the **Mineral Gallery** (http://mineral.galleries.com/) or another gallery. Learn about your birthstone. If you could have a stone from any birth month, which would you pick? Why? Find out about other minerals.

- Go to the **Amber Lady** (http://goldray.com/amberlady/) and find out about amber. Describe some of the insects that have been found in amber and how this relates to the movie Jurassic Park. What would you like to find preserved in amber? Why? What would you do with it?

- Go to the **Multimedia Minerals Site** (http://www.demon.co.uk:80/btlpub/Geog/Minerals/demo.html). Use the Mineral Identifier to see if your birthstone is on their list. To check, you'll need to know the cleavage, flame, hardness, and streak. What do these five words mean? You'll have to find out to use this identifier! Pretend that you've found the largest mineral of this type in the world. Write a paragraph about the mineral that might be used by the local newspaper to tell about your discovery.

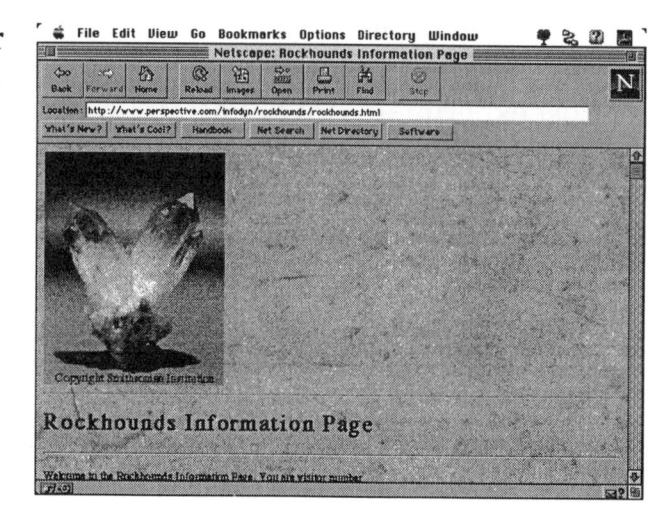

Earth/Space Science - Air

Air pollution, air quality, and other environmental concerns regarding our atmosphere can be found on the Internet.

Surfer Starters
Air
   http://www.erin.gov.au/air/air.html
Air project
   http://longwood.cs.ucf.edu:80/~MidLink/air.form.html
Office of Air and Radiation
   http://www.epa.gov/oar/oarhome.html
Ozone Depletion - Yahoo
   http://www.yahoo.com/Society_and_Culture/Environment_and_Nature/Ozone_Depletion/
Stratosphere Ozone
   http://www.epa.gov/docs/ozone/index.html

Other Information Resources
Ardley, Neil (1991) **Science Book of Air**. Gulliver/Harcourt Brace Jovanovich.
Atmosphere: On the Air (Videocassette) (1993) National Geographic.
Branley, Franklyn M. (1986) **Air Is Around You**. Crowell/ HarperCollins.
Cochrane, Jennifer (1987) **Air Ecology**. Watts.
Dolan, Edward F. (1991) **Our Poisoned Sky**. Cobblehill/Dutton.
Johnston, Tom (1985) **Air, Air Everywhere**. Gareth Stevens.
Murphy, Bryan (1991) **Experiment With Air**. Lerner.

Powerful Projects
Compare the air quality in your area with other students as part of an international email project.

Post experiments involving air on your web site. Include Quicktake pictures of your class completing the projects.

Write about the air quality problems being faced by a particular city. What's the problem and how can it be eliminated? What would you suggest to the city council that might be helpful in reducing the problem?

What's the ozone? Why should we be worried about the ozone? Use the following site to get started exploring this question.

   http://solstice.crest.org/environment/eol/ozone.html

Ridin' the Surf: Subject Area Activities

Visit the Stratosphere Ozone Site!
http://www.epa.gov/docs/ozone/index.html

Explore the Stratosphere Ozone Site! It has lots of information about our ozone problems and what you can do to help!

- Enter the art contest. You'll need to explore the site to find answers to the questions before entering the contest. Create a project in one of the following categories:
  The ozone layer: How does the ozone layer protect us from harmful UV rays from the sun?
  Ozone depletion: How do CFCs and other ozone-depleting substances harm the ozone layer?
  Scientists: How do scientists measure the ozone layer or ozone depletion?
  Protecting yourself from the sun: How can you protect yourself?
- Go to the **Resource Center** and explore the **Plain English Guide** to the Clean Air Act. Create a poster that tells people why they should be concerned about air pollution.
- Define **smog**. What causes smog? Where is smog a problem? Write a letter to a city that has a smog problem and explain how and why they need to stop their smog.
- Do cars, trucks, and other **vehicles** cause air quality problem? Why? Create a sign that could be posted at a local gas station that explains the problem and what motorists can do to help.
- What is **acid rain**? Do you need to worry about this problem? Who does? What will help stop acid rain? Why is Canada so concerned about acid rain? Create an animation in HyperStudio that shows how acid rain develops.
- Explore the **Ozone Depletion Science** area. What is ozone depletion? How does it occur? Create a list of common myths and the truth.
- Explore the **Methyl Bromide** area. What is methyl bromide and how is it harmful to the ozone layer? Are you causing part of the problem? What can you do to help?

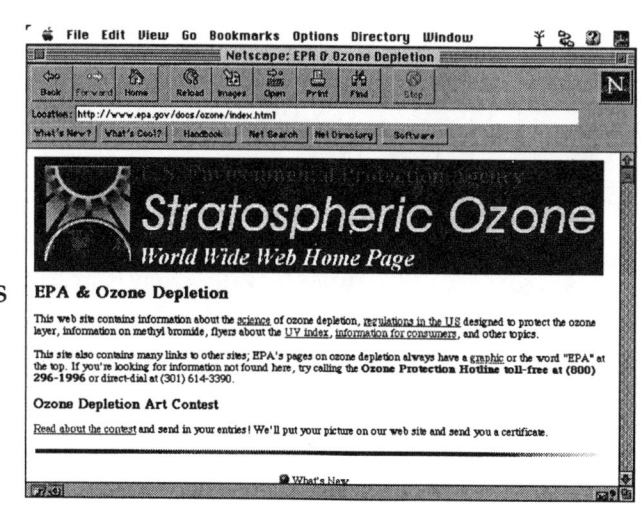

Earth/Space Science - Archaeology

Much of the information on archaeology is designed for older students, but much of it can be adapted for younger students. ArchNet is a good place to start. You'll find information about archaeological digs around the world. If you're interested in exploring US National Park and Monument sites, try GORP.

Surfer Starters

Archaeology Lesson Plans
>http://gnn.com/gnn/meta/edu/curr/rdg/gen_act/arch/index.html

ArchNet
>http://www.lib.uconn.edu/ArchNet/

Archaeology
>http://www.bergen.gov/Smithsonian/
>http://spirit.lib.uconn.edu/archnet/archnet.html
>http://atlantic.eusc.virginia.edu/julia/AncientWorld.html

Egyptian Art and Achaeology
>http://www.memst.edu/egypt/main.html

GORP National Sites
>http://www.gorp.com/gorp/resource/archaeol/main.htm

The Perseus Project
>http://www.perseus.tufts.edu/

Robot involved with archaeology project
>http://www.usc.edu/dept/raiders/

Other Information Resources

Cork, Barbara & Reid, Struan (1984) **Archaeology Discovering the Past with Science & Technology**. Usborne Publishing Ltd. London.

Hackwell, W. John (1986) **Digging To The Past Excavations in Ancient Lands**. Charles Scribner's Sons/New York.

Hayden, Brian (1993) **Archaeology The Science of Once And Future Things**. W. H. Freeman & Company New York.

Powerful Projects

Identify a current archaeological site. Describe the location, type of project, major finds, problems, current status, and factors that make this an important site.

Report on a famous archaeological area such as the Egypt, Easter Island, China, Mexico City, Rome, England, Scotland, or Greece.

Discuss a technique used in archaeology such as the electronic microscope.

Explore the Paleolithic cave art. Describe the problems of modern technology.

Discuss what future archaeologists would think of your garbage.

Ridin' the Surf: Subject Area Activities

Visit the ArchNet Site!
http://www.lib.uconn.edu/ArchNet/

Explore the ArchNet Site.

- Select **Resources by Region**. Select a part of the world to study. Create a map and show the location of an important archeological dig. What did they find? What plants, animals, and humans have lived in the area?
- Explore **Material by Subject**. Choose one aspect of archaeology to explore. Create a HyperStudio stack that defines your area and gives examples of the work. Link the stacks together with a main menu stack. Ideas are listed below:
  Archeometry: The scientific analysis of archaeological materials
  Botanical: Analysis of plant remains
  Ceramics: Analysis of ceramic artifacts
  Faunal: Analysis of animal remains from archaeological sites
  Geo-Archaeology: Sediments and site formation
  Historic Archaeology: Analysis of historic sites and artifacts
  Lithics: Analysis of stone tools
- Go to the **Museums**. Find a museum that has examples in the area you've been studying. For example, find a place with good ceramics or faunal. Examine one artifact and write a fictional story about how it came to rest at that location. Base your story on facts that you've gathered. Include a picture in your report.
- Explore a course that is taught on the web.
- Go to the **Academic Departments**. If you could spend the summer on an archaeological dig. Where would you go? Why? What do you think you'd learn?
- Explore one of the **new sites**. Write a news article announcing the new site and it's contributions.
- Go to the **email lists**. Write to a person who does the type of archaeological work you've been exploring. Ask about their career and education. Would you like their job?

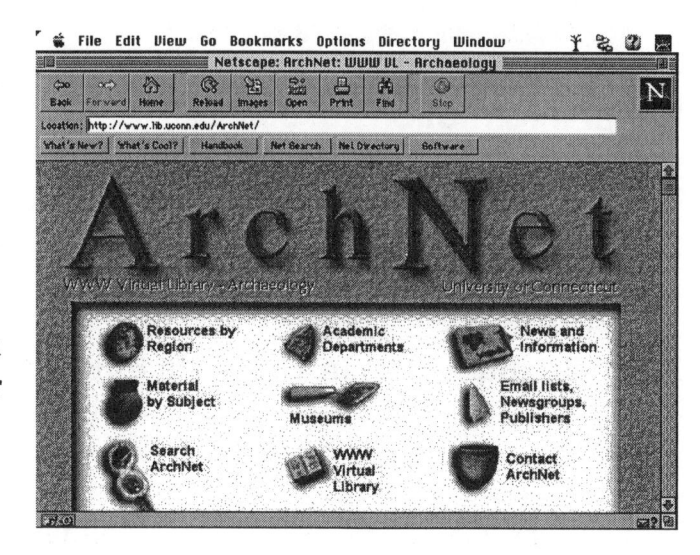

Earth/Space Science - Astronomy

The Internet is a great resource for information on astronomy. You can follow ongoing space projects, explore information about particular locations in space, or even use a robotic telescope! Use the Ask an Astronomer site to ask questions that you haven't been able to answer using traditional resources.

Surfer Starters

Ask an Astronomer
   http://www-hpcc.astro.washington.edu/k12/ask.html
Astronomy Sites
   http://www.injersey.com/Media/IonSci/features/perseids/perseids.html
   http://www.injersey.com/Media/IonSci/glance/news895/cometbop.html
   http://stardust.ipl.nasa.gov/planets
   http://seds.lpl.arizona.edu/nineplanets/nineplanets/nineplanets.html
   http://www-iwi.unisg.ch/~sambucci/space/index.html
   http://www.nosc.mil/planet_earth/planets.html
   http://www.eia.brad.ac.uk/btl/sg.html
   http://www.eia.brad.ac.uk/btl/m2.html
Middle School Student Project
   http://longwood.cs.ucf.edu:80/~MidLink/Mars.html
Telescopes
   http://ranier.oact.hq.nasa.gov/Sensors_page/Optics/TeleOV.html
Views of the Solar System
   http://bang.lanl.gov/solarsys/
Comets
   http://www.comet.arc.nasa.gov/comet/

Other Information Resources

   Asimov, Isaac (1982) **How Did We find Out About The Universe.** Walker.
   Berger, Melvin (1985) **Star Gazing, Comet Tracking & Sky Mapping.** Putnam.
   Berger, Melvin (1993) **Where Are The Stars During The Day? A Book About Stars.** Ideals.
   Beyer, Steven L. (1986) **Star Guide: A Unique System For Identifying The Brightest Stars In The Night Sky.** Little Brown.
   Brown, Peter Lancaster (1984) **Astronomy.** Facts On File.
   Darling, David J. (1985) **The New Astronomy: An Ever-Changing Universe.** Dillon.
   Gibbons, Gail (1992) **Stargazers.** Holiday House.
   Gustafson, John (1992) **Stars, Clusters, & Galaxies.** Messner.

Lampton, Christopher (1987) **Astronomy: From Copernicus to the Space Telescope**. Watts.

Lauber, Patricia (1989) **Voyagers From Space : Meteors & Meteorites**. Harper.

Moskin, Marietta D. (1985) **Sky Dragons, and Flaming Swords: The Story of Eclipses, Comets, & Other Strange Happenings in the Skies**. Walker.

Simon, Seymour (1986) **Stars**. Morrow.

Stars & Constellations (Videocassette) National Geographic.

CD-ROM Resources

Beyond Planet Earth, Discovery Channel
Planetary Taxi, Voyager
RedShift, Maxis
Space Shuttle, Mindscape

Powerful Projects

Below are topic ideas to get students started exploring the information found on the Web.

Compare and contrast theories on the beginning, ending, and size of space.

Trace the history of the telescope. Create a timeline showing the development.

Describe myths about astronomy. Write a myth.

Describe an ancient theory and compare it to modern theory.

Compare and contrast pulsars and quasars.

Trace a particular element of the space program and speculate on the future.

Trace the formation and evolution of an object such as a star or moon.

Describe the origins of objects in space such as planets, moons, start, quasars, or black holes.

Explore a "cool" feature of an object. For example, why does Saturn have rings? Why does a comet have a tail?

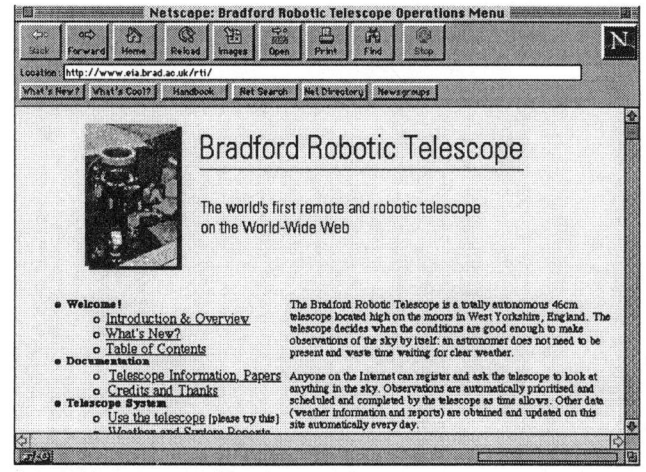

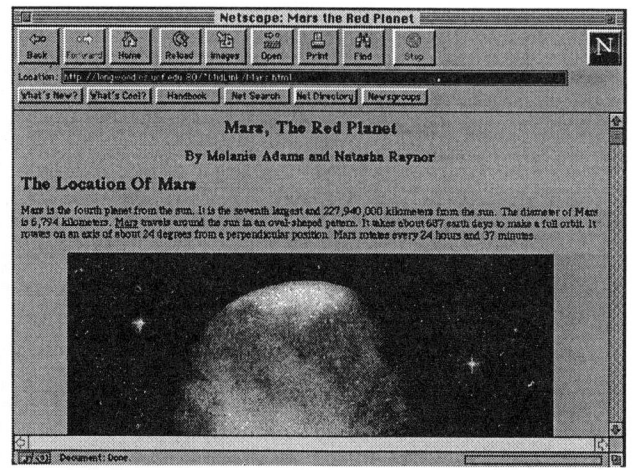

http://www.eia.brad.ac.uk/

http://longwood.cs.ucf.edu:80/~MidLink/Mars.html

Visit Views of the Solar System!
http://bang.lanl.gov/solarsys/

Explore Views of the Solar System.

Draw a picture of the solar system. Check your drawing against the information at this site. Change or add things to your diagram.

Create a mobile of the solar system.

Create a list of questions you have about our solar system. Use this resource to answer the questions.

Select a planet to explore. Create a HyperStudio stack that takes us on a trip to the planet and explains the features as we explore the planet.

Compare and contrast two planets in our solar system. If you had to live on one, which would you choose? Why?

Create a list of the greatest resources available on each planet. Create a game that asks players to identify the planet with the riches resources in a particular area.

Examine the information about comets, meteoroids and meteorites. Why do comets have tails? Will a comet ever wipe out the earth? What's the difference between a comet and a meteoriod? Which would cause more damage?

Explore a person or event from the history of our solar system. Why do you think people remember this person or event?

What questions weren't answered at this site? Use the Astronomy links to explore other informational sites.

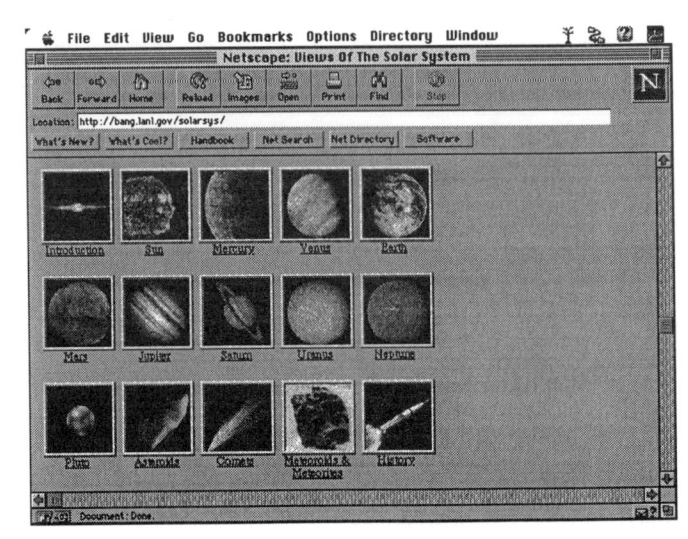

Earth/Space Science - Water

Water is an important part of life. Rivers, streams, and wetlands are essential to humans, plants, and animals. There are lots of water projects to explore.

Surfer Starters
Adopt-A-Watershed
   http://www.tcoe.trinity.k12.ca.us/aaw/adopt.html
EcoNet: Water
   http://www.igc.apc.org/igc/www.water.html
GREEN: Global Rivers Environmental Education Network
   http://www.igc.apc.org/green/green.html
Hydrology
   http://www.uwin.siu.edu/ucowr/hydro/index.html
Four Mile Run Project
   http://128.143.238.20/nvpdc/4MileRun/
Los Angeles River
   http://www.lalc.k12.ca.us/laep/smart/river/riverweb.html
Rivers
   http://solstice.crest.org/environment/eol/water/water.html
   http://www.umich.edu/~nppcpub/nppc.htm/#top
Texas River Project
   http://chico.rice.edu/armadillo/Ftbend/rivers.html
University Council on Water Resources
   http://www.uwin.siu.edu/ucowr/index.html
Water Resources of the United States
   http://h2o.usgs.gov/
Water - Student Projects
   http://web.cal.msu.edu/kc/Water.html
Water Terms
   http://www.tec.org/tec/terms2.html

Other Information Resources

Amos, William Hopkins (1981) **Wildlife of The Rivers.** H.N. Abrams.
Bellamy, David J. (1988) **The River**. C.N. Potter.
Cherry, Lynne (1992) **River Ran Wild: An Environmental History. Gulliver?** Harcourt Brace Jovanovich.
Court, Judith (1985) **Ponds & Streams.** F. Watts.
Fresh Water: Resource At Risk (Videocassette) (1993) National Geographic.
Hoff, Mary King (1991) **Our Endangered Planet: Groundwater**. Lerner.
Hoff, Mary King (1991) **Our Endangered Planet: Rivers & Lakes**. Lerner.
Lystak, Karen (1991) **Saving Our Wetlands & Their Wildlife.** Watts.
Madison, Lawrence (1988) **Trout River.** H.N. Abrams.
McCauley, Jane R. (1988) **Let's Explore A River.** National Geographic Society.
Parker, Steve (1988) **Pond & River.** Knopf.
Our Watery World (Videocassette) (1991) AIT/Slim Goodbody Corp.
Source of Water? Water In Our Environment (Videocassette) (1992) Rainbow Educational Video.

Powerful Projects

Go on a virtual tour of a river. Two are listed below.
Four Mile Run Project
> http://128.143.238.20/nvpdc/4MileRun/

Los Angeles River
> http://www.lalc.k12.ca.us/laep/smart/river/riverweb.html

Create a virtual tour of a river near you!

Explore information on water and the environment.

> http://solstice.crest.org/environment/eol/water/water.html

Select one fact that you found the most interesting about water and the environment. Find another source that supports this idea.
Find out what other countries are doing to conserve water.
Write a news article about what countries are doing about acid rain.

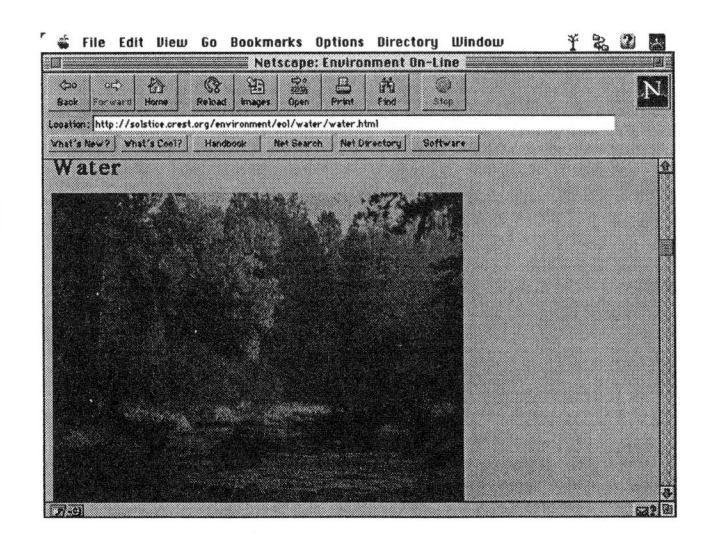

Visit the Hydrology Site!
http://www.uwin.siu.edu/ucowr/hydro/index.html

Visit the Hydrology Site!

Explore the **Introduction**. Why is water important? List all the things you do that involve water.

Find out about **Water and People**. Why do people need water? Create a chart showing how much water people use. How much do you use in a day? Keep track for a week. Compare your water use with your classmate.

Answer the question: **What Is Hydrology**? Create a poster showing examples.

Find out **What Hydrologists Do**. Would you like to be a hydrologist? What kind of skills do you think they need for their job?

Learn about **Surface Water** and **Groundwater**. What's the different between surface and ground water? Is one more important than the other? Where do they originate?

Explore water in **Agriculture**. What happens when there's not enough water?

What can we do to help **Flood Control**? It seems like there are floods all the time. What can we do to control floods? Find out about flood control in your area.

Learn about water and **Energy**. How can water be used as a source of energy? Is it used as an energy source in your area? Why?

Learn about how water moves, it's called **Navigation**. Find a river in your area to explore. Has it always had the same path? How has the river changed over time?

Is there enough **Water for Tomorrow**? What would happen if we ran out of water? Is that possible? What would life be like without water?

Explore **Careers in Hydrology**. Find out more about one of the careers.

Explore other water sites. Select a kinds of water source and learn more about how it is used.

Read more about hydrology at the USA Today Hydrology Page.

http://web.usatoday.com/weather/whydro00.htm

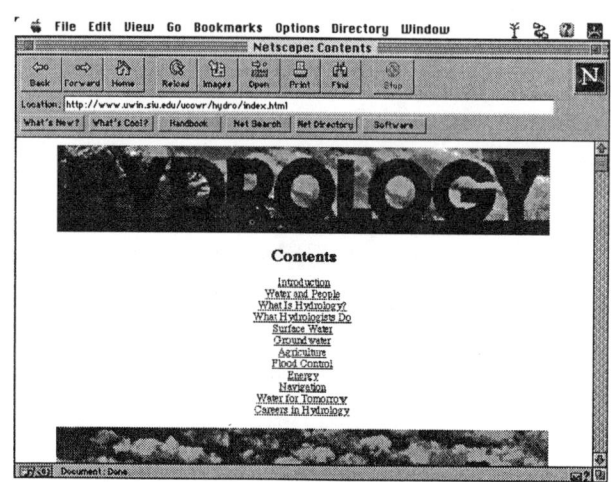

Earth/Space Science - Weather

Weather is one of the best topics to explore on the Internet. Information changes constantly. You can follow the progress of a thunderstorm, the development of a hurricane, or the path of a tornado.

Surfer Starters

AccuWeather
   http://www.accuwx.com/
CNN Weather
   http://www.cnn.com/WEATHER/index.html
Weather lesson ideas
   http://gnn.com/gnn/meta/edu/curr/rdg/gen_act/weather/index.html
   http://faldo.atmos.uiuc.edu/WEATHER/weather.html
K-12 school weather project
   http://nis.accel.worc.k12.ma.us/WWW/Projects/WeatherWeb/weather.html
USA Today Weather
   http://web.usatoday.com/weather/wfront.htm
Weather Information Superhighway
   http://thunder.met.fsu.edu/nws/public_html/wxhwy.html
Weather
   http://www.intellicast.com/
   http://www.osc.on.ca/Weather/html/wfhome.htm
   http://rs560.cl.msu.edu/weather
   http://www.mit.edu:8001/usa.html
   http://cirrus.sprl.umich.edu:80/wxnet/tropical.html
Weather - Bad Science
   http://www.ems.psu.edu/~fraser/Bad/BadRain.html
Weather Sites
   http://www.yahooligans.com/Science_and_Oddities/Weather/

Other Information Resources

Flint, David (1991) **Weather & Climate.** Gloucester/Watts.
Ford, Adam (1982) **Weather Watch.** Lothrop, Lee, & Shepard.
Gallant, Roy A. (1979) **Earth's Changing Climate.** Macmillian.
Gibbons, Gail (1987) **Weather Forecasting.** Four Winds/Macmillan.
Kohl, Jonathan D. (1992) **Weatherwise: Learning About The Weather.** Lerner.
Lambert, David (1984) **Weather & Its Work.** Facts On File.

McMillan, Bruce (1991) **Weather Sky.** Farrar, Straus & Giroux.
Zim, Herbert (1987) **Weather**. Western Paper.

Educational Software
Five-Star Forecast (1990) MECC.

Powerful Projects

Keep track of your local weather for a week. Compare it with your email penpal. Where would you rather live for the nicest weather this time of year? What factors impact the weather where you live?

Follow a storm as it develops. Use a resource like Accuweather to identify storms that may be developing.

http://www.accuwx.com/

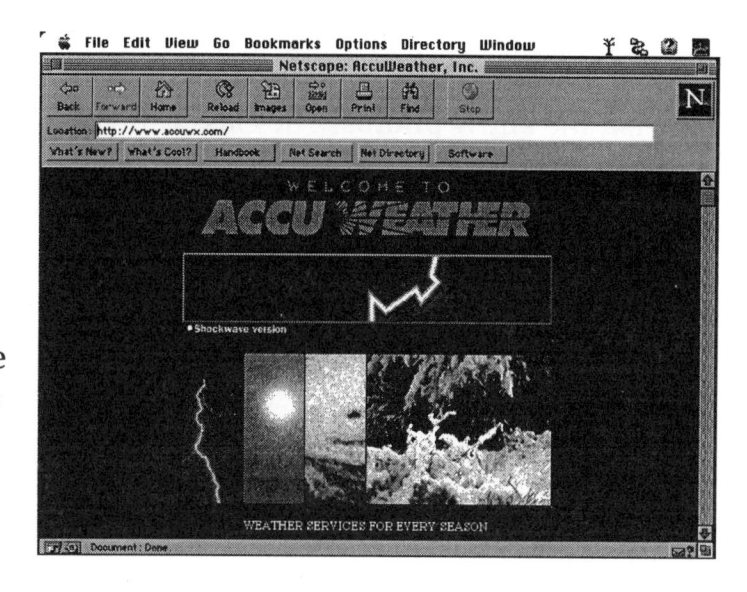

Use resources like the following to track a storm like Hurricane Marilyn as shown:

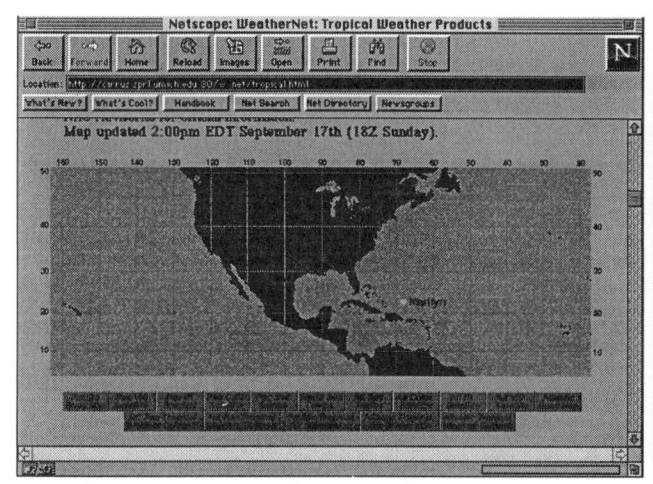

http://cirrus.sprl.umich.edu:80/wxnet/tropical.html

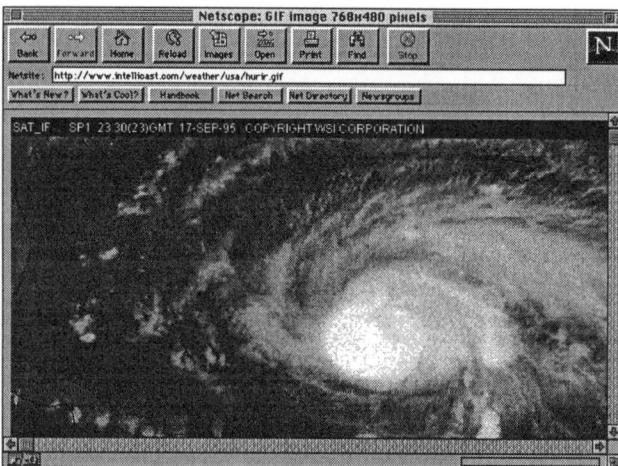

http://www.intellicast.com/weather/usa/hurir.gif

Visit the Snow Pages!
http://www.alaska.net/~mteel/kids/kids.html

Visit the Snow Pages.

Draw a picture of each **type of snow crystal**: needles, columns, plates, columns capped with plates, dendrites and stars.

Visit the **snow photos**. The class can vote on their favorite.

Try the **snow experiment**. What happened? Share your results with an epal!

Create **snow flakes**. Do they look real? Why or why not?

Read the **Snow Maiden** and make up your own ending.

Read the **Snow Queen** and each of the endings. Which is your favorite? Why? Would you write a different ending?

Read **The Snow Storm**. Which of the three pictures fits best with the poem? Why? What other kinds of pictures could you add to this story?

Read **The White Silence** and **To Build a Fire**. Which story did you like better? Why? Which character did you like best and least?

Go to the **second snow page**. Use each of the **snow words** in a short story set in Alaska.

There are many more **activities**. Try them out! Share your favorite with your epal.

Create your own snow activity.

Some children have never played in snow. Write about the best part of playing in the snow.

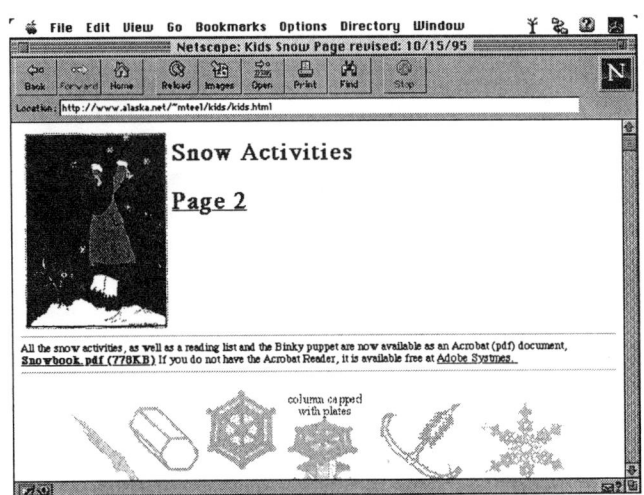

Ridin' the Surf: Subject Area Activities

Life Science - Anatomy, Biology

Text, graphics, line art, animation, and video clips are just a few of the information formats you can find in the area of anatomy and biology. Students can dissect frogs, explore parts of the human body, and view animated simulations of experiments through some of the Internet resources listed below.

Surfer Starters

Biology Education
 http://www-hpcc.astro.washington.edu/scied/bioindex.html
Biology Teachers
 http://www.gene.com:80/ae/
Biology Sites
 http://www.einet.net/galaxy/Science/Biology.html
 http://www.cs.brown.edu/people/art035/Bin/science.html
Bugs in the News
 http://falcon.cc.ukans.edu/~jbrown/bugs.html
Center for Disease Control
 http://www.cdc.gov
Dictionary of Cell Biology
 http://www.mblab.gla.ac.uk/~julian/Dict.html
Frog Dissection
 http://curry.edschool.Virginia.EDU/go/frog/
 http://george.lbl.gov/ITG.hm.pg.docs/dissect/info.html
Human Cross Section
 http://www.meddean.luc.edu/lumen/MedEd/GrossAnatomy/cross_section/index.html
Human Heart
 http://sln.fi.edu/biosci/biosci.html
Human Skeleton
 http://www.cs.brown.edu/people/art035/Bin/skeleton.html
Medical Illustrator
 http://www.mednexus.com/med_illustrator/links2.html
MicrobeZoo
 http://commtechlab.msu.edu/CTLProjects/dlc-me/index.html
Microbial Underground
 http://www.ch.ic.ac.uk/medbact/
Microbiology Course
 http://yoda.ucc.uconn.edu/VirtualClass/MCB/index.html
Visual Human Site
 http://www.nlm.nih.gov/research/visible/visible_human.html

Visit the Cells Alive site!
http://www.comet.chv.va.us/quill/

Visit the Cells Alive site! This site contains lots of video clips and 3D animation. You many need to download software to make them work.

Explore each of the following topics. Choose one to explore in depth through the use of Internet and other resources. Use the pictures, animation, or video clip in a HyperStudio project addressing the importance of this idea.

Guest scientist. Explore the dynamic redistribution of the cytoskeleton during phagocytosis.
Growing bacteria. Find out why we aren't knee-deep in bacteria.
Apoptosis. Watch what happened when a cell commits suicide.
Swimmin' E. coli. Explore how E.coli move.

Explore **Jim's Links.** Find a site that contains an area of biology you find interesting. Write a review of the site and what it contains.

Brainstorm biology questions that you have. Use Jim's Links to find the answers.

Examine the following topics. Select one that you think people would find interesting. Write about the information in language that "regular people" would understand. Why is it important that people know this information?

Chemotaxis
Cytotoxic T lymphocyte
Human macrophage
How big is a virus
The Parasites
Group A Strep pyogenes
How white blood cells kill microbes
How penicillin kills bacteria
CRYSTALS alive!

Life Science - Genetics

Genetics is an interesting topic for students of many ages. Start with Genetics 101 to learn the basics. Learn more about genetics through the study of flies.

Surfer Starters

Charles Darwin: Origin of the Species Text
   http://www.wonderland.org/Works/Charles-Darwin/origin/
Flybase
   http://morgan.harvard.edu/
Genetics 101: By a Ninth Grade Student!
   http://w3.trib.com/~rstokes/index.html
MendelWeb
   http://www.netspace.org/MendelWeb/
Mutant Fruit Flies
   http://www.exploratorium.edu/imagery/exhibits/mutant_flies/mutant_flies.html
Virtual Fly Lab Site
   http://vflylab.calstatela.edu/edesktop/VirtApps/VflyLab/Design.html

Other Information Resources

Arnold, Caroline (1986) **Genetics: From Mendel To Gene Splicing.** Watts.

Asimov, Isaac (1983) **How Did We Find Out About Genes?** Walker & Co. NY.

Berg, Paul (1992) **Dealing With Genes The Language of Heredity.** University Science Books Mill Valley, California.

Bornstein, Jerry & Sandy (1980) **What Is Genetics?** Julian Messner: New York.

Cooper, Kay (1988) **Where Did You Get Those Eyes? A Guide To Discovering Your Family History.** Walker.

Lee, Thomas F. (1993) **Gene Future-The Promise & Perils of the New Biology.** Plenum Press New York & London.

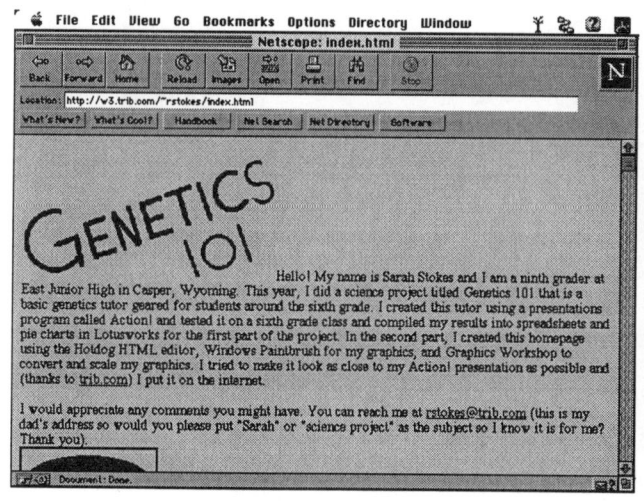

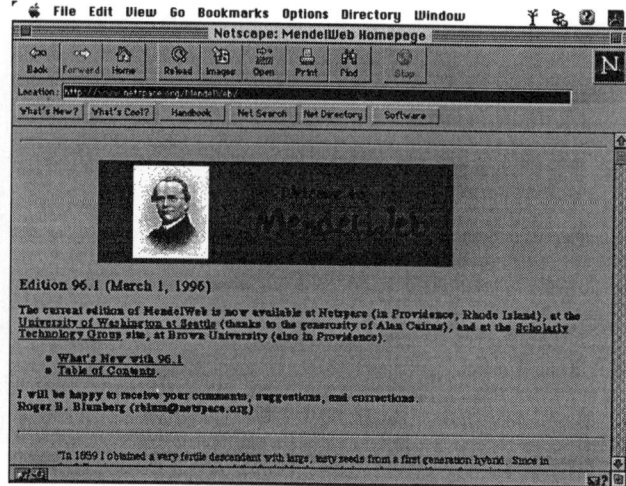

Visit the Fruit Fly Sites!
http://vflylab.calstatela.edu/edesktop/VirtApps/VflyLab/Design.html

Explore the genetics of fruit flies. Two sites contains great information and activities to help you explore the world of the fruit fly.

Explore the Mutant Fruit Flies

http://www.exploratorium.edu/imagery/exhibits/mutant_flies/mutant_flies.html

Create a chart showing the different fruit fly characteristics. Investigate both graphics and closeups.
Compare normal fruit flies to these fruit flies.
What do you think will happen when we mate fruit flies with particular traits?

http://www.exploratorium.edu/imagery/exhibits/mutant_flies/mutant_flies.html

Explore the **Virtual Fly Lab**.

http://vflylab.calstatela.edu/edesktop/VirtApps/VflyLab/Design.html

As a large group review each characteristic.
In small groups, create your own fruit fly family. Create a diagram of the generations.

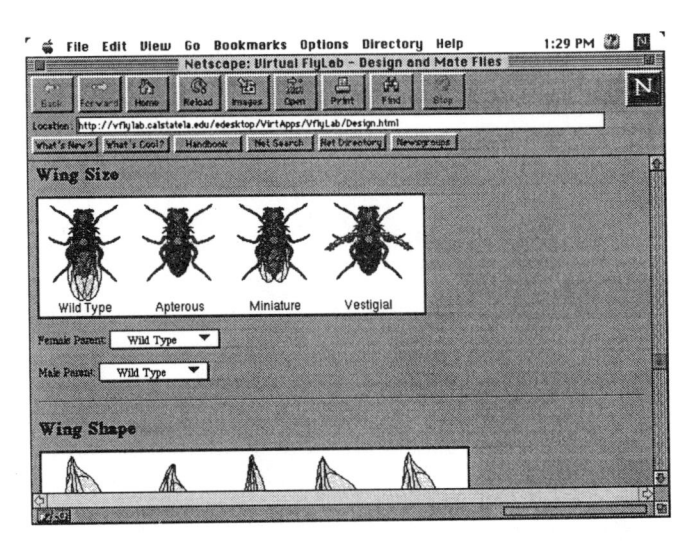

http://vflylab.calstatela.edu/edesktop/VirtApps/VflyLab/Design.html

Ridin' the Surf: Subject Area Activities

Life Science - Insects

Bugs to butterflies, you'll find all your favorites on the Internet. There are lots of sites that contain pictures and information about all kinds of insects.

Surfer Starters

Bees
   http://cvs.anu.edu.au/andy/beye/beyehome.html
Bug Watch
   http://cnj.digex.net/~lgbrossa/
Bugs - Cultural Entomology
   http://www.insects.org/
Butterflies
   http://mgfx.com/butterfly/
   http://www-swiss.ai.mit.edu/~philg/photo/butterflies/
   http://ns9000(a)furman.edu/~snyder/butterfly/index.html
Cockroach World
   http://www.nj.com/yucky/roaches/index.html
Insect Pages
   http://www.minnetonka.k12.mn.us/groveland/insect.proj/insects.html
   http://mgfx.com/insect/
Lesson Ideas
   http://www.hmco.com/hmco/school/links/theme_9.html
   http://www.ed.uiuc.edu/YLP94-95/Mini-units/Griffin.Insects/Monarch Watch Project
   http://129.237.246.134/
Cool bug stuff!
   http://www.colostate.edu/Depts/Entomology/ent.html
   http://www.public.iastate.edu/~entomology/ResourceList.html
   http://gears.tucson.ars.ag.gov/
   http://www.injersey.com/Media/IonSci/features/roach/roach.html
   gopher://ftp.bio.indiana.edu/11/Other-Gophers-and-Things/Images
Spiders
   http://www.ufsia.ac.be/Arachnology/Arachnology.html

Other Information Resources

Fischer-Nagel, Heiderose (1989) **Ant Colony**. Carolrhoda.
Gibbons, Gail (1989) **Monarch Butterfly**. Holiday House.
Lavies, Bianca (1992) **Monarch Butterflies: Mysterious Travelers**. Dutton.
Overbeck, Cynthia (1982) **Ants**. Lerner.

Powerful Projects

Use the Web to find information about an insect. Then, create a model of the insect in its habitat. What does it eat? What does it do all day?

Create a chart showing "helpful" and "harmful" insects. Use the Internet to find good pictures to include in your chart.

Learn about the migration patterns of the monarch butterfly. Join a monarch project.

Go to **Bug Watch** and explore the bugs. Choose a bug. Why do you think this insect exists? What's its life cycle? What does it eat? Create a bug box filled with information about your insect along with pictures to share.

Go to **Bugs - Cultural Entomology** and find out about how bugs impact our daily lives. There are movies and TV shows about bugs. We use bug words in our language, and sometimes even act like bugs.

Read an article from the **Cultural Entomology Digest**. Write your own article about bugs in your life.

Visit Cockroach World!
http://www.nj.com/yucky/roaches/index.html

Visit Cockroach World to learn about the world's most famous bug!

Explore the **Inside Story**. It shows you a bug body upclose. Choose another bug and create an Inside Story on that bug! How is your bug like and unlike the cockroach?

Visit **Cockroaches around the World**! Explore all the roaches and try the game. Make a Roach Roster and add everyone's score.

Explore a **Day in the Life** of a cockroach. Explore the Internet for a picture of a bug you like. Write a day in the life of your bug. Remember to include factual information about your bug.

Find out **How to** get rid of cockroaches. Compare and contrast the contents of popular bug sprays, roach houses, and other methods of removal. Which would be most effective? Why? Write an advertisement that explains why one product would be more effective than another based on facts about roaches.

Build a roach trap! If you caught one, what would you do with it?

Read **Tall Tales** about cockroaches. Write your own tall tale and send it in.

Explore **Cockroach Facts**. Post **Fun Facts** on a roach board. Compare a cockroach with your favorite bug. **Ask Betty** a question about cockroaches!

Use the yucky rustling sounds of cockroaches or a cute cockroach QuickTime movie in a HyperStudio stack on the world's yuckiest bug. Include your favorite project from this site.

Test your knowledge of roaches at the roach **quiz**!

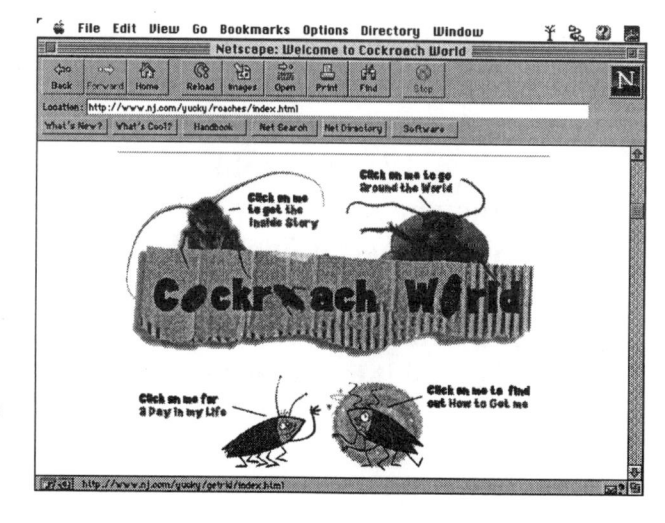

Visit Butterfly World!
http://mgfx.com/butterfly/

Butterflies are beautiful and helpful creatures. Visit Butterfly World!

- Go to the **Nature Store** and locate a book you'd like to read.
- Read the poem **Butterfly in My Back Yard** by a Chinese professor. Select a butterfly that fits with the poem. What butterfly would you choose? Why? Write your own butterfly poem and email it to the author.
- Select **Landscaping for Butterflies**. What kind of landscape do you need to attract butterflies? Design a butterfly area for your school. What plants would you include? What kinds of butterflies would you attract? What time of year do you need to plant the flowers, trees, or bushes? When will the butterflies come?
- Explore **Conservation and Ecology**. Select one of the articles. What can you do to help?
- Go to **Articles and Other Information**. Select a topic you'd like to learn more about and share it with a friend.
- Explore the world of the **monarch butterfly**.
- Select **Raising Your Own Butterflies.** Create a plan for raising a butterfly.
- Go to the **Picture Gallery** and select a butterfly. Locate information about the butterfly. Create a HyperStudio stack!
- Find a **Butterfly Garden** anywhere in the world. What butterflies do they have there? How are they like and unlike the butterflies where you live. Create a map comparing the locations in the world. Compare and contrast the climate, geography, and other factors that might impact the types of butterflies that live there.
- Write to a **Butterfly Society** and ask for information about the organization. Would you like to join? Do they have student activities?
- Explore the **Special Events**. Join a contest.
- Develop a neat idea for a contest and email it to the webmaster.

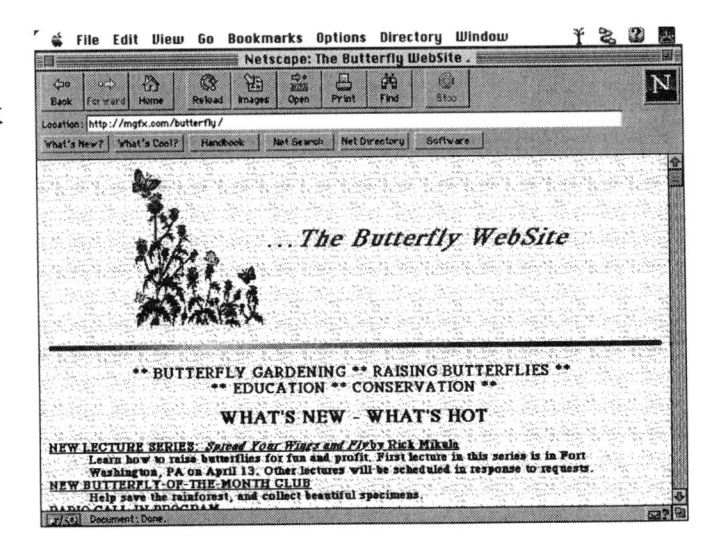

Life Science - Plant Life

Explore the world of plants. Apply what you learn about botany and horticulture to the development of gardens. Try your hand at traditional gardening or go to the tele-garden and use a robot-controlled gardener.

Surfer Starters - Botany

Botany
   http://www.euronet.nl/users/mbleeker/
Botany Sites
   http://www.bham.ac.uk/BUFAU/Projects/EAW/Themes/zoolab/botres.htm
Botany - Seeds of Life
   http://www.next.com/~jmh/SeedsOfLife/home.html

Surfer Starters - Horticulture

Garden Net
   http://www.olympus.net/gardens/home.htm
Plants
   http://bluehen.ags.udel.edu/grounds.html
Tele-garden - robot controlled garden
   http://www.usc.edu/dept/garden/
Botanical Gardens
   http://www.pathfinder.com/@@IjxPKKAMgglAQGOu/vg/Gardens/NYBG/index.html
The Electronic Garden
   http://pace1.cts.mtu.edu:8080/~alex/sustain.html
Roses
   http://www.halcyon.com/cirsium/rosegal/welcome.htm
Texas Wildflowers
   http://numedia.tddc.net/wildflowers/
Waterlilies
   http://www.h2olily.com/
Virtual Garden
   http://pathfinder.com/@@iLr7I6NAWQMAQOPB/vg/Welcome/welcome.html

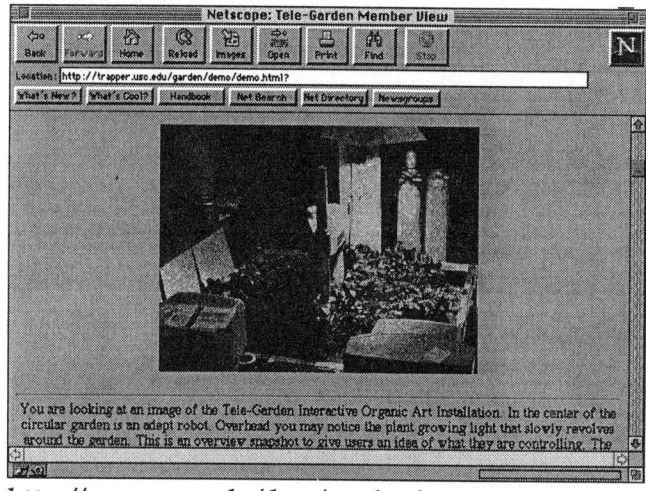

http://www.usc.edu/dept/garden/

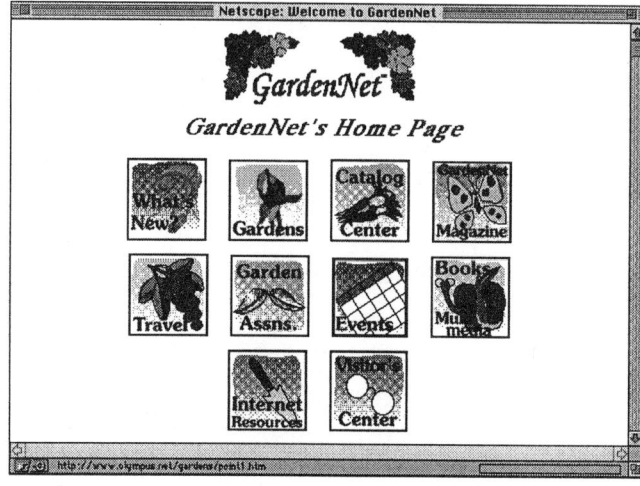

http://www.olympus.net/gardens/home.htm

Visit the Seeds of Life site!
http://www.next.com/~jmh/SeedsOfLife/home.html

Visit the Seeds of Life site and learn more about the important role of seeds in our life.

Explore the **Introduction**. Read the quote by Henry D. Thoreau. What do you think about this quote. Click on Thoreau to find out more about the person. How did seeds play a role in his life? Did he ever plant any seeds?

Select **Fruits and Seeds**. Create a table display that shows the four main fruit types. Create a chart that compares and contrasts each type of fruit. Which are your favorites? Compare and contrast fresh and dry fruits. Which do you like better? Why?

Go on a **Voyage**. Explore the different ways that seeds travel. Write a story about the life of three seeds. Each seed should travel a different way. How could each seed produce something different and all wind up on the same dinner plate in the future?

Learn about **Seeds and Man**. Grains play an important part in our lives. Create a timeline showing the history of seeds and humans. Create a list of all the things you eat in a day that include grain. Create a map showing grain production in a particular part of the country or world.

Answer the question: **What are these Seeds?** Examine each picture, do you know the seed? Email the author!

Go to the **Album** and pick a seed picture. Use the illustration in a HyperStudio stack that discusses the importance of the seed to humans and animals. Be sure to give credit to the photographer! Go to other **seed sites** to find information for your project.

Ridin' the Surf: Subject Area Activities 163

Visit the Missouri Botanical Garden Site!
http://cissus.mobot.org/MBGnet/

Visit the Missouri Botanical Garden Learning Network.

Explore the **Virtual Garden! - Desert** and do the following activities:
- What Is A Desert Like
- Types of Deserts
- What Causes Deserts
- Deserts of The World
- Desert Plants
- Desert Experiences
- Desert Links

Explore the **Biology of Plants**. Join the Card Contest!

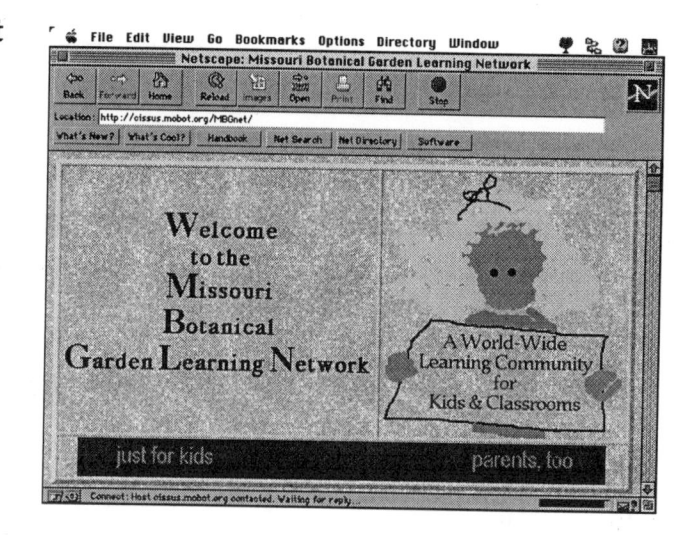

Try one of the following **Just For Kids Activities**: Making Rain, Osmosis, or Ink. How did it work? Send your comments to the MBG!

Join the **video contest** that deals with your area!

Explore **Blooms Across America**.

http://www.ibp.com/pit/blooms/

Get your community to join! Create your own local project that might be similar to Blooms Across America.

Physical Science

Physical science explores phenomena such as electricity, light, sound, magnetism, forces, energies, and heat. Many universities contain information on this topics, but many of these resources have tutorials and information that can be adapted for the K-12 classroom.

Surfer Starters

Chemistry
Chemistry
   http://www.cchem.berkeley.edu/Table/index.html
   http://www.shef.ac.uk/chemistry/web-elements/web-elements-home.html
   http://www.cs.ubc.ca/elements
Chemistry Education
   http://www-hpcc.astro.washington.edu/scied/chemistry.html
Chemistry Resources
   http://www.mbhs.edu/~pham/chem.html
Chemicool
   http://the-tech.mit.edu/~davhsu/chemicool.html

Physics
Particle Adventure
   http://pdg.lbl.gov/cpep/adventure.html
Physics
   http://cleopatra.berkeley.edu/Vol1/Contents.html
   http://www.duke.edu/~tj/hist/hist_mic.html
Physics Education
   http://www-hpcc.astro.washington.edu/scied/physics.html

Light & Sound
Lesson Plans
   http://ericir.syr.edu/Newton/Lessons/movisnd.html
How Light Works
   http://curry.edschool.virginia.EDU/murray/Light/How_Light_Works.html
Light Microscope
   http://www.duke.edu/~tj/hist/hist_mic.html
OpticsNet
   http://www.osa.org/index.html

   Ardley, Neil (1991) **Science Book of Color.** Bulliver/Harcourt Brace Jovanovich.
   Baker, Wendy (1993) **Sound.** Aladdin/Macmillan.

Broekel, Ray (1983) **Sound Experiments.** Childrens Press.
Catherall, Ed (1989) **Exploring Sound.** Raintree/Streck-Vaughn.
Color: Light Fantastic (Videocassette) National Geographic (1988).
Darling, David (1991) **Sounds Interesting: The Science of Acoustics.** Dillon.
Hoban, Tana (1989) **Of Colors & Things.** Greenwillow.
Lampton, Christopher (1992) **Sound: More Than What You Hear.** Enslow.
Taylor, Barbara (1990) **Color and Light.** Franklin Watts.
Devonshire, Hilary (1991) **Color.** F. Watts.
Smithsonian (1993) **Color and Light: Step-by-Step Science Activity Projects.**

Energy
Energy Quest
    http://www.energy.ca.gov/energy/education/eduhome.html
Atomic Energy - Student Project
    http://web66.coled.umn.edu:80/hillside/franklin/Atomic/Project.html
Einstein Online
    http://www.sas.upenn.edu/~smfriedm/einstein.html
Energy
    http://zebu.uoregon.edu/energy.html
Energy - Student Project
    http://k12.cnidr.org/gsh/schools/ny/che.html
Fermi Lab
    http://www.fnal.gov/fermilab_home.html
Fusion Page
    http://FusionEd.gat.com/
Nuclear Energy
    http://neutrino.nuc.berkeley.edu/neutronics/todd.html
Ardley, Neil (1991) **Science Book of Electricity.** Gulliver/Harcourt Brace.
Asimov, Isaac (1973) **How Did We Find Out About Electricity?** Walker.
Baker, Wendy (1993) **Electricity.** Aladdin/ Macmillan.
Berger, Melvin (1989) **Switch On, Switch Off.** Crowell/HarperCollins.
Boltz, C. L. (1985) **How Electricity Is Made.** Facts On File.
Cobb, Vicki (1986) **More Power To You.** Little Brown.
Cobb, Vicki (1990) **Why Doesn't The Sun Burn Out?** Lodestar/Dutton.
Fradin, Dennis B. (1987) **Nuclear Energy.** Childrens Press.
Gutnik, Martin J. (1986) **Electricity: From Faraday To Solar Generators.** Watts.
Lovins, L. Hunter (1986) **Energy Unbound.** Sierra Club Books.
Parker, Steve (1992) **Electricity.** Dorling Kindersley.
Math, Irwin (1981) **Wires & Watts Understanding & Using Electricity.** Scribners.
Vogt, Gregory (1986) **Electricity & Magnestism.** Watts.
Vogt, Gregory (1986) **Generating Electricity.** Watts.

Visit the Physical Science Sites!
http://pdg.lbl.gov/cpep/adventure.html

• •

Explore physical science through a variety of exciting sites!

Go on a **Partical Adventure**!

http://pdg.lbl.gov/cpep/adventure.html

Follow the directions and have a great adventure!

Explore **How Light Works**.

http://curry.edschool.Virginia.EDU/murray/Light/How_Light_Works.html

Learn about light and color. Try an experiment with light.

Explore how technology changes over time. Visit the Spotwood Pumping Station to learn about how plumbing has evolved.

http://www.mov.vic.gov.au/pumpstat.html

- How many different kinds of energy were used at this pumping station over time?
- Choose a technology and figure out how it works. Examine how it was changed over time.
- Trace the history of sanitation and toilets throughout history!

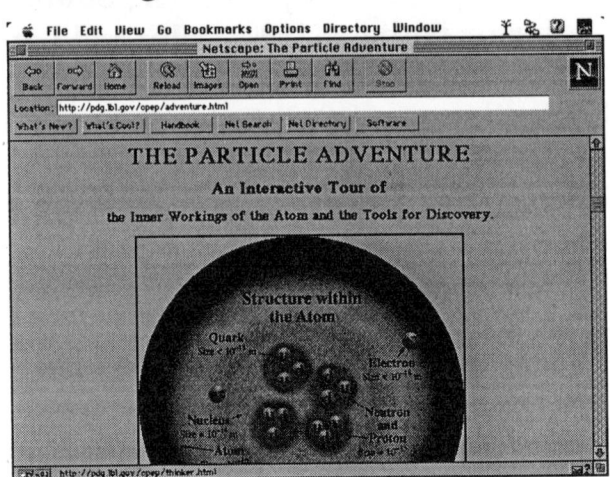

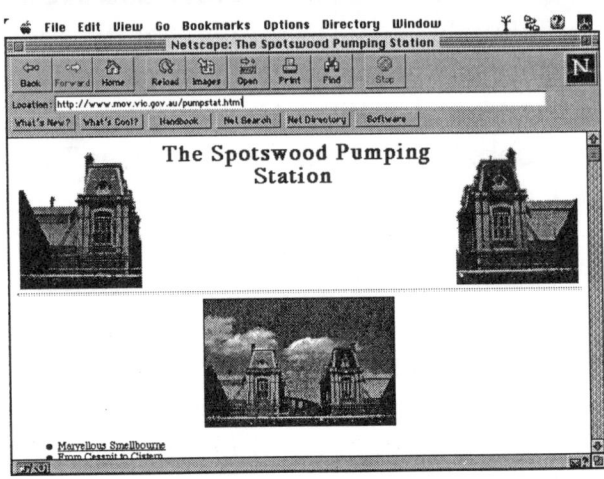

Social Studies - Continents & Countries

Use Internet to visit places around the world! You can take virtual visits to all the continents and hundreds of countries.

Surfer Starters
General Resources
Countries - Student Projects
   http://longwood.cs.ucf.edu:80/~MidLink/Australia.html
Planet Earth Home Page
   http://white.nosc.mil/info.html
United Nations
   http://www.amdahl.com/internet/events/un50.html
   http://www.undcp.or.at/unlinks.html
Virtual Tourist
   http://wings.buffalo.edu/world/
Yahoo's Country List
   http://www.yahoo.com/Regional_Information/Countries/
Yahooligans
   http://www.yahooligans.com/Around_the_World/Countries/

Countries and Regions of the World
Africa
   http://www.servtech.com/public/irony/intoafricia.html
   http://www.sas.upenn.edu/African_Studies/Home_Page/GIF_Images.html
Antarctica
   http://icair.iac.org.nz
   http://http2.sils.umich.edu/Antarctica/Story.html
Artic Project: expedition
   http://www.scholastic.com/public/IAP/IAP-Home.html
Bali (Indonesia)
   http://werple.mira.net.au/~wreid/bali_gal.html
Bermuda
   http://cousteau.uwaterloo.ca/u/kmayall/Bermuda/bda_images.html
Brazil
   http://darkwing.uoregon.edu/~sergiok/brasil.html
   http://www.deltanet.com/brazil/ag/ag.htm
Bulgaria
   http://ASUdesign.eas.asu.edu/~bliznako/Bulgaria/image/Canada
   http://www-nais.ccm.emr.ca/cgndb/geonames.html

Canada
    http://www.yahoo.com/Regional_Information/Countries/Canada/
China
    http://www.cnd.org/Scenery/index.html
Egypt
    http://www.mordor.com/hany/egypt/egypt.html
European Sites
    http://www.tue.nl/maps.html
European Union
    http://www.chemie.fu-berlin.de/adressen/eu.html
Finland
    http://www.travel.fi/int/Welcome.html
France
    http://dmf.culture.fr/culture/gvpda-en.htm
Greece
    http://velox.stanford.edu/hellas/tourist.html
    http://vislab-www.nps.navy.mil/~fapapoul/pictures.html
    http://www.stepc.gr/yannis/lesvos-m.html
Hong Kong
    http://sunsite.unc.edu/hkpa/
Hungary
    http://www.fsz.bme.hu/hungary/homepage.html
Iceland
    http://www.geog.ualberta.ca/als/icepics/eljpics.html
India
    http://spiderman.bu.edu/misc/india/index/images.html
    http://philae.sas.upenn.edu/Hindi/hindipix.html
Ireland
    http://celtic.stanford.edu/pmurphy/irish.html
    http://www.bergen.gov/AAST/Projects/Countries/Ireland/
Israel
    http://www.yahoo.com/Regional_Information/Countries/Israel/
    http://grafton.dartmouth.edu:8001/lrc/culture/mideast/israel.html
Italy
    http://www.webfoot.com/travel/guides/italy/italy.html

Japan
   http://www.cs.uidaho.edu/~marc9442/japan.html
Mexico - Yucatan
   http://www.netaxs.com/~jduncan/Yucatan.html
Mexico and Central America
   http://www.bergen.gov/~chrgre/mexcen/
Middle East
   http://tehran.stanford.edu/
   http://www.cs.cmu.edu/~anwar/kuwait.html
   http://www.wpi.edu/~zakharia/saudi-arabia.html
Morocco
   http://www.ece.scarolina.edu:80/~mouad/morocco.html
Nepal
   http://coos.dartmouth.edu/~rajendra/postcards/index.html
   http://www.eunet.fi/nepal/nep_kuve.htm
Netherlands
   http://www.eeb.ele.tue.nl/map/netherlands.html
New Zealand
   http://www.indirect.com/www/richardk/NZgraphic.html
Nordic Pages
   http://www.algonet.se/~nikos/nordic.html
Poland
   http://www.cs.put.poznan.pl/holidays/tatry/
Scotland
   http://www.cs.ucl.ac.uk/misc/uk/scotland_photos.html
South America
   http://www.bergen.gov/AAST/Projects/LatinAmerica/eritha/
Sri Lanka
   http://suif.stanford.edu/~lanka/sri_lanka.html
Vietnam
   http://sunsite.unc.edu/vietnam/vnpic.html
Slovenija
   http://www.ijs.si/slo.html

Other Information Resources

Bakken, Edna (1992) **Alberta**. Grolier.
Beaton, Margaret (1988) **Syria**. Childrens Press.
Burch, Joann J. (1992) **Kenya: Africa's Tamed Wilderness**. Dillon.
Charters, Dean (1973) **Mountie, 1873-1973: A Golden Treasury of Those Early Years**. Macmillian.
Chiasson, John (1987) **African Journey**. Bradbury.

Cobb, Vicki (1992) **This Place Is Crowded: Japan**. Walker.
Edwards, Frank B. (1993) **Ottawa A Kid's View**. Firefly.
Emmond, Ken (1992) **Manitoba**. Grolier.
Foster, Leila Merrell (1993) **Saudi Arabia**. Childrens Press.
Foster, Leila Merrell (1991) **Jordan**. Childrens Press.
Fox, Mary Virginia (1991) **Iran**. Childrens Press.
Fritz, Jean (1985) **China Homecoming**. Putnam.
Hargrove, Jim (1991) **Germany**. Childrens Press.
Harper, Paul (1990) **The Arab Israeli Conflict**. Watts.
Iraq In Pictures (1990) Lerner.
Jacobsen, Karen (1992) **Ghana**. Children's Press.
Kuwait In Pictures (1989) Lerner.
Laure, Jason (1988) **Zimbabwe**. Childrens Press.
Leigh, Nila K. (1993) **Learning To Swim in Swaziland: A Child's Eye View of a Southern African Country.**
Lotz, Jim (1992) **Nova Scotia**. Grolier.
MacKay, Kathryn (1992) **Ontario**. Grolier.
Meek, James (1990) **Land & People of Scotland**. HarperCollins.
Messenger, Charles (1987) **The Middle East**. Watts.
Paton, Jonathan (1990) **Land & People Of South Africa**. Lippincott.
Reynolds, Jan (1991) **Sahara: Vanishing Cultures**. Harcourt Brace.
Russia. (1992) Prepared By The Geography Dept. Lerner.
Stefoff, Rebecca (1988) **West Bank/Gaza Strip**. Chelses House.
Stegeren, Theo Van (1991) **Land & People of The Netherlands**. HarperCollins.
Vachon, Andre (1982) **Dreams of Empire: Canada Before 1700**. Public Archives.
Yusufali, Jabeen (1990) **Pakistan: An Islamic Treasure**. Dillon.

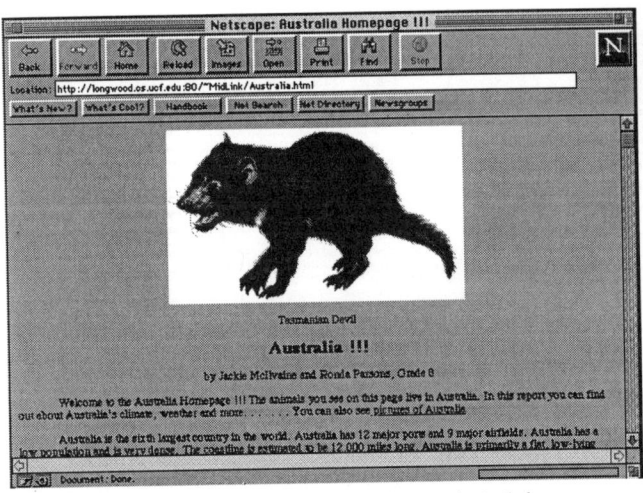

http://longwood.cs.ucf.edu:80/~MidLink/Australia.html

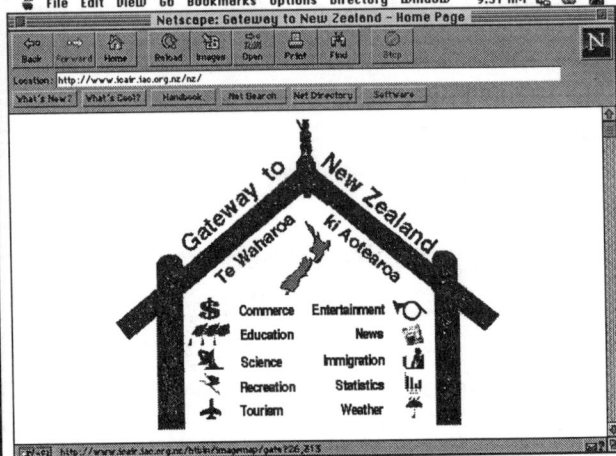

http://www.icair.iac.org.nz/nz/

Visit the Exploring Australia Pages!
http://www.com.au/aaa/Exploring.html

Visit the Exploring Australia Pages to learn more about this interesting country.

Select **Destination Australia**. Compare and contrast two different territories. Where would you like to visit? Why? Plan a trip to one of these territories Copy pictures and create your own scrapbook. Write about your virtual trip.

Learn about the **agriculture** in this country. Compare it to the agriculture in the United States. How is it alike? What products are different?

Compare the **history of the aboriginal people** to the Native American people. How are their histories alike and different?

Learn about the **music** of Australia, both past and present. How have Americans been influenced by Australian music?

If you were going to plan a trip, what types of things would you bring back? How much would they cost? What's the currency exchange rate right now? How much is the US dollar worth in Australia? What about in Canadian?

Sports are very popular in Australia. Select a sport and learn more about it. Do you think people in America would like the sport? How is it like and unlike sports we play in North America?

Australia has different **trees** than those in North America. They have similiar concerns about saving their forests. What kinds of trees do they have? What are they doing to preserve their forests?

Australia has interesting **plants**. Many of the flowers are different than the US. If you were going to create a flower arrangement to sent to your parents, what Australian flowers would you include? Why?

Australia has unique **animals**. Select an animal that's found only in this beautiful country and write about how you would protect it from harm.

Many of the **birds** in Australia look like the pets of the US. Select a bird that you think would make a great pet. What does the bird eat and where does it live?

The **history** of Australia is similiar to the US. Create a list of ways that the history of Australia and the US are alike and different.

What's **vegemite**? Australians eat it all the time. Do you think you'd like it?

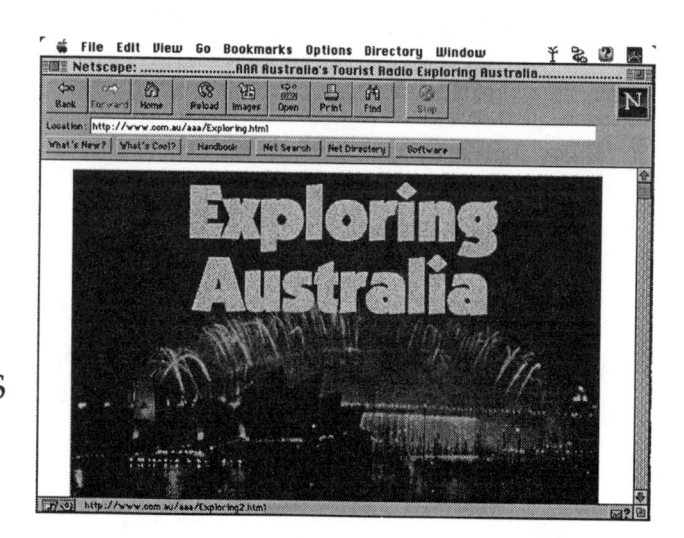

Visit the Wangaratta Australia Home Page!
http://www.ozemail.com.au/~ctech/acts.htm

The kids at Wangaratta School in Australia have developed a page for you to explore.

Listen to the **kookaburra**. Does it sound like a bird? Draw a picture of a made up bird. Give it a name. What would it sound like?

Do the **Aussie animals** word search. Create a word search for animals that live in your area.

Finish the **Dot-to-Dot**. Create a Dot-to-Dot for an animal that lives in your area. Ask someone else in the class to try it. If you use a sheet of plastic over the top of the paper you can use your dot-to-dot over and over again!

Rainbow **lorikeets** are very beautiful. Color the lorikeet. What kinds of birds do you have in your neighborhood? Draw a picture of one. Where do they live? What do they eat?

Make a **climbing koala**. Can you make a climbing animal from your area?

The **sugar glider** comes out at night. Are there any animals in your area that come out at night? Make the sugar glider kite! Write about an animal that roams your area at night. What does it do at night?

Make a **hopping kangaroo**. Write a skit that stars your hopping kangaroo.

When you get done, remember to fill out their **survey**!

Create your own page that has activities that show the kinds of plants, animals, and activities in your area!

Social Studies - Cities of the World

Many cities of the world have their own Web page. CityNet is a good place to start your exploration. CitySpace is a great way to get kids involved.

Surfer Starters
General Sites
CityNet - Index to Cities on the Web
   http://www.city.net/
CitySpace - Build a City Project
   http://cityspace.org/
How Far Is It?
   http://www.indo.com/distance/
Subway Navigator
   http://metro.jussieu.fr:10001/bin/cities/english
US CityLink
   http://banzai.neosoft.com/citylink/

Specific Cities
Bruges, Belgium
   http://www.webcom.com/~cleenwe/
Budapest, Hungary
   http://www.fsz.bme.hu/hungary/budapest/budapest.html
Cologne, Germany
   http://www.gmd.de/Misc/Cologne/IN/phototour.html
Cork City, Ireland
   http://symphony.ucc.ie/~niall/cork.html
Isfahan, Iran
   http://www.anglia.ac.uk/~trochford/isfahan.html
Kyoto, Japan
   http://woodpecker.dad.kit.ac.jp/serverFiles/virtualKyoto.html
Leipzig, Germany
   http://www.uni-leipzig.de/leipzig/
Madras, India
   http://www.eel.ufl.edu/~sriraj/madraspics.html
Milan, Italy
   http://www.dsi.unimi.it/Users/Students/markus/milan/milan.html
Oxford, England
   http://www.comlab.ox.ac.uk/archive/ox.html

Padua, Italy
   http://www.unipd.it/WWW_root/15.html
Paris, France
   http://www.paris.org/
   http://gopher.lib.utk.edu:70/0/Other-Internet-Resources/pictures/html-docs/flying/paris.html
Rio de Janeiro
   http://www.puc-rio.br/english/mapario.html
Seattle, Washington
   http://www.seanet.com/Seattle/SeattleHome.html
   http://www.vicnet.net.au/~theage/marmelb.htm

Other Information Resources

Adams Barbara Johnston (1988) **New York City**. Dillon.
Cotterell, Geoffrey (1972) **Amsterdam: The Life Of A City**. Little Brown.
Kuskin, Karla (1987) **Jerusalem**, Shining Still. HarperCollins.
Munro, Roxie (1992) **Inside-Outside Book of Paris**. Dutton.
Munro, Roxie (1989) **Inside-Outside Book of London**. Dutton.
Pollard, Michael (1986) **Cities of The World (The Face of the Earth)**. Schoolhouse Press Inc.
Sheldon, Walter J. (1962) **The Key To Tokyo**. Lippincott.
Ventura, Piero (1987) **Venice-Birth of a City**. Putnam.

CD-ROM Resources

SimTown, Maxis
SimCity 2000, Maxis

http://chico.rice.edu/armadillo/Rice/joelsclass/home.html

Ridin' the Surf: Subject Area Activities

Visit Cities Around the World!
http://www.city.net/

Explore cities of the world.

Use CityNet to find a city web page.

http://www.city.net/

Would you like to visit this city? Why or why not? Select the most important information for a person visiting the city and create a travel brochure.

Use US CityLink to locate a city near where you live or a city where you've visited.

http://banzai.neosoft.com/citylink/

Does the web page do a good job describing the city? What would you add to the description? Create a web page for your neighborhood, community, town, or city.

Create a list of five favorite cities in the world. Plan a trip. Draw lines between the cities. Estimate the distance. Use the following site to find the distances.

http://www.indo.com/distance/

Were your estimates close or not? If you were off, why do you think you misjudged the distances?

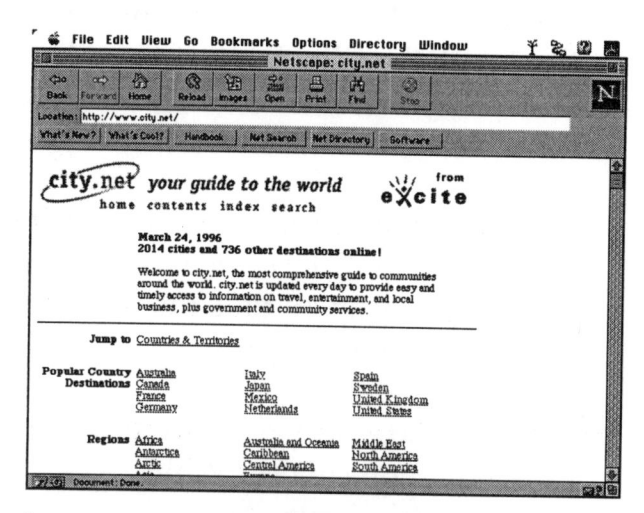

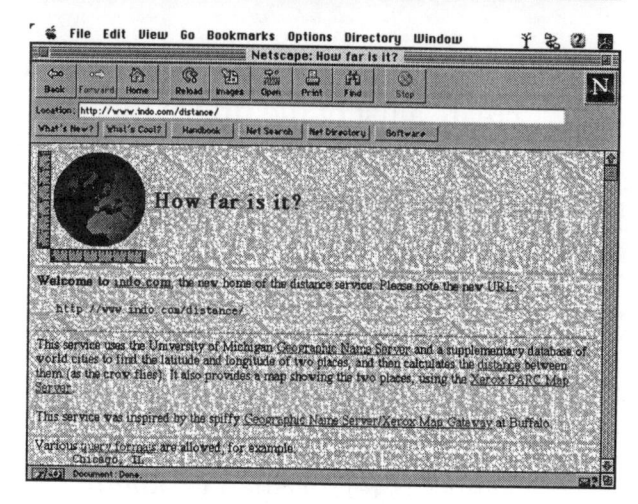

Visit the Paris Pages!
http://www.paris.org/

Visit the Paris Pages to learn more about this exciting city.

Start with the **City**. Explore the calendar and decide what events you'd like to see while you're in Paris. Find out what the weather will be like that time of year. What types of clothes will you need to take?

Browse the streets of Paris by examining the **Scenes of Paris**. Create a Paris Scrapbook. Select three pictures and write about what you might have been doing when you took the pictures. Create a map of Paris that shows where the pictures were taken.

Visit the **Cafes of Paris** and select one for lunch and one for supper. What foods would you choose? Why?

Select two **stores** you'd like to visit. Of course, you'll want to buy things for your friends. What kinds of things would you buy for your family and friends at these shops?

Explore the **Culture of the City** next. Select one place you would visit for the history, one for the art, and one for fun. How did you make your selections? Create a map showing their locations. How would you get from one to the other using public transportation?

Select a **hotel**. Use the currency exchange option to figure out the cost in American dollars.

Use the **French-English dictionary** to create a list of the fifteen most important words to know on your trip. Why are these important?

Use the **Travel Information** for the France page to find out about special considerations when traveling in France. What will you be watching out for while you're there? Is terrorism a problem? What about crime?

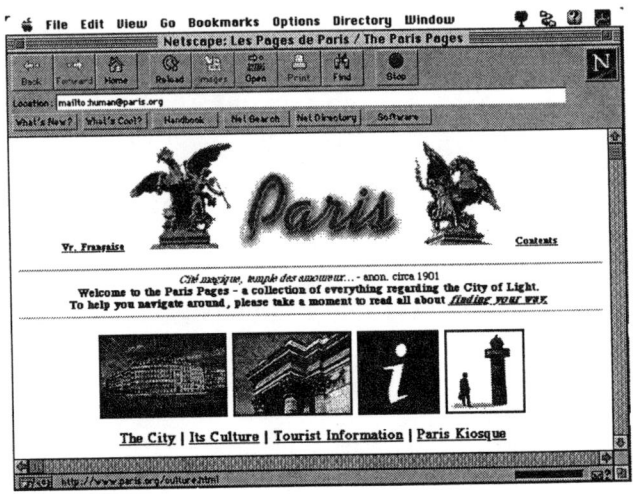

Ridin' the Surf: Subject Area Activities

Visit City Projects for Kids!
http://cityspace.org/

- -

Visit two kid projects that involve building cities.

Explore **CitySpace**.

http://cityspace.org/

Explore the projects that students have created. You may need to download graphics and movie resources to see some of the projects.

Which project do you like the best? Why? Write about the city you see in the picture. Who lives there? What would their lives be like?

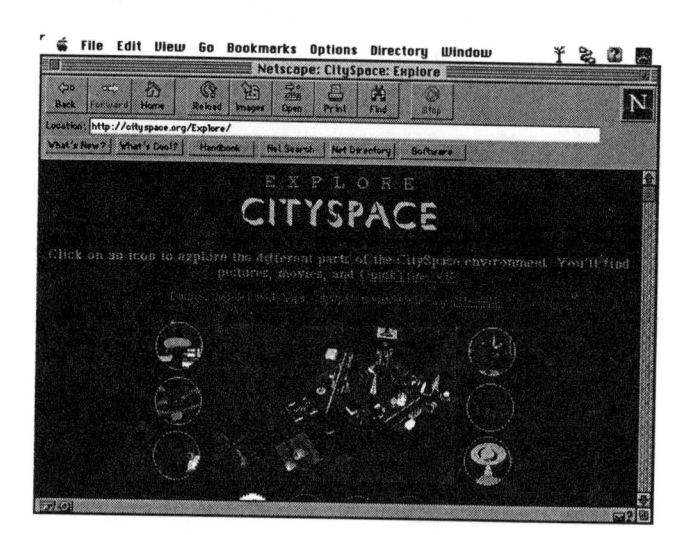

Create your own cityspace project and submit it to the project.

Explore the **Kids Space Web Kids' Village**.

http://plaza.interport.net/kids_space/village/village.html

Kids Space is working on a global village where students from around the world can post their home page in their favorite area of the village. How is the web kid's village like and unlike a real city? What's the definition of city? Could the global village be a city?

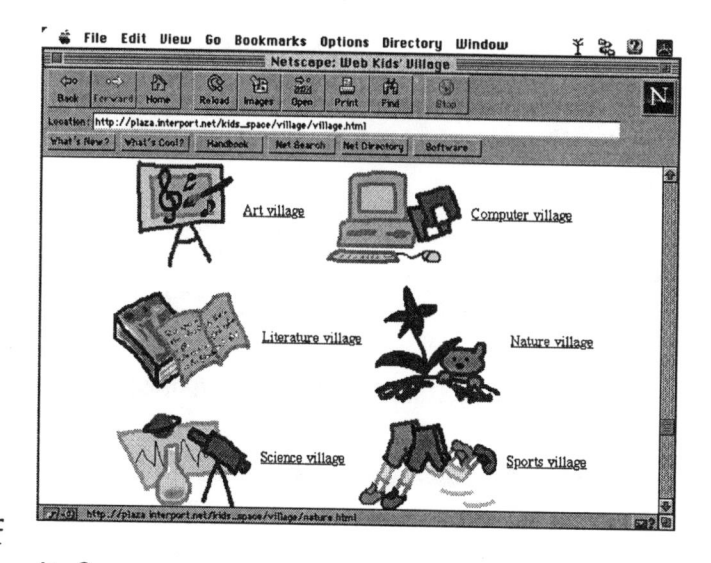

Social Studies - US States

Explore the United States. You'll find facinating information about each state.

Surfer Starters

General Sources
Flags of the United States
   http://asimov.elk-grove.k12.il.us/usflag/
Yahooligan's State List
   http://www.yahooligans.com/Around_the_World/U_S__States/
States, Capitals, and other information
   http://www.scottforesman.com/elpcapi.htm
   http://phoenix.ans.se/freeweb/holly/state.htm

Specific States
Alaska
   http://www.neptune.com/alaska/alaska.html
Arizona - Central
   http://www.azcentral.com/
California
   http://www.ca.gov/
   http://www.research.digital.com/SRC/virtual-tourist/California.html
Colorado
   http://www.state.co.us/
Florida
   http://orchid-isle.com/attr/attr.htm
Hawaii
   http://www.hcc.hawaii.edu/hawaii/
   http://www.mhpcc.edu/tour/Tour.html
   http://longwood.cs.ucf.edu:80/~MidLink/hawaii.ep.html
Idaho
   http://www.state.id.us/tourism.html
Kansas
   http://kicin.cecase.ukans.edu/kdoch/html/tour1.html
Maine
   http://www.state.me.us/decd/tour/welcome.html
Michigan
   http://www.lib.umich.edu/libhome/Documents.center/mich.html
Minnesota
   http://www.state.mn.us/welcome.html
Missouri
   http://www.missouri.edu/~c675032/index.htm

http://www.ecodev.state.mo.us/tou/home.htm
Nebraska
   http://www.state.id.us/tourism.html
New Hampshire
   http://www.nh.com/
North Carolina
   http://hal.dcr.state.nc.us/nc/cover.htm
Oregon
   http://www.teleport.com/~preore
Pennsylvania
   http://www.state.pa.us/
South Carolina
   http://www.state.sc.us/
South Dakota
   http://www.state.sd.us/
Tennessee
   http://www.state.tn.us/
Texas
   http://riceinfo.rice.edu/armadillo/tsir.html
Utah
   http://www.vii.com/~icis/kioskutah/home.htm
Vermont
   http://users.aol.com/frotz/vermont.htm
Washington
   http://www.wa.gov/
Wisconsin
   http://www.state.wi.us/
Wyoming
   http://www.state.wy.us/state/welcome.html

Other Information Resources

Brandt, Sue R. (1988) **Facts About The Fifty States**. Watts.
Dowden, Anne Ophelia (1978) **State Flowers**. Harper.
Gilfond, Henry (1984) **The Northeast States**. Watts.
Images USA (Laserdisc), Scholastic.
Landau, Elaine (1992) **State Birds: Including The Commonwealth of Puerto Rico**. Watts.
Perl, Lila (1992) **It Happened In America**. Henry Holt.
Ross, Wilma (1990) **Fabulous Facts About The Fifty States**. Scholastic Paper.
Shearer, Benjamin F. (1987) **State Names, Seals, Flags, & Symbols: A Historical Guide**. Greenwood Press.
Woods, Harold (1984) **The South Central States**. Watts.

Visit State Pages!
http://badger.state.wi.us/agencies/tourism/index.html

Every state has information on the web. Some states have an official page, while other states have information sponsored by schools or cities. Let's explore three states in different parts of the United States.

Explore the state of **Wisconsin**.

http://badger.state.wi.us/agencies/tourism/index.html

Find the Top Ten Best Bets in the tourism section. Locate them on a map. Which would you like to visit? Why?

Explore **Wyoming**.

http://www.state.wy.us/state/welcome.html

Go on the virtual tour of Wyoming. Pick two very different counties to explore. Why do you think they are so different even though they are in the same state?

Explore **Maine**.

http://www.state.me.us/decd/tour/welcome.html

The geography of Maine is very interesting. It was a coast, mountains, and farmland. Explore each region of the state. Which do you find most interesting? If you were going to move to Maine, which area would you choose? Why? Describe the area. Compare it to the place you live now.

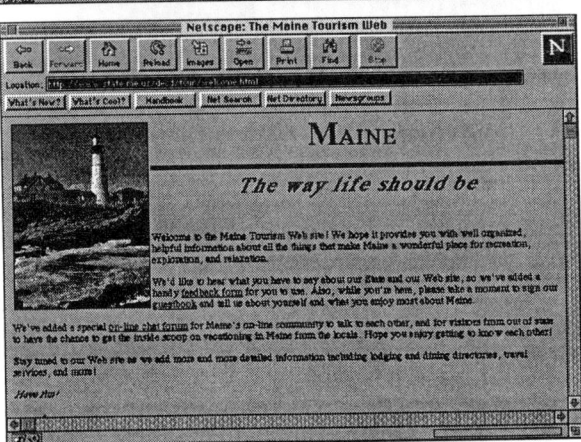

Ridin' the Surf: Subject Area Activities

Visit the CyberWest!
http://www.netway.net/cyberwest/archives.html

Visit the CyberWest magazine.

CyberWest magazine is a great way to learn about the western part of the United States. Each issue has exciting places to visit.

Select an **article** and learn more about the place that is described.

Select a **picture** and write a story about a day that you might spend there.

Many people think of the **Old West** when they hear about the west. Read an article about the Old West. How has the western part of the United States changed since the Old West. Is there still evidence of the Old West? Is the Old West a philosophy of life for some people in the west? How is this possible?

The West is full of **recreation**. Choose an article that describes a recreational interest. Write an article about that type of recreation. Use the Internet to find more information about this activity (http://www.yahooligans.com/Sports_and_Recreation/). Create a map that shows other places in the west you might visit for this type of recreation.

The West is full of **national forests and parks**. Read an article about one of these locations. Why do you think it is important to protect our forests and parks? Explore more information about our national parks at GORP (http://www.gorp.com/default.htm).

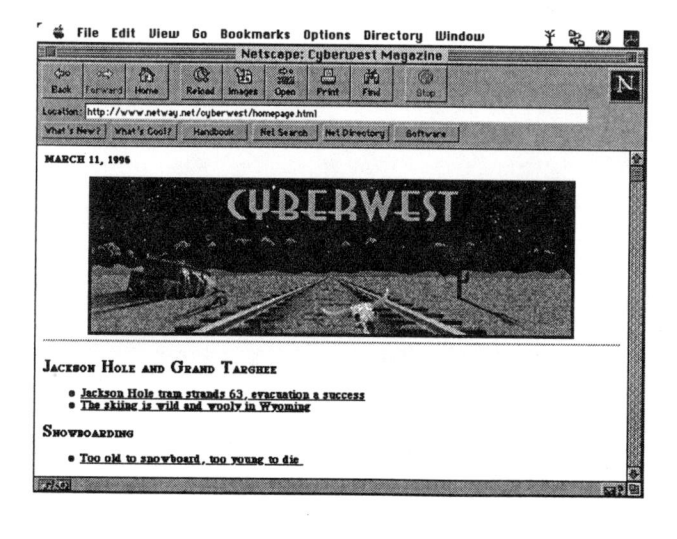

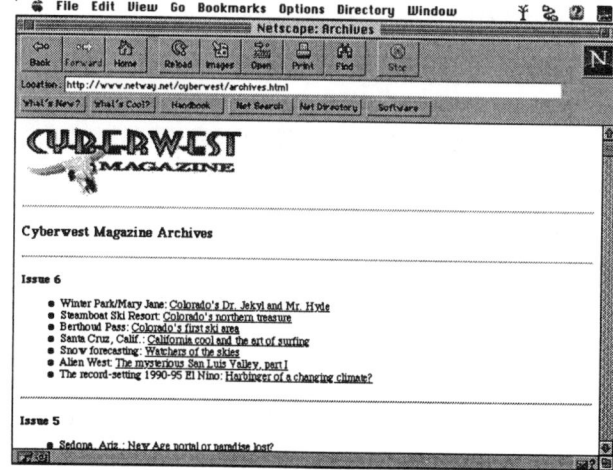

Social Studies - US History

Most popular US history events can be found on the Internet.

Surfer Starters

Amelia Earhart
   http://www-leland.stanford.edu/group/King/index.html
America History
   http://rs6.loc.gov/amhome.html
   http://kuhttp.cc.ukans.edu/history/
American History through Literature
   http://www.computek.net/public/barr/america.html
Biographies
   http://www.autobaun.com/~kbshaw/Biographies/BioLibrary.html
California History
   http://www.community.net/~stevensn/4thgrade.html
Clara Barton
   http://www.autobaun.com/~kbshaw/Biographies/Barton.html
Colorado History
   http://www.fortnet.org/~randyc/Colorado/colorado.html
Constitution of the United States
   http://www.cs.cmu.edu/afs/cs.cmu.edu/project/nectar/member/karl/html/general/constitution.html
Declaration of Independence
   http://www.cs.cmu.edu/afs/cs.cmu.edu/project/nectar/member/karl/html/general/constitution.html
Harriet Tubman
   http://www.autobaun.com/~kbshaw/Biographies/Tubman.html
Indiana History
   http://www.ihs1830.org/
Library of Congress - History
   http://lcweb.loc.gov/exhibits/
Martin Luther King Jr.
   http://www-leland.stanford.edu/group/King/index.html
Monticello - Thomas Jefferson
   http://www.monticello.org/
New Jersey History
   http://csbh.gbn.net/~dpost/njrw.html

Oregon Trail
   http://gsn.org/~jmeckel/oregon.html
Plymouth, Mass.
   http://media3.com/plymouth/
Susan B. Anthony
   http://www.history.rochester.edu/class/sba/first.htm

CD-ROM Resources

Compton's Encyclopedia of American History CD, Compton's New Media
History in Motion, Scholastic
Multimedia US History, Bureau of Electronic Publishing
Oregon Trail II CD, MECC
Point of View 2.0, Scholastic
Who Built America?, Voyager
Vital Links, Davidson (Multimedia packs)
Yukon Trail, MECC

Visit the Oregon Trail Information Center!
http://gsn.org/~jmeckel/oregon.html

Visit the Oregon Trail Information Center.

Select **Travel and Tourism**. Choose a state along the trail to study. How is the state different now than it was during the time when people were traveling the Oregon trail? What has remained the same?

Select **Museums**. In planning a trip on the Oregon Trail, there are many museums to visit. Examine the web sites. Which museums would you like to visit?

Examine the **Maps**. Compare and contrast two maps from different time periods. How did they change? What remained the same?

Explore **K.C. History Links**. Select three key historical events in KC history and examine what else was going on at the same time in the United States. Create a history page for your town.

Examine the **Oregon Trail Travel Info** and **Sites Along the Trail**. Select a picture and write about what may have happened on a day at this location during the Oregon Trail wagon trains.

Explore the **School Projects**. What can your class do to expand this project?

Find out what has happened to the **Wildlife** along the Oregon Trail? How has be wildlife changed?

Choose a book from the **Book List**. Create a book review and post it on the Internet!

Explore other Oregon Trail sites.
http://www.isu.edu/~trinmich/Oregontrail.html
http://www.teleport.com/~sligard/trail.html

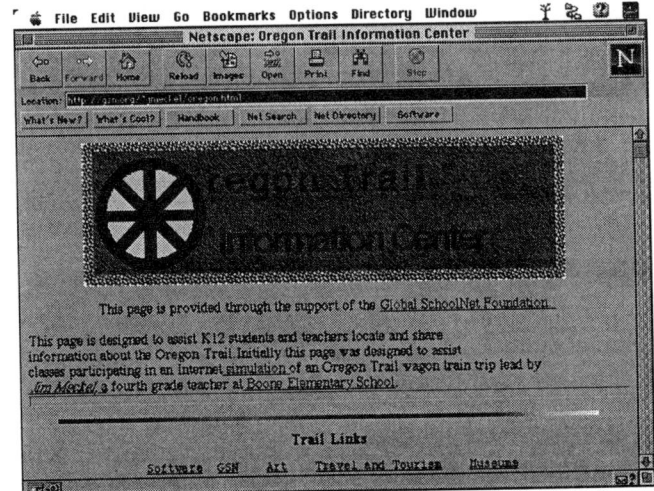

Visit the Presidents of the United States Page!
http://utkvx1.utk.edu/~razz2/uspres1.html

Visit the Presidents site! For more information on Presidents, check the US President's Site (http://chestnut.lis.utk.edu/~presidnt/USPres1.html).

Examine the life of three presidents from different time periods. Compare and contrast the presidencies. How did the "times" impact the effectiveness of the president? Would any of the presidents have been more effective during a different time period?

Andrew Jackson's nickname was Old Hickory. Examine the life of a president and give that person a nickname. Explain the reason for the nickname.

Read aloud a famous inaugural address and explain the important aspects that would shape that presidency.

Many of the presidents had interesting careers before entering the presidency. For example, Thomas Jefferson was skilled in dozens of areas. Choose a president and examine how his career influenced his skills in the presidency.

Examine a president. If you were designing a museum for this person what would you put in each room to represent his family, life, and career?

Pretend that you've been elected as president of the United States. Explore the inaugural addresses of other presidents and select three quotes that you might use in your address.

Create a list of characteristics that you think are important in a good president. Identify a president that demonstrates each characteristic and explain why.

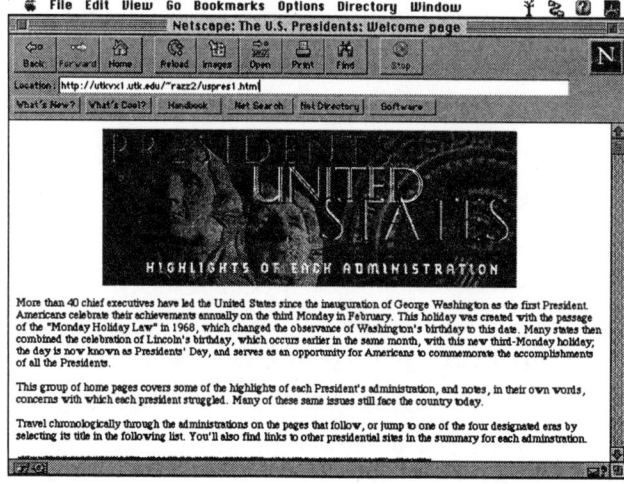

Visit From Revolution to Reconstruction Page!
http://grid.let.rug.nl/~welling/usa/revolution.html

Visit US History Pages. There are dozens of sites on US history. These two provide an good starting point for your exploration.

Explore the **Revolution to Reconstruction** Page.

http://grid.let.rug.nl/~welling/usa/ revolution.html

Write a children's book explaining one aspect of American History using the information in this site.

Select a key event in American History. How would the US be different if the event had turned out a different way?

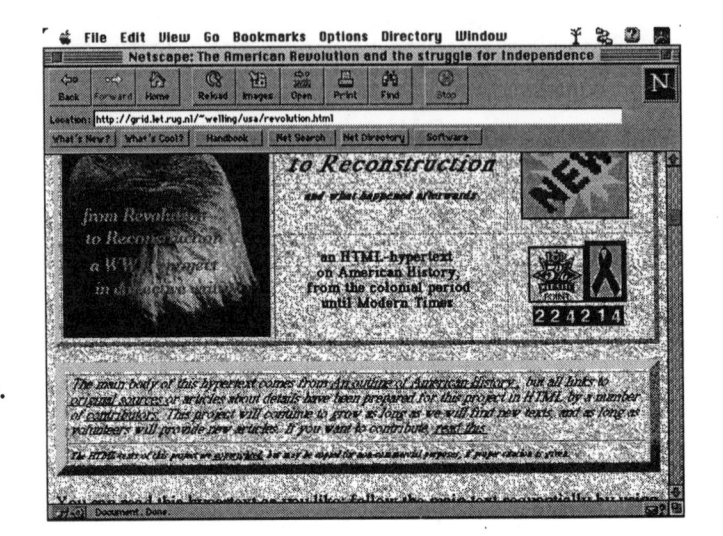

Select a favorite time period that has not been completed and create your own web page to submit.

The **Library of Congress** is a great place to explore information about US History.

http://lcweb2.loc.gov/ammem/ndlpedu/ index.html

Examine US history through the eyes of a particular group of people such as African-Americans or Irish Amerians.

Select an important US history event. Create a chart showing what was happening in a different part of the world during that time.

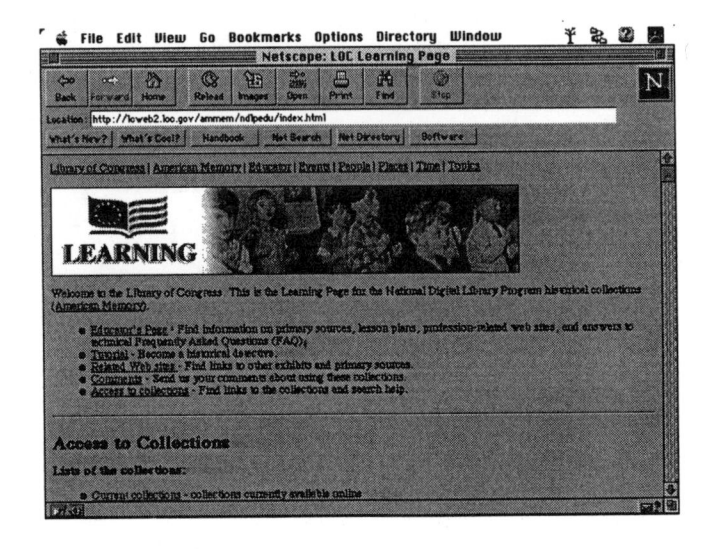

Social Studies - US History - Colonial America

Colonial America is an exciting time period for students to explore. Use the Internet to explore Colonial Williamsburg. You might want to try some of the teacher resources such as glossaries, historical documents, and lesson plans provided at the Colonial Williamsburg site. Also, use the resources to locate information about the arts and crafts of early America.

Surfer Starters
Colonial America
>   http://www.history.org/
>   http://www.abel-info.com/regguide/rechist.html
>   http://kuhttp.cc.ukans.edu/history/

Other Information Resources
> The Colonial Williamsburg site has an extensive bibliography.
> Alderman, Clifford Lindsey (1966) **Story of The Thirteen Colonies**. Random House.
> Perl, Lila (1975) **Slumps, Grunts, & Snickerdoodles: What Colonial America Ate & Why**. Clarion.
> Reische, Diana L. (1989) **Founding The American Colonies**. Watts.
> Madison, Arnold (1981) **How The Colonists Lived**. McKay.
> Siegel, Beatrice (1977) **New Look At The Pilgrims: Why They Came To America**. Walker.
> Tunis, Edwin (1976) **Colonial Craftsmen & The Beginnings of American Industry**. Harper.
> Tunis, Edwin (1976) **Colonial Living**. Harper.

http://homearts.com/cl/inns/09wilf1.htm

Visit the Colonial Williamsburg Site!
http://www.history.org/

Visit the Colonial Williamsburg Site. It contains information about Historic Williamsburg in addition to an interesting almanac of information.

Select **Visit Colonial Williamsburg**.
Plan a trip to Colonial Williamsburg. Create a map showing your driving route. How much will the trip cost? Include the cost for gas, hotels, food, and tickets to Williamsburg. Would you like to work at Colonial Williamsburg? Why or why not?

Explore one area of Colonial Williamsburg such as the Print Shop or Wig Shop. Write about a week in the life of the person who might have worked or lived there in Colonial Days. What would the person do during the day? What skills would they have? Where would they have learned these skills? Use books and other resources to learn as much as you can about life during that time period. Email your project to Colonial Williamsburg!

Select **Historical Almanack**.

Select **Meet the People**. Select an actual day in history to recreate. Develop a class play based on the people described in the almanac. Each student will select a role to play from the list of people described. In small groups write a skit that would include each person. Each member of group would play one of the roles, just like they do in historic Colonial Williamsburg. Create a playbill that includes a description of each character.

Select **See the Places**. Select a place. Create a model of the location and a one-page description that includes a timeline of the location and a description of its importance in Colonial Williamsburg history.

Select **Colonial Dateline**. Select three events on the timeline and describe what your character might think about what was happening.

Select **Experience Colonial Life**.
Choose a tool or skill area. Create a table display that includes pictures, diagrams, or models. Conduct a demonstration of the skill.

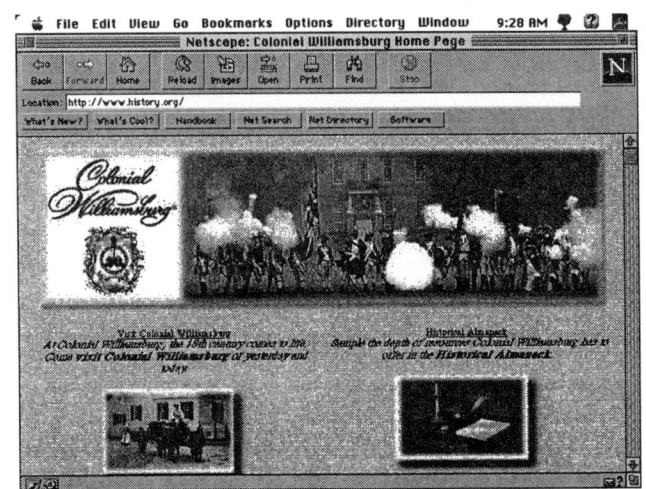

Ridin' the Surf: Subject Area Activities

Social Studies - US History - Civil War

You'll find an endless variety of information on the US Civil War! In addition to specific Internet sites, you'll find lots of discussion groups and email addresses. Use Civil War experts and history buffs as online experts to answer student questions. Consider an email project that connects students from the southern and northern states. Have a debate online! Develop projects that compare and contrast the letters written during different wars such as the Civil War and Vietnam.

Surfer Starters

American Civil War
> http://www.ucsc.edu/civil-war-letters/home.html
> http://rs6.loc.gov/cwphome.html
> http://www.access.digex.net/~bdboyle/cw.html
> http://kuhttp.cc.ukans.edu/history/milhst/civwar.html

American Civil War Timeline
> http://rs6.loc.gov:80/ammem/timeline.html

Illinois in the Civil War
> http://www.outfitters.com/illinois/history/civil/

Letter's from an Iowa Soldier
> http://www.ucsc.edu/civil-war-letters/home.html

Ohio in the Civil War
> http://www.infinet.com/~lstevens/a/civil.html

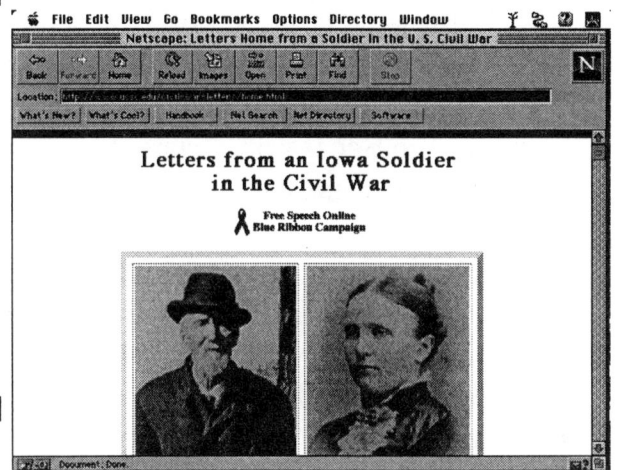

Other Information Resources

Allen, Thomas B. (1992) **The Blue & The Gray**. National Geographic Society.

Carter, Alden R. (1985) **The Civil War: American Tragedy**. Franklin Watts.

Chang, Ina (1991) **A Separate Battle : Women & The Civil War**. Atheneum.

Murphy, Jim (1980) **The Boys War-Confederate & Union Soldiers Talk About The Civil War**. Clarion Books.

O'Shea, Richard (1992) **American Heritage Battle Maps of The Civil War**. Council Oak Books.

Ray, Delia (1991) **Behind The Blue & Gray: The Soldier's Life in the Civil War**. Lodestar Books.

Robertson Jr., James I. (1992) **Civil War - America Becomes One Nation**. Alfred A. Knopf.

The Time - Life Series on Civil War. Time-Life Books.

Visit the American Civil War HomePage!
http://funnelweb.utcc.utk.edu/~hoemann/cwarhp.html

Visit the American Civil War HomePages. They contain tons of information on this war. You'll also want to check out the US Civil War Center (http://www.cwc.lsu.edu/).

Create a fictional character who participated in the war.

Explore the **timelines**. Create a Civil War timeline that includes important war events as well as personal events in your character's life.

Select a **graphic image** and use it in a short story that includes your character.

Read **letters, accounts, and diaries**. Create a sample journal entry for your fictional character. Who would the character write? Why?

Explore the **Secession Crisis**. Hold a class debate about the causes of the war. How are these causes like and unlike other American wars?

As a small group, select a **Civil War battle** to explore in depth. Each member of the group should take a different role such as union infantry, confederate officer, medic, local local shopkeeper, runaway, slave, or women alone on a farm. Find a picture to go with your character. Create a map showing the battle and location of each member of the group. Write about the battle from the perspective of your character. How does this battle reflect the entire war?

Trace the role of a particular group of people during the war such as women, teenagers, African Americans, Irish Americans, or Iowans.

Read an important **document or speech** from the Civil War period. What was the impact on the war? Does the document or speech still have relevance today? Why?

Explore the personal documents of an individual who participated in the war. How does the document reflect the events happening when the document was created? What happened before and after? Why?

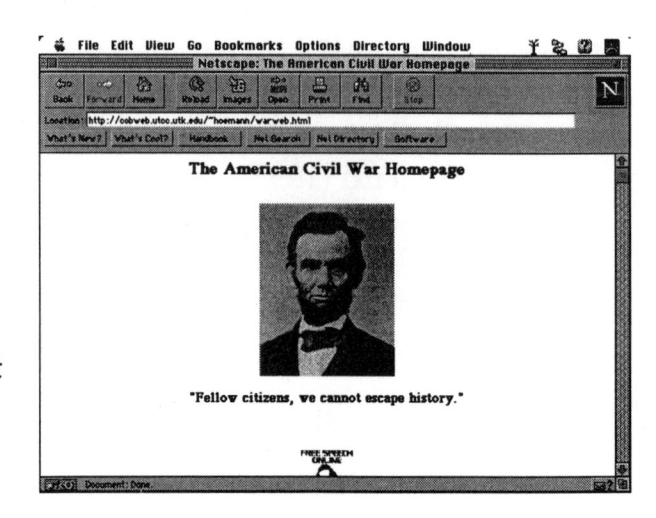

Ridin' the Surf: Subject Area Activities

World History

People from around the world are contributing to Internet sites on world history. Whether you're interested in ancient or modern history, you'll find it on the web. Consider starting your students with Yahooligan's History section.

Surfer Starters
Yahooligans - History
   http://www.yahooligans.com/Around_the_World/History/
World History
   http://kuhttp.cc.ukans.edu/history/
   http://neal.ctstateu.edu/history/world_history/world_history.html
   http://www.arts.cuhk.hk/His.html
   http://www.einet.net/galaxy/Social-Sciences/History.html
   http://204.225.221.7/csm/libraryh.htm#history
Historical government documents
   gopher://vax.queens.lib.ny.us/11[gopher._ss._histdocs]
Writings of Ancient Egypt
   http://odyssey.lib.duke.edu/papyrus/
Ancient Egypt
   http://www.gatech.edu/CARLOS/egypt.gal.html
Mayan Adventure
   http://www.ties.k12.mn.us:80/~smm/
Maya Quest
   http://howww.ncook.k12.il.us/docs/mayaquest.html
Russian History
   http://www.times.st-pete.fl.us/treasures/TC.Lobby.html
Celtic, Scottish, Anglo-Saxon, Welsh, and Viking information History
   http://www.mountain.net/hp/unicorn/
Canadian Museum of Civilization
   http://www.cmcc.muse.digital.ca/cmc/cmceng/exhibeng.html
Kelsey's On-line Museum
   http://classics.lsa.umich.edu/Kelsey/Outreach.html
School House Rock - America
   http://hera.life.uiuc.edu/america.html
Vatican
   http://www.ncsa.uiuc.edu/SDG/Experimental/vatican.exhibit/Vatican.exhibit.html
Viking History
   http://odin.nls.no/viking/vnethome.htm

Medieval Studies
   http://www.georgetown.edu/labyrinth/labyrinth-home.html
Holocaust
   http://www.cis.ohio-state.edu/hypertext/faq/usenet/holocaust/reinhard/part02/faq.html
   http://www.ushmm.org

Other Information Resources

Caselli, Giovanni (1985) **First Civilizations.** Peter Bedrick.
Caselli, Giovanni (1986) **Renaissance & The New World.** Peter Bedrick.
Crosher, Judith (1993) **Ancient Egypt.** Viking.
Dunrea, Olivier (1985) **Skar Brae: The Story Of A Prehistoric Village.** Holiday House.
Reeves, Nicholas (1992) **Into The Mummy's Tomb.** Scholastic.
Ventura, Piero (1987) **There Once Was A Time.** Putnam.

CD-ROM Resources

Age of Exploration, Entrex
Ancient Civilizations, Entrex
Ancient Lands, Microsoft
Dig It: Egyptians, Terrapin
Discoverers CD, Knowledge Adventures
Eyewitness History of the World CD, Dorling Kindersley
Leonardo the Inventor CD, SoftKey
MayaQuest, MECC
Multimedia World History, Bureau of Electronic Publishing
Nile: Passage to Egypt CD, Discovery Channel
Knights and Kings, Entrex
Stowaway CD, Dorling Kindersley

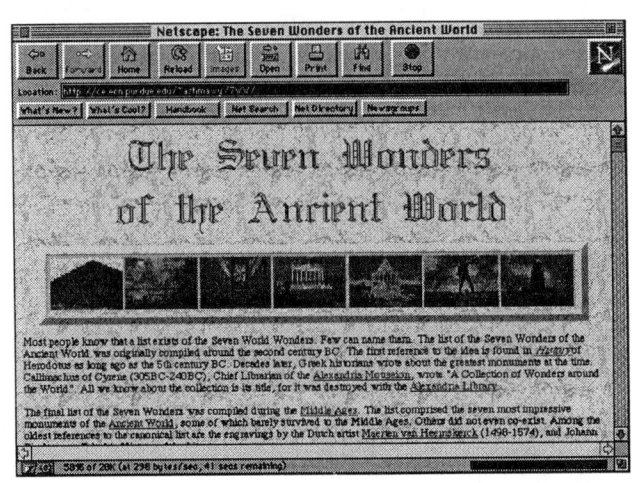

http://ce.ecn.purdue.edu/~ashmawy/7WW/

Ridin' the Surf: Subject Area Activities

Visit the French & Indian War Page!
http://web.syr.edu/~laroux/

Visit the French & Indian War page.

Find out if anyone with your last name fought in the war. What is the origin of your name? Where were your descendants during the war? What would their reaction have been to the war? Why?

Read one of the documents provided. Where does this document fit into the war? What was going on at the time that it was written? What does the document say about the author and the war?

As a small group, write two stories set during the war. One from the point of view of a French student your age. The other from the perspective of an Indian youth. How are their views alike and different?

Create a map of sites that you could visit that would relate to the war. Create a plan for visiting each site.

Take a virtual trip to **Fort William Henry** (http://www.adirondack.net/tour/fwh.html). Use the hotel information in planning a trip to this site. Create a brochure for people interested in visiting the site. Why is Fort William Henry an important part of the French & Indian War?

Create a model of the fort and reenact a battle.

Create a timeline showing what was happening in another part of the world at the same time as the French and Indian War.

Fort William Henry has a long history. Why do you think it was an important military location for so long? Select another site from history that has remained important for many years.

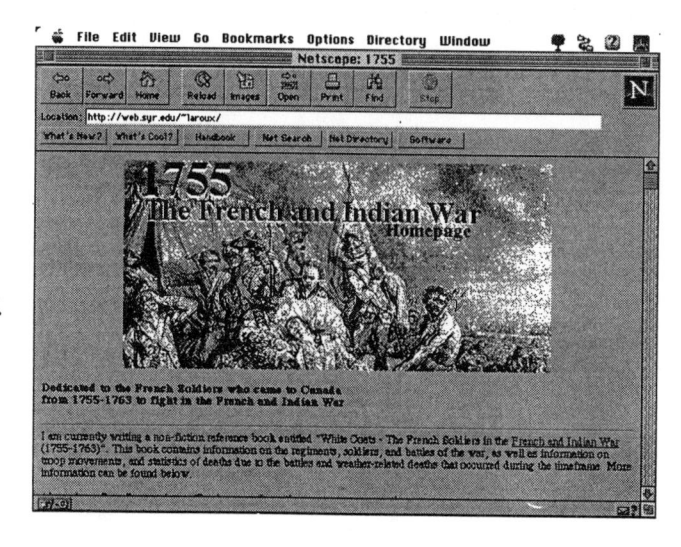

Visit the World War II Pages!
http://192.253.114.31/D-Day/Table_of_contents.html

Visit the World War II pages. They were created by the students and staff at The Patch American School in Germany.

Read an article from the **Stars and Stripes**. Create a HyperStudio stack that includes sound and video footage from the site. Why did you include those particular selections?

Read about the **Army's Women's Corps**. What roles did women play in the war? Was this important? Why or why not? If you were giving special women's duty awards, what group of women would you honor? Why? How have women's roles in the military changed since World War II? Hold a class debate about the role of women in the military.

Explore the **maps section**. Select a map and describe the events that took place in the area. Why were these events important to the war? Select another map. What would it have been like for the families who lived in these areas? Write a story from the perspective of a person your age living in the area at that time. How would they have felt about the war? Why? Conduct an "on-camera" interview of the youth that could have been held at that time if CNN were around.

Select a **speech**. Learn more about the speaker and that person's role in the war. How does the speech reflect the personality of this famous person? Is this their most famous speech? If not, why was another more important?

Explore other World War II links
   http://www.grolier.com/links/ww2link.html
   http://www.csi.ad.jp/ABOMB/index.html

Select one aspect of World War II and create a Web page. What do you want to tell the world about this person, place, or event? Why?

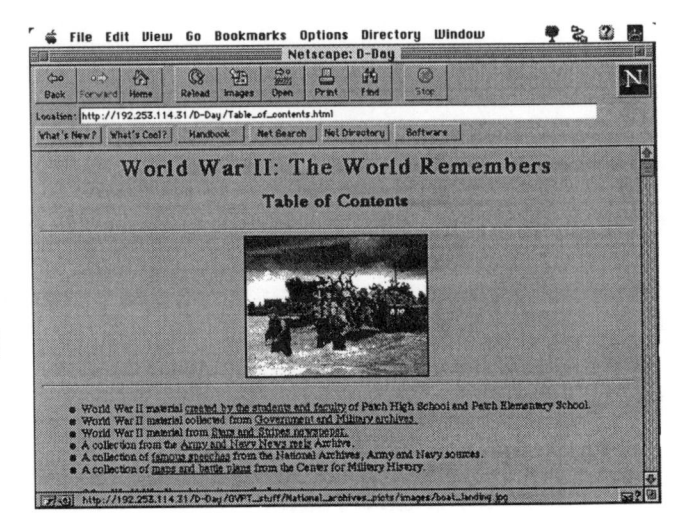

Ridin' the Surf: Subject Area Activities   195

Anthropology

Anthropology is the study of people and culture. Throughout the world, scholars are posting information about anthropology.

Surfer Starters
Anthropology
   http://www.usc.edu/dept/v-lib/anthropology.html
Stone age
   http://www.ncl.ac.uk/~nantiq/
Kinship and Social Organizations
   http://www.umanitoba.ca/faculties/arts/anthropology/kintitle.html
Center for Folklife
   http://www.si.edu/organiza/offices/folklife/start.htm
British Columbia Folklore
   http://www.islandnet.com/~shall/folklore/bcfolk.html
Oral Histories
   http://www.vsa.cape.com/~powens/Newfiles/

Other Information Resources
American Museum of Natural History (1993) **The Illustrated History of Humankind The First Humans Human Origins & History to 10,000 B.C.** Harper.

Asimov, Isaac (1979) **How did we find out about our human roots?** Walker & Company.

Howells, William (1993) **Getting Here The Story of Human Evolution.** The Compass Press.

Lambert, David & The Diagram Group (1987) **The Field Guide To Early Man.** Facts On File Publications.

Lewin, Roger (1988) **In The Age of Mankind-A Smithsonian Book of Human Evolution.** Smithsonian Books.

Sattler, Helen Roney (1988) **Hominids A Look Back At Our Ancestors.** Lathrop, Lee & Shepard Books.

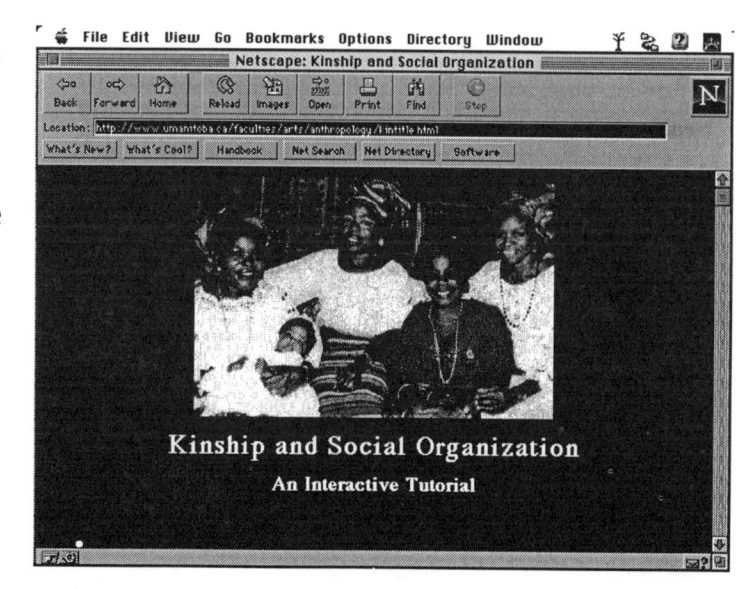

Wave Words
customs, tradition, folkways, folklore, evolution, myth, symbols

Powerful Projects
What was the importance of tool development to early humans? How did tools evolve over time? Why? What role do tools play in society in the past and present?

How did the discovery of fire change the life of early humans?

What is the definition of race? What are the current definitions of race and how have they changed?

Why did civilization evolve at different rates around the world?

What was life like for a particular group of people such as the Inca, Maya, or Aztecs?

How and why do rites vary from culture to culture? How do the funeral rites of different cultures compare? Why do they vary? What about the rites related to puberty?

What role did sports play in early and present civilizations?

How does the family structure of early people compare with today's families?

What techniques can be used to learn about culture today? Compare and contrast two of these techniques.

What roles do folkways, folklore, and myth play in culture? Explore this issue within a culture of your choice.

People of the World – Native Americans

There are many people and cultures around the world that are interesting to study. Start with the Native American people. Then compare the history and culture of these people with another somewhere else in the world such as the Aboriginal people of Australia. Explore how Native Americans live today. There are dozens of tribal sites to visit and many Native American students enthusiastic about sharing their heritage through email!

Surfer Starters

National Museum of the American Indian
   http://www.si.edu/nmai/
Index to Native American Studies
   http://hanksville.phast.umass.edu/misc/NAresources.html
Native Americans
   http://kuhttp.cc.ukans.edu/~marc/native_main.htm
Indigenous People's Literature
   http://kuhttp.cc.ukans.edu/~marc/natlit/native_lit_main.html
Native American Center
   http://www.powersource.com/powersource/gallery/
NativeWeb Home Page
   http://ukanaix.cc.ukans.edu/~marc/native_main.html
Oneida Indian Nation
   http://nysernet.org/oneida/
The Great Sioux Nation
   http://www.state.sd.us/state/executive/tourism/sioux/sioux.htm
Pueblo Cultural Center
   http://hanksville.phast.umass.edu/defs/independent/PCC/PCC.html
Great Lakes Regional Indian Network
   http://cedar.cic.net/glrain/
Tribal Voice
   http://www.tribal.com/
Native American Culture Home Page
   http://LAHS.LosAlamos.K12.nm.us/sunrise/work/piaseckj/homepage.html
American Indian Studies
   http://www.csulb.edu/gc/libarts/am-indian/index.html
American Indian Resources
   http://www.tucson.ihs.gov/Docs/Paths/Amerind/Amerind.html

Costanoan-Ohlone Indian Canyon ResourcePage
   http://www.ucsc.edu:80/costano/
Fourth World Documentation Project
   http://www.halcyon.com/FWDP/fwdp.html
Aboriginal Studies
   http://coombs.anu.edu.au/WWWVL-Aboriginal.html
Cree Indians
   http://www.lib.uconn.edu/ArcticCircle/CulturalViability/Cree/creeexhibit.html

Other Information Resources

Avery, Susan (1992) **Extraordinary Indians**. Childrens Press.
Gallant, Roy A. (1989) **Ancient Indians: The First Americans**. Enslow.
Harlan, Judith (1987) **American Indians Today: Issues & Conflicts**. Watts.
Ortiz, Simon (1988) **People Shall Continue**. Children's Book Press.
Sattler, Helen Roney (1993) **Earliest Americans**. Clarion.
Tunis, Edwin (1979) **Indians**. Crowell/HarperCollins.
Waldman, Carl (1988) **Encyclopedia of Native Americans**. Facts On File.
Waldman, Carl (1985) **Atlas of The North American Indians**. Facts On file.
Wheeler, J. J. (1983) **First Came The Indians**. Atheneum.

CD-ROM Resources

500 Nations, Microsoft

Powerful Projects

How are Native Americans preserving their heritage?
What happened to the Native Americans in the area where you live?
What is the traditional importance of animals to Native Americans?
Some people say that American Indians are the original "environmentalists." Why? Provide examples.
What art and customs are unique to particular tribes? Select an art or custom of a Native American group and describe how it is unique to their group. Examples: Apache skin painting, Navajo rugs, Mimbres pottery, Pueblo pottery. Have a cultural fair of reproductions of Indian art.
What was daily life like for a prehistoric Indian of the American West?
What is being done to preserve Indian sites and artifacts? Describe one location where preservation is taking place.
What is the controversy over Indian burial grounds? Why is it an important issue?

What are the social and health issues facing American Indians? How do these problems compare to the nation as a whole?

How do traditional American Indian medicine and modern medicine compare?

How are tribes similiar to and different from each other? Compare and contrast the religious beliefs of a number of tribes such as the Navajo and the Hopi.

Explore the myths of a particular Indian tribe. Write a myth that is based on the culture of that tribe. What elements did you include that are unique to their tribe?

Why did settlers want to relocate the Indian populations? Why were the settlers able to eliminate opposition from the Indians in the West?

How did the life of a particular Indian tribe change as white people came along?

Were American Indian reservations a successful solution to what was considered by many to be "The Indian Problem"? Why or why not? What were and are the alternatives?

What are the controversies surrounding natural resources on Indian land? Describe one particular case and describe how it is similiar to other problems.

Who should teach in tribal schools? What should be taught? What is the role of Indian culture in tribal schools?

What cultural adjustment problems are common among people who live on American's reservations?

What is it like to grow up on an Indian reservation? How is it like and unlike your life?

How are Native Americans using the Internet to make cultural connections? Explore Native American sites!

http://niikaan.fdl.cc.mn.us/~isk/kidpage.html

Visit the Native American Indian Stories Site!
http://indy4.fdl.cc.mn.us/~isk/stories/stories.html

Explore stories written about and by Native Americans.

Explore the stories of **Norma Jeam Croy** and **Leonard Peltier**. Learn more about their plight. Conduct a mock trail to debate their cases.

Learn about the **White Buffalo**. What do you think about the prophecy?

Read the **Death of an Eagle, My Blackfeet Grandma** and **How the Choctaws Lost It Bigtime**. Create a series of questions that might be answered by other class members. Write a story that reflects elements of your cultural heritage.

Explore **The Tribes Need Heroes--Where Are they Today**? Are heroes important? Why? Who are your heroes? Why? What makes them heroes?

Explore works written about native people around the world.

Read the **Mayan** stories. How do these reflect the Mayan culture?

Read **How Fly Saved the River**. Join their Australian writing project.

Read about **The Origin of Light** and compare it with other Alaskan stories you've read.

Read a traditional story from somewhere in the world. Read more about that part of the world. What elements can you pick out in the story that reflect the setting of the story?

Read a Native American story. Learn more about the tribe described in the story. How does the story reflect the culture of the tribe? Write and submit your own story set within this tribe.

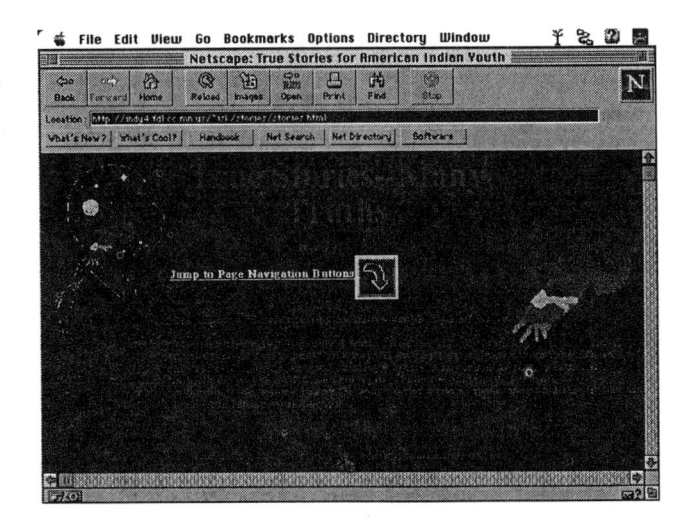

Ridin' the Surf: Subject Area Activities

Law, Political Science, and Government

Many government resources are being placed on the Web. For example, you can get information from the US Department of Education about school grants and programs. You'll also find many sites that focus on political issues. Many of these are sponsored by lobbyist groups, so it's important that students understand that they'll find bias, opinion, and misinformation on the Internet. Students need experiences separating fact from opinion and making effective decisions based on the information they find on the Internet.

Surfer Starters

General Government Links
> **http://www-hpcc.astro.washington.edu/scied/democracy.html**

Legislative Information on Internet: Find out how bills are made
> **http://thomas.loc.gov/**

CSPAN: Campaign information, contact legislators
> **Explore the CSPAN lesson plans**

Public Affairs Hot List: Individuals, Parties, Special Interests
> **http://www.c-span.org/congress/hotlinks.htm**
> **http://www.c-span.org/**

Presidential candidates
> **http://www.c-span.org/campaign/prescand.htm**

FedWorld Government Information (government guide)
> **http://www.fedworld.gov/**

Federal Law and Information Page
> **http://www.law.emory.edu/FEDERAL/**

Declaration of Independence
> **http://www.law.emory.edu/FEDERAL/independ/declar.html**
> **http://www.law.cornell.edu/lii.table.html**
> **http://www.law.uc.edu/Diana**
> **http://www.yahoo.com/Law/**

US Courts
> **http://www.uscourts.gov/**

Federal Courts
> **http://www.law.emory.edu/FEDCTS/**

Democratic Party Page
> **http://www.webcom.com/~digitals/**

GOP Online
> **http://www.gop.org**

FBI
> http://www.fbi.gov/

Military
> http://www.ncts.navy.mil
> http://white.nosc.mil/army.html
> http://www.yahoo.com/Humanities/History/Military_History/

Vote Smart Web
> http://www.vote-smart.org/

Mock Trial
> http://www.bergen.gov/AAST/Projects/MockTrial/

Other Information Resources

Blue, Rose (1993) **U. S. Air Force**. Millbrook.

Byam, Michele (1988) **Arms & Armor**. Knopf.

Hewett, Joan (1991) **Public Defender: Lawyer for the People**. Lodestar/Dutton.

Hyde, Margaret O. (1983) **Juvenile Justice & Injustice**. Watts.

Kurtz, Henry I. (1993) **U. S. Army**. Millbrook.

Meltzer, Milton (1990) **Bill of Rights: How We Got it & What It Means**. Crowell/Harper Collins.

Naden, Corinne J. (1993) **U. S. Navy**. Millbrook.

Rose, Charles Jules (1983) **Careers in Law**. Messner.

Surge, Frank (1990) **The Law & Economics: Your Rights As A Consumer**. Lerner.

Walz, Michael K. (1990) **The Law & Economics: Your Rights As A Consumer**. Lerner.

Visual Dictionary of Military Uniforms (1992) Darling Kindersley.

Warner, J. F. (1991) **U. S. Marine Corps**. Lerner.

Zerman, Melvyn Bernard (1981) **Beyond a Reasonable Doubt: Inside the American Jury System.** Crowell/Harper Collins.

http://www.webcom.com/~digitals/

Ridin' the Surf: Subject Area Activities

Visit the Thomas Site!
http://thomas.loc.gov/

Explore the Thomas Site for information about legislative issues.

Read the **Constitution and Bill of Rights**. Are they in any particular order? Reorder the Bill of Rights by importance. Justify your top three. Hold a class debate to determine the three most important rights.

Read **How Our Laws are Made**. Create a flowchart showing the life of a bill. Select one aspect of the bill to explore indepth. What makes this element of the process important? Could we eliminate your step? Why or why not?

Explore a bill currently before Congress. Who is sponsoring the bill? What are the issues for and against the proposal? Is it likely to pass? Why or why not?

Find the email address of a person you think would have some clout with this bill. Email this person your position on the bill.

Follow the progress of five bills before Congress. Each small group should be in charge of tracking their bill. What issues impact the movement of a bill through Congress? Track the path of each bill on a bulletin board.

Read a report written by an advisory committee. Was this report a good use of time? Why or why not? Summarize the document into two short paragraphs.

Explore the **Library of Congress**. Why is this an important service of our government?

Explore the **US Courts** site (http://www.uscourts.gov/). Read **Understanding the Federal Courts**.

Find the **US Federal Court** for your area (http://www.law.emory.edu/FEDCTS/). Read about a recent decision. What was the issue? Do you agree or disagree with the decision? Why?

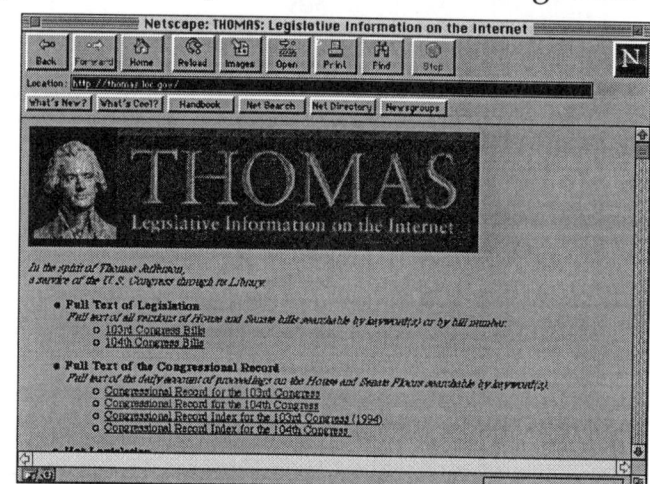

Economics

Many Internet sites can be used for economics projects. Start by browsing popular financial magazines online:

    http://pathfinder.com/fortune/index.html
    http://pathfinder.com/money/moneyhome.html

Visit the **US Census Bureau**.
    http://www.census.gov/ftp/pub/econ/www/

    Explore US Economics from the perspective of the US Census Bureau. Select one of the following areas to explore: **Agriculture, Manufacturing, Construction, International Trade** and **Retail-Wholesale**. Explore issues related to **income and poverty**. Chart **Price Indexes, Wages, and Unemployment**.

Visit the **American Stock Exchange**.
    http://www.amex.com/

    Select a company and make predictions about its performance. Track class progress on a "STOCK STATS" bulletin board.

Visit **Finance Net**.
    http://www.financenet.gov/

    Select a government job and find out about the education needed and salary schedule. Would you want this job? Why or why not?

    Explore the finanical statement of a government agency. What elements go into a financial report? Discuss some aspect that you think should be changed in the agency? Why?

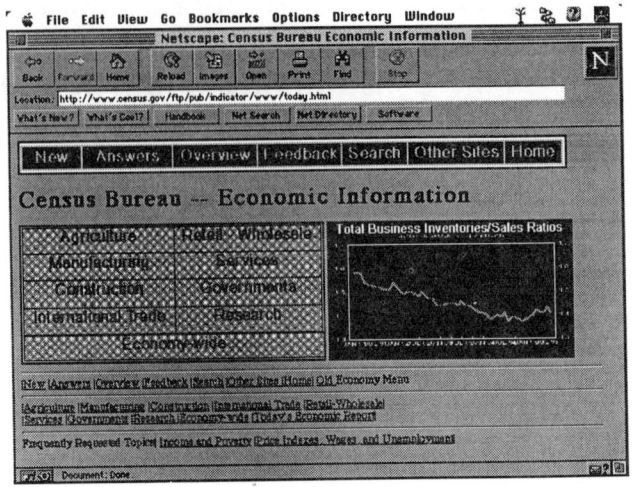

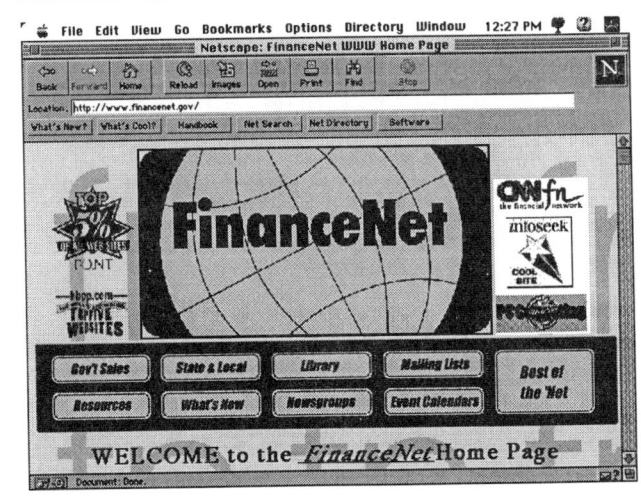

Ridin' the Surf: Subject Area Activities

Psychology

Psychology is a popular topic on the Internet. Teacher might want to start with the Secondary Teachers of Psychology page (http://cscc.clarion.edu/mitchell/topss.htm). You may even want to join the PsycList Project.

Visit PsychWeb.
http://www.gasou.edu/psychweb/psychweb.htm

Explore brochures and articles on various topics. Try the quiz questions!

Visit the Self Help and Psychology site
http://www.well.com/user/selfhelp/

Explore the PsychToons. Copy one into a word processor. What does it have to do with psychology? Why do you think it's a PsychToon?

Explore Links and the Psychology WEB pointer. Select a topic. Why is this topic important to you? Create a top 10 list of things you think people should know about this topic.

Visit the Jean Piaget Society site.
http://vanbc.wimsey.com/~chrisl/JPS/index.shtml

Read the biography. Jean Piaget was born 100 years ago, why has his work remained so popular?

Explore an online Psychology textbook.
http://web.wwnorton.com/norton/grip.html

Choose an area and compare the online textbook with your print textbook.

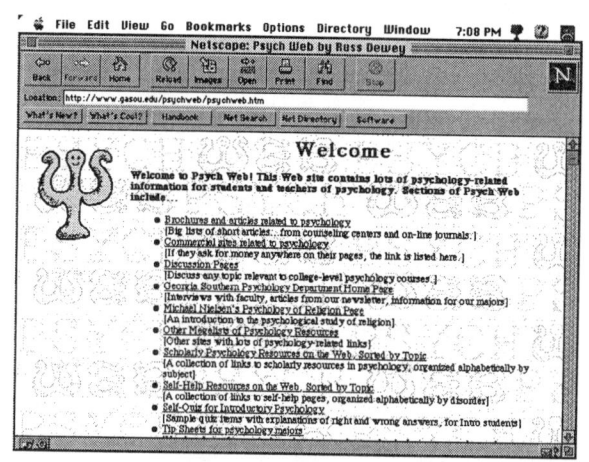

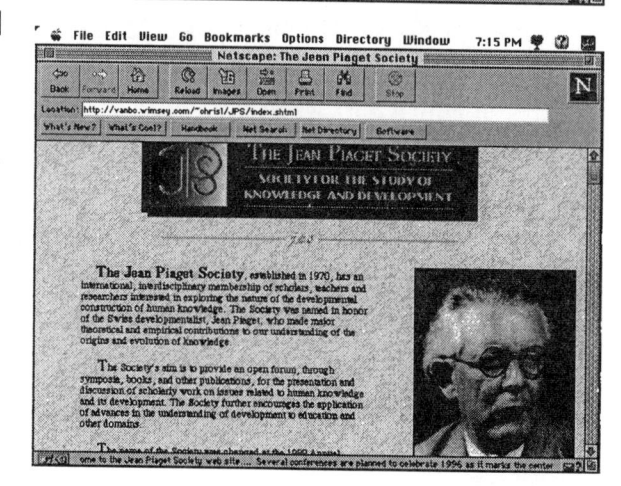

Literacy - Authors

Learn more about your favorite author. Use the Internet to ask authors questions and identify answers to your questions.

Surfer Starters

Ask the Author
   http://ipl.sils.umich.edu/youth/AskAuthor/
Children's Authors
   http://www.yahoo.com/Arts/Literature/Children/Authors/
   http://www.weblust.com/NS/BuildPadPage/Books
   http://www.lehigh.edu/jil4/public/www-data/pooh.html
Children's Literature
   http://www.ucalgary.ca/~dkbrown/index.html
Kid Lit Page
   http://mgfx.com/kidlit/
The OZ Page
   http://seamonkey.ed.asu.edu/oz/
Sources of Electronic Books
   http://nickel.ucs.indiana.edu/~lwolfgra/english.html
Ink Spot - Authors Page
   http://www.interlog.com/~ohi/inkspot/authors.html
Author Sketches - Literature Land
   http://204.225.221.7/csm/authors.htm
   http://204.225.221.7/csm/libraryh.htm#25
Authors
   http://ipl.sils.umich.edu/youth/AskAuthor/
   gopher://scholastic.com:2003/11/Scholastic%20Internet%20Libraries/Reading%20and%20Language%20Arts%20Library/All%20About%20Authors/Authors%20and%20Illustrators
   http://www.li.net/~scharf/writers.html
   http://www.books.com/author1.htm
Poets
   http://www.ece.ucdavis.edu/~darsie/library.html
English Teachers Resource
   http://nickel.ucs.indiana.edu/~lwolfgra/english.html
English Server
   http://english-www.hss.cmu.edu/

Author Pages
CS Lewis
>http://cc.usu.edu/~slq9v/cslewis/index.html

Emily Dickinson
>http://www.cc.columbia.edu/acis/bartleby/dickinson/

Edgar Allan Poe
>http://www.et.byu.edu:80/~conradt/poepage.html

Mark Twain
>http://web.syr.edu/~fjzwick/twainwww.html

J.R.R. Tolkien
>http://csclub.uwaterloo.ca/u/relipper/tolkien/rootpage.html

Walt Whitman
>http://www.cc.columbia.edu/acis/bartleby/whitman/

JRR Tolkien
>http://www.lights.com/tolkien/rootpage.html

William Shakespeare
>http://the-tech.mit.edu/Shakespeare/works.html

Dr. Seuss
>http://www.afn.org/~afn15301/drseuss.html

Lewis Carroll
>http://www.students.uiuc.edu/~jbirenba/carroll.html

C.S. Lewis
>http://www.cache.net/~john/cslewis/index.html

Roald Dahl
>http://www.nd.edu/~khoward1/Roald.html

Other Information Resources

Carpenter, Humphrey, & Mari Prichard (1984) **The Oxford Companion To Children's Literature**. Oxford University.

Gallo, Donald R. ed. (1990) **Speaking for Ourselves**. NCTE.

Greenfield, Howard (1989) **Books: From Writer To Reader**. Crown.

Hackwell, W. John (1987) **Signs, Letters, Words: Archaeology Discovers Writing**. Macmillan.

Jones, Delores Blythe (1994) **Children's Literature Awards & Winners: A Directory of Prizes, Authors, & Illustrators**. Neal-Schuman Publishers.

CD-ROM Resources

Great Literature Plus, Bureau of Electronic Publishing
History of English Literature, Clearvue
Monarch Notes, Bureau of Electronic Publishing
Science Fiction, Grolier
Twain's World
Women in Literature, Clearvue

Visit the Ask the Author Site!
http://ipl.sils.umich.edu/youth/AskAuthor/

Explore the Ask the Author site.

Use **Ask the Author** to ask an author a question. New authors being added are Daniel Pinkwater, Gary Paulsen, Katharine Paterson, Phyllis Root, Ashley Bryan, Joan Blos and Seymour Simon.

Explore one of the following authors: Matt Christopher, Lois Lowry, Robert Cormier, Jane Yolen, and Avi. Read about the author, then read a book by the author.

Identify an author not included in the Ask the Author site. Create a list of questions you would have for the author. Find information about this author on Internet or using other resources. Write an interview that includes the questions and answers you found. If you couldn't find the answers, speculate about what the author might have said.

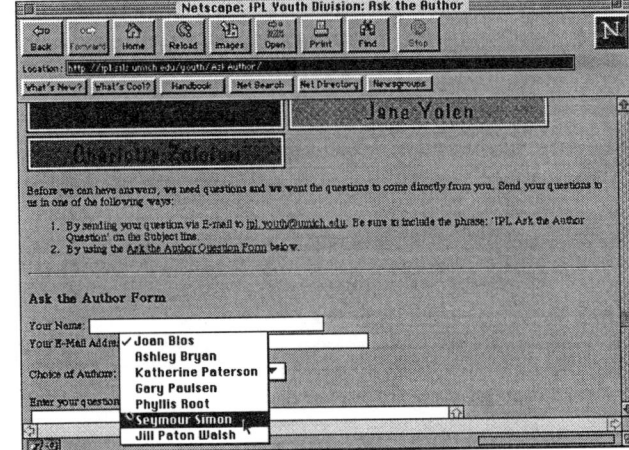

Ridin' the Surf: Subject Area Activities

Visit Early Childhood Sites!
http://www.ucalgary.ca/~dkbrown/authors.html

Explore the worlds of Pooh and Cat in the Hat. You'll find many more authors at the Children's Literature Web Guide.

There are tons of Winnie the Pooh sites (http://www.catt.ncsu.edu/users/tyche/pooh/elsewhere.html).

Winnie the Pooh
http://www.lehigh.edu/~jbh6/jbh6.html
http://www.public.iastate.edu/~jmilne/pooh.html

Find the Answers to Frequently Asked Pooh Questions
http://www.aber.ac.uk/~prs/pooh/faq/faq.html

Visit the 100 Acre Woods
http://www.catt.ncsu.edu/users/tyche/pooh/index.html

Try the trivia questions. Vote for your favorite character.

Dr. Seuss is everywhere on the Web!
http://www.afn.org/~afn15301/drseuss.html

Read a Dr. Seuss story online.
Go to GrinchNet. Do you like or hate the Grinch? Why?
Vote in the great Grinch debate.

Visit Seussville.
http://www.seussville.com/
Create a new Seuss character and enter the Seuss Content!
Chat with the Cat!

Visit Elementary Author Sites!
http://www.scholastic.com/public/Goosebumps/Stine-Home.html

Explore favorite elementary author sites.

Start with the Goosebumps page and the life of R.L. Stine.

http://www.scholastic.com/public/
Goosebumps/Stine-Home.html

Write a question for R.L. Stine.
Create a storyline for a new Goosebumps book.
Answer the following questions:
Why do you like R.L. Stine and his books?
What other authors do you think are similiar to R.L. Stine?

Caroline Arnold has written lots of nonfiction books for children. Find one in your school library. Find out about the author.

http://www.geocities.com/Athens/1264/

Read about one of her books and how she got her ideas. Try writing your own nonfiction book.

Caroline Arnold has lots of projects and activities for you to try. Check out her **Projects** page!

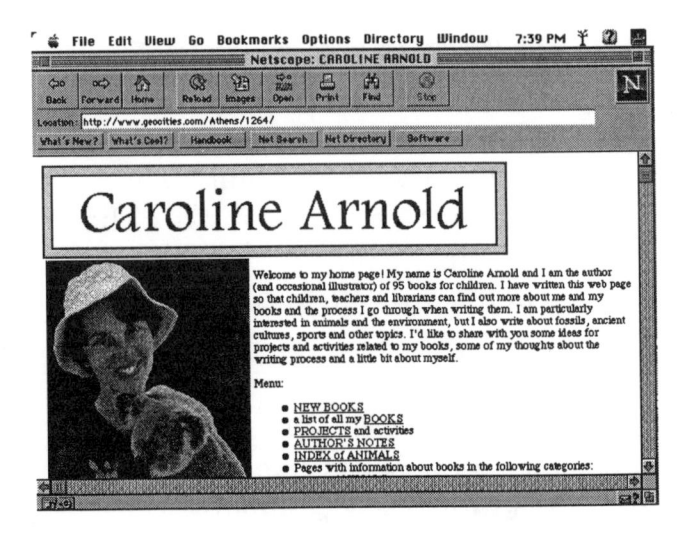

Ridin' the Surf: Subject Area Activities

Visit the Series Lovers Sites!
http://www.ucalgary.ca/~dkbrown/authors.html#series

There are many series for children and young adults to enjoy. Learn about some of these book series through the Internet!

Boy Series
   http://members.aol.com/biblioholc/bseries.html
Girl Series
   http://members.aol.com/biblioholc/gseries.html
Nancy Drew
   http://ils.unc.edu/nancy.drew/ktitle.html
Goosebumps
   http://scholastic.com/public/Goosebumps/Cover.html
Laura Ingalls Wilder
   http://vvv.com/~jenslegg/
Series Origins
   ftp://members.aol.com/sharonr899/library/StratemeyerFAQ.txt

Read a series of books and explore the following questions.
What makes reading a series so much fun?
What things happen in every book?
Select a character and describe how he or she evolved through the series.
Create a timeline showing each book and the main plot.
Create a plotline for another book in the series.
Develop an idea for a spinoff series using one of the characters or settings in the book.
Develop your own series. Describe the characters and setting of the series.
Create a rating system for your series. List your top three books in the series on a poster.

Visit Middle School Author Sites!
http://www.cache.net/~john/cslewis/index.html

Explore the worlds of L.M. Montgomery and C.S. Lewis.

Visit the C.S. Lewis Site.

http://www.cache.net/~john/cslewis/index.html

Describe your favorite C.S. Lewis book. Why do you think it is still popular so many years after it was written?

Write a short story set in the closet of your bedroom.

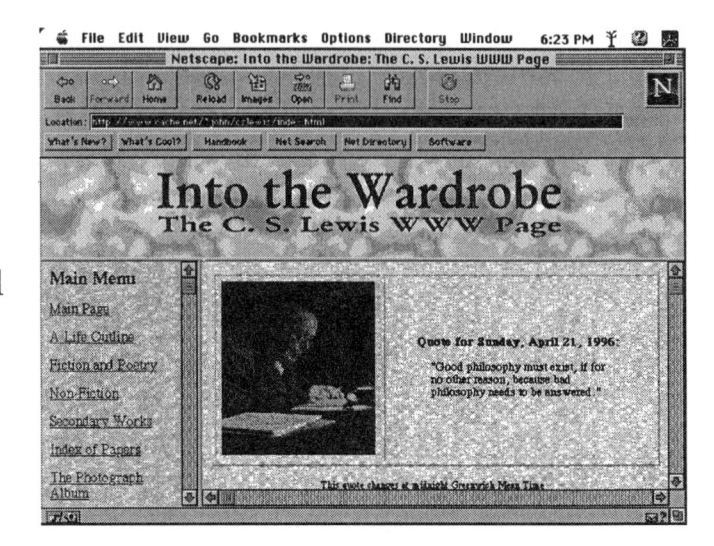

L.M. Montgomery is one of Canada's most famous authors. Learn more about her at the Kindred Spirits site. Create a timeline of Montogmery's works and life.

http://www.upei.ca/~lmmi/cover.html

Visit the L.M. Montomery pages on Prince Edward Island.

http://www.gov.pe.ca/vg/al.html

Create a list of things you would do if you could visit the setting of L.M. Montgomery's books.

Draw a map of the island and show the location of the fictional Avonlea.

Create a fictional character that might live in your town. Where would the person live? Why?

Ridin' the Surf: Subject Area Activities

Visit Secondary Authors Sites!
http://the-tech.mit.edu/Shakespeare/works.html

Let's explore popular authors from the past and present.

There are dozens of sites that contain good Shakespeare resources. The main Shakespeare home page is at MIT.

http://the-tech.mit.edu/Shakespeare/works.html.

There are lots of activities for Shakespeare in the classroom at the following page.

http://www.computek.net/public/barr/shakespeare.html.

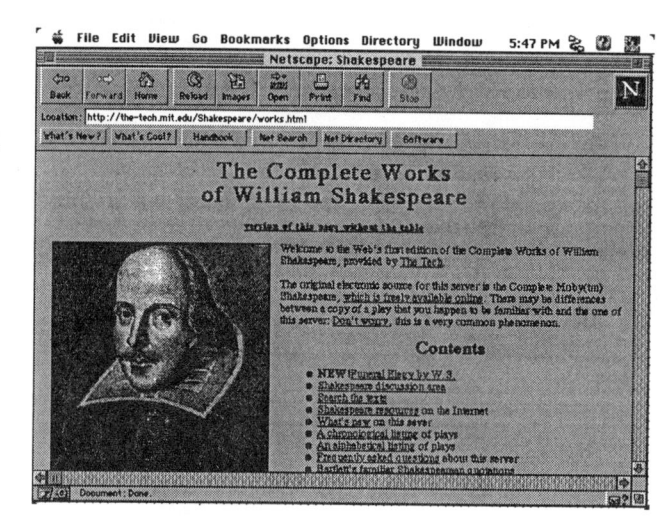

Stephen King is one of the most popular authors around. There are lots of Internet sites that contain good information. A few are listed below.

http://wwwcsif.cs.ucdavis.edu/~pace/king.html
http://www.acs.appstate.edu/~pl7714/sking_html/
http://callisto.girton.cam.ac.uk/users/jls20/sk.html

Explore his new series The Green Mile.
http://www.greenmile.com/

Read about why he developed the series. Do you like this concept? Email him your opinion. Read his responses to questions.
Write your own "Constant Reader." Just start with one episode.

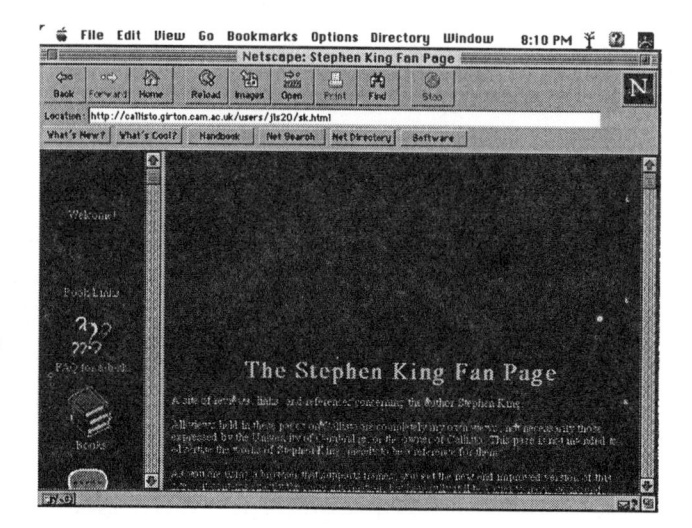

Visit the Tales of Wonder Site!
http://www.ece.ucdavis.edu/~darsie/tales.html

Explore folk and fairy tales from around the world. The Tales of Wonder Site contains a collection of stories from many part of the world.

Select tales from one of the following areas:
- Russia
- Siberia
- Central Asia
- China
- Japan
- Middle East
- Scandinavia
- Scotland
- England
- Africa
- India
- Native American

Try some of the following activities:

Create a class map and label the location where your tales take place. Learn about that area of the world. What does the tale say about the country, setting, and people who live there?

Find other tales from the same area in a book. Compare the tales you read on Internet with one in a book.

Illustrate one of the tales.

Compare two stories set in the same country.

Compare tales written in differenet countries.

Read a tale that contains animal characters. Are the animals more like real animals or like humans? What characteristics do they have that are like humans? Why do you think people like to read tales about animals?

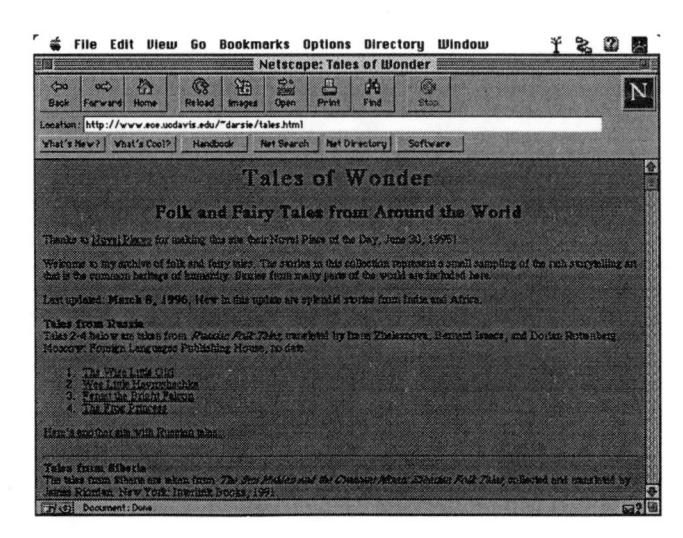

Visit Poetry Sites!
http://iquest.com/~e-media/kv/poetry.html

You can read poems, write poems, learn about poetry and poets all on the Internet! Try some of the following sites about poems and poetry. Start with Positively Poetry which was created by a 13 year old interested in poetry!

Visit the Poetry Garden.
http://sashimi.wwa.com/~uschwarz/poetry/grc000.html

Explore these funny poems. Read humorous poems by other poets like Jack Prelutsky and Shel Silverstein.

Visit the I Live On A Raft poetry page.
http://www.iatech.com/books/rafttoc.htm

Visit the Haiku site.
http://mikan.cc.matsuyama-u.ac.jp:80/~shiki/

Try writing some Haiku.

Visit KidzPage for lots of poetry by and for kids!
http://web.aimnet.com/~veeceet/kids/kidzpage.html

Visit the world of Walt Whitman.
http://www.liglobal.com/Walt/

Read his biography and poetry. How do his poems reflect his background? Give an example. Write and illustrate your own poem.

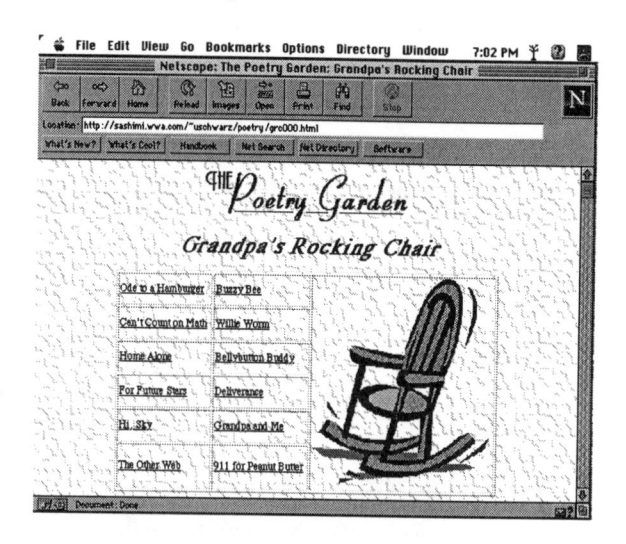

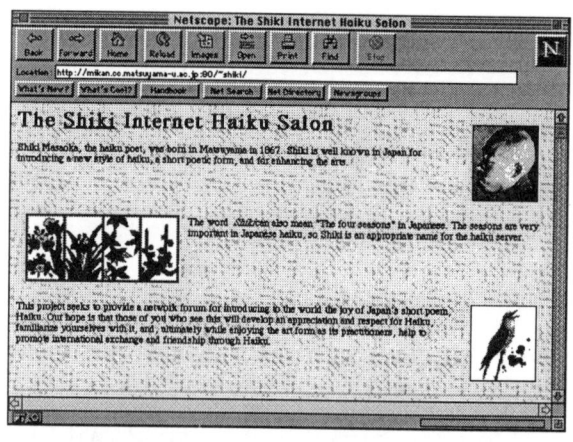

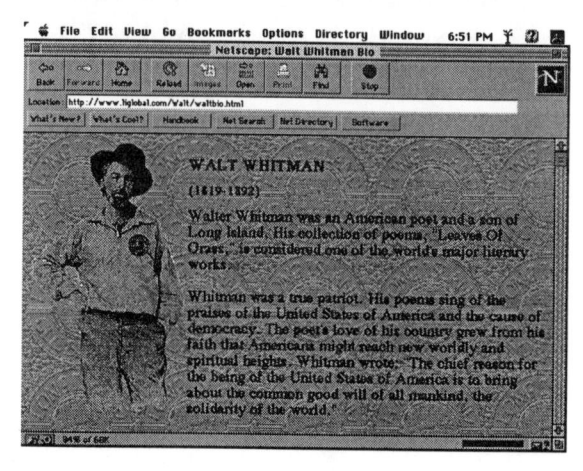

Visit Mark Twain Sites!
http://web.syr.edu/~fjzwick/twainwww.html

Explore the life and works of Mark Twain. There are many excellent resources for information on Mark Twain.

http://web.syr.edu/~fjzwick/twainwww.html
http://cadswes.colorado.edu/twain/
http://web.mit.edu/linguistics/www/forum/twainweb.html

Try some of the following activities:

Create a map showing all the places that Twain lived and how his works related to places he lived.

Visit the home town of Mark Twain.
http://www.webcom.com/~twainweb

How did his boyhood impact his writing?

Explore the world of Huck Finn. Read the text and explore the issues surrounding the book.
http://etext.lib.virginia.edu/twain/huckfinn.html

Some of Mark Twain's books have been banned. Explore the issue of censorship.
http://web.syr.edu/~fjzwick/twain_html/denvpost.html

Do you think Huck Finn should be banned? Why or why not?

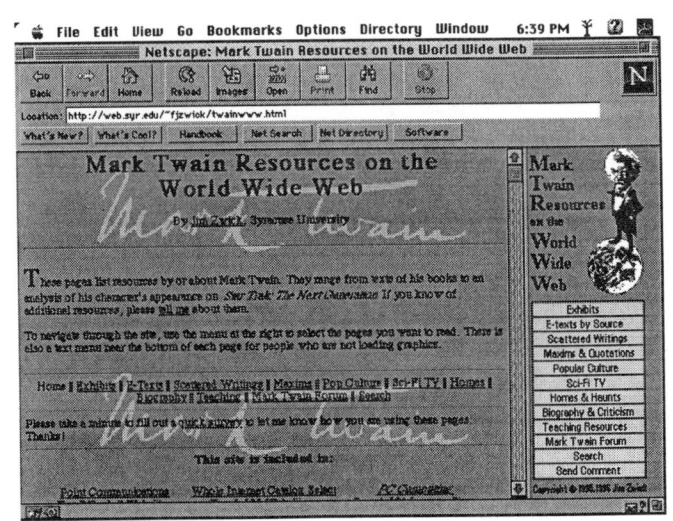

Visit Mythology and Folklore Pages!
http://www.pantheon.org/myth/

Explore Mythology and Folklore Pages.

Visit **Mythology and Folklore**.
http://pubweb.acns.nwu.edu/~pib/myth.htm

Read about the meaning of myths and folklore.
Read stories about Bigfoot. What do you think? Write your own story about a creature that might live in your area.

Visit the **Encyclopedia Mystica** site.
http://www.pantheon.org/myth/

Read a work of mythology from one of the following areas.
- Greek mythology
- Latvian mythology
- Norse mythology
- Other mythologies
- Folklore and legends
- Occult and mysticism

Write a myth in an area of interest and submit it for publication.

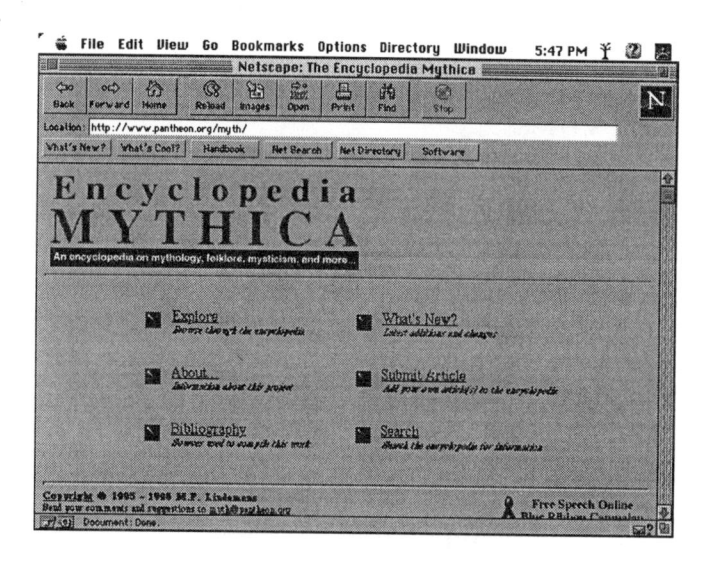

Visit **Princeton's Mythology Page**.
http://www.princeton.edu/~markwoon/Myth/

Visit **Barr's English Literature Page** on Mythology.
http://www.computek.net/public/barr/classic.html

Select one of the following works and explore the assigned locations.
- Edith Hamilton: Mythology
- Homer: Odyssey
- Sophocles: Antigone
- Coleridge: The Rime of the Ancient Mariner
- Shakespeare: A Midsummer's Night's Dream

Reading Comes Alive!

You'll find lots of online stories on the Web. Sometimes they link to other sites, let you choose an ending, or even let you make your own ending.

Internet Resources

Candlelight Stories
   http://users.aol.com/cimal/candlelight/candle.htm
Children's Literature
   http://www.ucalgary.ca/~dkbrown/index.html
Online Children's Stories
   http://www.ucalgary.ca/~dkbrown/stories.html
Realist Wonder Society
   http://www1.rrnet.com/~nakamura/
Buzz Rod and the Light: An Interactive Story
   http://hillside.coled.umn.edu/class1/Buzz/Story.html
Grin's Message
   http://indy.opennet.com/schoolhouse/grin/Welcome.html
Tales of Wonder
   http://www.ece.ucdavis.edu/~darsie/tales.html
Aesop's Fables
   gopher://spinaltap.micro.umn.edu/11/Ebooks/By%20Title/aesop
The Neverending Tale
   http://sarcazm.resnet.cornell.edu/~gila/tale/
Dodoland in CyberSpace
   http://www.swifty.com/azatlan/
The Hole Dewey Dug
   http://headbone.com/text/dewey/dewey.html
Storyweb
   http://www.webspace.com/~storyweb/welcome.htm
Noonie
   http://csclub.uwaterloo.ca/u/cbnorman/Noonie/noonie.html
Time Tag
   http://www.autobaun.com/~kbshaw/TimeTag/TimeTag.html
KidzPage
   http://web.aimnet.com/~veeceet/kids/kidzpage.html

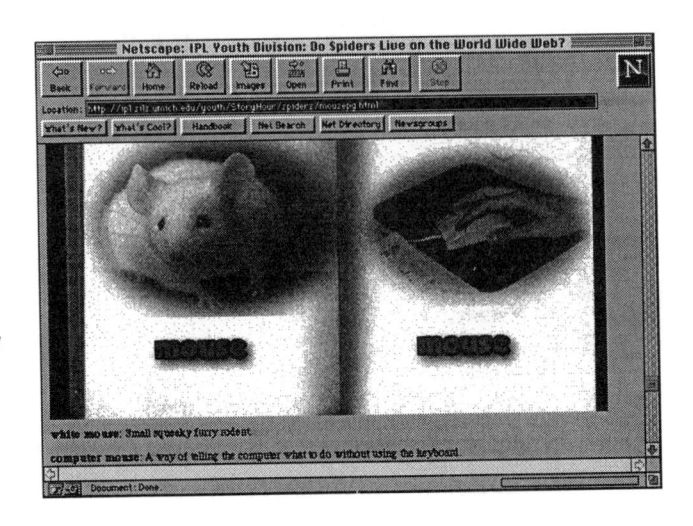

Ridin' the Surf: Subject Area Activities

Beginning Readers
Dinosaur Story
   http://www.echonyc.com/~spingo/Matt/Mike2.html
My Blue Suitcase
   http://www.iatech.com/books/mbstoc.htm
Madeline's Books
   http://www.bemelmans.com/

CD-ROM Resources
   Stories
      Broderbund Living Books: Harry and the Haunted House
      DISCUS Books: Tell-Tale Heart
      Magic Tales Interactive Storybooks: Imo and the King-African Folk Tale
      Of Mice and Men
      Puddle Books: After the Beanstalk
   Creativity Tools
      Amazing Writing Machine
      HyperStudio
      Imagination Express
      KidPix Studio
      Wiggleworks

Powerful Projects

The computer can bring words alive through sound, video, animation, and writing extensions. Do these extras add to or distract from the original intent of the writer? Explore some of these literature extensions and create your own! Compare the online interactive stories with the CD-ROM and print books.

Create your own storybook web pages.

Write to the authors of the on-line books. Provide alternative conclusions or ask the authors questions about their work.

Read and write your own stories (http://www.digikids.com/wms/wmskids.html).

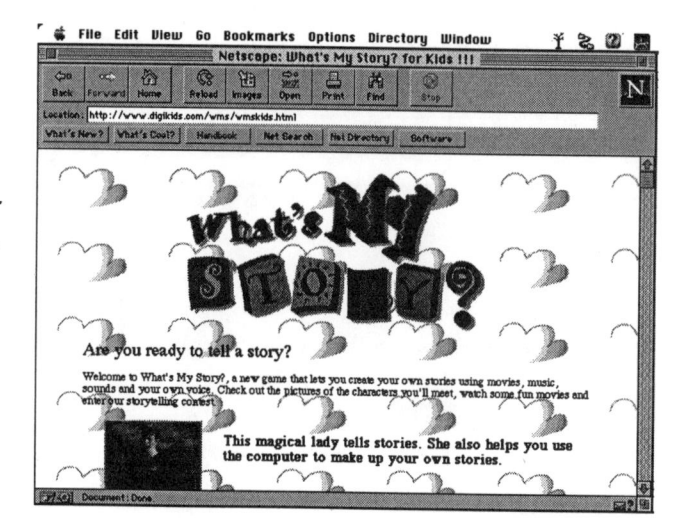

Visit Parents and Children Together Online!
http://www.indiana.edu/~eric_rec/fl/pcto/menu.html

Explore the Parents and Children Together Online site. It contains lots of creative interactive stories for children.

Go to the Fall 1995 Issue
Read the Stories for Grades 1-3. Read **BobTail Charlie's New Job**! Create your own interactive story. Create links to information that might be interesting. For example BobTail Charlie's New Job links to information the Circus and Trains.

Read the **Stories for Grades 4-6**. Which story do you like best? Why? Write a sequel to one of the stories. Include the same characters in a new situation.

Read the **Articles**. Explore the web for more information about one of the topics discussed.

Can you read **Spanish**? See how many English looking words you can pick out in the story Tomasita y El Gran Oso Negro.

Read the **Classic** stories from past issues. Write a review of one of the stories.

Write your own story and submit it for a future issue!

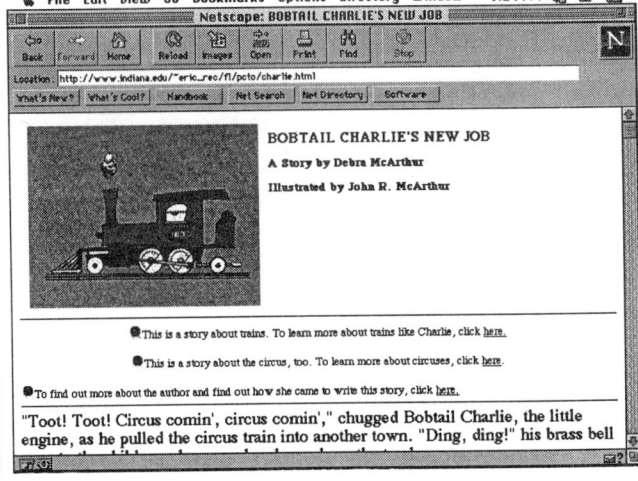

Ridin' the Surf: Subject Area Activities

Visit the Storyhour Page!
http://ipl.sils.umich.edu/youth/StoryHour/

Explore some story sites for kids!

Visit StoryHour.

http://ipl.sils.umich.edu/youth/StoryHour/

Read the following stories.
The Tortoise and the Hare
Molly Whuppie
Do Spiders Live on the World Wide Web?
The Fisherman and His Wife
The Boy Who Drew Cats

Write a new ending for one of the stories.
Draw a picture to go with the story.
List words associated with the story.
Change the characters in one of the stories. How would that change the story?

Visit Webtime Stories.
http://www.web-concepts.com/wts.htm

Read a story. Create a list of things you liked and disliked about the story. Would you change the ending? Why and how?
Write a story using one of the characters in a story that you've read. Send your story to the web page.
Draw a picture to go with one of the stories that you've read.
Would you like to be a web crawler? Create your own webcrawler creature. What's his or her name? What does this webcrawler do all day? How is a web crawler like and unlike a real spider?

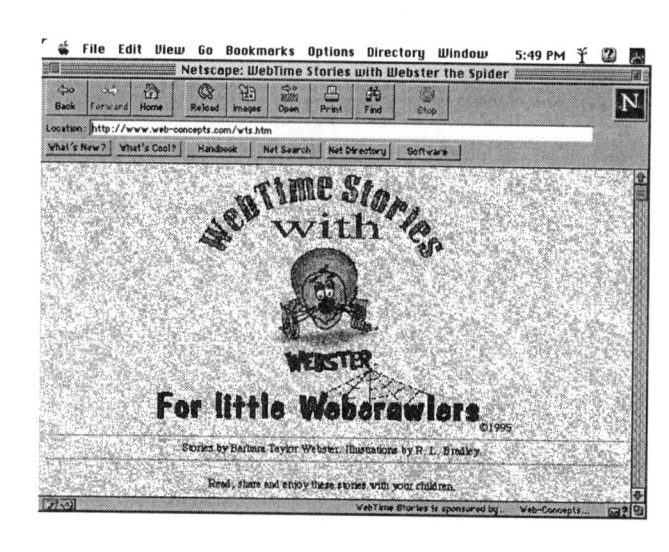

Visit the World of Reading Site!
http://ipl.sils.umich.edu/youth/WorldReading/

Explore literature sites!

Explore the World of Reading
http://ipl.sils.umich.edu/youth/WorldReading/

Choose a topic, read a book review, then read the book.

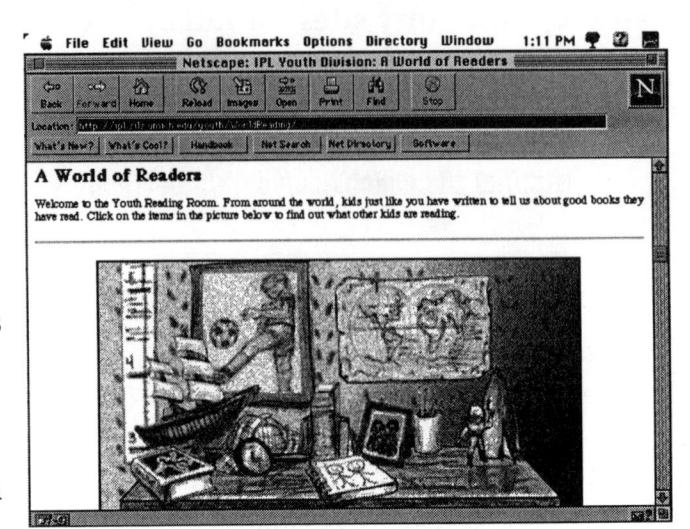

- Adventure
- Classic
- Friendship
- History/Folklore
- Scary Stories
- Sports
- Writing
- Animal Stories
- Family
- Growing Up
- Mystery
- Science Fiction
- Suspense

Read a book that wasn't reviewed. Write your own review and sent it in!

Visit Literature Land for books that are available online.
http://204.225.221.7/csm/books.htm

Read an author review. Use it as a model to create your own author review.

Read a book review. Read the book. Do you agree or disagree with the review? Provide specific examples from the book to support your idea.

Read a short story or poem. Copy and paste a passage from the text that is a good example of the author's abilities in each area below. Why did you choose the passage and how does it represent the author's work?:

- Plot
- Setting
- Character
- Technique (i.e., irony, satire)

Visit Teen Ezines!
http://www.acpl.lib.in.us/young_adult_lib_ass/yateens.html

Explore Teen magazines online. These ezines contain serious and fun articles and activities to explore. You can find a good list of teen sites at http://www.acpl.lib.in.us/young_adult_lib_ass/yateens.html.

Here are some of the most popular sites for teens:

FishNet
> http://www.jayi.com/

Girl Interwire
> http://www.girlgamesinc.com/interwire.html

High School Central
> http://www.azc.com/client/enn2/hscentral.htm

NetChick Clubhouse
> http://www.cyborganic.com/People/carla/

React
> http://www.react.com/

Reverse Link
> http://www.io.org/~sward/

Spank Zine
> http://www.cadvision.com/spank/spank.htm

Slummit
> http://spider.netropolis.net/slummit/

Stranger than Fiction
> http://www.connect.org.uk/merseyworld/stf/

Teen Page
> http://www.1starnet.com/teen

Teen Zine
> http://www.cyberspace.org/~teenzine/current/magazine.html

Yo: Youth Outlook
> http://www.pacificnews.org/yo/

Other Resources for Teens
> http://www.slip.net/~scmetro/forabout.htm

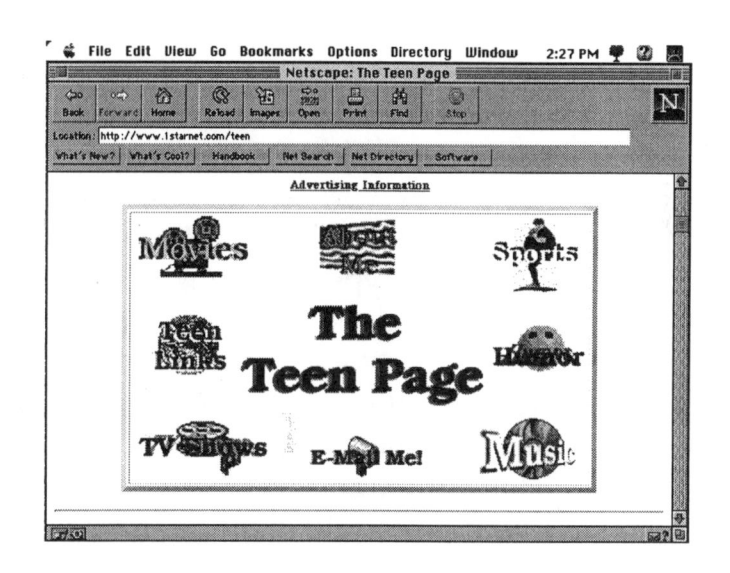

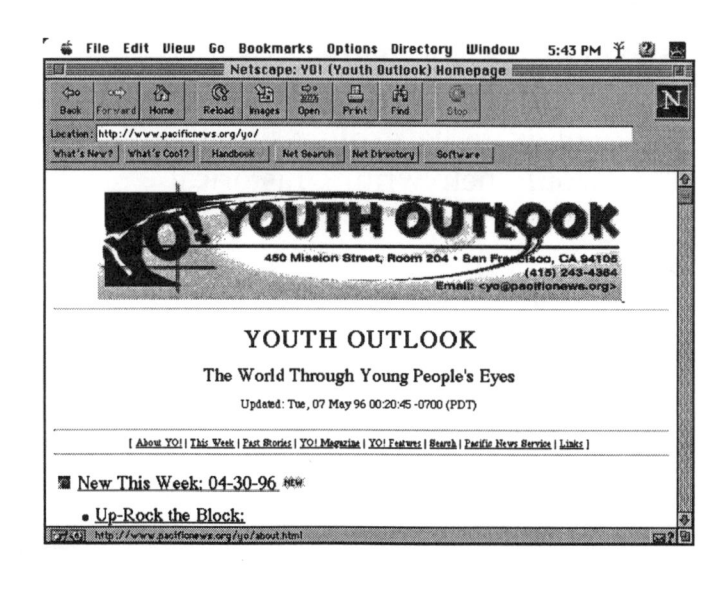

Visit the Resources for Young Writers Page!
http://www.inkspot.com/~ohi/inkspot/home.html

Explore InkSpot's resources for writers!

Explore the **Resources for Young Writer's Page.** Read the article on becoming a screenwriter. Create a story outline for one of your favorite television shows. Or, develop an idea for a movie sequel.

Explore the **Marketplace**.

Select an ezine and read at least three articles from different issues. Develop an idea for a piece of writing you could submit to this ezine. Why do you think your prose would fit the needs of this publication?

Submit a piece of work to a writing contest.

Select a writing genre. Explore **back issues of Inklings** to detemine how you might get this type of writing published. Create a plan for writing and publishing an article, short story, or other type of prose. Create a query letter that you could send to a potential publisher.

Read a **feature article**. Discuss how this information might be useful in your own writing activities.

Explore the **author and illustrator directories**. Use information from one of these sites for a poster highlighting this person and the contribution writers make to society. Use some of the writer's clip art in your poster.

Explore the results of one of the **writer's polls**. Select three ideas that you could use. How could these ideas help you in your writing? Add your own idea to the list. Write a short article using the information from the poll to help young writers.

Explore specific **genres** to learn about about writing in the area. For example, explore sites that would help writing historical fiction!

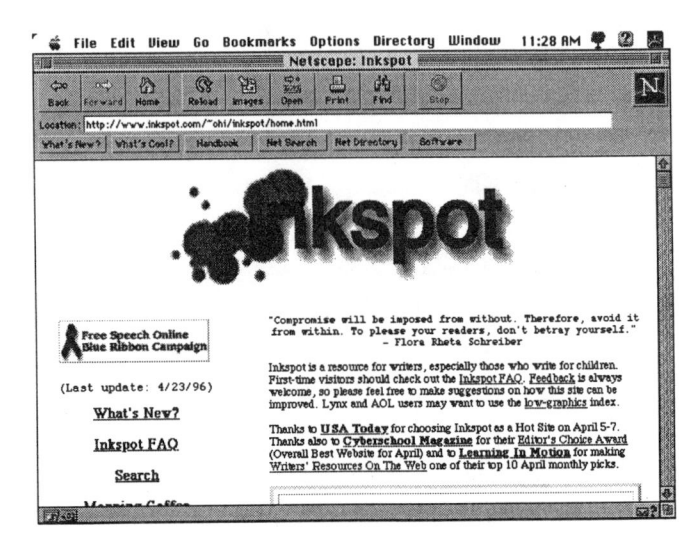

Visit the Bartleby Library!
http://www.cc.columbia.edu/acis/bartleby/

Explore the Bartleby Library and try the following activities.

Select **Barlett's Familiar Quotations**. Find a quote by one of your famous authors. How is the quote a reflection of this person and his/her work?

Think about a report or term paper you've done recently. Look for quotes that might have gone with the topic.

Create a sign containing a favorite quote.

Select a favorite historical figure and select a quote that represents some aspect of this person's career. How do you think it reflects their chosen occupation?

Select a poet and read a series of his/her poems. Compare this poet to another poet you've already studied. How are they alike and different?

Go to William Skrunk's **The Elements of Style**. Select five things you've always had difficulty with regarding use of language. Compare your list with others in class. Come up with a class "help sheet" of the most common class language concerns. You might want to explore other grammar and style writing sites (http://www.inkspot.com/~ohi/inkspot/style.html).

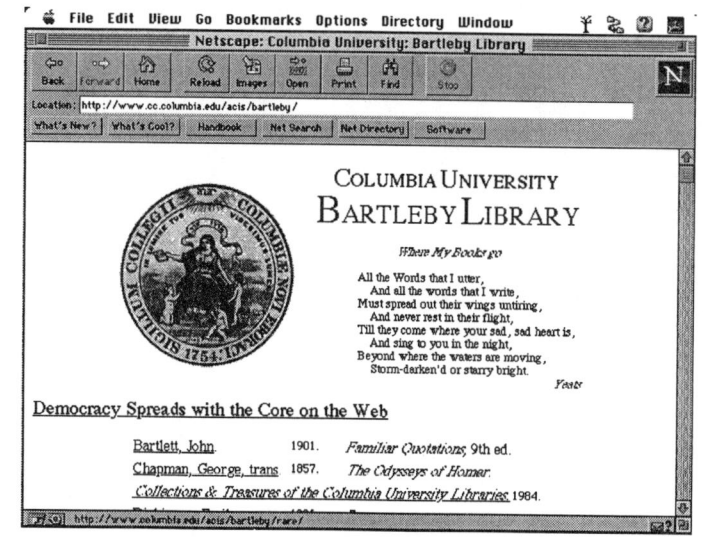

Visit Writing Help Pages!
http://www.computek.net/public/barr/works.html

Start with Barr's Writing Resources. Explore resources to assist with writing assignments. Also try some of the sites below.

English Resources
   http://nickel.ucs.indiana.edu/~lwolfgra/english.html
The English Server
   http://english-www.hss.cmu.edu/
College Board Exams
   http://www.collegeboard.org/

After writing a paper, use some of the following resources in the editing process. Cite the resources that were most helpful.

Writing Helpers
   http://www.inkspot.com/~ohi/inkspot/style.html).
Copy Editing Ideas
   http://www.access.digex.net/~bwalsh/editing.html
Elements of Style
   http://www.cc.columbia.edu/acis/bartleby/strunk/
Writing Lab
   http://owl.trc.purdue.edu/by-topic.html

Explore reference materials available on the web. Create your own "book shelf" list of the most valuable resources. Use Planet Earth as a place to start.

Planet Earth Home Page
   http://www.nosc.mil/planet_earth/books.html

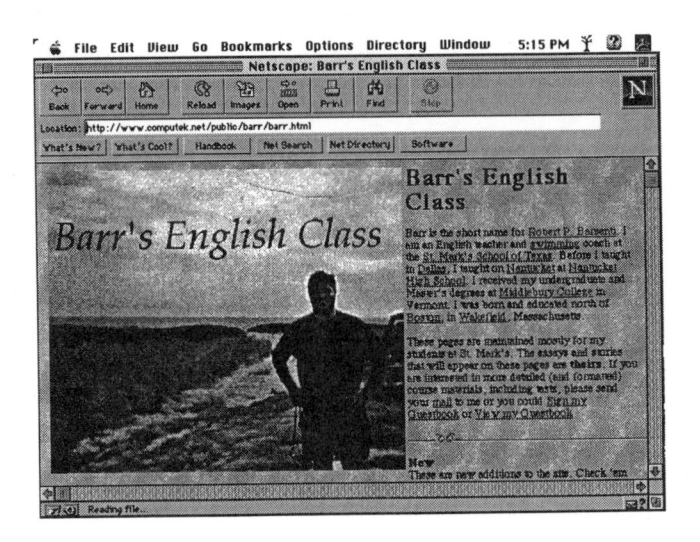

Ridin' the Surf: Subject Area Activities

Visit Fun English Sites!
http://www.dtd.com/excuse/

Explore the following fun English Sites.

Visit the **Excuse Generator**.

http://www.dtd.com/excuse/

Try the excuse generator.
Create your own story builder for another topic.

Explore the **Heretical Rhyme Generator**.

http://zenith.berkeley.edu/seidel/poem.html

Write a poem!

Visit **Grammar Rock**.

http://hera.life.uiuc.edu/grammar.html

Write your own "rock" song for learning a style of poetry.

Visit **Susie's Place** for some word games.

http://www.primenet.com/~hodges/susplace.html

Create your own word game.

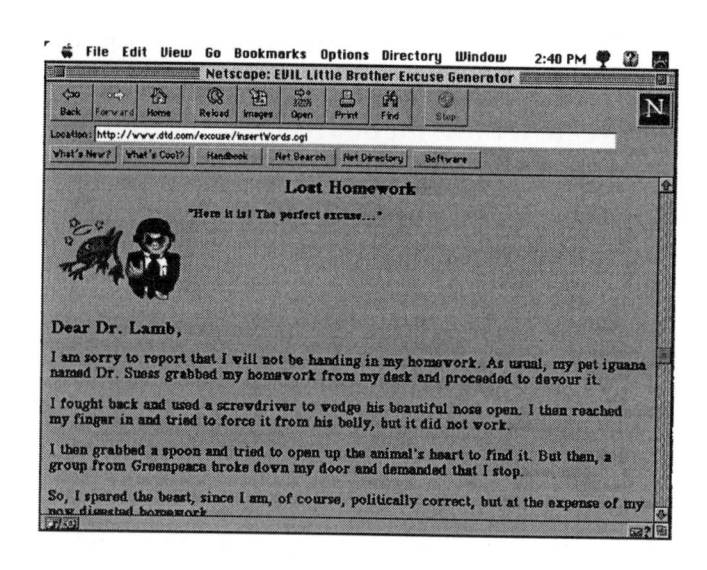

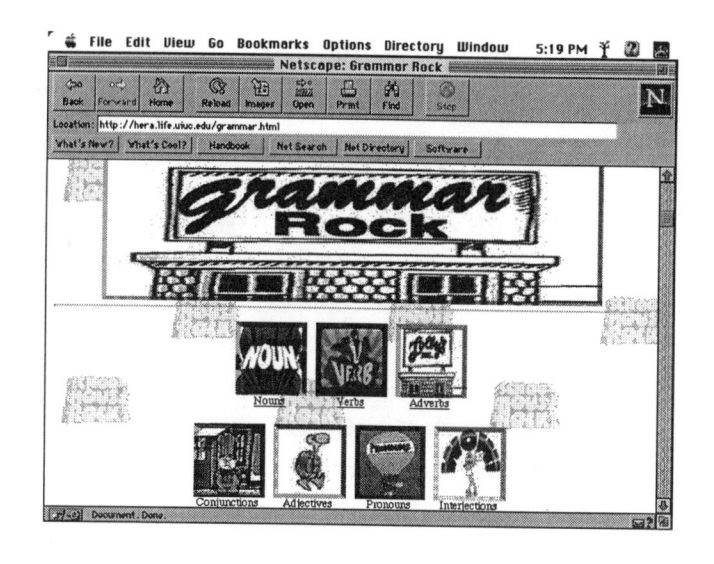

Visit the Banned Book Site
http://www.cs.cmu.edu/Web/People/spok/banned-books.html

Visit the Banned Book site to begin your exploration of censorship issues.

- Do you have any of these "banned books" in your school? Why or why not?

- Create a bulletin board that highlights the Library Bill of Rights, and titles of banned books.

- Hold a mock trial for a banned book. Discuss each side of the issue of banning books in schools.

- Select a related censorship issue such as Internet, television, or art.

- Explore freedom of expression issues in Canada (http://insight.mcmaster.ca/org/efc/pages/chronicle/chronicle.html). How are the issues similiar and different from concerns in the US?

- Explore the **Electronic Frontier Canada** Site (http://insight.mcmaster.ca/org/efc/efc.html) to learn about Internet censorship concerns.

- Read **Book Banning, Burning, and Censorship** (http://www.banned.books.com/). Select one aspect of the article to explore indepth.

- Visit **24 Hours of Democracy** to learn about what law students are doing about Internet Censorship (http://www.hotwired.com/staff/userland/24/). What could you do at your school to promote freedom of speech?

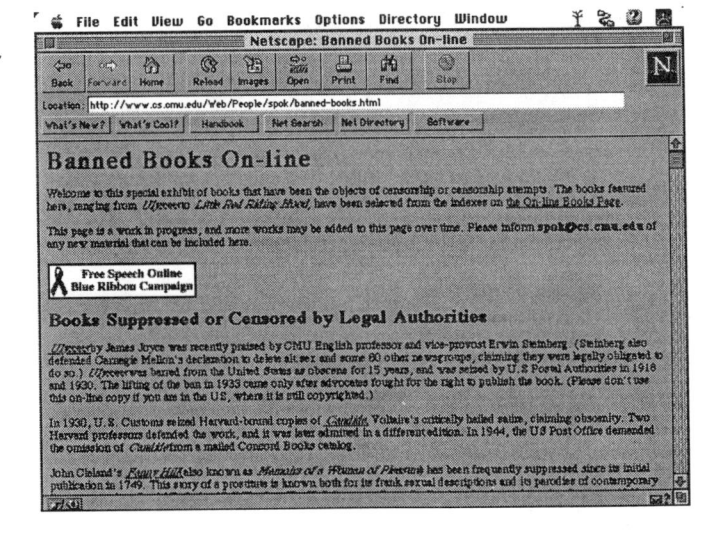

Ridin' the Surf: Subject Area Activities

Health and Fitness

Health and Fitness is a topic that crosses subject areas including nutrition, health, and physical education.

Surfer Starters
Kathy Schrock's Health and Fitness List
    http://www.capecod.net/Wixon/health/fitness.htm
Health
    http://www.cdc.gov/cdc.html
    http://www-sci.lib.uci.edu/HSG/Ref.html
    http://ificinfo.health.org/10tipkid.htm
    http://vm.cfsan.fda.gov/label.html
    http://128.196.106.42/nutrition.html
    http://debra.dgbt.doc.ca/~mike/healthnet
    http://www.nlm.nih.gov:82/
Good Health Web
    http://www.social.com/health/index.html
Band-Aids
    http://www.northcoast.com/savetz/bandaid/bandaid.html
The Heart
    http://sln.fi.edu/biosci/biosci.html
Dole 5 A Day
    http://www.dole5aday.com/
Tossed Salad
    http://www.tossed-salad.com/
Health and Fitness WorldGuide
    http://www.worldguide.com/Fitness/hf.html
Health Touch
    http://www.healthtouch.com/
Virtual Kitchen
    http://pathfinder.com/twep/kitchen/
Cooking Light
    http://pathfinder.com/cl/
CDC
    http://www.cdc.gov/

Other Information Resources

Ardley, Neil (1982) **Health & Medicine**. Watts.
Berger, Melvin (1982) **Sports Medicine**. Harper.
Fekete, Irene & Ward, Peter D. (1985) **Disease & Medicine**. Facts On File.
Jackson, Gordon (1984) **Medicine: The Body & Healing**. Watts.
Karlsberg, Elizabeth (1991) **Eating Pretty**. Troll.
Lambert, Mark (1986) **Medicine In The Future**. Watts.
Nutrition To Grow on (Videocassette) (1988) Human Relations Media.
Patent, Dorothy Hinshaw (1992) **Nutrition, What's in the Food We Eat.**
Parker, Steve (1990) **Food & Nutrition**. Watts.
Seixas, Judith S. (1984) **Junk Food-What It Is, What It Does**. Greenwillow.
Silvestein, Alvin (1992) **Vitamins & Minerals.** Millbrook.
Ward, Brian R. (1987) **Diet & Nutrition**. Watts.
Wickham, Nicholas (1986) **Medival Technology**. Watts.

CD-ROM Resources

ADAM
BodyPark
BodyWorks
Compton's 1995
Crunchers
Encarta 1995
The Magic School Bus Explores the Human Body
Mayo Clinic
Ultimate Human Body

Wave Words

Substance abuse   Medicine
Health   Nutrition
Exercise   Physical conditioning
Genetics   Diet

Powerful Projects

Explore all aspects of wellness including health, nutrition, exercise, and physical conditioning. Are you doing everything you can to stay "well"? Start with some of the following questions:

What are the effects of substance abuse, lack of exercise or obesity?
What are the latest findings regarding cholesterol, fats, and heart disease? Why is this important?

Have you been drawn in by health product fads and frauds. Why do we have these trends?

Are food additives harmful? Why do people take dietary supplements? Should you take vitamins? Why or why not?

What are the pros and cons of cosmetic surgery? Is it safe? Would you have it? Why or why not?

What are Health Maintenance Organizations (HMOs)? Are they good or bad? How are they viewed by patients and doctors? How are they different from traditional health care?

What are preventative health services? Are flu shots effective? Who should have them? Why?

What contributes to a long life? What can you do now to live longer? Do you want to live to be very old?

Are Xray machines, video displays, microwaves, and other machines safe? Why or why not? Are you worried?

What are the most dangerous occupations? Why? What are safety issues related to a particular career?

Use Healthtouch (http://www.healthtouch.com/) and other health and fitness resources to answer the following questions:

Explore your medicine cabinet and learn about the contents of the drugs you have at home. What are their uses, abuses, and side effects? Should they be in your cabinet where young children could find them? Why or why not? What would you do if a child accidenty took an overdose of one of these drugs?

Select a health topic, disease, or illness and find a health organization that provides information. Create a folded brochure that could be used by the organization to provide information for the public. Use the links at this site to locate information you could use in the brochure.

Read an article from the Health Living Ezine at (http://pathfinder.com/HLC/).

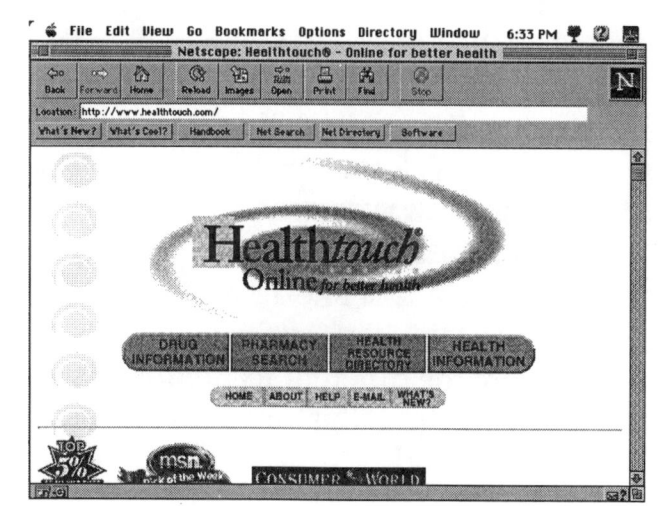

Visit First Aid Sites!
http://www.wps.com.au/business/firstaid/firstaid.htm

Visit First Aid Sites. The First Aid Online site also links to other good information about first aid.

- Explore one of the following areas:
   - Blistering, burns and frostbite
   - Breathing difficulty, choking and fainting
   - Bruising and puncture wounds
   - Ears, eyes and nose
   - Poisoning and Bites
   - Sprains and fractures
   - Shock
- Create a poster that illustrates what to do in a medical emergency.
- Develop a skit that shows the correct and incorrect actions in handling first aid.
- Make a chart showing the common poisons and how to handle them.
- Create a poster warning people about a particular type of creature bite.
- Select a season of the year and identify the most common accidents that occur during that time of year. Create a list of problems and remedies for each situation.
- Make a video showing the proper technique for handling a sprain or fracture.
- Choose a common sport. What type of first aid is often needed for injuries related to the sport? Create a first aid booklet for people who play that sport.
- Explore the medical illustrator's site. It contains lots of cool pictures.
   http://www.mednexus.com/med_illustrator/index.html
- Copy a piece of line art and write about the illustration.
- Explore the different techniques used by medical illustrators to express their work.

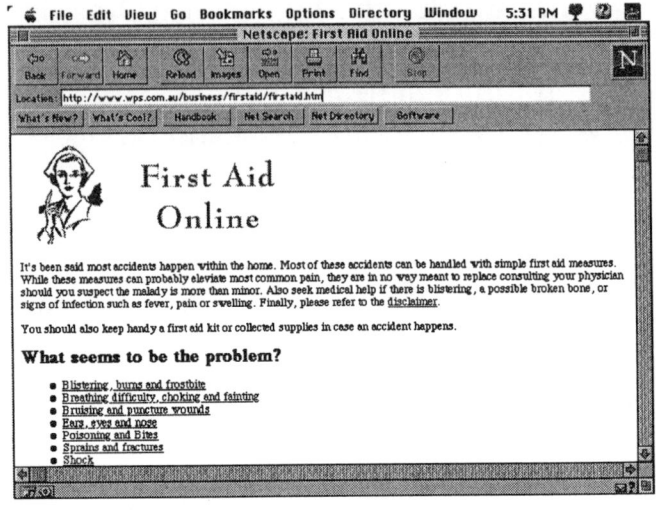

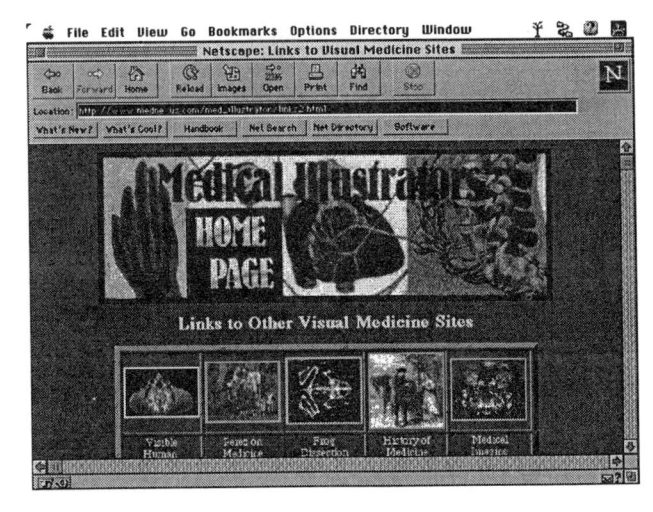

Ridin' the Surf: Subject Area Activities

Visit Nutrition Sites!
http://www.tossed-salad.com/

Explore nutrition with the Tossed Salad and 5 A Day Sites.

Visit the **Tossed Salad** site.
http://www.tossed-salad.com/

Healthy Herb stands for good nutrition. Create your own nutrition character. What important things would he or she tell children about nutrition?

Download and color one of the pages from **Health Herb's coloring book**. Write a paragraph about nutrition to go with the page.

Read the story **1-2 Tree**. What happens next? Write your own ending for the story. Create a web with the question "How do I play with a tree?" in the middle. Brainstorm ideas related to the question.

Visit the **Virtual Playground** and explore foods. Create your own information page for a healthy food you enjoy. Tell Healthy Herb about your food.

Visit **Dole 5 A Day** site.
http://www.dole5aday.com/

Explore the **Nutrition Center**. Create a chart showing information about your favorite fruit or vegetable.

Try the following **Fun** activities.
   How'd You Do Your 5 Today?
   Play the 5 A Day Game!
   Bobby Banana and Friends
   Meet the 5 A Day Fruit and Vegetable Characters!
   Fun with Fruits and Vegetables Kids Cookbook

Teachers should explore the School projects.

Visit the Health and Fitness WorldGuide Site!
http://www.worldguide.com/Fitness/hf.html

Explore the Health and Fitness WorldGuide site.

Anatomy: Explore the human anatomy page. Write down and define each term. If you were going to create an exercise program for yourself, what areas of the body would be your priority? Why?

Strength Training: Try each of the recommended exercises. Create a program for yourself that includes those exercises that focus on your priority areas.

Cardiovascular Exercise: Explore the activites that they recommend for a healthy heart. Pick an activity that you would choose for a family member. Why do you think this would be a good choice for their health? How would you convince them to try it?

Eating Well: Do you eat right? Describe your eating habits. What areas are your strengths? Where do you need to improve your nutritional habits? Create a plan for improving your eating habits over the next two weeks.

Sports Medicine: What's your body fat? What body type are you? Compare yours with another person in class. Choose one of the body fat myths and discuss it in a small group. Do you think most people believe these myths? Create an advertising campaign to help eliminate a myth. Create a poster that demonstrates the RICE principle.

Highplanet: Explore the online magazine. Write a fitness article for the magazine.

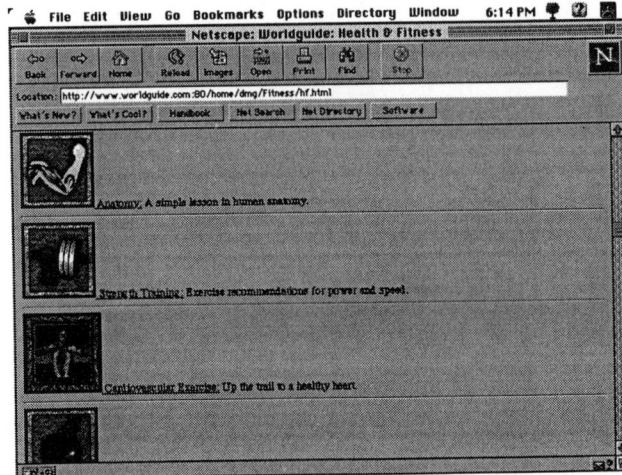

Section 4

Hangin' Ten: Interdisciplinary Thematic Units

I want students actively involved with real-world problems and issues. What kinds of projects work well for the Internet?

How can I use Internet as a resource for bringing content from different subjects together?

I'll looking for projects that go beyond traditional paper and pencil activities. I want students to become more effective problem-solvers and communicators. Can Internet help?

This section will address each of these questions. Rather than emphasizing a particular subject area, broad areas of interest that cross disciplines will provide the basis for a variety of activities. We'll explore interdiscplinary thematic units that incorporate a lot of different resources and challenge students to solve problems and communicate their ideas to others.

In this section of the book we'll focus on activities that cross subject areas and use a variety of technologies. Students "hang-ten" on the waves of technology by using Internet as only one of many tools and resources for addressing issues, answering questions, and solving problems. Rather than focusing on Internet, select the best resource for the particular activity. For example, a book, video, laserdisc, CD-ROM, or Internet site might be used as the springboard or focal point for an activity.

As you identify activities, develop units, and create lessons, focus on learner-centered activities that involve students in synthesizing information from a variety of resources. Each student or team may focus on a different problem or issue related to the same theme. Encourage students to follow their interests and design unique ways to communicate their ideas. Experienced Internet users will be ready to go beyond the suggested resources and explore related topics and sites.

Hangin' Ten Topics and Activities

Our Global Community
  Connections
    Global Community Pages!
    United Nations
    Human Rights
  What's It Like Where You Live?
    Great Globe Gallery
    Mapmaker
  Travel
    Getting Around the Planet
    US Dept of Transportation
  Where We Live
    This Old House
  Cultural Diversity
    Black History
    American Immigration

Our Environment
  The Great Outdoors
    GORP
    Wilderness through Literature
    National Wildlife Federation
  Mostly Ocean!
    Underwater World
  The Impact of Disasters
    VolcanoWorld
    Earthquakes
  Let's Save It!
    Envirolink

Exploration and Development
  Early Developers
    Institute of Egyptian Art
    Jorvik Viking Centre
    Pirates of the Caribbean
  America's Development
    Lords of the Earth
    History of the NW Coast
  Beyond Our Planet
    NASA
    SpaceLink
    Science Fiction
    Bermuda Triangle

Imagine, Investigate, Invent
  Inventors
    Famous Inventors
    Be an Inventor
    Creativity Web
    Invention Dimension
  Inventions
    Innovation
    Energy Quest

Our Global Community

Our global community is the first of four themes explored in this section of the book. We're part of a global community. Explore how people around the world work, learn, and play. Make connections with other cultures to learn about how people are alike and different. Celebrate diversity and shared ideas about humanity.

This theme contains five main elements:

Connections
Internet is a great way to help students become part of the global community. Epals can connect your students with others throughout the world. Start with activities that help students get to know other children their age at a personal level. Then expand their interactions to include discussions on important world issues such as human rights.

What's It Like Where You Live?
Help students gain a global perspective by exploring the geography of our world through globes and maps. These activities are exciting when students collaborate on projects with their epals in other parts of the world.

Travel
Once students have made connections, discussed issues, and explored the world, it's time to do some planning. Students enjoy making travel plans and it's a great way to explore transportation options and the mathematics of distance and financing travel.

Where We Live
Many students don't realize that everyone doesn't live in a house in the suburbs. Help students explore the meaning of "home" in different parts of the world.

Cultural Diversity
We're all part of the human race, but diversity makes our world interesting. Help students explore their heritage through the study of family history or cultural exploration.

Global Community: Connections

Encourage students to explore the world through Internet. Epals can help students reach out and explore issues, concerns, and life in other parts of the world. Go beyond personal communication and encourage students to discussion relevant issues related to understanding their role in the global community. Your class may want to focus on cultural issues within their own community, region, or country before reaching out and exploring worldwide concerns.

Surfer Starters

Contacts made by students

CyberKids Interactive
  http://www.cyberkids.com/cyberkids/Interactive/Interactive.html
Kid's Page Mail Office - International Kids Space
  http://plaza.interport.net/kids_space/mail/mail.html
Email KeyPal Connection
  http://www.comenius.com/keypal/index.html
The Kid's Place
  http://www2.islandnet.com/~bedford/kids.html

Contacts made with teacher help

Net Contacts
  http://gnn.com/gnn/meta/edu/dept/contacts/contacts.html
Intercultural Email Classroom Connect
  http://www.stolaf.edu/network/iecc/
  http://www.start.com/start

Tool for Finding School Pages

Web66 - School Pages
  http://web66.coled.umn.edu/schools.html
Classroom Connect - ClassroomWeb
  http://www.wentworth.com/classweb/
Launchpad - School Pages
  http://www.weblust.com/NS/BuildPadPage/Schools
Middle Schools
  http://longwood.cs.ucf.edu:80/~MidLink/middle.home

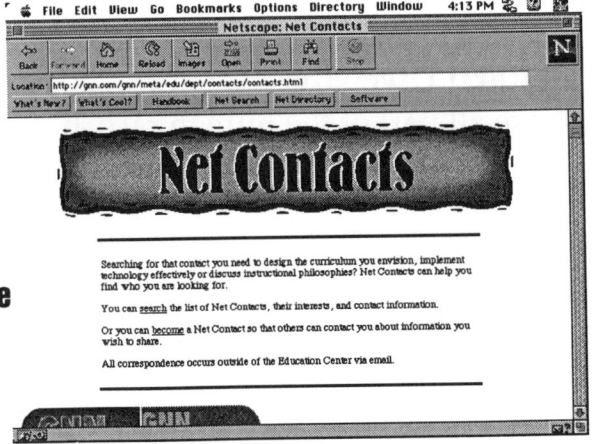

School Sites
Hillsdale School
   http://hillside.coled.umn.edu/
Fairbanks Alaska School
   http://www2.northstar.k12.ak.us/schools/upk/upk.home.html
Japanese Middle School
   http://www.nptn.org/cyber.serv/AOneP/schools/ukima/home.html

Global Connections
United Nations
   http://www.un.org/
International Simulations Page
   http://www.lib.umich.edu/libhome/Documents.center/intsim.html
Mexico and Central America
   http://www.bergen.gov/~chrgre/mexcen/
South America
   http://www.bergen.gov/AAST/Projects/LatinAmerica/eritha/

Social Issues Sites
Life Education Network
   http://www.lec.org/
Human Rights Page
   http://www.traveller.com/~hrweb/hrweb.html
Homelessness
   http://ecosys.drdr.virginia.edu/ways/list.html
   http://ecosys.drdr.virginia.edu/ways/1.html

CD-ROM Resources
   Amnesty Interactive
   Crunchers
   Encarta
   Material World: Global Family Portrait

Wave Words
   International Pen Pals
   Homelessness
   Human Rights
   Cultural Diversity
   Multicultural
   Social Issues

Powerful Projects

Begin your exploration of the global community with a discussion of diversity in your own community, region, and country. What different cultures are represented? How are these like and unlike your own? Explore issues related to stereotyping, racism, and prejudice. Use epals as a way to explore feelings and attitudes about cultures that are different from those represented in the classroom. For example, a rural class could communicate with an urban class. A class from the southern part of the US could compare ideas with students from the north. Consider a project that would pair students from eastern and western Canada.

Start your exploration of the global community by getting to know the geography of the world through epals. Encourage students to get to know their epal on a personal basis before beginning content-related activities. Students can share information about their daily lives, the climate where they live, and the geography of the area. Once students feel comfortable with on-line communication, move to other projects. For example, young children might compare the animals that live in their area with the animals that live in another country.

Students enjoy learning about other cultures. Use **Material World** as a focal point for exploration of life in another country. Use Internet pen pals to compare the families they read about on the CD with real students around the world.

Use the **Amnesty Interactive** CD to provide information about human rights concerns around the world. Are children in other parts of the world concerned about human rights? Are their concerns like or unlike theirs?

Compare the "quality of life" and economics of different countries. Use the **Crunchers** software to gather and analyze statistics about different areas.

Explore Visions of Liberty (http://www.tech21.org/yany/Index.html). Share your ideas on the importance of liberty in a global society.

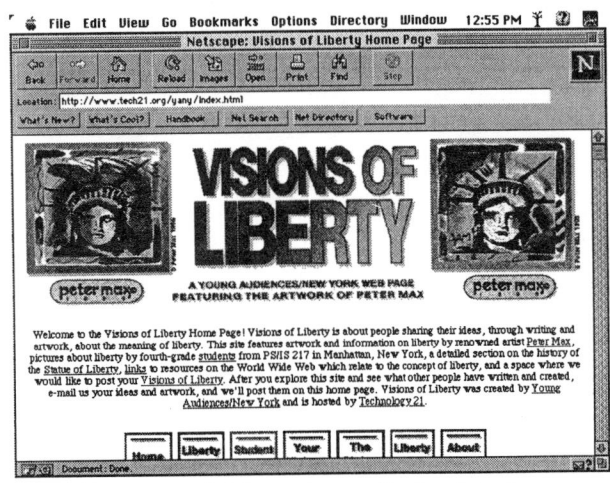

http://www.tech21.org/yany/Index.html

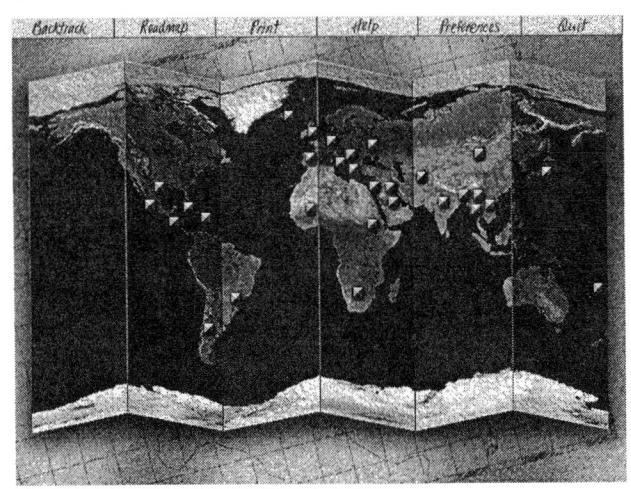

Material World CD-ROM

Visit Global Community Pages!
http://www.scholastic.com/public/Network/GlobalComm/index.html

Explore global communities on the web and through email.

Join the **Global Community Project**.

http://www.scholastic.com/public/Network/GlobalComm/index.html

Explore the characteristics of other communities.
Share the characteristics of your community including:

Community Information
Local Economy
Community History and Lore
Community Images
Information about Students

Explore the HUT Internet Writing Projects.

http://www.hut.fi/~rvilmi/email-project.html

Select a topic for discussion on the **HUT Internet Writing Project**:

Contacting My Culture
Communicating Across Cultures
Problems in Society
Ethical Issues
Personal Philosophies
Education and Social Causes
Entertainment and the Arts
Media Regulation
Careers

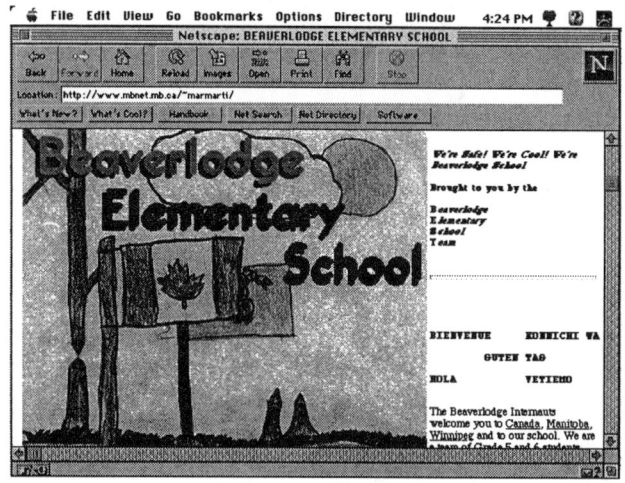

Visit the United Nations Page!
http://www.un.org/

Explore global issues through exploration of the United Nations and other international agencies.

Explore the **United Nations Site**.

http://www.un.org/

Select an issue of global interest such as drug abuse or space exploration. What is the position of the United Nations related to this issue? Do you agree or disagree with their position? What action would you like to see the United Nations take in this area? How does your epal stand on the issue?

Explore the **International Simulations Page**. You'll find lots of information to help understand our global community.

http://www.lib.umich.edu/libhome/Documents.center/intsim.html

Explore the Subject Background area.

Select an International Agency and determine their role in the global community.

Explore information about the country where your epal lives.

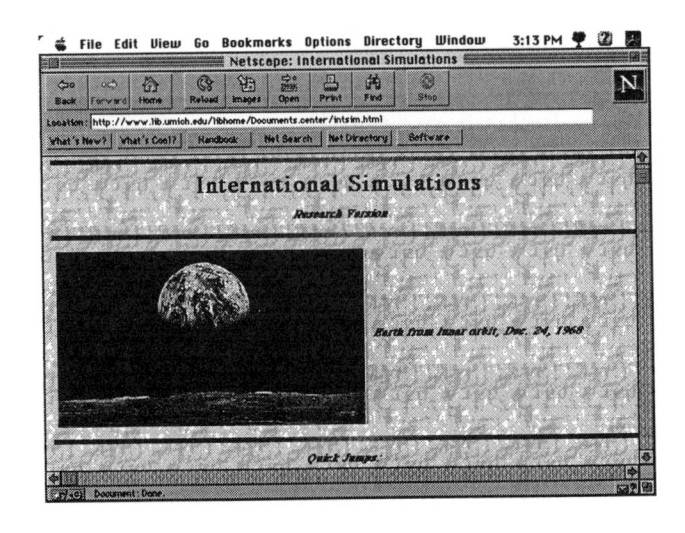

Visit Human Rights Pages!
http://www.amnesty.org/

Explore issues related to human rights. What do people around the world think about human rights?

Explore the **Amnesty International Page**.

http://www.amnesty.org/

Create a world map that shows locations of current human rights concerns.

Read about Amnesty International. Do you think this is an important organization? Why or why not?

Explore the **Human Rights Web**.

http://www.traveller.com/~hrweb/

Read the section called **What are Human Rights?**
Discuss the definition of human rights with a student from another country.

Explore the history of the human rights movement. If you could give an award for the person who best represented the human rights movement. Who would you pick? Why?

Explore **legal documents** related to human rights. How do different countries view human rights? What about the United Nations?

Find out **What can I do to Promote Human Rights?**

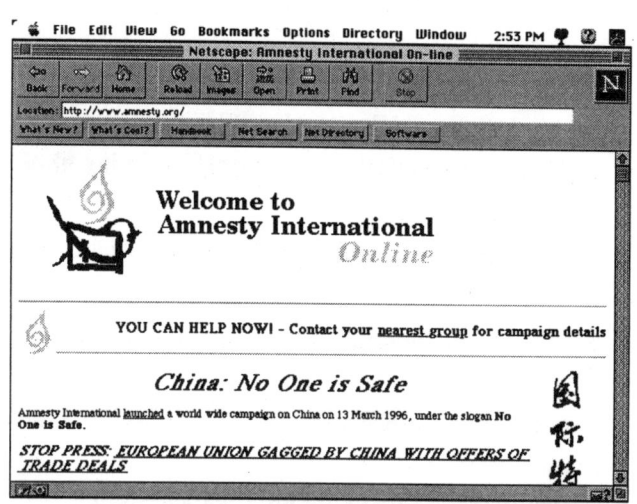

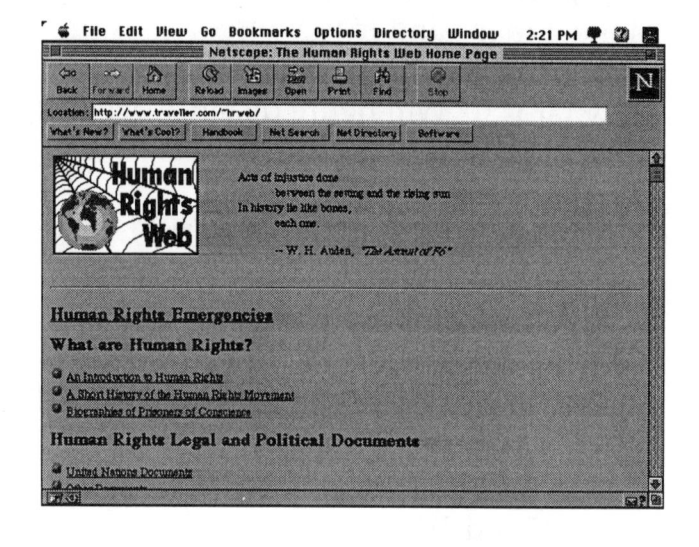

Global Community: What's It Like Where You Live?

Explore where people live. Help students make national and international connections to help them compare where they live with where others live.

Surfer Starters
What's It Like Where Your Live?
   http://www.mobot.org/MBGnet/live/index.html
Cultural Connections
   http://www.cs.uidaho.edu/~connie/interests-geography.html
Color Landforms
   http://fermi.jhuapl.edu/states/states.html
Maps Lessons
   http://info.er.usgs.gov/education/teacher/what-do-maps-show/index.h
Canadian maps
   http://www-nais.ccm.emr.ca/schoolnet/
Making maps and map words
   http://loki.ur.utk.edu/ut2kids/maps/map.html
How far is it? Will figure distance between two locations
   http://gs213.sp.cs.cmu.edu/prog/dist
Globes
   http://hum.amu.edu.pl/~zbzw/glob/glob1.htm
US Map
   http://www.zilker.net/~hal/apl-us/
Global Positioning
   http://wwwhost.cc.utexas.edu/depts/grg/gcraft/notes/gps/gps.html
Using a Map and Compass
   http://internet.er.usgs.gov/fact-sheets/finding-your-way/finding-your-way.html
Virtual Field Trips
   http://www.terraquest.com/
   http://astro.uchicago.edu/cara/vtour/mcmurdo/

Hangin' Ten: Interdisciplinary Thematic Units

Other Information Resources

Abell, Neill (1982) **Book Of Where, Or How To Be.** Naturally Geographic. Little Brown.

Carey, Helen H. (1983) **How to Use Maps & Globes.** Watts.

Couper, Heather (1987) **Telescopes & Observatories.** Watts.

Finding Your Way: Using Maps & Globes (Videocassette) (1990) Rainbow Educational Video.

Hogan, Paula Z. (1982) **The Compass.** Walker.

Knowlton, Jack (1985) **Maps & Globes.** Crowell/Harper Collins.

Madden, James F. (1977) **The Wonderful World of Maps.** Hammond.

Pollard, Michael (1986) **Finding The Way.** Schoolhouse Press, Inc.

Snow, Jon (1987) **Atlas of Today The World Behind The News.** Warwick Press.

Weiss, Harvey (1991) **Maps: Getting From Here To There.** Houghton Mifflin.

CD-ROM Resources

US Atlas 6.0, Mindscape
World Atlas 6.0, Mindscape
Children's Atlas of the United States CD, Rand McNally
Tripmaker, Rand McNally
Cartopedia CD, Dorling Kindersley
Small Blue Planet, Now What Software

Powerful Projects

Start with some teacher ideas at Missouri Botanical Garden Site (http://www.mobot.org/MBGnet/live/index.html).

Create maps showing when epals live. Include different types of maps such as political, weather, and topographical. Compare and contrast animals, plant life, food and water sources, weather, and other features.

Try virtual field trips to explore different parts of the world. Design a virtual field trip of the area where you live to share with others!

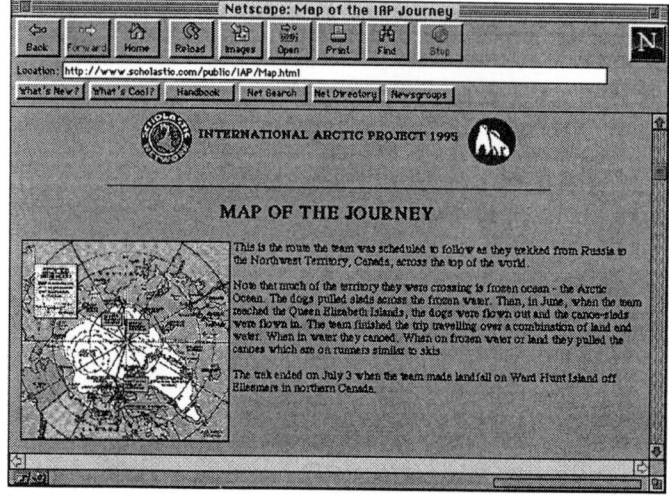

http://www.scholastic.com/public/IAP/Map.html

Visit the Great Globe Gallery!
http://hum.amu.edu.pl/~zbzw/glob/glob1.htm

Explore different types of globes through the Great Globe Gallery!

In North American we're used to seeing the globe from our perspective. Look at **different views of the globe**. Identify the continents and a few of the countries. Describe which globe people in other parts of the world might choose and why. Ask your epal about their ideas about globes.

Use the **cloud globe** picture in a report that addresses the following questions:
Why don't clouds fly off into space?
Why are there different types of clouds?
How do the clouds hold rain?
Where do thunder and lightening come from?

Examine the **seafloor globe**. Isn't it strange seeing the globe like this? Draw a picture of a globe for a fictional planet. What might the countries look like? Explain how the land and water forms evolved.

Explore the **timezone globe**. In small groups, each member should select a location and figure out the current time. Figure out a time when everyone would probably be awake for a "conference call."

Pick your **favorite globe** and describe why you think it should be the Official World Globe.

Go to **discoveries globe.** Identify who made the discoveries shown on the map.

Go to the **historical globe** and compare one of them to our current globe. Create a globe for the past, present, or future.

Explore a globe related to **weather**. Why do you think this type of globe might be useful to scientists?

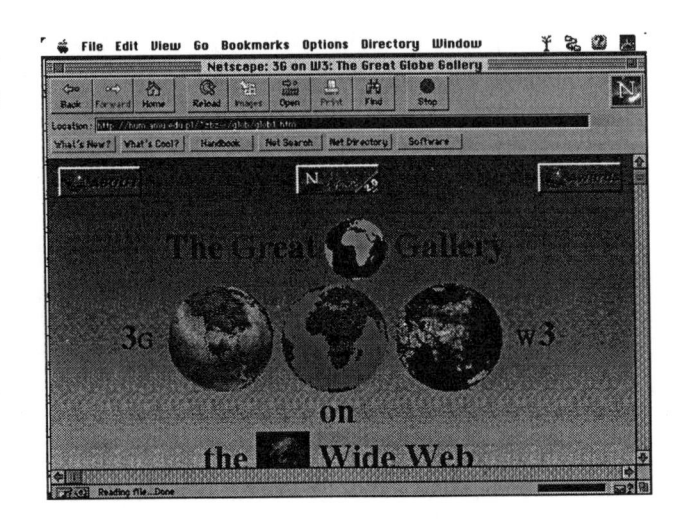

Visit the Mapmaker Site!
http://loki.ur.utk.edu/ut2kids/maps/map.html

Visit the Mapmaker, mapmaker, make me a map site!

- Make a map! Use the directions on this page to help. Make sure you include all the elements of an effective map.

- Explore the Peter Pan and Oz maps. Can you create a picture that will get you to a fictional place? Try Over the river and through the woods!

- Draw a pirate map and write a story about the treasure and how it was hidden.

- What is a cartographer? What do you like and dislike about this job? Would you like to be a cartographer? What kinds of skills would you need to be a good cartographer?

- Find the latitude and longitude of where you live and compare this with a place you'd like to visit anywhere in the world. Get help from the US Geological Survey (http://wings.buffalo.edu/geogw). You could also get a picture from the Xerox PARC (http://pubweb.parc.xerox.com/map).

- Explore the different types of maps: political, physical, road, thematic, or weather. Select a topic and create one of these maps to show it. Then write a story that includes features from the map.

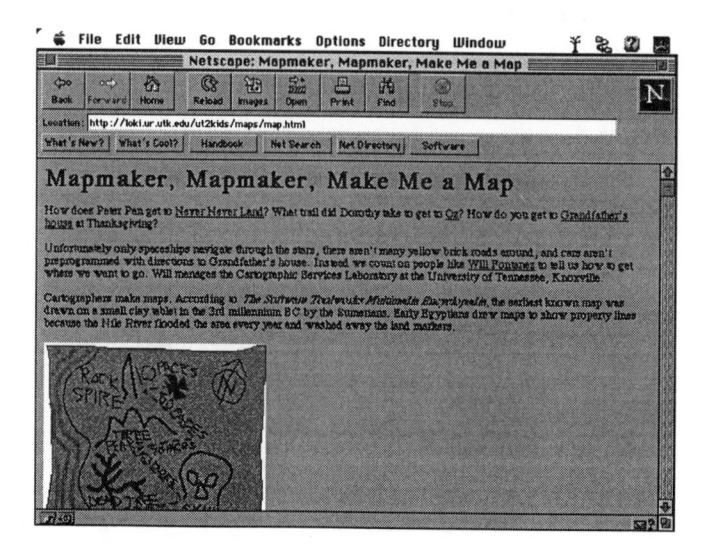

Global Community: Travel

Wouldn't it be fun to visit your epals all over the world? How do people travel from place to place?

Surfer Starters
Getting Around the Planet
   http://pathfinder.com/Travel/index.html
The Avid Explorer
   http://www.explore.com/index.html
Einet Galaxy
   http://www.einet.net/galaxy/Leisure-and-Recreation/Travel.html
The Global Network Navigator
   http://gnn.com/cgi-bin/gnn/currency/
GNN Traveler's Center
   http://nearnet.gnn.com/gnn/meta/travel/index.html
   http://gnn.com/gnn/meta/travel/index.html
The Subway Navigator
   http://metro.jussieu.fr:10001/bin/cities/english
World Traveller Books and Maps
   http://www.explore.com/wtbm/wtbm.html
GORP (Great Outdoor Recreation Page)
   http://www.gorp.com/
Traffic Site
   http://tdg.uoguelph.ca/g-police/kid_intr.html
Canadian Airlines International
   http://www.cdnair.ca
Cathay Pacific Airways
   http://www.cathay-usa.com/
Lufthansa
   http://www.tkz.fh-rpl.de/tii/lh/lhflug.html
Travel Agencies
   http://www.travelweb.com/
   http://www.charm.net:80/~aesu/
   http://mmink.cts.com/mmink/kiosks/costa/costatravel.html
   http://www.explore.com/ece.html
   http://www.happy-tours.com/
   http://www.explore.com/mat/matterhorn.html

http://www.neptune.com/index.html
http://www.explore.com/ncl/ncl.html

Grand Canyon Trip Planner
http://star.ucc.nau:80/~grandcanyon/TripPlanner/

City.Net World Map - Vitural Tourist II
http://wings.buffalo.edu/world/vt2

RailServer
http://rail.rz.uni-karlsruhe.de/rail/english.html

Florida
http://thunder.met.fsu.edu/explores/explores.html

Journey to Beijing
http://metrotel.co.uk/jvt/china1.htm

Flying Machines
http://cellini.leonardo.net/museum/flying.html#flying

Water Travel
http://www.princeton.edu/~rcurtis/rivplan.html
http://www.yahoo.com/Entertainment/Outdoors/Canoeing_Kayaking_

Sailing Page
http://www.cs.yale.edu/HTML/YALE/CS/HyPlans/loosemore-sandra/sail.html

Student project on jet aircraft.
http://longwood.cs.ucf.edu:80/~MidLink/jet.aircraft.html

Air Travel
http://www.qadas.com/airparts/
http://aviation.jsc.nasa.gov

Transportation & the Environment
http://itre.uncecs.edu/itre/cte/cte.html

US Dept of Transportation
http://www.dot.gov/

Sources of Highway Information
http://cti1.volpe.dot.gov/ohim/resource.html

Other Information Resources

Ancona, George (1985) **Freighters: Cargo Ships & The People Who Work Them**. Crowell/HarperCollins.

Bailey, Donna (1991) **Canoeing**. Steck-Vaughn.

Berliner, Don (1990) **Distance Flights**. Lerner Publications Co. Minneapolis.

Graham, Dan (1989) **Submarines**. Gloucester.

Gunning, Thomas G. (1992) **Dream Planes**. Dillon Press.

Humble, Richard (1991) **Ships, Sailors & The Sea**. Watts.

Jackson, Donald Dale (1980) **The Aeronauts**. Time-Life.
Kentley, Eric (1992) **Boat**. Knopf.
Huff, Barbara A. (1987) **Welcome Aboard: Traveling On An Ocean Liner**. Clarion.
Lincoln, Margarette (1992) **Amazing Boats**. Knopf.
Moolman, Valerie (1980) **The Road To Kitty Hawk**. Time-Life Books.
Moran, Tom (1984) **Canoeing Is For Me.** Lerner.
Pollard, Michael (1986) **Travel By Air** (Moving Around The World). Schoolhouse Press, Inc.
Steele, Philip (1991) **Boats**. Crestwood House.
The Present Day. Greenwich House.
Weiss, Harvey (1990) **Submarines & Other Underwater Craft**. HarperCollins.
Wohl, Robert (1994) **A Passion For Wings Aviation and the Western Imagination 1908-1918**. Yale University Press.

Powerful Projects

Investigate one of the following problems:

How and why do objects like planes, gliders, helicopters and other aircraft fly?

How do you fly an airplane or other type of air machine? Create step by step instructions.

Why are there more cars than planes? Will we ever have a plane in everyone's driveway? Why or why not?

What kind of equipment would make airplanes more safe? How could you make certain that everyone would survive a plane crash? What would you do in a plane crash?

How fast can planes fly? How does supersonic flight work? What's the problem with supersonic flight?

How did human flight evolve through history? Trace the history of one aspect of aviation such as hot air balloons. Compare modern aircraft with the ideas of Leonardo Da Vinci.

Which are safer, small or large planes? Why? How does weather impact air safety?

If you could visit your epal, what kind of transportation would you use from your home to their home?

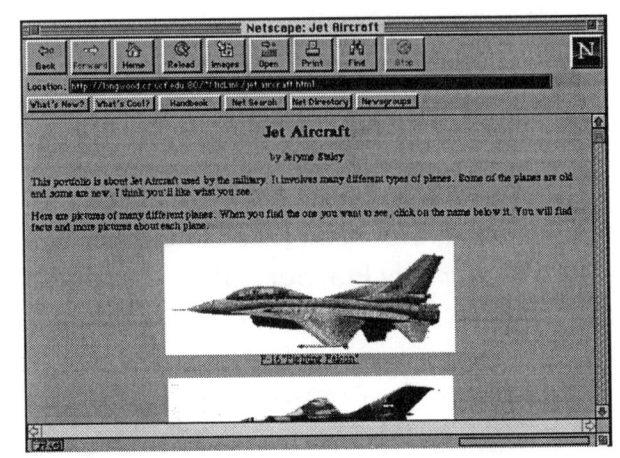

http://longwood.cs.ucf.edu:80/~MidLink/jet.aircraft.html

Create a transportation project and submit it to Midlink!

Visit the Getting Around the Planet Site!
http://pathfinder.com/Travel/index.html

Visit the Getting Around the Planet Site. If you have trouble getting in, start with pathfinder. com.

- Explore the **Bulletin Board**. Read some questions and answers. Can you help anyone? Do you have a question to post? Create a bulletin board of travel questions and answers in your classroom.

- Explore the **Travel & Leisure** magazine (http://pathfinder.com/Travel/TL/index.html). Read an article about a place you'd like to visit. Write an article about a place you've read about, a place that your epal lives, or a place you'd like to visit. Search the web to find pictures you might include in your article. Use Planet Profiles for information about specific places (http://pathfinder.com/Travel/Profiles/index.html). Be sure to include a map of your area!

- Choose a country to visit where the native language is not English. Go to the **language** section (http://pathfinder.com/Travel/language/index.html) and learn some basic words. Create a booklet of words that you think will be most valuable on your trip. Practice the words using the sound generator.

- Explore the **currency converter** (http://www.olsen.ch/cgi-bin/exmenu/pathfinder). Let's say you're buying the following items: T-shirt, Can of Coke, Candy Bar, Newspaper, Music CD, and a Book. How much would these items cost in your country's money? What about in the country you plan to visit?

- Plan a trip. Find out what the **weather** is like this time of year. Find out how much a **flight** would cost. Be sure to print out a **map** and trace the flight path!

- Try the chat section to chat with other people around the world!

Visit the US Dept of Transportation Site!
http://www.dot.gov/

Visit the US Dept of Transportation Site!

Choose a type of transportation to explore:

Bureau of Transportation Statistics - BTS

Federal Aviation Administration - FAA

Federal Highway Administration - FHWA

Federal Railroad Administration - FRA

Federal Transit Administration - FTA

National Highway Traffic Safety Administration - NHTSA

Maritime Administration - MARAD

Research & Special Programs Administration - RSPA

United States Coast Guard - USCG

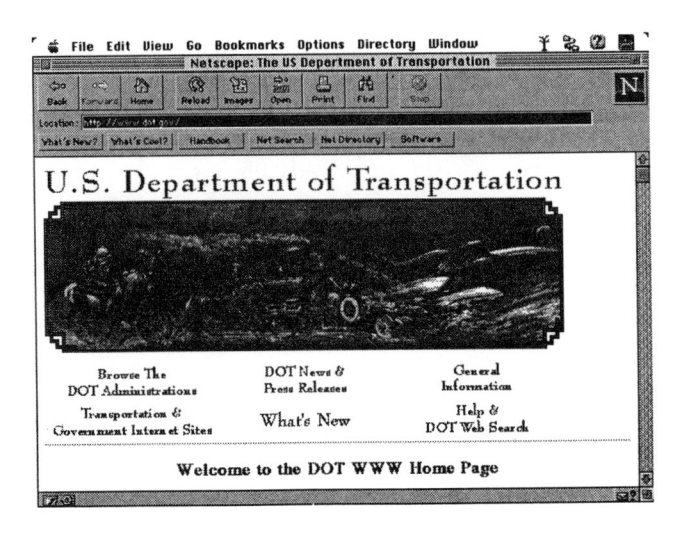

Global Community: Where We Live

Where do you live? People throughout the world live in many different types of homes. They are made of many different materals. Explore the places where people live. Use epals to collect and share information about the places we live.

Surfer Starters
Architecture
   http://darkwing.uoregon.edu/~struct/
   http://www.clr.toronto.edu:1080/VIRTUALLIB/archALL.html
Student project from Houston
   http://chico.rice.edu/armadillo/Rice/joelsclass/skyscraper.html
Castles
   http://www.nectec.or.th/rec-travel/europe/castles
   http://www.gmd.de/GMD/Schloss.en.html

Other Information Resources
Baker, John (1994) **American House Styles: A Concise Guide.** W.W.Norton.
Brand, Stewart **How Buildings Learn: What Happens After They're Built.** Viking.
Ceserani, Gian Paolo, & Ventura, Piero (1983) **Grand Constructions.** Putnam.
Clements, Gillian (1990) **Truth About Castles.** Carobehoda.
Goodall, John S. (1986) **Story of a Castle.** McElderry.
Hale, Jonathan (1994) **The Old Way of Seeing.** Houghton Mifflin.
Isaacson, Philip M. (1988) **Round Buildings, Square Buildings, & Buildings That Wiggle.** Knopf.
James, Alan (1989) **Castles & Mansions.** Lerner.
James, Cary (1990) **Julia Morgan: Architect.** Chelsea House.
Macaulay, David (1977) **Castles.** Houghton Mifflin.
MacDonald, Fiona (1990) **Medieval Castle.** Peter Bedrick.
Michael, Duncan (1987) **How Skyscrapers Are Made.** Facts On File.
Sancha, Sheila (1982) **The Castle Story.** Harper.
Sharp, Dennis (1991) **Twentieth Century Architecture: A Visual History.** Facts On File.
Smith, Beth (1988) **Castles** Watts.
Wilcox, Charlotte (1990) **Skyscraper Story.** Carolrhoda.
Wood, Tim (1990) **Castles.** Warwick/Watts.

CD-ROM Resources
Imagination Express: Castles CD, Edmark

Powerful Projects
Investigate one of the following problems:

What do the words shelter, home, and environment mean? Can you help the homeless find shelter and a home? Design an environment for the homeless.

How would you go about fixing up a historial site? Would you choose renovation, restoration, or reconstruction? Why? Explore some of the National Historic sites to find out how this is done.

What kind of building do you like the best? Explore famous castles, cathedrals, or other types of famous buildings.

How are houses designed? Compare different types of housing construction and design such as a log house, skyscraper, or underground house.

What would you like to design? Design a shopping mall, vacation resort, or amusement park.

How would you design a museum? Choose a person, place, or topic and design a museum.

What are the different forms of architecture? Describe the rise and fall of a popular type of architecture such as Baroque, Byzantine, or Gothic architecture. Create you own type that combines the best of your favorite styles.

What can people do to help their homes withstand natural disasters such as fires, floods, earthquakes, or hurricanes? Choose a disaster and describe what you would do when designing a new house or updating an older house.

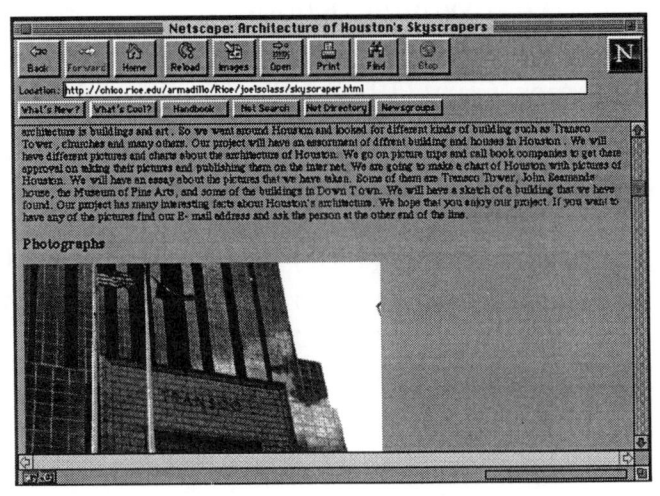

http://chico.rice.edu/armadillo/Rice/joelsclass/skyscraper.html

Hangin' Ten: Interdisciplinary Thematic Units

Visit the This Old House Site!
http://pathfinder.com/TOH/

Explore information about architecture and building homes. If you have trouble getting into pathfinder, start at the main page at pathfinder.com.

Explore the **This Old House Site!**
http://pathfinder.com/TOH/

Go to the **Bulletin Board**. Select a topic of interest. Read the discussion and ask a question! Start a "home helps" column for parents in your school newspaper.

Explore the **Encyclopedia**.
Can you find something that helps answer a question you have about where you live?

Try the Trivia Quiz.

Explore Interesting Links. Plan an extension to the place where you live. How much would it cost? Read the Money article about financing for remodeling.

Visit the Frank Lloyd Wright Site.
http://flw.badgernet.com/flw

Why do you think he's called the greatest 20th century architect? Do you like his work? Why or why not? Design a shelter applying some of his techniques.

Choose a picture from is gallery that you think reflects Wright's best work. Why do you think this is a good example of his work?

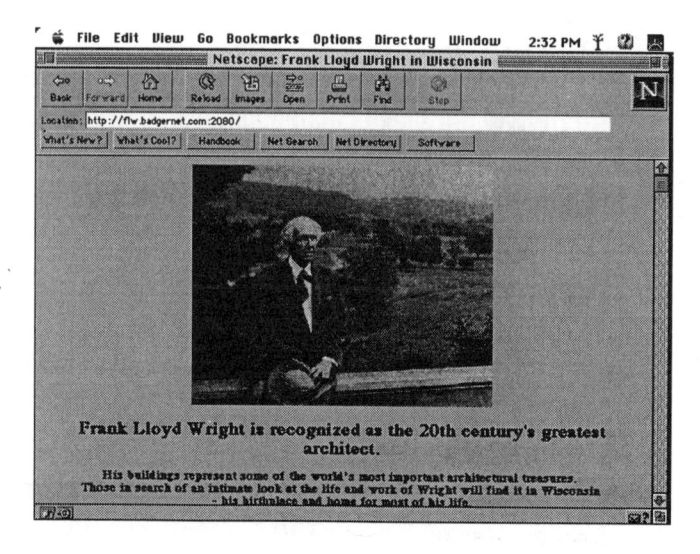

Global Community: Cultural Diversity

The global community starts with your family. Who are members of your immediate family? What about your extended family? Where are your family's roots? Are these roots important? Why or why not? Explore the world of family.

Surfer Starters

Genealogy and Families

Family and Genealogy Sites
   http://WWW.Trinity.Edu/~mkearl/family.html

Emigration/Immigration
   http://www.usc.edu/users/help/flick/Reference/immig_main/html
   http://rs6.loc.gov/wpaintro/wpahome.html

Families Lessons
   http://gnn.com/gnn/meta/edu/curr/rdg/gen_act/family/index.html

White House: First family
   http://www.whitehouse.gov/White_House/Family/html/Life.html

Geneology
   http://www.xmission.com/~Jayhall/
   http://alexia.lis.uiuc.edu/~helm/si.html
   http://www.ncgr.org:80/sigma/home.html
   http://alexia.lis.uiuc.edu/~helm/genealogy.html

Ellis Island Virtual Museum
   http://wwwald.bham.wednet.edu/museum/museum.htm

Multicultural Sites

African-American Experience
   http://lcweb.loc.gov/exhibits/African.American/intro.html
   http://www.hotwired.com/rough/usa/south/basics.html

African Americans: Universal Black Pages
   http://www.gatech.edu/bgsa/blackpages.html

African American Pioneers
   http://www.localnet.com/~adonis/pioall.htm

Continuum
   http://www.tcm.org/clubhouse/projects/continuum/index.html

Multicultural
   http://www.bin.com/
   http://lcweb.loc.gov/exhibits/African.American/intro.html
   gopher://marvel.loc.gov:70/11/global/socsci/area/afro

Civil Rights Museum
   http://d0sgi0.fnal.gov/~oconnell/support/mac/net/WEB/NCRM/NCRM.HTM

Other Information Resources
Genealogy and Families
Berger, Melvin (1993) **Where Did Your Family Come From? A Book About Immigrants**. Ideals.

Bresnick-Perry, Roslyn (1992) **Leaving for America**. Childrens Book Press.

Caney, Steven (1978) **Steven Caneys Kid's America.** Workman.

Cooper, Kay (1988) **Where Did You Get Those Eyes?** Walker.

Fisher, Leonard Everett (1986) **Ellis Island Gateway to the New World**. Holiday House.

Gamlin, LInda (1988) **Life On Earth**. Gloucester.

Jacobs, William Jay (1990) **Ellis Island: New Hope In A New Land.** Scribners.

Kurelek, William (1985) **They Sought A New World: The Story Of European Immigration To North America**. Tundra.

Martinet, Jeanne (1992) **The Year You Were Born 1984, 1985, 1986, 1987**. Tambourine.

Perl, Lila (1989) **Great Ancestor Hunt: The Fun of Finding Out Who You Are**. Clarion.

Rosenberg, Maxine B. (1986) **Making A New Home in America**. Lothrop, Lee, & Shepard.

Paten, Dorothy Hinshaw (1989) **Grandfather's Nose: Why We Look Alike Or Different**. Watts.

Wolfman, Ira (1991) **Do People Grow On Family Trees? Geneology For Kids & Other Beginners - The Official Ellis Island Handbook**. Workman.

Multicultural Resources
Brown, Tricia (1991) **LeeAnn, The Story Of A Vietnamese-American Girl**. Putnam.

Hamilton, Virginia (1993) **Many Thousand Gone: African Americans from Slavery To Freedom**. Alfred A. Knopf.

Hewett, Joan (1990) **Hector Lives In The United States Now: The Story Of A Mexican-American Child.** Lippincott/ Harper Collins.

James, Portia P. (1989) **The Real McCoy: African-American Invention & Innovation 1619-1930.** Smithsonian Institution.

Katz, William L. (1993) **A History of Multicultural America - Minorities Today**. Raintree Steck-Vaughn.

Katz, William Loren (1990) **Breaking The Chains: African-American Resistance**. Atheneum.

Kosof, Anna (1989) **The Civil Rights Movement and It's Legacy**. Franklin Watts.

Meltzer, Milton (1984) **Black Americans: A History In Their Own Words 1619-1983**. Crowell/ HarperCollins.

Pascoe, Elaine (1985) **Issues in American History - Racial Prejudice**. Franklin Watts.

Meltzer, Milton (1984) **Black Americans: A History in Their Own Words**. Harper-Collins.

Meltzer, Milton (1982) **Jewish Americans: A HIstory In Their Own Words**. 1650-1950). HarperCollins.

Meltzer, Milton (1980) **Chinese Americans**. HarperCollins.

Mettger, Zak (1994) **Till Victory Is Won: Black Soldiers In The Civil War**. Lodestar Books Dutton.

Reynolds, Barbara A. (1988) **And Still We Rise: Interviews with 50 Black Role Models**. USA Today Books.

Smead, Howard (1989) **The Afro-Americans Series: The Peoples of North America** Chelsia House.

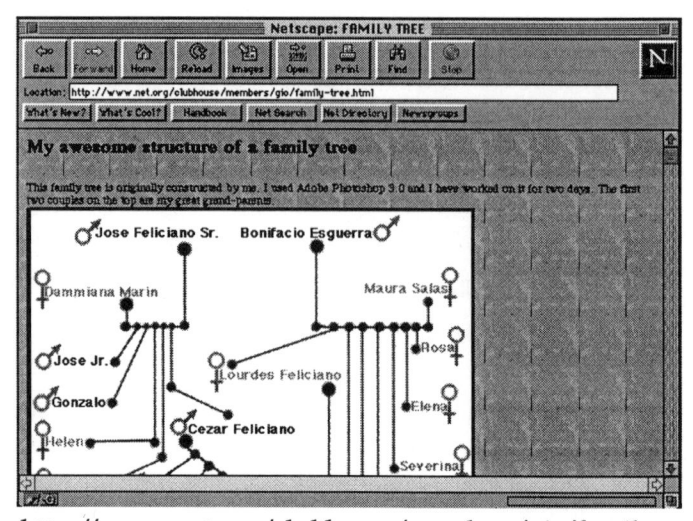

http://www.net.org/clubhouse/members/gio/family-tree.html

Visit Black History Page!
http://pathfinder.com/pathfinder/features/blackhistory/

Explore the Black History Page.

http://pathfinder.com/pathfinder/features/blackhistory/

Take a virtual visit of the **Savory Gallery**. Which work of art did you enjoy the most? Why? Who was the artist? Why do you think he or she choose this particular subject? How does this work reflect the heritage of the artist?

Read the chat with **Darrell Dawey**. What would you like to ask this person? What do you think he'd say? Do you agree with his perspectives? Why or why not?

Explore the **Savory Poll**. Select one of the top twenty people to explore. Why do you think this person is in the top twenty? Why do you think this person has had an impact on our world? What personal characteristics make this person special? If you were going to nominate someone from your community for an award that would reflect his or her contributions, who would you choose? Why?

Examine the photographs of Harlem. What would you take pictures of in your community? Why?

Explore NetNoir (http://www.netnoir.com/index.html). Identify those aspects of the sight that reflect African-American culture.

Read African stories (http://www.netnoir.com/emp/edu/story/index.html). Explore how stories change as they move from culture to culture. Contact an epal in another country. Are any of their folktales similiar to the ones you've read as a child? What themes appear around the world?

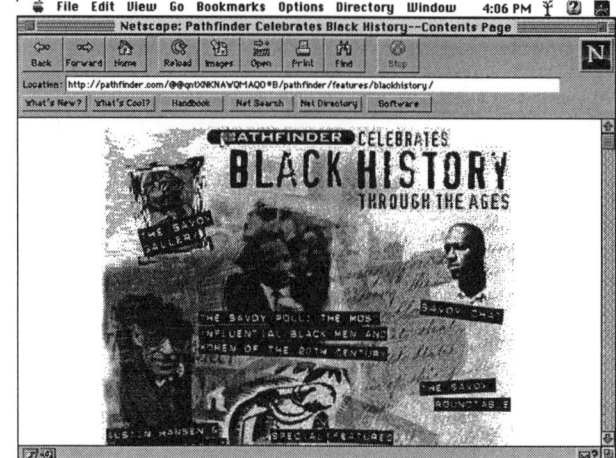

Visit the American Immigration Site!
http://www.bergen.gov/AAST/Projects/Immigration/index.html

Explore the American Immigration Page.

In small groups, explore one of the following time periods:

1607-1830   1830-1890   1890-1924   1968-Present

Explore the following topics for your time period:

Reasons for immigration
Who were/are the immigrants to the U.S.?
Peaks/waves of immigration
Methods of transportation and ports of arrival
Process of entering the U.S.
Destination/places where they settled
Treatment/reception by other Americans
Effects/impact on America (positive and negative)
Opportunities for and success of immigrants
Assimilation? If so, to what degree?
What did/do immigrants find distinctive about America?
Legal vs. illegal immigrants
Laws restricting immigration

Our Environment

People, plants, and animals all live in a precious environment. It's our responsiblity to protect our environment for future generations. Our second thematic project explores issues related to our environment.

This theme contains four main elements.

The Great Outdoors
We begin with an exploration of the great outdoors. The Internet contains lots of information about parks and recreation areas. You can also explore the wilderness through literature. Information about authors and their works is available online. There are many groups that post information about the environment including all types of creatures and their habitats.

Mostly Ocean!
A large part of our world is under water. These activities explore life in our rivers, seas, and oceans.

The Impact of Disasters
Natural and human made disasters have a major impact on our environment. Explore the world of volcanoes and earthquakes.

Let's Save It!
Students can play an important role in saving our fragile planet. Encourage students to become involved through exploration of Internet sites that promote taking action to save the environment.

Our Environment: The Great Outdoors

Students enjoy exploring nature and the great outdoors. Projects that encourage students to explore parks and other natural resources can incorporate all subject areas.

Surfer Starters
http://www.gorp.com/gorp/resource/US_national_park/main.htm
http://www.nbs.nau.edu/Parks/parks.html
http://www.mindspring.com/~ahearn/smoky.html

Grand Canyon
http://www.kbt.com/gc/gc_home.html
http://star.ucc.nau.edu:80/~grandcanyon/TripPlanner/

GORP
http://www.gorp.com/gorp/resource/main.htm

National Wildlife Federation
http://www.igc.apc.org/nwf/

Other Information Resources

America's Western National Parks (Videocassette) (1990) Finley-Holiday Films.
Arnold, Caroline (1988) **Walk On The Great Barrier Reef**. Carolrhoda.
Frew, Tim (1991) **America's Natural Wonders**. Gallery Books.
Gregson, Lionel (1985) **Wonders of The World**. Gallery Books.
Kids Explore America's National Parks (Videocassette) (1991) Children's International Network.
Mackintosh, Barry (1987) **The National Park Service**. Chelsea House.
Mattews, Rupert (1988) **The Atlas of Natural Wonders**. Facts On File.
O'Neill, Catherine (1984) **Natural Wonders of North America**. National Geographic Society.
Sierra Club Desert Southwest (1984) Stewart, Tabori & Chang.
Sierra Club (1984) **Rocky Mountains & The Great Plains**. Stewart, Tabori & Chang.
Siy, Alexandra (1991) **Artic National Wildlife Refuge**. Dillon.
Smallwood, Carol (1989) **Educational Guide to the National Park System**. Scarecrow.
Stone, Lynn M. (1989) **Deserts**. Rourke.
Stone, Lynn M. (1989) **Mountains**. Rourke.
Whitney, Stephen (1982) **Field Guide To The Grand Canyon**. Quill/ Morrow.
Young, Donald (1990) **Sierra Club Book of Our National Parks**. Sierra Club.

Visit the GORP!
http://www.gorp.com/default.htm

Explore the GORP page and try the following activities. Use the words in bold to help you find the information you need for each activity. This web site contains lots of graphics, so it may be slow.

Go to the attractions and read about some of the National Parks. Select one you would like to visit and one you wouldn't want to visit. Explain why.

Visit some of the **National Forests**. It's important to save our forests. Create a poster for one of these forests. Describes it's features and the importance of saving it.

Visit the **US Wilderness Areas**. Select one area and describe the animals that live there. Write about a day in the life of one of these animals.

Visit a **US Wildlife Refuge**. What's the purpose of a wildlife refuge? Discuss an animal that lives in one of these refuges and why this is important.

Visit the **National Monuments**. Plan a trip to visit three of these national monuments. You only have four days. Will you fly or take a car? Why did you pick these three monuments?

Visit the **Archeological & Paleontological Sites**. Learn more about the people or creatures that once lived at one of these sites. Draw a picture of what the area might have looked like when it was "alive" with activity.

Visit the **National Historic Parks**. Write down the address and write a letter to one of the parks asking for more information.

Visit the **National Recreation Areas**. Locate one of these areas on a map. If you could spend the weekend at this site, what would you do?

Visit the **National Seashore Area**. Locate one of these areas on a map. Describe the sea creatures that live in this area. Create a chart showing the life cycle of one of these creatures.

Visit the **National Battlefield Parks**. Create a timeline showing when this battle took place in comparison to other battles of the war. Why was this battle important enough to become a National Battlefield?

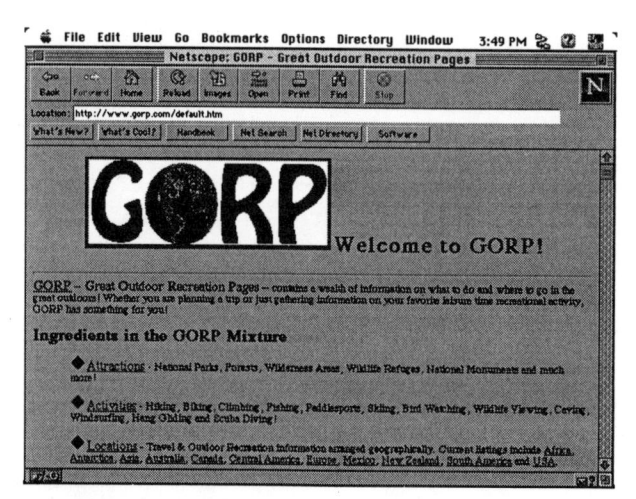

http://www.gorp.com/

Visit the Wilderness through Literature!
http://www.computek.net/public/barr/wilderness.html

Explore the Wilderness through Literature. This web site has a wealth of resources and activities related to the wilderness and literature.

Select one of the following areas to explore:

  Edward Abbey

  Willa Cather

  Emerson and Thoreau

  Moby Dick

  Robert Frost

  Edgar Allen Poe

Identify your own example of wilderness in literature. Why did you choose this area? Does the person or work take a particular enviromental position? Provide examples.

Select a book for younger children related to the wilderness. How could you use this piece of literature to promote environmental awareness?

Have people's attitudes about the role of the environment changed over the years? Compare works written during different times in our history.

Create a bulletin board that shows the best of wilderness literature. You might include authors, titles of works, poems, reviews, and quotes.

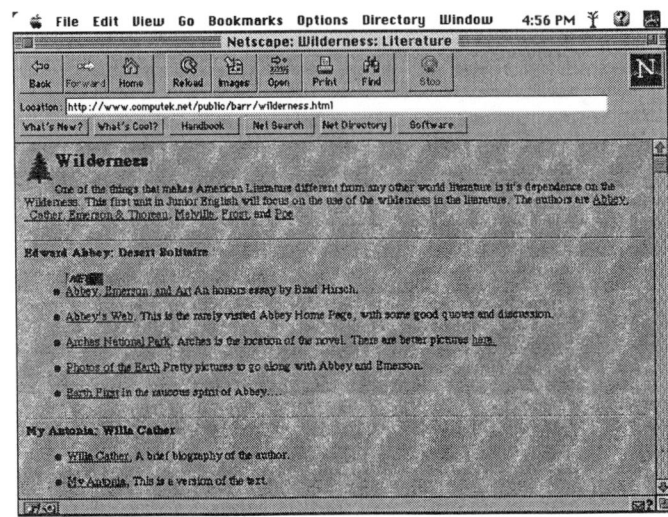

Visit the National Wildlife Federation!
http://www.igc.apc.org/nwf/

Explore the National Wildlife Federation.

Select one of the following areas to explore:

Issues and Actions: Check the Action Alert area for current topics of concern. Select a topic that concerns you personally and find out how you can take action. Create a plan for presenting your ideas to a local, regional, or national group who might be able to implement your change.

In the Classroom: Find out about one of the following areas: Air, Habitat, People and the Environment, Wildlife and Endangered Species or Water.

On-line Library:
Read one of the National Wildlife Federation Position Papers in the online reports section. Do you agree or disagree with their stand on the issue? Hold a class debate. Each person should represent the position of a different person that would be affected by any proposed change.
Explore one of the following magazines - Ranger Rick, National Wildlife, International Wildlife, or Your Big Backyard. Write an article about an issue that could be published in one of these magazines.

Adventure and Entertainment: Explore the activities that are available. If you could participate in one of these programs, which would you choose? Why?

For Kids! Games and Riddles: Just for fun, play some games. Which are your favorite? Rate the games and share your favorites with a friend. Create your own wildlife game!

Wetlands Project: Explore the wetlands pages. Are there areas near you that need to be protected? Take action on an environmental project close to home!

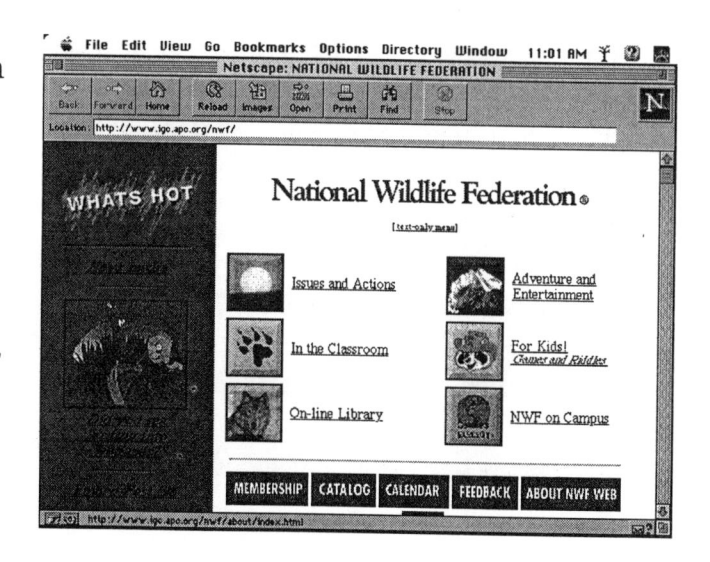

Our Environment: Mostly Ocean!

Much of our world is covered with water. Oceans cover much of our planet and are an exciting topic to explore.

Surfer Starters

Lesson plan and classroom ideas
   http://www.hmco.com/hmco/school/links/theme_14.html
Safari Splash
   http://oberon.educ.sfu.ca/splash.htm
Great Barrier Reef
   http://www.erin.gov.au/portfolio/gbrmpa/gbrmpa.html
Research Ship
   http://longwood.cs.ucf.edu:80/~MidLink/baldrige.home.html
Deep-sea diving expedition - Jason Project
   http://seawifs.gsfc.nasa.gov/JASON/HTML/JASON_7_HOME.html
Ocean Links
   http://seawifs.gsfc.nasa.gov/JASON/HTML/JASON_7_LINKS.html
Student project on whales and dolphins
   http://longwood.cs.ucf.edu:80/~MidLink/whale.html
Whales Adoption Project
   http://www.webcom.com/~iwcwww/whale_adoption/waphome.html
Whales Thematic Unit
   http://www.webcom.com/~iwcwww/whale_adoption/waphome.html
Dolphins
   http://wjh-www.harvard.edu/~furmansk/dolphin.html
Student project on marine life
   http://longwood.cs.ucf.edu:80/~MidLink/marine.life.html
Oceans
   http://seawifs.gsfc.nasa.gov/ocean_planet.html
Oceania
   http://oceania.org/
FINS: Everything you want to know about fish
   http://www.actwin.com/fish/index.html
Explore a fish tank
   http://oberon.educ.sfu.ca/splash/tank.htm
Sea World
   http://www.bev.net/education/SeaWorld/

TOPEX/Poseidon Project
    http://quest.arc.nasa.gov/topex/welcome.html
Oceanography
    http://www.rsmas.miami.edu/iof.html
Underwater World
    http://pathfinder.com/pathfinder/kidstuff/underwater/

Other Information Resources

Jaspersohn, William (1982) **Day In The Life of a Marine Biologist**. Little, Brown.
Mattson, Robert A. (1991) **Living Ocean**. Enslow.
Oceans: Exploring Earth's Last Frontier (Sound Filmstrip) (1986) National Geographic.
Rice Tony (1991) **Ocean World**. Dorset Press.
Simon, Seymour (1990) **Oceans**. Morrow.
Souza, D. M. (1992) **Powerful Waves**. Carolrhoda.
Snyderman, Marty (1991) **Ocean Life-Discovering The World Beneath The Seas**. Publications International.
Wu, Norbert (1991) **Life in the Oceans**. Little, Brown.

CD-ROM and Laserdisc Resources

Eco-adventures in the Oceans
The Great Ocean Rescue, Laserdisc
Imagination Express: Oceans
In the Company of Whales
Ocean Escape
Ocean Planet
Oceans Below
Microsoft Oceans
Sharks
Sumeria's Ocean Life: Hawaiian Island
Sumeria's Ocean Life: Caribbean
Tale of the Whale
Undersea Adventure
Whales and Dolphins 2.0

Oceans Below

Powerful Projects

Explore life under the oceans by examining some of the following questions:

What's an ocean? What lives in the ocean? Why? What's at the bottom of the ocean?

How do ocean currents effect land formations?

What kinds of creatures live near the coral reef?

What are the food web and food chain of the ocean.

How do sea creatures relate to each other? Describe relationships among sea creatures.

How are dophins like humans? How do whales and dolphins communicate?

What happens during an oil spill? How does it impact the environment? What are other causes of water pollution? How can humans prevent ocean pollution?

What are the concerns involved with seal hunting, whale hunting, and other water-related hunting issues? What role do groups such as Greenpeace play in the protection of our oceans?

http://www.actwin.com/fish/index.html

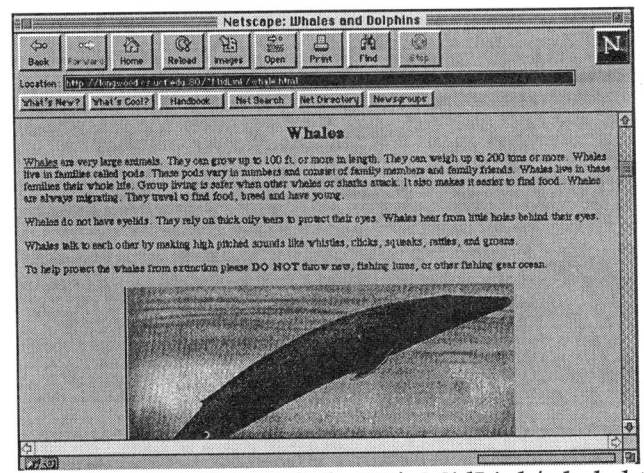

http://longwood.cs.ucf.edu:80/~MidLink/whale.html

Visit the Underwater World Site!
http://pathfinder.com/pathfinder/kidstuff/underwater/

Visit the Underwater World Site!

Explore the **Lost in a Forgotten Sea: A Diving Adventure**.
Create a map showing the location of your underwater adventure.
Choose one of the sea creatures from your dive and learn more about it. How does it move? How does it protect itself? Who are its friends and enemies? Create a HyperStudio stack that uses the picture from your dive.

Explore the **Monterey Bay Aquarium**.
Choose one sea creature from the aquarium. Draw a picture showing the habitat where this creature lives.
Label all the elements of the habitat. What types of fish would you put into an aquarium?

Explore some **Fishy Questions**! Try the quiz. Create a bulletin board showing the questions and answers.

Explore **How Big Is It's Bite?** Draw a picture of your teeth next to shark teeth. How are our teeth like and unlike a shark's tooth? If you were a shark, which type would you be, why?

Explore the **Freaky Fishes Family Album**. After you've studied the different kinds of sea creatures, use this section to match the pictures and names!

Our Environment: The Impact of Disasters

Disasters have an impact on people, places, and things. Explore science and social issues related to natural disasters. Discuss disaster preparation.

Surfer Starters

Disaster Links
  http://www.hmco.com/hmco/school/links/theme_3.html
Disaster Preparation
  http://www.ag.uiuc.edu/~disaster/resource.html
Japanese students write about the impact of the earthquake on their lives
  http://www.kobe-cufs.ac.jp/kobe-city/school/fukiai/opinion.html
General Disaster Information
  http://www.redcross.org/disaster/comm_ed/community.html
  gopher://nisee.ce.berkely.edu/
  http://vulcan.wr.usgs.gov/home.html
  http://www.med.umich.edu/aacap/after.disaster.html
  http://wcmc.org.uk:80/~latenews/
  http://www.alaska.net/~ospic/
  http://www.alaska.net/~ospic/status.html
  http://www.intellicast.com/weather/intl/wxintl.html
Hurricane Chart
  http://lumahai.soest.hawaii.edu/Tropical_Weather/atlantic_track.gif
Earthquakes
  http://wwwneic.cr.usgs.gov/
  http://www.injersey.com/Media/IonSci/features/quakes/quakes.html
  http://quake.wr.usgs.gov/
  http://www.geophys.washington.edu/seismosurfing.html
Hurricanes
  http://www.injersey.com/Media/IonSci/features/hurr/hurr.html
  http://mizar.crossnet.org/arc/what/disaster/hcane.htm
  http://www.fema.gov/fema/hurricaf.html
Hurricane Student Project
  http://longwood.cs.ucf.edu:80/~MidLink/hurricanes.html
Jason Project: Volcano in Hawaii
  http://seawifs.gsfc.nasa.gov/JASON/HTML/JASON_6_HOME.html
Volcanoes
  http://vulcan.wr.usgs.gov/photo_list.html
  http://www.rspac.ivv.nasa.gov/space/hawaii/virtual.field.trips.html

    http://volcano.und.nodak.edu/
Floods
    http://www.amdahl.com/internet/events/ca-1-95-floods.html
National Severe Storms Laboratory
    http://www.nssl.uoknor.edu/
Tsunami
    http://tsunami.ce.washington.edu/tsunami/general/historic/historic.html
Earthquake Animation
    http://www.abag.ca.gov/bayarea/eqmaps/animation.html
El Nino Watch
    http://topex-www.jpl.nasa.gov/ninowatch/index.html

Other Information Resources

Arnold, C. (1988). **Coping With Natural Disasters**. Walker & Co.
Berger, M. (1981). **Disastrous Floods and Tidal Waves**. Watts.
Berry, J. (1990). **About Disasters**. Childrens Press.
Billings, H. (1990). **Great Disasters**. Steck-Vaughn.
Boehm, B. (1980). **Connecticut Low**. Houghton Mifflin.
Coatsworth, E. (1974). **All-of-a-Sudden Susan**. Macmillan.
Fodor, R.V. (1980). **Angry Waters: Floods and Their Control**. Dodd, Mead.
Fradin, D. (1982). **Floods**. Childrens Press.
Gilson, J. (1989). **Hobie Hanson, Greatest Hero of the Mall**. Lothrop, Lee and Shepard Books.
Lyon, G.E. (1990). **Come a Tide**. Orchard Books.
Markle, S. (1993). **A Rainy Day**. Orchard Books.
Milton, H. (1983). **Tornado!** Watts.
National Geographic Society (1982). **Our Violent Earth**. National Geographic Society.
Olesky, W. (1982). **Nature Gone Wild!** Messner.
Parker, M.J. (1990). **City Storm**. Scholastic.
Ruckman, I. (1984). **Night of the Twisters.** Crowell.
Ruckman, I. (1988). **No Way Out**. Crowell.
Stolz, M. (1988). **Storm in the Night**. Harper & Row.
Sobol, D. (1979). **Disaster**. Pocket Books.
Wignell, E. (1989). **Escape By Deluge**. Holiday House.

Visit VolcanoWorld!
http://volcano.und.nodak.edu/

Explore the world of volcanoes. Teachers can explore lots of great lesson plans to go with this site (http://volcano.und.nodak.edu/vwdocs/vwlessons/lesson.html)!

- Create a wall chart and model showing how a volcano works! Use the information in **What is VolcanoWorld?** for help!
- Create a world map showing recent volcanic activity. Use **Volcanoes of the World** for ideas. In small groups, study a part of the world where a volcano is active. Email someone in the area and see what they think about living so close to an active volcano. Are they worried? Are they ready for an eruption? How are they preparing for a possible eruption?
- Where is the closest **Volcanic Park or Monument** from where you live? How far is it from where you live? If the volcano erupted, would you see evidence where you live? What and how?
- Study the **impact of volcanoes** in our world. Choose one of the following areas to explore: plant succession, animal behavior, evolutionary and geologic processes, ecology, weather patterns and environmental issues.
  Create a two-sided hanging poster that shows "before" and "after".
  Make a timeline showing the long term impacts of volcanoes.
- Explore the **glossary**. Create an alphabet book for younger students that uses each letter of the alphabet to explain volcanic terms. How could you explain to students in pictures and words the impact of a volcano?
- Explore the **Mount St. Helen's Volcano** site. How did the Mount St. Helen's volcano change the people who live in the area? Email students at a school near the volcano and ask them about the disaster.
- Read some **student projects** about volcanoes. Pick a topic and send in your own ideas!
- Explore **other volcano sites**. Create a set of questions to go with one of the volcano sites. Create a HyperStudio stack containing questions and answers about your favorite volcano.
- Join the **volcano contest**!
- Learn about becoming a **volcanologist** and ask a volcanologist a question!

Visit Earthquake Sites!
http://www.injersey.com/Media/IonSci/features/quakes/quakes.html

Explore the impact of earthquakes on people and the places they live.

Explore the **Earthquake Site**.
http://www.injersey.com/Media/IonSci/features/quakes/quakes.html

- Learn about the history of earthquakes. Create a timeline showing some of the worst earthquakes. Create a world map showing the most likely places for earthquakes. Why are there so many earthquakes in these areas?
- What would happen if an earthquake hit your area? Are you prepared? How would you prepare your family for a disaster?
- Contact an epal and ask about disaster dangers where they live. How are their preparations alike and different from the ones you've developed for your disaster.
- Learn about how and why earthquakes happen. Create a HyperStudio stack on earthquakes. include the animations that show how the earth moves.

Find out about the **Impact of Earthquakes** on people.
http://www.kobe-cufs.ac.jp/kobe-city/school/fukiai/opinion.html

- Read the stories by Japanese students about their experiences during the great earthquake.
- Write about your experiences dealing with disaster. Or, write a fictional story based on a real-life disaster.

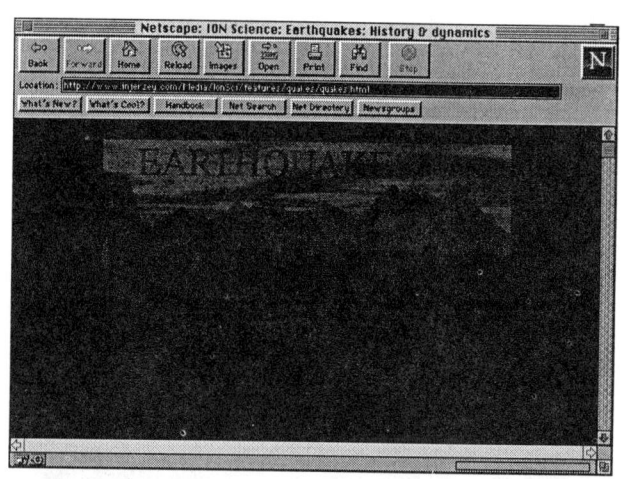

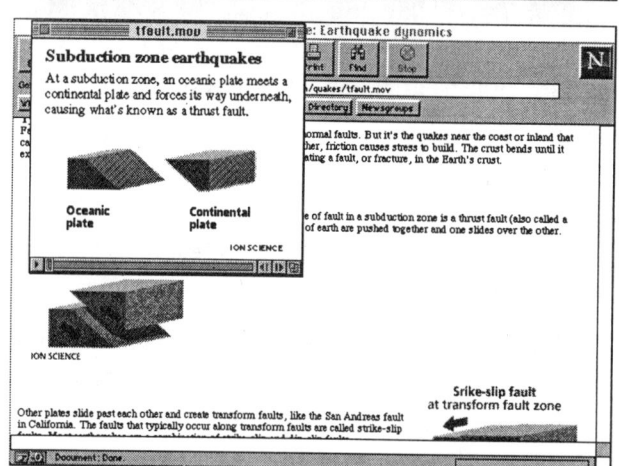

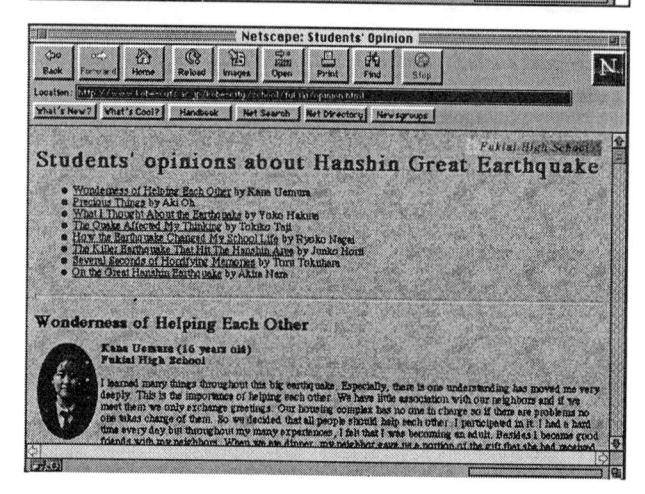

Our Environment: Let's Save It!

Use Internet to explore issues related to saving our environment.

Surfer Starters

Children and the Environment
- http://snowwhite.it.bton.ac.uk/icc/icc.html
- http://solstice.crest.org/environment/eol/resources/resources.html
- http://solstice.crest.org/environment/eol/energy/energy.html
- http://mh.osd.wednet.edu/

Environmental Awareness Lessons
- http://gnn.com/gnn/meta/edu/curr/rdg/gen_act/earth/index.html
- http://www.nceet.snre.umich.edu/index.html

Envirolink
- http://www.envirolink.org/about.html

SeaWorld Alerts
- http://www.bev.net/education/SeaWorld/nature_at_risk/natendang.html

ERIN (Australian Environmental Group)
- http://www.erin.gov.au/erin.html

Student project
- http://longwood.cs.ucf.edu:80/~MidLink/conserv.html

Jason Project
- http://seawifs.gsfc.nasa.gov/JASON/HTML/JASON_5_HOME.html
- http://llmh.osd.wednet.edu/
- http://www.igc.org/ran/kids_action/index.html
- http://www.bev.net/education/SeaWorld/tropical_forests/tropicalfor.html

Rainforest Action Network
- http://www.ran.org/ran/kids_action/animals.html

Environment
- http://snowwhite.it.bton.ac.uk/icc/icc.html
- http://solstice.crest.org/environment/eol/resources/resources.html
- http://solstice.crest.org/environment/eol/energy/energy.html

Forests
- http://www.sky.net/~emily/plant-it.html
- http://solstice.crest.org/environment/eol/forests/forest.html

Tree of Life
- http://phylogeny.arizona.edu/tree/phylogeny.html

Wetlands
- http://www.globalone.net/fcar/

Other Information Resources

Banks, Martin (1989) **Conserving Rain Forests.** Steck-Vaughn Library.

Branley, Franklin M. (1989) **What Happened To The Dinosaurs.** HarperCollins.

Dorros, Arthur (1990) **Rain Forest Secrets.** Scholastic.

Druse, Kenneth (1994) **The Natural Habitat Garden.** Clarkson Potter.

George, Jean Craighead (1990) **One Day In The Tropical Rain Forest.** Crowell/Harper Collins.

Gibbons, Gail (1994) **Nature's Green Umbrella: Tropical Rain Forests.** Morrow Junior Books.

Greenaway, Theresa (1994) **Jungle.** Knopf.

Grove, Noel (1984) **Wild Lands For Wildlife: America's National Refuges.** National Geographic.

Gutnik, Martin (1984) **Ecology.** Watts.

Hacker, Randi (1992) **Habitats: Where The Wild Things Live.** J. Muir Pub.

Hoff, Mary King (1991) **Our Endangered Planet; Life On Land.** Lerner.

Hiscock, Bruce (1991) **Big Tree.** Atheneum.

Jaspersohn, William (1980) **How The Forest Grew.** Greenwillow.

Jorgenson, Lisa (1992) **Grand Trees of America: Our State & Champion Trees.** Roberts Rinehart.

Lambert, David (1985) **Planet Earth 2000.** Facts On File.

Landau, Elaine (1990) **Tropical Rain Forests Around The World.** Watts.

Lerner, Carol (1987) **Forest Year.** Morrow.

Lewis, Scott (1990) **Rainforest Book: How You Can Save The World's Rainforests.** Living Planet Press.

Little, Jr., Elbert L. (1980) **Audubon Society Field Guide To North American Trees Eastern Region.** Knopf.

McVey, Vicki (1993) **The Sierra Club Kid's Guide To Planet Care & Repair.** Sierra Club books For Children.

Nations, James D. (1988) **Tropical Rainforests: Endangered Environment.** Watts.

Patent, Dorothy Hinshaw (1991) **Challenge Of Extinction.** Enslow.

Peacock, Graham (1993) **Exploring Habitats.** Raintree Steck-Vaughn.

Pearce, Fred (1991) **The Big Green Book.** Grosset & Dunlap.

Pollock, Steve (1993) **Ecology.** Dorling Kindersley.

Pringle, Laurence (1987) **Restoring Our Earth.** Enslow.

Pringle, Laurence (1991) **Living Treasure: Saving Earth's Threatened Biodiversity.** Morrow.

Rinard, Judith E. (1987) **Wildlife, Making A Comeback: How Humans Are Helping.** National Geographic.

Schoonmaker, Peter K. (1990) **Living Forest.** Enslow.

Simon, Noel (1987) **Vanishing Habitats.** Gloucester Press.
Smith, Howard Everett (1987) **Small Worlds: Communities of Living Things.** Scribner.
Steele, Philip (1991) **Extinct Insects & Those in Danger of Extinction.** Watts.
Tesar, Jenny E. (1992) **Endangered Habitats.** Facts On File.
Thornhill, Jan (1992) **Tree In A Forest.** Simon & Schuster.
Zim, Herbert S. (1991) **Trees: Guide To Familiar American Trees.**

CD-ROM Resources

Animals 2.0
Dangerous Creatures
Eco-adventures in the Rainforest
HyperStudio
Microscope Nature Explorer
Rainforest Explorer

Compton's 1995
Earth Explorer
Eyewitness Encyclopedia of Nature
Imagination Express: Rainforest
Rainforest
Zurk's Rainforest Lab

Laserdisc Resources

Race to Save the Planet, Scholastic laserdisc.
Animal Pathfinders, Scholastic laserdisc.

Powerful Projects

Explore an issue related to saving our environment.
Create a **HyperStudio** stack to debate both sides of the issue.
Create a **HyperStudio** stack to explain an environmental problem and provide specific solutions.
Explore organizations that work to save the environment. Develop a plan to join one of their projects.

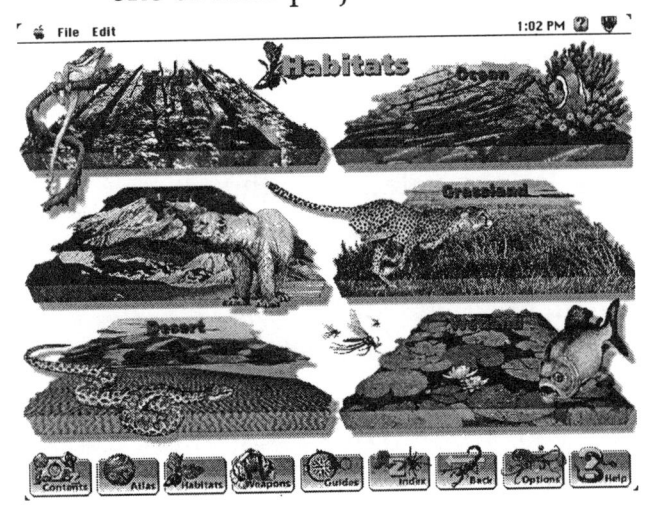

Dangerous Animals CD

HyperStudio Student Project

Visit the Envirolink Site!
http://envirolink.org/

Explore environmental issues that are of concern to children and young adults.
Visit **Envirolink**.

- Explore the **Envirolink Library** for information about an environmental topic in one of the following areas.
  Air, Water, Fire, Flora & Fauna, Earth
- Write about your stand on an issue of concern. Could you have an impact on this issue from where you live or will you need help? Find an epal living in an area affected by your environmental concern. Develop a joint plan of action!
- Read about **Actions You Can Take**! Explore the **Education** programs. Try one!
- Use the **News** selection of Envirolink to keep a bulletin board of up-to-date statistics about the environment.
- Explore the **Boycotts**. Create a list of things you use that they suggest harm the environment. What will you do? Explore the Green Marketplace. Which of these products do you use? Why?
- Explore a student project on conservation.
  http://longwood.cs.ucf.edu:80/~MidLink/conserv.html
- Create your own report that examines some aspect of saving the environment. Send your project to the Evergreen Dispatch!
  http://www.mobot.org/MBGnet/environment/evergreen/evergreen.html

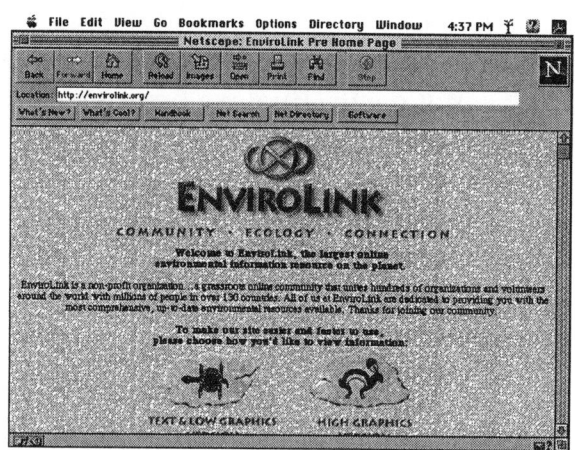

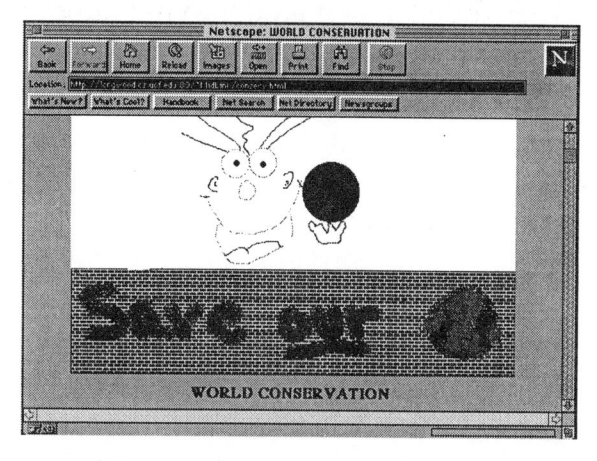

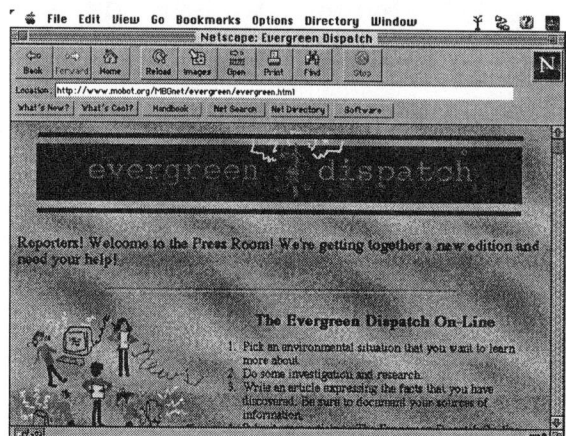

Exploration and Development

Our world expands daily through exploration, discovery, and development. Connect the past, present, and future by investigating famous explorers from the past and present. Compare and contrast the missions, roles, and purposes of explorers through history. Examine how and why different cultures "reached out" to discovery and settle new lands. Find out about how space explorers are discovering worlds off our planet earth. Explore how we're making new discoveries all the time. Speculate on the future of exploration.

This theme contains three main elements.

Early Developers
Start with an exploration of early development including Egyptians, Vikings, and Pirates. Is discovery always good? How does it impact the people, animals, and plantlife that live in the area? Were Vikings a positive or negative influence on the areas they "discovered"? What about the Puritans?

America's Development
Trace the development of North America. Investigate issues related to exploration and discovery. For example, explore how the word discovery is defined. How does perspective play a role in discovery and history? Did Columbus "discover" America? Weren't there already people there?

Beyond Our Planet
Explore the world beyond Earth. The exploration of space has become the center of many debates about exploration and discovery. Why do people want to explore new worlds? What have we learned from the past regarding the potential and consequences of exploration that we should consider as we explore the universe?

How have science fiction authors viewed space exploration? How has science fiction evolved with the development of science facts?

Exploration: Early Developers

Explore early discovery and development of civilization. Connect the past, present, and future by investigating famous explorers from the past and present. Compare and contrast the missions, roles, and purposes of explorers through history. Examine how and why different cultures "reached out" to discover and settle new lands.

Surfer Starters

History
   http://neal.ctstateu.edu/history/world_history/world_history.html
   http://www.einet.net/galaxy/Social-Sciences/History.html

Historical government documents
   gopher://vax.queens.lib.ny.us/11[gopher._ss._histdocs]

Writings of Ancient Egypt
   http://odyssey.lib.duke.edu/papyrus/

Pyramid
   http://www.woodwind.com/mtlake/CyberKids/Issue1/Crossword.html

Acropolis Page
   http://www.mechan.ntua.gr/webacropol/

Ancient Egypt
   http://www.gatech.edu/CARLOS/egypt.gal.html

7 Wonders of the World
   http://ce.ecn.purdue.edu/~ashmawy/7WW/

Russian History
   http://www.times.st-pete.fl.us/treasures/TC.Lobby.html

Celtic, Scottish, Anglo-Saxon, Welsh, and Viking information History
   http://www.mountain.net/hp/unicorn/

Canadian Museum of Civilization
   http://www.cmcc.muse.digital.ca/cmc/cmceng/exhibeng.html

Viking History
   http://odin.nls.no/viking/vnethome.htm

Jorvic Viking Center
   http://www.demon.co.uk/tourism/jvc/

Medieval Studies
   http://www.georgetown.edu/labyrinth/labyrinth-home.html

Explorers
   http://thunder.met.fsu.edu/explores/explores.html

Pirates
   http://tigger.cc.uic.edu/~toby-g/pirates.html

Egypt
   http://www.memphis.edu/egypt/main.html

Other Information Resources

Ancient Monuments & Mysteries (Sound Filmstrip) (1978). National Geographic.
Blumberg, Rhoda (1987) **Incredible Journey of Lewis & Clark**.
Caselli, Giovanni (1985) **First Civilizations**. Peter Bedrick.
Caselli, Giovanni (1986) **Renaissance & The New World**. Peter Bedrick.
Collins, James L. (1989) **Exploring The American West**. Watts.
Crosher, Judith (1993) **Ancient Egypt**. Viking.
Dunrea, Olivier (1985) **Skar Brae: The Story Of A Prehistoric Village**. Holiday House.
Fisher, Leonard Everett (1986) **Great Wall of China**. Macmillan.
Grosseck, Joyce & Attwood, Elizabeth (1988) **Great Explorers**. Gateway Press Inc.
Hauser, Hillary (1987) **Call To Adventure**. Bookmakers.
Lomask, Milton (1989) **Great Lives: Exploration**. Macmillan.
Macaulay, David (1980) **Unbuilding**. Houghton.
Matthews, Rupert (1991) **Explorer** (Eyewitness Books) Alfred A. Knopf.
Morley, Jacqueline (1991) **Egyptian Pyramid**. Peter Bedrick.
Reeves, Nicholas (1992) **Into The Mummy's Tomb**. Scholastic.
Ventura, Piero (1987) **There Once Was A Time**. Putnam.
Sandak, Cass R. (1983) **Explorers & Discovery**. Watts.
Simon, Charnan (1990) **The World's Great Explorers-Explorers of The Ancient World**. Childrens Press.
Stevens, Joseph E. (1988) **Hoover Dam: An American Adventure**. University of Oklahoma Press.

CD-ROM Resources

Age of Exploration
Ancient Civilizations
Compton's 1995
Dig It: Egyptians
Discoverers
Explorers of the New World
Eyewitness History of the World
How Would You Survive?
Knights and Kings
Microsoft Ancient Lands
Multimedia World History
Nile: Passage to Egypt
Stowaway
Timeliner

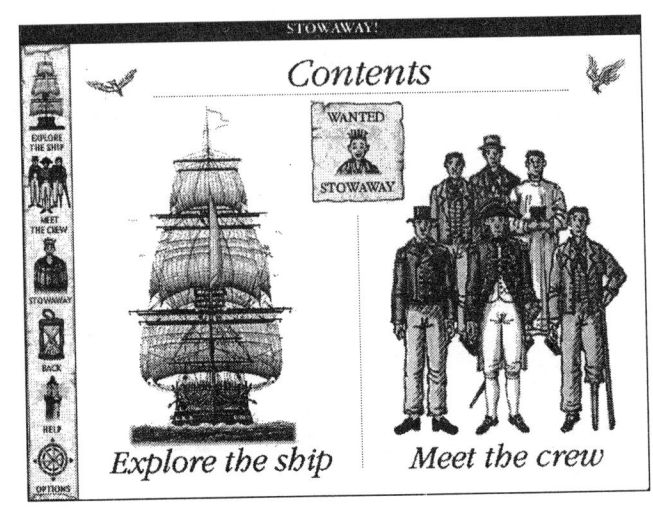

Stowaway

Visit Institute of Egyptian Art & Archaeology
http://www.memphis.edu/egypt/main.html

The Institute of Egyptian Art and Archaeology is a great place to start an exploration of the life of early Egyptians!

Find out about the **Egyptian artifacts** they've collected. Create a timeline showing each artifact. Select one of the artifacts and learn more about how it fit into the development of Egyptian culture.

Go on the **color tour of Egypt**. Select one of the sites and locate it on a map. Create a sketch of one of the items that you find.

At the top and bottom of many of the Web pages, you'll see a series of pictures called hieroglyphs. Can you figure out what any of these pictures mean? Create your own border for a Web page that contains hieroglyphs.

You can translate your name into hieroglyphs by visiting the following site :

http://weblifac.ens-cachan.fr/Portraits/S.ROSMORDUC/nomhiero.html

Here's the one for Annette!

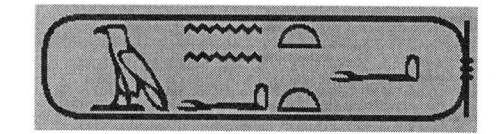

Visit other Egyptian pages.

http://www.teleport.com/~ddonahue/egyptol.html

Read about the Egyptian gods .

http://www.contrib.andrew.cmu.edu/~shawn/egypt//gods.html

Write a myth that includes at least three of these gods.

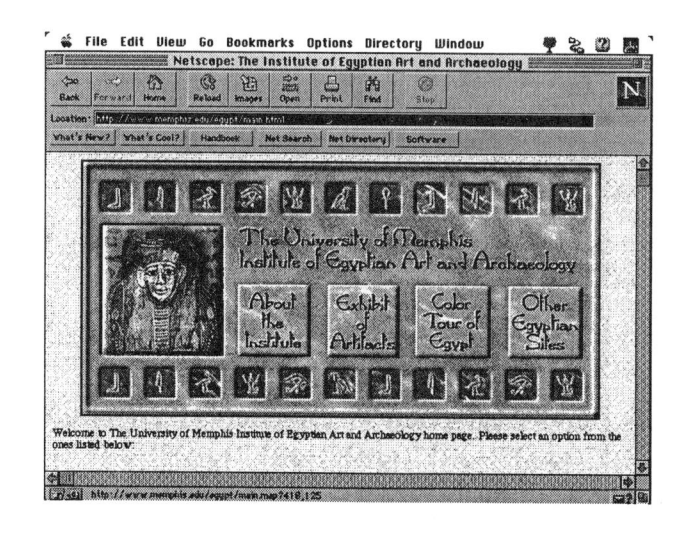

Visit the Jorvik Viking Centre!
http://www.demon.co.uk/tourism/jvc/

The Jorvik Viking Centre have lots of great information on Vikings!

Select **Jorvik Viking Festival.** Create a poster for the annual festival. Select an event and learn more about it in order to create an effective advertisement for the event.

Select **Facing the Past.** The Jorvik Centre has accurately recreated Vikings through a really neat technique. It's called facial imaging. Learn about the steps in recreating a Viking from a human skull. In what other areas would this technique be useful?

Select **The World of Vikings.** Find out about the Kensington Runestone (http://www.sound.net/~billhoyt/kensington.htm). Do you think it's fact or fraud? Take a position and support it with facts from the article.

Download a Runic font (http://babel.uoregon.edu/Yamada/fonts/runes.html) and try writing a sentence in the language.

Like many cultures, the Vikings had their own sayings. Learn about the sayings of the Vikings (http://iceweb.ismennt.is/g/gudrun/Welcome_uk.html). Read the two sayings a create your own.

Read an article or story about Early Medieval Europe (http://www.ftech.net/~regia/). Create your own short story that incorporates some of the ideas from your readings.

Learn about reenactments of Medieval times (http://www.biochem.ucl.ac.uk/~davis/vikings.html). Read about their combat and daily lives. What do you think would be the most difficult part to reenact? Use the images they provide in a multimedia project that discusses a day in the life of a Viking.

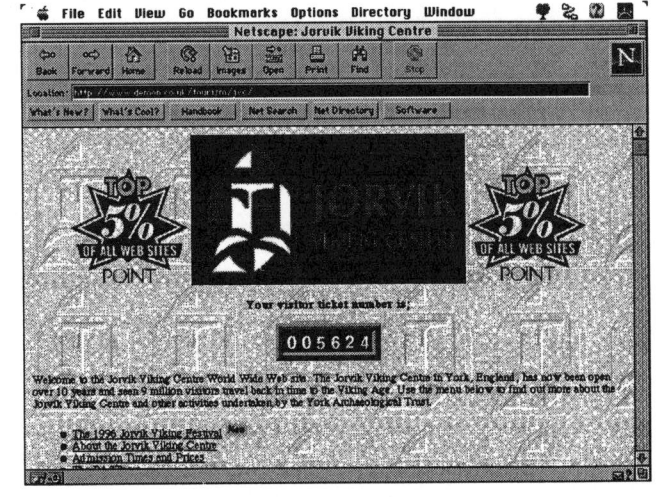

Visit the Pirates of the Caribbean!
http://tigger.cc.uic.edu/~toby-g/pirates.html

Explore the Pirate Web page and try the following activities.

Visit the **Pirates of the Caribbean**.
http://tigger.cc.uic.edu/~toby-g/pirates.html

Explore the bibliography and read a book or online story that includes pirates.

Read about a pirate's life. Write a short story following one person on an adventure. Incorporate each pirate area. Read about the famous locations for pirate activities and use one of these as the setting for your story.

Create a poster that compares and contrasts the life of a privateer, pirate, and buccaneer.

Explore pirate ships. Select one and give it a name. Create a log book and map of your travels. Write a short story about one of your adventures.

Examine the weapons used by pirates. What type of weapon would you choose?

Look at the Jacks (Flags). Create a flag for your pirate ship. How does it reflect your group's activities?

Read about each of the famous pirates. Which pirate would you like to meet on the high seas? Why? Build this character into a story.

Are there modern day pirates?

Visit the **Piracy** Page.
http://www.filmzone.com/cutthroat/highseas/highseas.html

Explore the rouges, justice, and father of pirary. Would you want to be a pirate? Why or why not?

Explore the characters (Rouges) of Cutthroat Island. Create your own character.

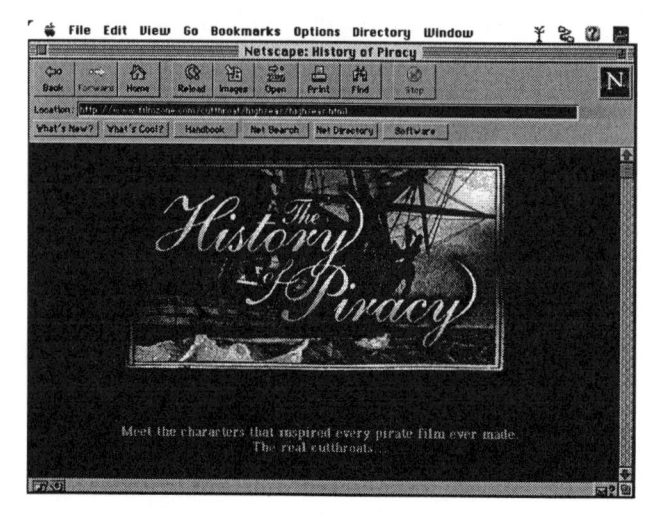

Exploration: America's Development

Trace the history of exploration in America from the Mayans to the Westward Movement. How has America developed through the centuries? How has it survived?

Surfer Starters
American History
   http://rs6.loc.gov/amhome.html
   http://www.msstate.edu/Archives/History/USA/19th_C./nineteen.html
Library of Congress History Information
   http://lcweb.loc.gov/exhibits/
California Missions
   http://www.tsoft.net/~cmi/
Wild West
   http://uts.cc.utexas.edu/~sring/DIARY/welcome.html
History
   http://www.msstate.edu/Archives/History/USA/19th_C./nineteen.html
   http://www.einet.net/galaxy/Social-Sciences/History.html
Mayan Adventure
   http://www.ties.k12.mn.us:80/~smm/
Maya Quest
   http://howww.ncook.k12.il.us/docs/mayaquest.html
Canadian Museum of Civilization
   http://www.cmcc.muse.digital.ca/cmc/cmceng/exhibeng.html
Explorers
   http://thunder.met.fsu.edu/explores/explores.html
Maya, Aztec, Inca
   http://www.realtime.net/maya/index.html
Gallery of the Frontier
   http://www.unl.edu/UP/gof/home.htm
1492
   http://sunsite.unc.edu/expo/1492.exhibit/Intro.html

Other Information Resources
Alter, Judy (1989) **Growing Up in the Old West**. Watts.
Alter, Judy (1989) **Women of the Old West**. Watts.
Blumberg, Rhoda (1987) **Incredible Journey of Lewis & Clark**.
Burdoch, David H. (1993) **Cowboy Eyewitness Books**. Alfred A. Knopf New York.

Collins, James L. (1989) **Exploring The American West**. Watts.
Dillon, Richard (1993) **Western Quotations Famous Words From the American West**. Four Peaks Press.
Freedman, Russell (1983) **Children of the Wild West**. Clarion.
Freedman, Russell (1985) **Cowboys of the Wild West**. Clarion.
Into The Shining Mountains (Videocassette) (1991) WNET/ dist by PBS Video.
Landau, Elaine (1990) **Cowboys**. Franklin Watts.
Lomask, Milton (1989) **Great Lives: Exploration**. Macmillan.
Marrin, Albert (1993) **Cowboys, Indians & Gunfighters The Story of the Cattle Kingom**. Atheneum.
Matthews, Rupert (1991) **Explorer** (Eyewitness Books) Alfred A. Knopf.
Matthews, Leonard J. (1988) **Cowboys**. Rourke.
Matthew, Leonard J. (1988) **Pioneers**. Rourke.
Morris, Michele (1993) **The Cowboy Life**. Simon & Schuster.
Perl, Lila (1977) **Hunter's Stew & Hangtown Fry: What Pioneer America Ate & Why**.
Pioneer Community At Work (Videcassette) (1987) National Film Board of Canada/McIntyre Visual Publications.
Rounds, Glen (1991) **Cowboys**. Holiday House.
Sandak, Cass R. (1983) **Explorers & Discovery**. Watts.
Stevens, Joseph E. (1988) **Hoover Dam: An American Adventure**. University of Oklahoma Press.
Tunis, Edwin (1961) **Frontier Living**. Crowell/Harper Collins.
Yancey, Diane (1991) **Desperadoes & Dynamite: Train Robbery in the United States**. Watts.

CD-ROM Resources

Age of Exploration
Microsoft Ancient Lands
Compton's 1995
Discoverers
Explorers of the New World
Eyewitness History of the World
How Would You Survive?
KidPix Studio
MayaQuest
Multimedia US History
Oregon Trail
Timeliner

Wyatt Earp's Old West
Yukon Trail
Vital Links
Who Built America?

Laserdisc Resources
Point of View 2.0
History in Motion

Powerful Projects

Explore the past by becoming part of the past. Start with the CD-ROM **Wyatt Earp's Old West**. Each student takes on the role of a person in an Old West Town. Create a map of the town on a bulletin board. Each student creates a diorama of their area such as the general store or blacksmith's shop.

Create a timeline tracing the movement of people in America from ancient times to the present. What happened to all these people? Is there still evidence of their lives?

Explore the CD titled **How Would You Survive?** Then, explore the links at (http://www.grolier.com/links/survlink.html).

Wyatt Earp's Old West

Hangin' Ten: Interdisciplinary Thematic Units

Visit Lords of the Earth Site!
http://www.realtime.net/maya/index.html

These pages include history, geography, geology, astronomy, archaeology, anthropology and art forms related to the Americas before Christopher Columbus's discovery.

Explore the **Meso-American Exchange Center**. How does the Mixtec Nuttall Codex star grid system compare to ours? Did the roof combs on the Maya temples relate to the Nuttall Grid Roof Patterns in this story? Were they star tracking forms also?

Explore the **Maya Exchange Center**. Why did the Maya become the followers of Kulkukan, the Maya version of Quetzal/Serpent god?

Explore the **Aztec Exchange Center**. Did Tepotzlan, The City of Wonder contain miracles or just miraculous primitive technology? Check out the mysteries found here with the 1523 map of Texcoco. and an Ancient Pre-Columbian Map. What do you think?

Explore the **Andean Exchange Center**. What do you think of the glyphs in this section? All Gods have a purpose in the culture where they are found. What do you think the purpose was?

Explore the **Inca Exchange Center**. What's the purpose of the Weeping God of the Andes? Does it relate to the Inca story of the Moon?

Explore the **Amerian Indian Exchange Center**. Compare the information here with information at other American Indian sites.

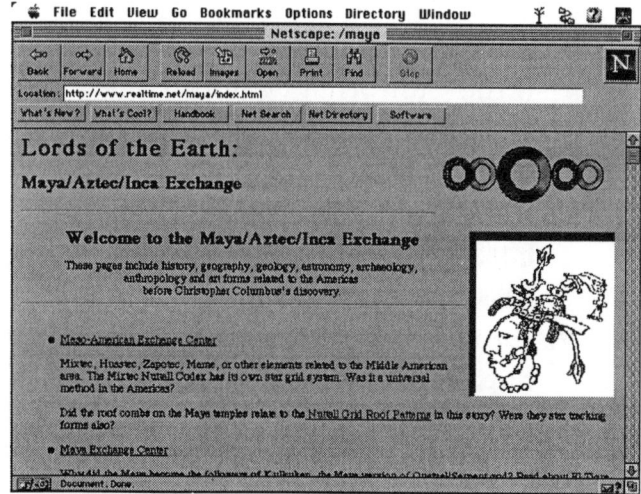

Visit History of the NW Coast Site!
http://www.hallman.org/~bruce/indian/history.html

Explore the History of the Northwest Coast of the United States.

Explore the history of the European/Indian contact on the Northwest Coast.
  Select one contact to explore. Was this a postive or negative contact with the native people? How did this contact change the future of the area? Compare this contact with one from another part of the United States.

Compare life in the area during three different time periods. How and why did everyday life change over time?

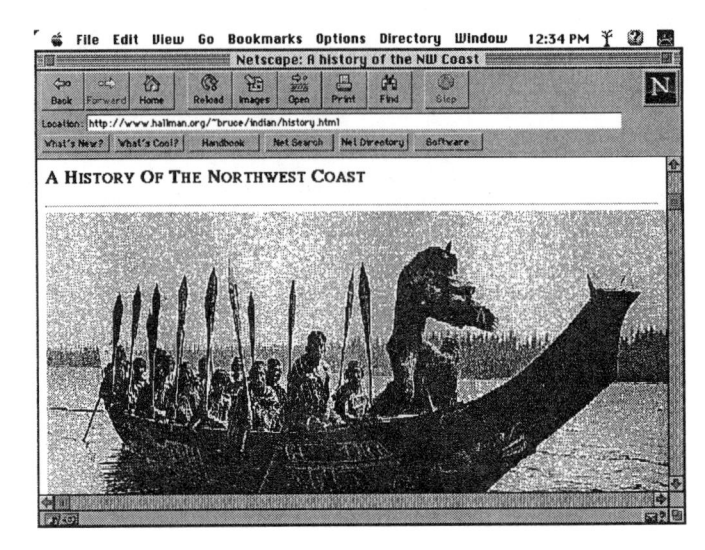

Read **The Story of the Old Shaman**. Can you identify ways that people from the outside have impacted the native culture?

Explore a Native American group that lived in the area. Trace their history.

Explore the foods and food preparation of the people who lived in the area. How does it reflect the area where they live? Compare the foods with a native group from another part of the United States.

Explore histories developed for other parts of the United States:

Visit the California History Page.
  http://www.community.net/~stevensn/4thgrade.html

Visit the Colorado History Page.
  http://www.fortnet.org/~randyc/Colorado/colorado.html

Visit the Texas History Page.
  http://riceinfo.rice.edu/armadillo/Texas/history.html

Create your own History page reflecting the development of the area where you live.

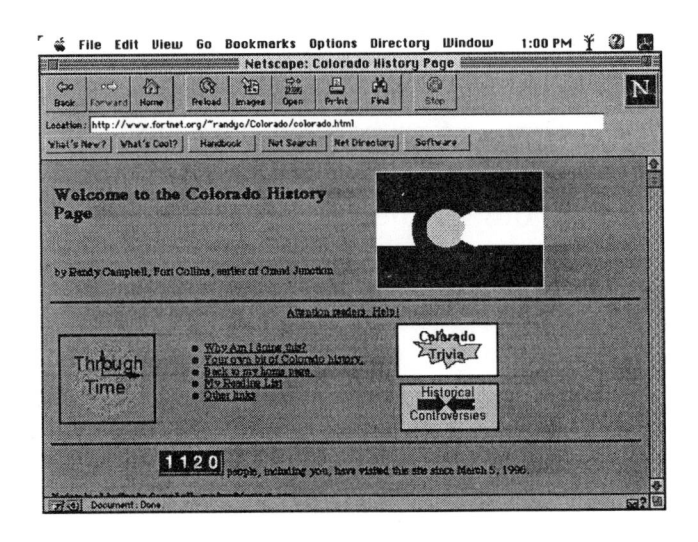

Hangin' Ten: Interdisciplinary Thematic Units

Exploration: Beyond Our Planet

Explore the world beyond our planet. Space exploration is the next frontier. What does it have to offer? Explore science fiction for some speculations.

Surfer Starters

Places to Start
   http://www.yahooligans.com/Science_and_Oddities/Space
StarChild
   http://guinan.gsfc.nasa.gov/K12/StarChild.html
Students for the Exploration and Development of Space
   http://www.seds.org/
Space resources
   http://liftoff.msfc.nasa.gov/
K-12 online space projects
   http://quest.arc.nasa.gov/interactive.html
Space
   http://shuttle.nasa.gov/
   http://nssdc.gsfc.nasa.gov/planetary/lunar/apollo_25th.html
   http://Seds.lpl.arizona.edu/nineplanets/nineplanets/spacecraft.html
   http://www.ksc.nasa.gov/ksc.html
   http://www.JSC.nasa.gov/JSC_homepage.html
   http://newproducts.jpl.nasa.gov/calendar/
Explore Apollo 13 with Jim Lovell
   http://www.mcn.org/Apollo13/Home.html

Other Information Resources

Baker, David (1988) **I Want To Fly The Shuttle.** Rourke.

Berliner, Don (1993) **Living in Space.** Lerner.

Branley, Franklyn M. (1986) **From Sputnik To Space Shuttles: Into The New Space Age.** Crowell/HarperCollins.

Branley, Franklyn M. (1987) **Planets In Our Solar System.** Crowell/HarperCollins.

Dolan, Edward F. (1989) **Famous Firsts in Space.** Cobblehill/Dutton.

Embury, Barbard (1990) **Dream Is Alive: A Flight of Discovery Aboard The Space Shuttle.** HarperCollins.

Harris, Alan W. (1990) **Great Voyager Adventure: A Guided Tour Through The Solar System.** Messner.

Kettelkamp, Larry (1993) **Living In Space.** Morrow.

Lauber, Patricia (1991) **Journey To The Planets**. Crown.
Rathburn, Elizabeth (1989) **Exploring Your Solar System**. National Geographic.
Ride, Sally (1986) **To Space And Back**. Lothrop, Lee, Shepard.
Robinson, Fay (1993) **Space Probes To The Planets**. Whitman.
Seevers, James A. (1988) **Space**. Raintree.
Simon, Seymour (1992) **Our Solar System**. Morrow.
Smith, Howard E. (1987) **Daring The Unknown: A History of NASA**. Gulliver/ Harcourt Brace Jovanovich.
Today & Tomorrow In Space: The Space Shuttle & Beyond (sound filmstrip) National Geographic (1983).
Vogt, Gregory (1991) **Apollo And The Moon Landing.** Millbrook.
Vogt, Gregory (1990) **Space Stations.** Watts.
Vogt, Gregory (1991) **Viking & Mars Landing.** Millbrock.

CD-ROM Resources

Where in Space is Carmen Sandiego?, Broderbund
Beyond Planet Earth, Discovery Channel
Journey to the Planets, Discovery Channel
The Great Solar System Rescue Laserdisc, Tom Snyder
Destination Mars!, Compu-teach
Space Shuttle, Mindscape
The Magic School Bus Explores the Solar System CD, Microsoft

Powerful Projects

Explore the StarChild Project (http://guinan.gsfc.nasa.gov/K12/StarChild.html) for background information about space.

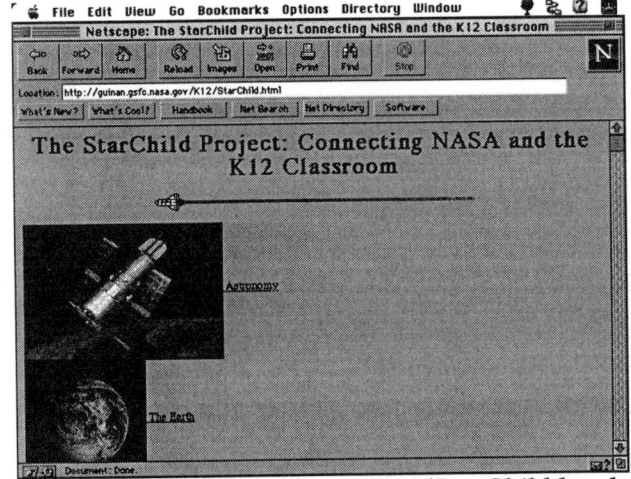

http://guinan.gsfc.nasa.gov/K12/StarChild.html    http://shuttle.nasa.gov/

Visit the NASA Home Page!
http://www.gsfc.nasa.gov/NASA_homepage.html

Explore the NASA Home Page.

Welcome: Read NASA's mission. Do you agree or disagree with the mission? If you had to convince Congress to eliminate or continue funding NASA's programs, what would you say? Write a position paper stating your perspective. Use examples to support your ideas.

Today@NASA: Identify a mission that your class can follow. Plan activities that will go with a live mission.

NASA Organization: Explore one of NASA's many departments. Most people think of the space shuttle, but did you know that NASA is involved with this many different activities. Select an activity that you think is important. Why do you think it is important? Create a plan for advertising this program.

Gallery: Find a picture in the gallery that you can use in your advertising campaign.

Questions and Answers: Explore some area of Space Science that you find interesting. Use this section to create a set of trivia questions to share with your class.

Aeronautics: How is this research important to the global community?

Space Science: How is the NASA cooperating with other space agencies around the world?

Mission to Planet Earth: Why do you think that NASA is involved with earth concerns when its emphasis is on space exploration?

Technology Development/Human Space Flight: Select a product developed by NASA. How was its development important for our daily life?

NASA Centers: Every NASA center has cool activities for students. Explore the centers and choose a project to try. Create your own guide to the best of NASA sites.

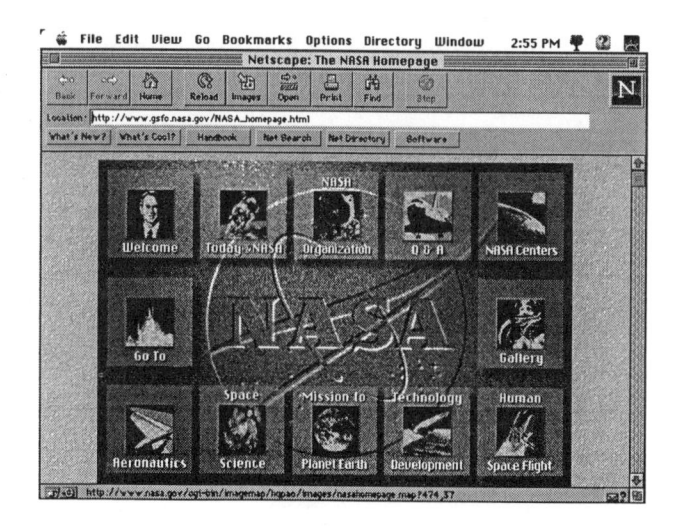

Visit the SpaceLink Page!
http://spacelink.msfc.nasa.gov/

Explore the SpaceLink for information about space programs. Then, examine the Space Activism Page to learn what you can do to promote the space program.

Explore **SpaceLink's Hot Topics**.

http://spacelink.msfc.nasa.gov/html/
Spacelink.Hot.Topics.html

Explore some aspect of the space program. Some areas are listed below:

Shuttle Missions
Spacehab Space Research Lab
Earth Asteroid Rendezvous
The Night of the Comet
The Galileo Spacecraft
Hubble Space Telescope
Women of NASA Project
Chiron Perihelion Campaign

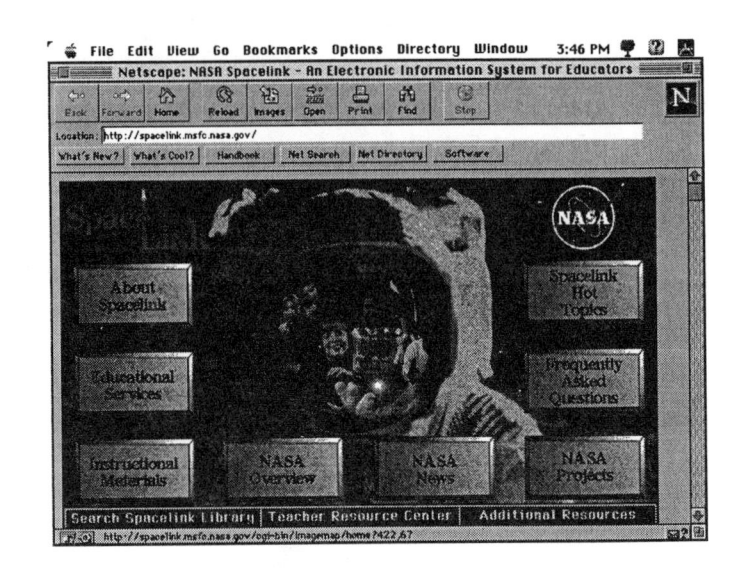

Visit the **Space Activism Page**.

http://muon.qrc.com/space/start.html

What do you think is the most important direction for space research and exploration? Use the Space Activism Page to explore ways to express your ideas.
Follow the guidelines for effective activism for your space project.

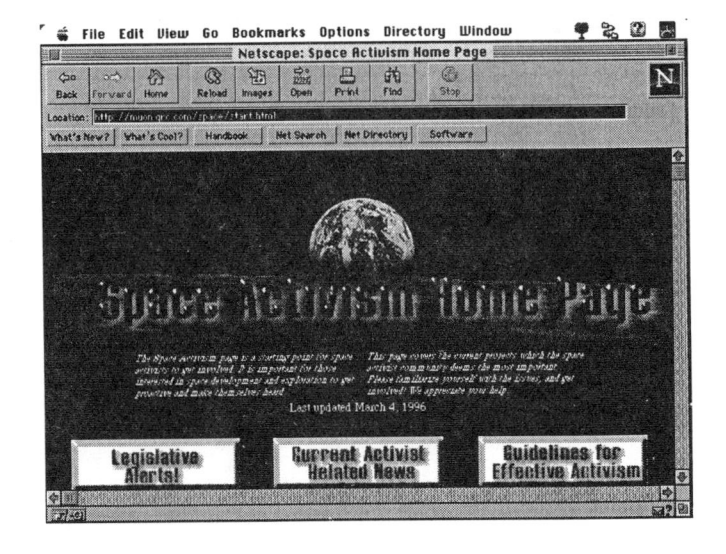

Hangin' Ten: Interdisciplinary Thematic Units

Visit Science Fiction on the Web!
http://www.umich.edu/~umfandsf/links/

Explore space exploration through Science Fiction on the Web.

Start with a good list of links.
http://www.umich.edu/~umfandsf/links/
http://lacon3.worldcon.org/www/Hazel/SFRG/sf-resource.guide.html
http://sflovers.rutgers.edu/Web/sf-resource.guide.html

Explore a science fiction book that became a movie. Which did you like better, the book or the movie? What are the advantages and disadvantages of the print media over the movie media?

Trace the history of science fiction related to space exploration. Compare a work written in the 1940's with a work written recently. How did the science of the time impact the author's perspective?

Explore space exploration and science fiction art. Use a piece of art as the basis for a science fiction short story.
Chesley Bonestell (http://www.secapl.com/bonestell/top.html)
Image Gallery (http://www.novaspace.com/)

Read about a Science Fiction author. Write a speech that might be used in an introduction for an award you might give to this person. What might the award represent?
http://lacon3.worldcon.org/www/Hazel/SFRG/sfrg05.html#Authors
http://www.interlog.com/~ohi/www/sf.html
http://www.yahoo.com/Arts/Literature/Science_Fiction__Fantasy__Horror/Authors/

Learn about Speculative Fiction.
http://206.101.96.68:8001/
sf-clearing-house/

What's speculative fiction? Are you a fan? Why or why not? Which elements do you like and dislike?

Write your own story focusing on some aspect of space exploration. Combine fiction with scientific facts.

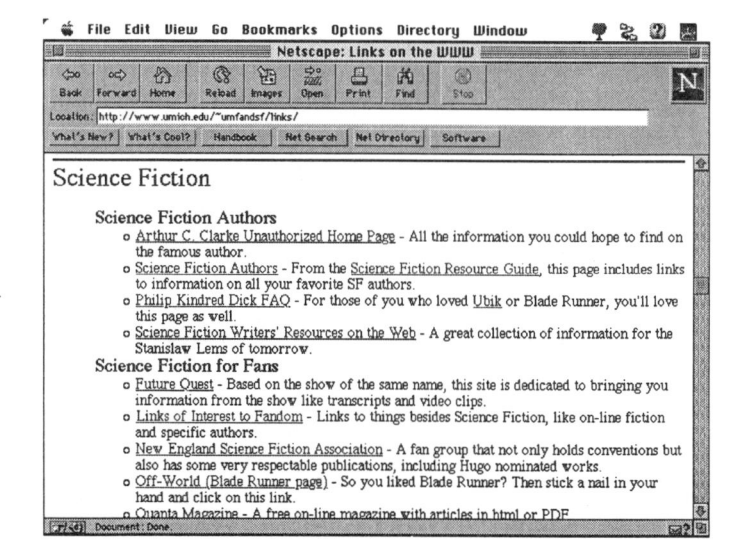

Visit the Bermuda Triangle!
http://tigger.cc.uic.edu/~toby-g/tri.html

Explore the mystery of the Bermuda Triangle!

Create a map showing where in the world the Bermuda Triangle is located.

Create a map showing the depth of the sea in the area of the Bermuda Triangle.

Do you agree with the authors conclusions about the Bermuda Triangle? Why or why not? What makes the author a good or poor resource for information on this topic?

Create your own mystery about a part of the world. Name it another shape. Create a map and short story to go along with your tale.

How are **Christopher Columbus** and the Bermuda Triangle connected? Can you find facts in other resources to back up this story?

Read **The Biggest Mystery Flight 19**. Do you agree or disagree with the authors conclusions? What do you think happened?

Read about **The Mary Celeste** and **The Disappearance of NC-16002**. Select one of the stories and write a fictional ending about what happened.

Locate other resources on the Internet (http://www.grolier.com/stories/g07847.html). Compare this information with the information provided by Bubba, the salty dog and author of this Bermuda Triangle page.

Search for information on another mystery such as Big Foot or the Loc Ness Monster. Compare that page with this one.

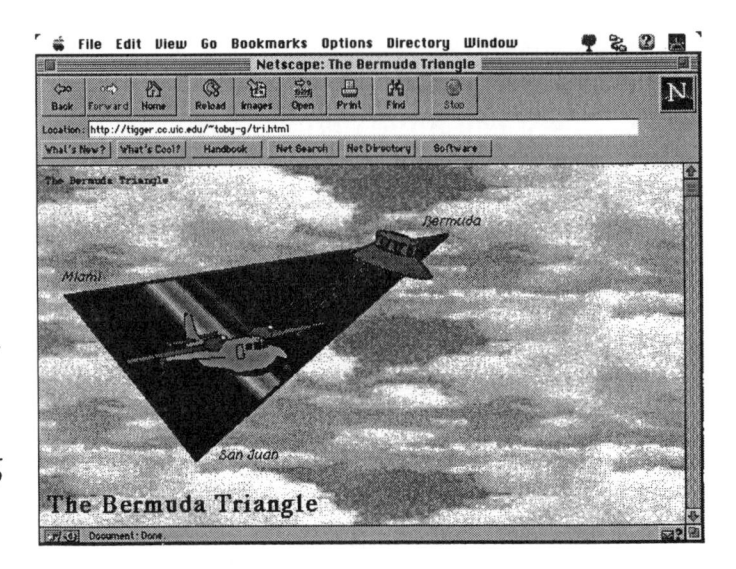

Imagine, Investigate, Invent

How was the television invented? What about all the other machines we use everyday? The books we read, the bikes we ride, and the food we eat were all created by someone, sometime. Who, what, when, where, and why? The final thematic area is titled imagine, investigate, invent. It explores inventors, inventions, creativity, and innovation. The activities encourage students to be proactive in the development of unique ideas and projects.

This theme contains two main elements:

Inventors
Start with an exploration of famous inventors. Would you make a good inventor? What are the characteristics of an inventor? Get your creative juices flowing with activities at the Creativity Web and explore the development of inventions at the Invention Dimension

Inventions
How do you develop an idea for an invention? Where are new innovations needed? Can you create a plan for addressing an important worldwide concern such as energy?

Imagine, Investigate, Invent: Inventors

Explore famous inventors and their inventions. What does it take to become an inventor?

Surfer Starters

Albert Einstein Page
http://www-groups.dcs.st-and.ac.uk/~history/Mathematicians/Einstein.html
http://www.sas.upenn.edu/~smfriedm/einstein.html

Thomas Edison
http://userwww.sfsu.edu/~markd/TheFatherofLight.html

Community of Inventors
http://medoc.gdb.org/work/invent.html

Creativity
http://www.quantumbooks.com/Creativity.html

Dead Inventor's Corner
http://www.discovery.com/DCO/doc/1012/world/inventors/week0896/inventors.html

Great Minority Inventors
http://www-groups.dcs.st-and.ac.uk/~history/Mathematicians/Einstein.html

Invention and Design
http://jefferson.village.virginia.edu/~meg3c/id/id_home.html

Invention Lesson Ideas
http://gnn.com/gnn/meta/edu/curr/rdg/gen_act/invent/index.html

Inventure Place: Inventor's Hall of Fame
http://www.invent.org/inventure.html

Psychology of Invention
http://hawaii.cogsci.uiuc.edu/invent/invention.html

Canadian Young Inventor's Site
http://www.ideas.wis.net//cyif.html

Inventor's Site
http://mustang.coled.umn.edu/inventing/inventing.html

Young Inventors
http://www.ideas.wis.net/cyif.html
http://www.rfcc.cse.uconn.edu/www/Inventors/Inventors.html

Invention Dimension
http://web.mit.edu/afs/athena.mit.edu/org/i/invent/

Leonardo da Vinci
   http://cellini.leonardo.net/museum/main.html

Other Information Resources

AAseng, Nathan (1991) **Twentieth Century Inventors**. Facts On File.
Haskins, James (1991) **Outward Dreams: Black Inventors & Their Inventions**. Walker.
Invent It (Videocassette) (1988) Insights Visual Productions 401.
Jones, Charlotte Foltz (1991) **Mistakes That Worked**. Doubleday.
Lomask, Milton (1991) **Great Lives: Invention & Technology**. Scribners.
Olsen, Frank H. (1991) **Inventors Who Left Their Brands On America**. Bantam.
Richardson, Robert O. (1990) **Weird & Wondrous World of Patent**s. Sterling.
Taylor, Barbara (1987) **Be An Inventor.** Harcourt Brace Jovanovich.

CD-ROM Resources

Amazing Writing Machine
Microsoft Ancient Lands
Eyewitness Encyclopedia of Science
How Things Work
Leonardo the Inventor
The Way Things Work
What's My Secret #1 and #2

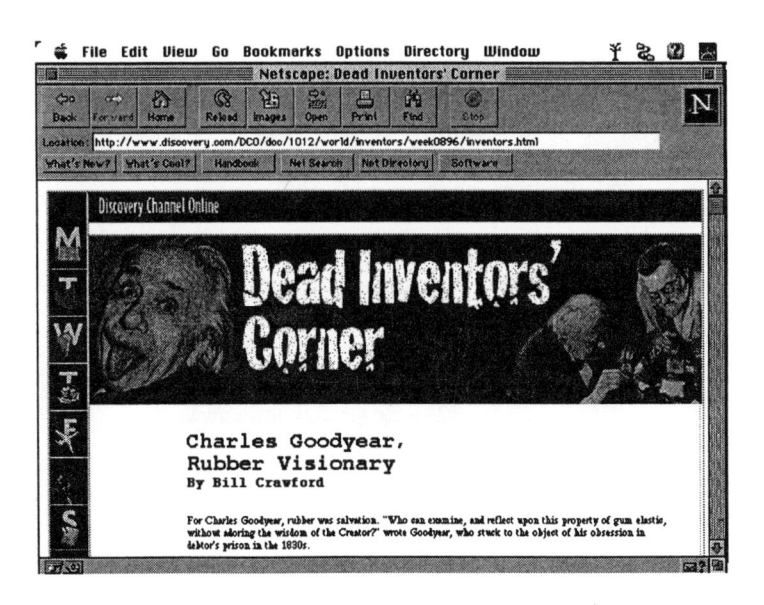

Visit Famous Inventor Sites!
http://www.clark.net/pub/kight/clearview/inventions.html

Start your exploration of inventors and inventions at a celebration at Clearview Elementary School.

Read the instructions and join their invention project.

Select a famous inventor to explore:
  Benjamin Franklin
  John Pemberton
  Spencer Silver
  Richard James
  Alexander Graham Bell
  Sir Isaac Newton
  Lumiere Brothers
  Sir Alexander Fleming
  Peter Hodgson
  Wright Brothers

Create a table display highlighting some of this person's ideas.

Visit the sites of some very early inventors such as Leonardo Da Vinci and Galileo. How many of their ideas are still used today? Compare and contrast these two early inventors.

Visit the Leonardo da Vinci Site.
  http://cellini.leonardo.net/museum/main.html

Visit the Galileo Site.
  http://galileo.imss.firenze.it/museo/b/egalilg.html

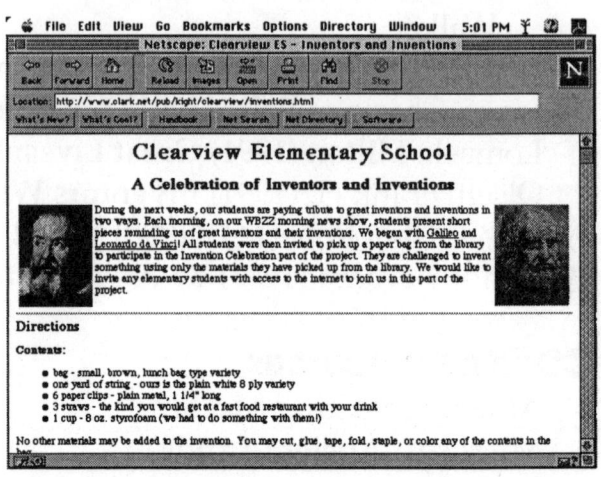

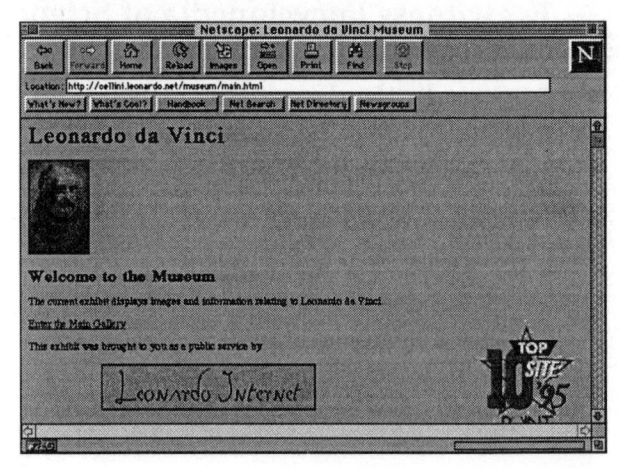

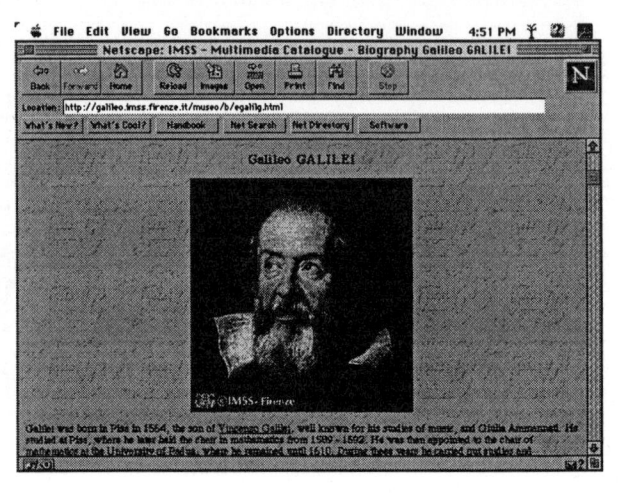

Visit the Be An Inventor Site!
http://mustang.coled.umn.edu/inventing/inventing.html

Visit the Be An Inventor's Site and learn about what it takes to become an inventor.

Create a chart showing the skills you already have that will make you a good inventor. Then, make a list of those areas you need to work on if you want to be an inventor.

Compare and contrast two famous inventors: **Benjamin Franklin** and **Richard G. Drew,** the Inventor of SCOTCH Tape. How are these people alike and different? Why do you think they were so successful?

Write a **Report about an Inventor**. Follow the directions at the Inventor's Site. Be sure to include information about the inventor's personality, life, family inventions, and the impact on society.

Follow the directions to become a scout, wizard, critic, and trail blazer.

Become a Scout: What should we invent?

Become a Wizard: How do we use the problem we have chosen to create our invention?

Become a Critic: Will my invention be successful?

Become a Trail Blazer: How do I market my invention?

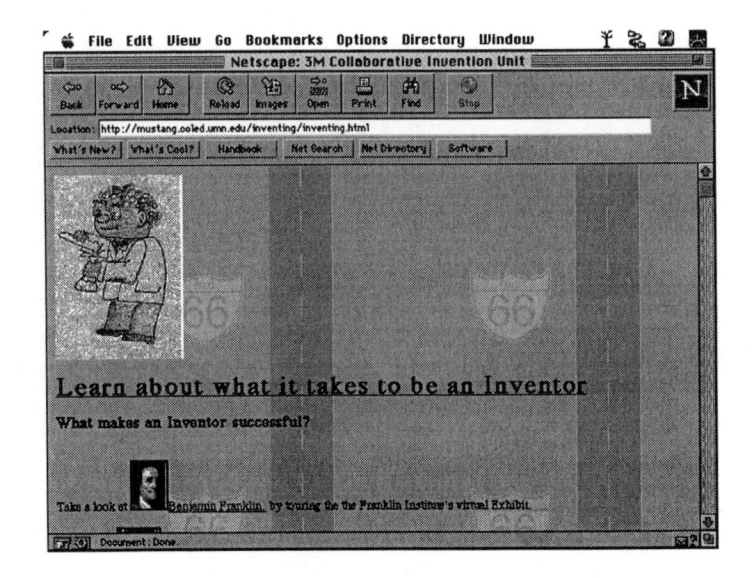

Visit the Creativity Web Site!
http://www.ozemail.com.au/~caveman/Creative/

Be creative! Explore the Creativity Web Site!

- Start with **The Big Picture**. Read the Definitions and Questions section. Are you creative? Why or why not? What are obstacles to your creativity? What can you do to stimulate your creative thinking?

- Go to the **Famous People Section** and choose a person to explore. Use the web to find out about this person. Do you think this person is creative? Why or why not? Give an example to share with the class.

- Learn a creativity **method**. Teach this technique to someone else in the class.

- Try some of **Edward de Bono's** Ideas. Learn about his Six Thinking Hats. Choose a topic and as a small group, try each of the six hats.

- Make a **Mind Map** for your favorite topic, a unit you just completed, or an issue you're interested in exploring. Compare your map with another person's. How are they alike and different?

- Explore **Quotations** and **Affirmations**. Create a poster containing your favorite creativity quote or affirmation.

- Learn about the **Brain**. Are you good to your brain? Draw a picture of your brain highlighting those areas you use the most and least? Also, show the positive things you do to "feed" your brain.

- Explore some of the other web resources on creativity. Select one to share with the class.

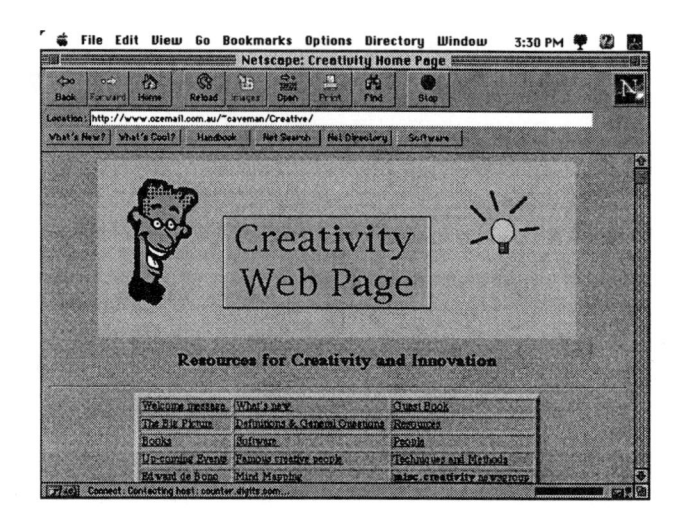

Visit the Invention Dimension!
http://web.mit.edu/afs/athena.mit.edu/org/i/invent/

Visit the Invention Dimension and learn about American inventors and their discoveries. A different American inventor is highlighted every week.

Explore the **Inventor of the Week** area each week and post the information about the person on a special bulletin board!

Explore the **Inventor of the Week** archives. Select a past inventor of the week. How is this person like and unlike you? What did you learn about the person as you examined the information? What else would you like to learn about this person? Search the Web for more information about this inventor.

You could be an inventor too! Pretend that you created an invention, what would your Inventor of the Week page look like?

Visit the **Invention Dimension Hotlist**. Explore the Copyright and Patent area. What's the difference between a copyright and a patent? Which will you need for the invention you're going to develop?

Explore the **Research Laboratories** around the world. Which lab would you like to visit? Who would you like to talk to and what would you ask them? If you could work there what would you like to do?

Explore the **Timelines Extensions**. Create a chart showing the history of Apple Computer. Where do you think they'll go in the future? Why?

Go to the **Community of Science Inventions**. Explore other inventions that are similiar to the one you'd like to create.

Explore the **Creativity Site**. Do you have what it takes to be creative? Do you agree with their philosophy?

Examine the **Dead Inventor's Corner**. Find a favorite inventor. What makes a good inventor?

Explore the **Internet Invention Store**. Would you buy any of these inventions? Create a rating system and rate the inventions. What criteria are you using to evaluate the inventions?

Explore **Invention and Innovation at MIT**. Which invention do you think has the best chance? Why? Would you buy one?

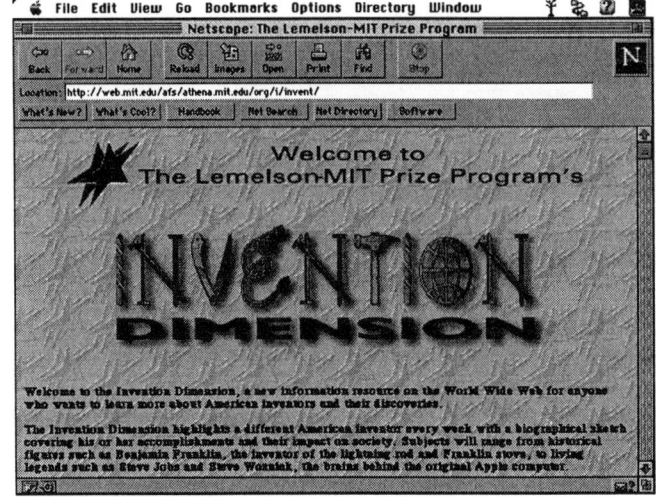

Imagine, Investigate, Invent: Inventions

Explore the world of inventions. How do things work? Why?

Surfer Starters

Creativity
   http://www.quantumbooks.com/Creativity.html
Invention and Design
   http://jefferson.village.virginia.edu/~meg3c/id/id_home.html
Make a Robot Move
   http://telerobot.mech.uwa.edu.au/
Run a Robotic Telescope
   http://www.eia.brad.ac.uk/rti/
Robot-controlled garden
   http://www.usc.edu/dept/garden/
Archaeology robot project
   http://www.usc.edu/dept/raiders/

Other Information Resources

Cooper, Chris & Tony Osman (1984) **How Everyday Things Work**. Facts On File.
Horvatic, Anne (1989) **Simple Machines**. Dutton.
Introducing Simple Machines (Sound Filmstrip) (1984) Society for Visual Education (3-6)
Invent It (Videocassette) (1988) Insights Visual Productions 401.
Jones, Charlotte Foltz (1991) **Mistakes That Worked**. Doubleday.
Macaulay, David (1988) **The Way Things Work**. Houghton.
Machines, Power, & Transportation.(1984) Arco.
Push & Pull: Simple Machines At Work (Videocasettes) (1990) Rainbow Educational Video.

CD-ROM Resources

The Way Things Work, DK
What's the Secret, 3M

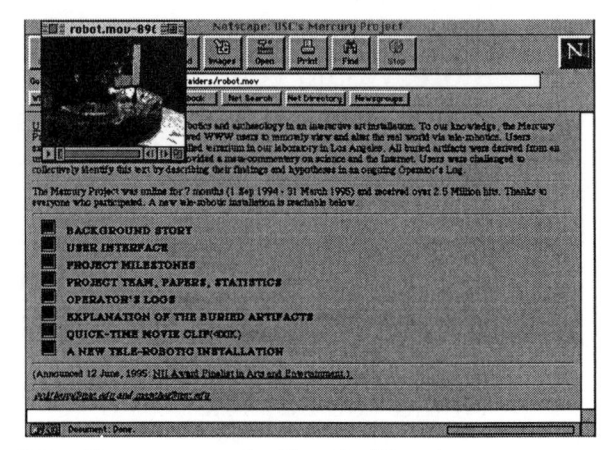

http://www.usc.edu/dept/raiders/

Visit the Innovation Pages!
http://www.exploratorium.edu/publications/Hands-On_Science/Hands-On_Science.html

Explore the world of science, invention, and innovation.

- Start with some "warmup" experiments at the Exploratorium pages.
  http://www.exploratorium.edu/publications/Hands-On_Science/Hands-On_Science.html
- Learn about robotics at the following pages. You can even try running a remote robot.
  http://piglet.cs.umass.edu:4321/robotics.html
  http://www.robotics.com/robomenu/
- Try running a remote robot in Australia.
  http://telerobot.mech.uwa.edu.au/
- Try Bill Nye's experiments with simple machines.
  http://nyelabs.kcts.org/nyeverse/shows/tryit.wav
- Explore the possibilities of Omniscience Futureneering which involves science, inventing, and engineering.
  http://www.webcom.com/sknkwrks/
- Try some engineering projects.
  http://www.sme.org/memb/neweek/hpact.htm
- Explore the Ornithopter Home Page.
  http://www.bucknell.edu/~chronstr/orn.html
- Create your own invention that involves flapping flight.
- Make some paper airplanes.
  http://pchelp.inc.net/paper_ac.htm
- Design your own paper airplane.

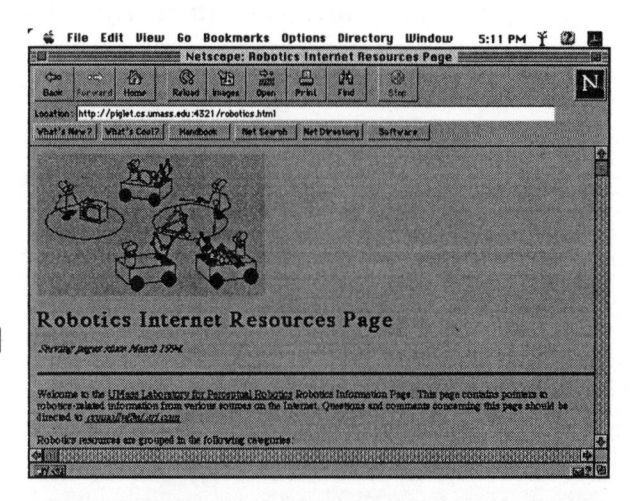

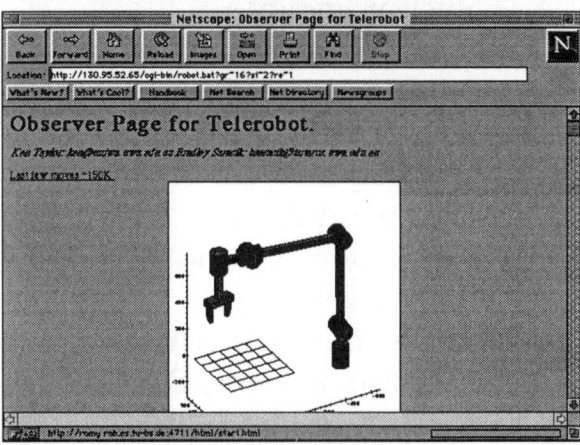

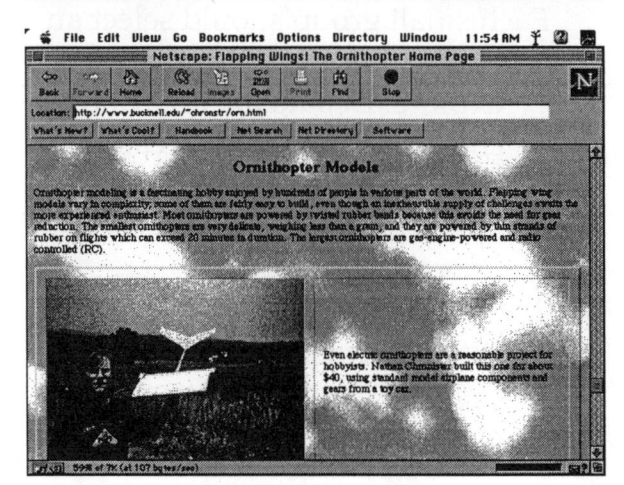

Visit the Energy Quest Site!
http://www.energy.ca.gov/energy/education/eduhome.html

Explore alternative forms of energy. Our future will depend on identifying new forms of energy and reexamining our current energy resources.

- Choose one of the following projects:
    - Percy's Puzzles
    - Poor Richard's "Energy" Almanac
- Choose an easy activity:
    - Biomass Energy
    - Discover California's Energy
    - Energy Patrol
    - Fossil Fuels
    - Geothermal Energy
    - Hydro-electric Energy
    - Nuclear Energy
    - Saving Energy (Energy Conservation)
    - Solar Energy
    - Wind Energy
    - Choose a medium activity:
    - The Energy Story
    - Alternative Fuel and Electric Vehicles
    - Energy Safety
- Choose a difficult activity:
    - California's Energy Policy
    - The Sun's Joules
- Each small group should select an alternative energy source to explore. Debate the pros and cons of each source. Create a class plan for our energy future and send it to the Department of Energy.
- Try the energy scavenger hunt (http://trms.k12.ga.net/~jtucker/lessons/sc/electricitydir.html).

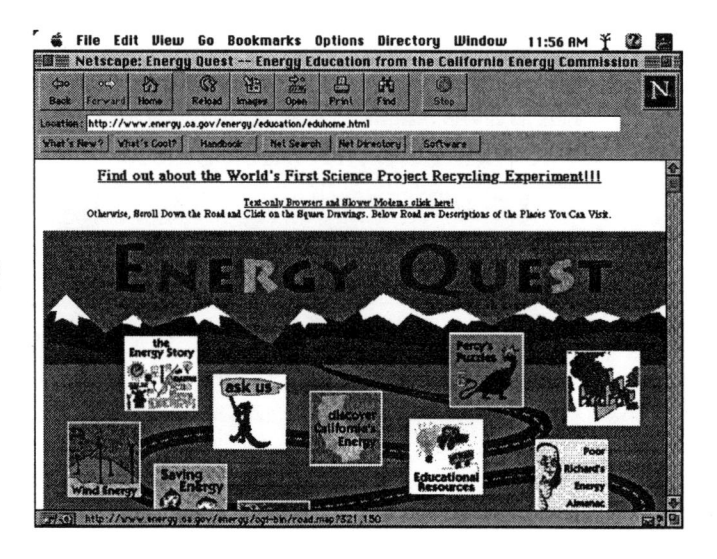

References

Armstrong, T. (1994). Multiple intelligences: seven ways to approach curriculum. **Educational Leadership**, 52(3), 26-33.

Berge, Zane L. & Collins, Mauri P. (1995). **Computer-Mediated Communication and the Online Classroom**. Cresskill, NJ: Hampton Press.

Breivik, Patricia Senn & Senn, J.A. (1993). **Information Literacy: Educating Children for the 21st Century**. New York: Scholastic.

Dyrli, O. (1994). Riding the Internet schoolbus: places to visit and things to do. **Technology & Learning**. 15(2), 32-40.

Ellsworth, Jill H. (1994). **Education on the Internet: A Hands-on Book of Ideas, Resources, Projects, and Advice**. Indianapolis: Sams.

Gardner, H. (1983). **Frames of Mind.** New York: Basic Books.

Gardner, H. (1991). **The Unschooled Mind.** New York: Basic Books.

Haggerty, B. (1995). **Nurturing Intelligences: A Guide to Multiple Intelligences Theory and Teaching**. Addison-Wesley.

Kuhlthau, C. C. (1993). **A Process Approach to Library Skills Instruction. In Information Literacy: Learning How to Learn**. Chicago, IL: American Library Association (p. 35-40).

Lamb, Annette (1996). **Building Treehouses for Learning: Technology in Today's Classrooms**. Evansville, IN: Vision to Action.

Lamb, Annette & Johnson, Larry (1996). **Cruisin' the Information Highway: Internet in the K-12 Classroom**. Evansville, IN: Vision to Action.

Marjorie Pappas (1994). Information skills process models and electronic resources. **Indiana Media Journal**, 16(4), 39-45.

Miller, Elizabeth B. (1994). **The Internet Resource Directory for K-12 Teachers and Librarians**. Englewood, CO: Libraries Unlimited.

Nelson, K (July/August 1995). Seven ways of being smart. **Instructor**. 26-34.

Pappas, M. & Tepe, A. (1993). Information skills model. In Angle, M. **Teaching Electronic Information Skills**. McHenry, IL : Follett Software Company.

Williams, Bard (1995). **The Internet for Teachers.** Indianapolis, IN: IDG Books.

Wisconsin Educational Media Association. (1993). **Information Literacy: A position paper on information problem solving.** Chicago, IL : American Association of School Librarians, American Library Association.

Index

AARP 96
Abbreviations 30
Abbey, Edward 264
ABC Educational Games (Website) 5
Aboriginal people 171
Aboriginal Studies (Website) 198
Abortion 111-12
Abuse of Power in Literature (Website) 93
Abuse, physical and emotional 94
Abuse Survivor's Page (Website) 94
Academy One (Website) 37
Acid rain 141
Accuracy of information (see Reliability)
AccuWeather (Website) 150-1
Achoo (Website) 93, 97
Acropolis Page (Website) 279
Act Locally (Website) 88
Action verbs for objectives 2
Activism, Social (Website) 88
Adams Collection, Ansel (Website) 118
Addictions 108-9
Address, email 30
Adopt-A-Watershed (Website) 147
Adoption and foster parenting 104-5, 111-2
Aeronautics 291
Aesop's Fables (Website) 218
Aging 95-6
Africa 167
African-American experience 256
African-Americans: Universal Black Pages (Website) 256
African American Pioneers (Website) 256
African Art (Website) 118
African stories 259
AID S97
Aha (Website) 5
Air (Website) 140
Aircraft, jet 249
Airlines and air travel 248-9
Airplanes, paper 303
Alabama 51

Al-anon (Website) 108-9
Alaska 34, 44, 178, 239
Alcohol abuse 108-9
Algebra For Everyone Home Page (Website) 129
All-In-One (Search engine) 72
Alta Vista (Search engine) 72
Alzheimer's Disease (Website) 95
Amber Lady (Website) 139
American Cancer Society (Website) 98
American Civil War HomePage (Website) 190
American Civil War Timeline (Website) 189
American Diabetes Association (Website) 102
American History 182, 284
American Immigration (Website) 260
American Indian Exchange Center 287
American Indian Resources (Website) 197
American Indian Studies (Website) 197
American Stock Exchange (Website) 204
Amnesty International (Website) 243
Amphibians (see also reptiles) 46
Ancient Egypt (Website) 279
Andy Warhol (Website) 118
Antarctica 167
Anorexia Nervosa 103
Anatomy, frog 153
Anatomy, human 153, 234
Andean Exchange Center 287
Anglo-Saxon history 191, 279
Animals 4, 44-55
Animals, Australia 171-2
Ansel Adams Collection (Website) 118
Anthony, Susan B. 183
Anthropology 195-6
Anti-Smoking Site, Master (Website) 107
Apollo 13 (Website) 289
Apoptosis 154
Aquarium 44, 48, 53, 266, 269

Archaeology 142-3
Archaeology robot project (Website) 302
Architecture 253, 255
Arizona 178
Armadillo 45
Army's Women's Corp 194
Arnold, Caroline (Website) 210
Art, arts 115-128, 142, 259
Arts and Art Education (Website) 118
Art galleries, museums 118-9, 123, 259
ArtSource (Website) 118
Artic 167
Asian Arts (Website) 118
Ask the Author (Website) 206, 208
Ask the Dietitian (Website) 103
Ask-An-Expert (Website) 77-8
Ask the Mad Scientists (Website) 78
Astronomer, Ask-An (Website) 78, 144
Atlanta Reproductive Health Center (Website) 111
Atomic energy 165
Aunt Annie's Craft Page (Website) 17
Audience identification 88
Australia 34, 48, 171-2, 274, 303
Australia money 130-1
Authors 113, 206-13
Author, science fiction 293
Authority 77
Auto racing 20-1
Aviation Administration, Federal (FAA) 252
Avid Explorer, The (Website) 248
Aztec Exchange Center 287

Bacteria 154
"Bad Science" Site (Website) 132
Bali (Indonesia) 167
Band-Aids (Website) 229
Banned Book Site (Website) 228
Barbie (Website) 16
Barr's English Literature Page on Mythology (Website) 217
Barr's Writing Resources (Website) 226

Barry's Clip Art (Website) 42
Bartlett's Familiar Quotations 225
Bartleby Library (Website) 225
Barton, Clara 182
Baseball 20-1
Baseball cards 14
Basic Prose Style and Mechanics (Website) 84
Bayeux Tapestry 118
Beakman's World (Website) 132, 135
Be An Inventor (Website) 299
Bees 48, 157
BeforeNet and AfterNet (Website) 92
Beijing 95 (Conference) 113
Belgium 173
Bell, Alexander Graham 298
Bermuda 167
Bermuda Triangle (Website) 294
Best Sites for Kids, Berit's (Website) 59
Bias 77
Bicycles 17, 23
Bibliographic Citations (Website) 84
Bill Nye the Science Guy (Website) 132, 135, 303
Bill of Rights 203
Binge Drinking (Website) 108
Biological diversity 50
Biology 153
Birds 46, 48-50
Birds, Australia 171-2
Birmingham Zoo 51
Biographies 182
Biology, plant 163
Birth control 112
Black History (Website) 259
Blood Alchohol Concentration (Website) 108
Blood cells, white 154
Blues music 124
Boba World Searcher (Search engine) 72
Bonestell, Chesley (Website) 293
Book of Kells 118
Book series 211

Index

Botanical gardens 161, 163
Botany 161
Bowling 20-22
Brainstorming 68
Brazil 167
Bright Ideas (Website) 5
British Columbia Folklore (Website) 195
Bruges, Belgium 173
Budapest, Hungary 173
Bugs 153-4, 157
Bug Watch (Website) 157
Bulgaria 167
Bullimia Nervosa 103
Bureau of Justice Statistics (Website) 99-100
Bureau of Missing Socks (Website) 7, 9
Bureau of Transportation Statistics 252
Butterfly 157, 160
Butterfly World (Website) 160
Buzz Rod and the Light: An Interactive Story (Website) 218

Calculus 129
California 147-8, 178, 182, 269
California History Page (Website) 288
California Missions (Website) 284
'Call for projects' 29
Camping 17
Canada 12, 168
Canadian Airlines International (Website) 248
Canadian Centre on Substance Abuse (Website) 108
Canadian maps 244
Canadian Museum of Civilization (Website) 191, 284
Canadian National Zoo 51
Canadian SchoolNet (Website) 12
Canadian Young Inventor's Site (Website) 296
Cancer 98
Cancer Guide (Website) 98
CancerNet (Website) 98

309

Candlelight Stories (Website) 218
Carl Hayden Bee Research Center (Website) 48
Carlos' Coloring Page 5
Car racing (see Auto racing)
Carroll, Lewis (Website) 207
Cartoons and cartooning 119, 122
Castles 253
Cathay Pacific Airways (Website) 248
Cather, Willa 264
Cats 54
CDC (Website) 229
Celtic, Scottish, Anglo-Saxon, Welsh, and Viking Information History (Website) 191, 279
Cell Biology 153-4
Censorship (see also Banned Books site) 228
Center for Disease Control (Website) 153
Center for Folklige (Website) 195
Center for Studies on Aging (Website) 95
Central America 169
Chemicool (Website) 164
Chemistry 164
Chemotaxis 154
Childbirth, Pregnancy & (Website) 111
Child custody 104-5
Children and the environment 274
Children home pages / websites 35
Children's art projects 119, 121
Children's literature 206-7, 210-2, 214, 218-21
Children's Theatre (Website) 128
China 168, 249
China, Art of (Website) 118
Chris Rywalt's game 8
Citing Electronic Information, Guide for (Website) 84
Cities 173-7
CityLink, US (Website) 173, 175
CityNet (Website) 173, 175
CityNet World Map - Virtual Tourist II (Website) 249

CitySpace (Website) 173, 177
Civil Rights Museum (Website) 257
Civil War 189-90
Classifying information 73, 75
Classroom Connect (Website) 34
Classroom Connect's Fun Links (Website) 5
Classroom projects 37
Clip art 42-3
CNN Weather (Website) 150
Coast Guard, US 252
Cockroach Lady, Ask Betty the (Website) 78
Cockroach World (Website) 157, 159
Collections 14-6
College Board Exams (Website) 226
Cologne, Germany 173
Colonial America 187-8
Colonial Williamsburg 187-8
Color 164-5
Color Landforms (Website) 244
Colorado 178, 182
Colorado History Page (Website) 288
Comets (Website) 144
Community of Inventors (Website) 296
Compare / contrast information 81-3
Composing Good HTML (Website) 87
Composing music 124
Composers, classic music 126
Computer Clubhouse (Website) 37
Computer Games 17
Condoms and Safe Sex (Website) 97
Conflict and resolution 99
ConflictNet (Website) 99
Conservation 50, 160
Constitution, US 182, 203
Continents and countries 167-72
Continuum (Website) 256
Cooking 229
Cooking Light (Website) 229
Cool Links for Kids, Tessa's (Lists of Lists) 12, 72
Copy Editing Ideas (Website) 226
Copyright Information (Website) 84

Cork City, Ireland 173
Costanoan-Ohlone Indian Canyon Resource Page (Website) 198
Courts, Federal (Website) 201
Courts, US (Website) 201
Courtship and Pairing 104-5
Crafts 17
Crayola Site (Website) 5, 118
Creative writing 39
Creativity (Website) 302
Creativity Web Page (Website) 296, 300
Cree Indians (Website) 198
Crime 99-100
Criminal Justice 99
Crisis, Grief, and Healing (Website) 101
Crossword puzzles 6
Crystals 154
C-SPAN (Website) 201
Cultural Connections (Website) 244
Cultural diversity 256-60
Cultural Entomology 157-8
Currency converter 251
Customs 195-6
CyberCitations (Website) 84
CyberKids (Website) 5, 37-8, 89
CyberKids Interactive (Website) 24-5, 238
CyberPet (Website) 54-5
CyberSeas Treasure Hunt (Website) 5
CyberTrail (Website) 87
CyberWest (e-magazine) 181
CyberWest (Website) 181
Cycling (see Bicycles)
Cytoskeleton 154
Cytotoxic T lymphocyte 154

Dahl, Roald (Website) 207
Darwin, Charles 155
Dave's Story (Website) 139
da Vinci, Leonardo (Website) 297-8
Dawey, Darrell 259
Dead Inventor's Corner (Website) 296, 301
Death and dying 101, 105
Death penalty 99

Index

de Bono, Edward 300
Declaration of Independence 182, 201
Deep-sea diving 266, 269
Democratic Party Page (Website) 201
Desert Project (Website) 136
Deserts 163
Design 296, 302
Design, On (Website) 87
Diabetes 102
Dickinson, Emily (Website) 207
Dictionary, Math 129
Dietician, Ask the (Website) 103
Dinosaurs 56-8
Dinousaur Story (Website) 219
Disaster information sites 270
Disaster Links (Website) 270
Disaster Preparation (Website) 270
Discover Magazine (Website) 132
Discovery Channnel (Website) 135
Disney 15, 62
Distance between two locations 173, 175, 244
Diving (see Deep sea diving)
Divorce 104-5
Dodoland in CyberSpace (Website) 218
Dogs 55
Dole 5 A Day (Website) 229, 233
Dolls 14, 16
Dolphins 266
Domestic violence 94
Drew, Nancy (Website) 211
Drew, Richard 299
Dr. Suess 209
Drug abuse 108-9

Eagle 49-50
Earhart, Amelia 182
Earthquakes 270-1, 273
Earthquakes (Website) 273
Earthquake Animation (Website) 271
Earth science 136-7, 140, 147-52
Earth Scientist, Ask-An (Website) 78
Eating disorders 103

E.coli 154
Ecology 160
EconNet: Water (Website) 147
Economics 204
Edge (Website) 89
Edison, Thomas (Website) 296
Editorial guidelines 89
Egypt (Website) 280
Egypt, Writings of Ancient (Website) 191, 279
Egyptian Art and Archaeology (Website) 142, 281
Egyptian gods (Website) 281
Einet Galaxy (Website) 248
Einstein, Albert 296
Einstein Online (Website) 165
Eldercare 95-96
Elder Care Web (Website) 95
Elderhoste 196
Electronic Books, Sources of (Website) 206
Electronic communications 33
Electronic Frontier Canada (Website) 228
Electronic Garden, The (Website) 161
Electronic Newstand (Website) 89
Elementary student pages 37-8
Elements of Style (Website) 225-6
Ellis Island Virtual Museum (Website) 256
El Nino Watch (Website) 271
Email 30-3
Email address 30
Email KeyPal Connection (Website) 238
Emerson and Thoreau 264
Emigration/immigration 256
Emoticons (see Smilies)
Emotional Support Guide (Website) 101
ENC (Eisenhower) (Website) 132
Encyclopedia Mystica (Website) 217
Endangered species 48
Energy 165-6
Energy scavenger hunt (Website) 304
Energy Quest (Website) 165, 304
Engineering projects 303
England 173

English 227
English Server (Website) 206, 226
English Resources (Website) 226
English Teachers Resource (Website) 206
Entertainment 13
Entomology, cultural 157
Envirolink (Website) 274, 277
Environment 147-8
Environment, Our (Thematic unit) 261-78
Environmental awareness lessons 274
Environmental Protection Agency (Website) 132
ERIN, Australia (Website) 274
ESPNet SportZone (Website) 22
Europe 168
Evaluate your project 91-2
Evergreen Dispatch (Website) 277
Excuse Generator (Website) 227
Explore a fish tank (Website) 266
Exploration and Development (Thematic unit) 278-94
Exploration and Development of Space, Students for (Website) 289
Exploratorium (Website) 132, 303
Explorer, The Avid (Website) 248
Explorers (Website) 279
Explorer Home Page (Website) 129
Ezines (See also Online magazines) 88-9, 223

Families Lessons (Website) 256
Family, family relationships (Website) 104
Family and Genealogy (Website) 256
Family Violence Prevention Fund (Website) 94
Family home pages / websites 35
Family Surfboard (Website) 12
Fairytales 214
Federal Aviation Administration (FAA) 252
Federal Bureau of Investigation (FBI website) 99-100, 202

Federal Courts (Website) 201
Federal Highway Administration (FHWA) 252
Federal Law and Information Page (Website) 201
Federal Railroad Administration (FRA) 252
Federal Transit Administration (FTA) 252
FedWorld Government Inforamtion (Website) 201
File user responsibility 33
Finance Net (Website) 204
Financial magazines online 204
Finland 167
FINS: Everything you want to know about fish (Website) 266
First Aid Online (Website) 232
First family (White House website) 256
Fish 44, 46, 266, 269
Fishing 20
Fermi Lab (Website) 165
Ferrets 54
Figure skating 20, 22
FishNet (Website) 223
Five (5) W's & H 68, 71
Flags (Website) 5
Flags, US 178
Flash (Website) 89
Fleming, Sir Alexander 298
Flies 155
Floods 271
Florida 178, 249
Flying Machines (Website) 249
Folklife, Center for (Website) 195
Folklore 195-6, 217
Folklore Folk, Ask-The (Website) 78
Folk Song Database, Traditional (Website) 125
Folktales 214
Forests (see also national forests, trees) 274
Fort William Henry (Website) 193
Foster parenting 104-5
Four Mile Run Project (Website) 147-8

1492 (Website) 284
Fourth World Documentation Project (Website) 198
France 123, 168, 174, 176
Franklin, Benjamin 298-9
French-English dictionary 176
French & Indian War (Website) 193
French painting 118
Frogs 54
Frog dissection 153
Frost, Robert 264
Fruit flies 155-6
Fruits 162
FTP (file transfer protocol) 33
Fun and games (Website) 5-6
Fun and games 8, 17-9, 26
Fun links, Classroom Connect's (Website) 5
Funny poems 215
Fusion 165
Future Place (Website) 62
FUTURES II: Teacher's Guide (Website) 129

Galileo (Website) 298
Gallery 291, 293
Gallery of the Frontier (Website) 284
Gallup Poll (Website) 73, 76
Games 5-6, 8, 17-8, 26
Games, math 129
Games and riddles 265
Gangs 99-100
Garbage 27
Garden, robot-controlled 302
Gardens 161
Garden Net (Website) 161
Garden, butterfly 160
Gems (Website) 136
Gender 113
Genealogy 256-8
General Government Links (Website) 201
General Music Guide (Website) 124
General science 132
Genetics 155-6

Geography Forum (Website) 129
Geography game 26
Geologist, Ask-A (Website) 78
Geology 56, 136, 139
Germany 173
Getting Around the Planet (Website) 248, 251
Girl Interwire (Website) 223
Global Community, Our (Thematic unit) 237-60
Global Community Project (Website) 241
Global Network Navigator (Website) 248
Global Positioning (Website) 244
Global Show & Tell (Website) 37, 41, 90
Global youth dialog (Kidlink) 77, 79
Globes (Website) 244, 246
GNN Traveler's Guide (Websites) 248
Go Ask Alice (Medical Expert Website) 78
Good Health Web (Website) 229
Goosebumps (Website) 210-1
GOP Online (Website) 201
GORP - Great Outdoor Recreation Page (Website) 142, 248, 262-3
Government 201-3
Government Documents, Historical (Website) 279
Goya, Francisco 118
Graffiti wall 26
Grains 162
Grammer Rock (Website) 227
Grand Canyon 262
Grand Canyon Trip Planner (Website) 249
Great American Smoke Scream (Website) 107
Great Barrier Reef (Website) 266
Great Globe Gallery (Website) 246
Great Lakes Regional Indian Network (Website) 197
Great Minority Inventors (Website) 296
Great Sioux Nation (Website) 197
Greece 168
GREEN: Global Rivers Environmental Education Network (Website) 147

Grief 101
Grin's Message (Website) 218
Grolier, Crossword puzzles by (Website) 6
Grolier Online (Website) 139
Grooves Online Music Magazine (Website) 124, 126
Gun Control (Website) 99

Haiku (Website) 215
Hawaii 178
Health and fitness 93, 95-8, 102-12, 229-34
Health and Fitness WorldGuide (Website) 229, 234
Health Care of Elderly (Website) 95
Health Living Ezine (Website) 231
Healthtouch (Website) 229, 231
Heart, The (Website) 229
Heart, human 153
Heretical Rhyme Generator (Website) 227
Hieroglyphs 281
High School Central (Website) 223
Highway Administration, Federal (FHWA) 252
Highway information sources 249
Highway Traffic Safety Administration, National (NHTSA) 252
Historical Almanack 188
Historical government documents (Website) 191, 279
(History website) Ask-The-Curator 78
History 279-80
History, American 182, 284
History, Australia 171
History, California 182, 288
History, Celtic, Scottish, Anglo-Saxon, Welsh, and Viking Information (Website) 191
History, Colorado 182, 288
History, Indiana 182
History, Kansas City 184
History, Library of Congress 182
History of Mathematics (Website) 129
History, New Jersey 182

History of the Northwest Coast of the United States (Website) 288
History of Rock and Roll (Website) 124
History, Russian 191, 279
History, Texas 288
History, US 186-90
Hobbies (See also Crafts, Fun, games, recreation, sports) 17-8
Hodgson, Peter 298
Holidays 6, 13
Hole Dewey Dug, The (Website) 218
Holocaust 192
Homelessness 239
Hometown Free Press (Search engine) 72
HomeWork Page (Lists of Lists) 12, 72
Homework hotlines 28
Hong Kong 168
Horticulture 161
Hotlist: Kids Did This! (Website) 37, 90
Hot wheels 14
Housing 253-5
HTML language 87
HTML Guide 87
HUB Math/Science (Website) 132
Huck Finn (Website) 216
Human Rights Page (Website) 93, 239, 243
Hungary 168, 173
Hurricane 151, 270
HUT Internet Writing Project (Website) 241
Hydrology 147, 149
HyperStudio Projects (Student productions for downloading) 37

Iceland 168
Icon Science (Website) 133
Idaho 178
Identify audience 88
I Live On A Raft (Website) 215
Illinois in the Civil War (Website) 189
Illuminated manuscript (Les Tres Riches Heures of the Duc de Berry) 118
Illustrator, medical (see also Medical Illustrators) 153

Index

Image Gallery (Website) 293
Imagine, investigate, invent (Thematic unit) 295-304
Immigration 256, 260
Impact of earthquakes on people 273
Impressionist art 118
Inappropriate humor 7
Inca Exchange Center 287
Index to Native American Studies (Website) 197
India 168, 173
Indiana 182
Indigenous People's Literature (Website) 197
Info Zone (Website) 85, 91-92
Information resources 72
Information-rich projects 64-65
Information Skills Rating System 91
Information SuperLibrary (Website) 88
Inklings 224
Ink Spot - Authors Page (Website) 206
Insects 46, 144, 157-8
Intellicast 151
Intercultural Email Classroom Connections (Website) 24, 29, 238
International E Club (Website) 24
International Kids Space (Website) 6, 24, 27, 40, 90
International Simulations Page (Website) 239, 242
Internet Citations (Website) 84
Internet search tools 68, 72
Internet sleuth (search engine) 72
Internet Underground Music Archive (Website) 24
Inventor, Be An (Website) 299
Inventors 296-7
Inventors Site (Website) 296, 298
Invention and Design (Website) 296, 302
Invention Dimension (Website) 296, 301
Invention Lesson Plans (Website) 296
Invention, Psychology of (Website) 296

Inventure Place: Inventor's Hall of Fame (Website) 296
Iowa 189
Iran 173
Ireland 168, 173
Isfahan, Iran 173
Israel 168
Italy 168, 173-4

Jackson's Page for Five Year Olds (Website) 6
James, Richard 298
Japan 34, 169, 173, 239, 270
Jason Project 266, 270, 274
Jazz music 125
Jean Piaget Society (Website) 205
Jefferson, Thomas 182
Jokes 10
Jorvic Viking Center (Website) 279, 282
Journal Writing (Website) 67
Journey to Beijing (Website) 249
Justice Information (Website) 99
Juvenile Justice (Website) 99

Kangaroo 172
Kansas 178
Kansas City 184
Karate 20-21
Kathy Schrock's Lists of Lists (Website) 12-13, 17, 59, 66, 72
Kathy Schrock's Evaluation Page (For webpages) 77, 80
Kathy Schrock's Health and Fitness List (Website) 229
Keating's Peer Evaluation 91
Kelsey's On-line Museum (Website) 191
Kensington Runestone (Website) 282
Keyboard symbols 30
Key pal 26
Kidopedia (Website) 90
KidsCom (Website) 6, 12, 24, 26
Kid's Corner (Website) 6
Kid's Crambo Games (Website) 6

KidKash Questions 26
Kidlink (see also Global Youth Dialog) 91
Kid Lit Page (Website) 206
Kid's Net (Website) 6
Kid News (Website) 37, 39, 90
KidPub (Website) 37, 90
Kids on the Web, The (Website) 12
Kid's Page, Uncle Bob's (Lists of Lists) 12, 72
Kid's Page Mail Office (Website) 24, 238
Kid's Place, The (Website) 24, 238
Kids Space (Website) 177
KidsWeb (Website) 12, 35
Kids Web - Math (Website) 129
KidzMagazine (Website) 89
KidzPage (Website) 215, 218
King, Martin Luther Jr. 182
King, Stephen (Websites) 213
Kinship and Social Organizations (Website) 195
Koala 172
Kookaburra 172
Krannert Art Museum (Website) 118
K-12 CyberTrail (Website) 34
K-12 online space projects 289
K-12 school weather project 150
Kyoto, Japan 173

LaughLink, The (Website) 10
Launchpad (Website) 34, 59, 238
Law 201-3
Learner-centered projects 64-65
Legislative information, issues 201, 203
Lego 17
Leipzig, Germany 173
Lesson ideas on inventions 296
Lesson plans 266
Lessons and Appetizers for Math (Website) 129
Lessons, environmental awareness 274
Les Tres Riches Heures of the Duc de Berry 118
Letters from an Iowa Solder (Website) 189

Lewis, CS (Websites) 207, 212
Library of Congress 182, 186, 203, 284
Library of Music Links (Website) 124
Light 164-6
Life Education Network (Website) 93, 239
Life Science 153-63
LinkUp (Website for secondary students' projects) 37-8
Listserv 33
Lists of Lists 12, 72
Lite Brite Online (Website) 6
Literature 206-17
Literature, American history 182
Literature, Children's (Website) 206-7, 210-2, 214, 218-21
Literature, Indigenous People's (Website) 197
Literature Land (Website) 222
Literature, Loss of Innocence in (Website) 93
Literature, Abuse of Power in (Website) 93
Literature, Visit the wilderness through 264
Literature, Women Studies through (Website) 113
Llama 45, 48
Lords of the Earth (Website) 287
Lorikeets 172
Los Angeles River (Website) 147-8
Loss of Innocence in Literature 93
Louvre 123
Lovell, Jim 289
Lufthansa (Website) 248
Lumiere Brothers 298

Macrophage, human 154
Madeline's Books (Website) 219
Madras, India 173
Magazines 13, 133, 223
Magazines, student 38
Magic 19
Mailing lists 33
Maine 178, 180
Make a Robot Move (Website) 302

Index

Making maps and map words 244, 247
Making the Most of the Web (Website) 87
Mammals (see also animals) 45-6
Mapmaker, Mapmaker, Make Me a Map (Website) 247
Maps 184, 194, 244, 248, 251
Maps, Canadian 244
Maps Lessons (Website) 244
Maps, US (Website) 244
Maritime Administration (MARAD) 252
Marriage and Family (Website) 104
Massachussetts, Plymoth 182
Mathematics 129-32
Mathematics history 129
Mayan Adventure (Website) 191, 284
Maya Exchange Center 287
Maya Quest (Website) 191, 284
Medical expert website 78
Medical Illustrators (Website) 153, 232
Medicare 96
Medieval Europe 282
Medieval Studies (Website) 192
MendalWeb (Website) 155
Mental Health Net (Website) 93
Mentoring 28
Meso-American Exchange Center 287
Metacognition map 68, 70
Methyl bromide 141
Mexico 169
Mexico and Central America (Website) 239
Michigan 178, 239
Microbes 154
MicrobeZoo (Website) 153
Microbial Underground (Website) 153
Microbiology 153
Middle East 169
Middle schools 12, 34, 37-8, 238, 239
Middle School Student Project (Website) 144
MidLink Magazine (Webmagazine for Middle school students) 37-8, 89
Milan, Italy 173

Military 202
Mind map 81, 300
MindTools (Website) 84
Mineral Gallery (Website) 139
Minnesota 34, 178
Minority Inventors, Great (Website) 296
Missions, California (Website) 284
Missouri 178
Missouri Botanical Garden (Website)1 63, 245
MLA Style Guide (Website) 84
Moby Dick 264
Mock Trial (Website) 202
Model trains 17
Monarch butterfly 158, 160
Money - Australia (Website) 130-1
Monterey Bay Aquarium 269
Montgomery, L.M. (Websites) 212
Monticello - Thomas Jefferson (Website) 182
Motorcycles 20
Morocco 169
Mountain biking 17, 23
Mount St. Helen's 272
Movies (entertainment films) 61
Mr. Edible Starchy Tuber Head (Website) 8
Multicultural sites 256-60
Multimedia Minerals Site (Website) 139
Multiple generation families 105
Multiple intelligences (Gardner's) 63
Muppets 14
Museums 133, 184, 191, 256-7, 297-8
Music 124-7
Music (Australia) 171
Mutant Fruit Flies (Website) 156
My Blue Suitcase (Website) 219
Myths 195-6
Mythology and Folklore (Website) 217

Names Project: Quilts Memorial (Website) 97
NASA Homepage (see also Spacelink)(Website) 291

National AIDS Clearinghouse, CDC (Website) 97
National Clearinghouse for Drug and Alcohol Abuse (Website) 108
National Highway Traffic Safety Administration (NHTSA) 252
National Institue on Alcohol Abuse and Alcoholism (Website) 109
National Institute on Drug Abuse (Website) 108
National Museum of American Art (Website) 119
National Museum of the American Indian (Website) 197
National Osteoporosis Foundation (Website) 95
National forests and parks 181, 262
National Science Museum (Website) 133
National Severe Storms Laboratory (Website) 271
National Wildlife Federation (Website) 44, 262, 265
Native American Center (Website) 197
Native American Culture Home Page (Website) 197
Native Americans 197-200, 287-8
NativeWeb Home Page (Website) 197
Nature Links (Website) 44
Nebraska 179
Nepal 169
NetChick Clubhouse (Website) 223
Net Contacts (Website) 24, 28, 238
Net Full of Animals (Website) 48
Netherlands 169
Netiquette 31
NetNoir (Website) 259
Neverending Tale (Website) 218
New Hampshire 179
New Jersey 182
"New Stuff For Kids" 26
Newton's Apple (Website) 133, 135
Newton, Sir Isaac 298

New Zealand 169
Newspapers 13
Newspapers and publications (student productions) 37-9
Nikolai's Web Site 6
Nine Planets: Earth (Website) 136
Noonie (Website) 218
Nonprofit Profits (Website) 85-6
Nonviolence Resources (see also Peacenet) (Website) 99
Nordic Pages (Website) 169
North Carolina 179
Northwest Coast US, History of (Website) 288
Nuclear energy 165
Nutrition (see also Health and fitness) 233

Objectivity 77
Observation 67
Oceania (Website) 266
Oceanography (Website) 267
Oceans (Website) 266-7
Ocean Links (Website) 266
Office of Air and Radiation (Website) 140
Ohio in the Civil War (Website) 189
Omniscience futureneering 303
On Design (Website) 87
Oneida Indian Nation (Website) 197
Online Children's Stories (Website) 218
Online magazines 88-9, 133
Online Magazines for Kids (Website) 89
Online magazines for students 37-9
Online Writery, The (Website) 84
Ontario Science Museum 133
OpticsNet (Website) 164
Oral Histories (Website) 195
Oregon 179
Oregon Trail Information Center (Website) 182, 184
Organize information 81
Origin of the species 155
Ornithopter Home Page (Website) 303

Osteoporosis 95
Outdoors (see GORP)
Oxford, England 173
Ozone 140-1
OZ Page (Website) 206

Padua, Italy 174
Paleontology 56
Paper airplanes 303
Parasites 154
Parenting 104-5
Parents and Children Together Online (Website) 220
Paris, France 174, 176
Parks (see national parks)
Parrots 49
Particle physics 164, 166
PeaceNet (Website) 93, 99-100
Peace in Pictures (Website) 37
Pemberton, John 298
Penicillin 154
Pennsylvania 179
Pen Pal Connections (Website) 24
Pen pals (E-pals) (see also Teacher to teacher connections) 24, 26-7
Peregrine Fund, the (Website) 50
Perseus Project (Website) 142
Pets 26, 44, 54-5
Phagocytosis 154
Photography 118
Physical Science 164-6
Physics 164, 166
Piaget, Jean 205
Pioneers, African-American (Website) 256
Pioneers, women 113
Piracy & Pirates (Website) 279, 283
Place for Math Resources 130
Planet Earth Home Page (Website) 167, 226
Planned Parenthood Online (Website) 111
Plant life 161-3, 171
Plumbing 166
Plymouth, MA (Website) 182

Poe, Edgar Allen (Website) 207, 264
Poetry 215, 227
Poetry by kids 215
Poetry Garden (Website) 215
Poets (Website) 206-7
Poland 169
Political parties 201
Political science 201-3
Polls and surveys 27, 259
Poseidon Project, TOPEX (Website) 266
Potatohead, Mr. (see Mr. Edible Starchy Tuber Head)
Pregnancy (Website) 111-2
Presidential candidates 210
Presidents of the US 185
Press Return (Website) 37, 90
Princeton's Mythology Page (Website) 217
Products, student 3, 85
Project-based learning 63-65
Project evaluation 91
Project on Death in America (Website) 101
Projects 5
Projects K-12 on space 289
Project Watch (Website) 37
Psychology 93, 205
Psychology of Invention (Website) 296
Psych Web (Website) 205
Public Affairs Hot List: Individuals, Parties, Special Interests (Website) 201
Public opinion polls (see Gallup Poll)
Publishing on the Web 88-90
Pueblo Cultural Center (Website) 197
Puppets Page (Website) 6
Puzzles 5
Pyogenes, group A 154
Pyramid (Website) 279

Quilt analogy 81
Quilts memorial (Names Projects) 97
Quotations, Bartlett's Familiar (Website) 225

Rabbits 54
Raccoons 47
Racing, Indy / car (see auto racing)
Railroad Administration, Federal (FRA) 252
RailServer (Website) 249
Raindrop (Website) 101
Rainforest Action Network (Website) 274
React (Webmagazine for secondary students) 37-8, 89, 223
Reader's Theatre Scripts (Website) 128
Reading 218-22
Reading and Writing, Tools for (Website) 84
Realist Wonder Society (Website) 218
Recreation 5, 181
Recycling 27
Reed Interactive Subject Guide (Website) 130
Reference / research / library research materials 72, 92
Relevance 77
Reliability 77
Reproductive Health Center, Atlanta (Website) 111
Reptiles 45-6
Republican party 201
Research & Special Programs Administration (RSPA) 252
Research Ship (Website) 266
Resources for young writers 224
Retirement 96
Reverse Link (Website) 223
Revolution to reconstruction 186
Riddles 10
Rio de Janeiro, Brazil 174
Rivers 147-8
Roaches 157, 159
Robots 142, 302-3
Rockhounds 136, 139
Rodeo 20, 22
Rock and roll 124, 127

Rock & Roll Hall of Fame & Museum (Website) 127
Roses 161
Rules for Internet 33
Run a Robotic Telescope (Website) 302
Runestone, Kensington (Website) 282
Runic font 282
Russian History (Website) 191, 279

Safari Splash (Website) 266
Safety Net (Website) 94
Safe sex 97
Sailing Page (Website) 249
Sample student products 3, 37-8
Savory Gallery (art) 259
Savory Poll 259
Schoolhouse Project (Lists of Lists) 12, 72
Schoolhouse Rock - America (Website) 191
Schoolhouse Rock - Math (Website) 130
Schoolhouse Rock - Science Rock (Website) 132
School pages / sites 34, 239
Schrock's (Kathy) Website (see Kathy Schrock's Lists of Lists)
Science, earth 136-7, 140, 147-52
Science fiction 293
Science, life (See Life Science)
Science, physical (See Physical Science)
Science, space 136-7, 140, 147
Scotland 169
Scottish history 191, 279
Scripts, Reader's Theatre 128
Search engines 72, 92
Searching the Net (Website) 92
Seattle, WA 174
Sea World (Website) 44, 51, 53, 266
Sea World Alerts (Website) 274
Secondary student pages 37-8
Seeds 162
Seeds of Life (Website) 162
Select information 81
Self Help and Psychology (Website) 93, 205

Index

Seven Effective Steps to Library Research 92
(Seven) 7 Wonders of the World (Website) 279
Sexual Assault (Website) 99
Shakespeare, William (Websites) 207, 213
Share and collaborate 77
Show-n-Tell (see Global Show-n-Tell)
Silent Witness (Website) 94
'Silly surfin' sites' 5-6
'Silly' projects 7
Silver, Spencer 298
Single parenting 104-5
Sistine Chapel, The (Website) 119
Skeleton, human 153
Slash (Website) 89
Slovenija 169
Slummit (Website) 223
Smilies 30
Smog 141
Smoky Mountains 262
Smoking 107-9
Snow 152
Social Activism 88
Social issues 93-114
Social Services for Teens (Website) 93
Socks 9
Solar system 144, 146
Sound 164-5
Sounds, animal 44
Sources of Electronic Books (Website) 206
Sources of Highway Information (Website) 249
South America 169
South America (Website) 239
South Carolina 179
South Dakota 179
Space exploration 289-92
SpaceLink (Website) 292
Space science 136, 140-1, 147, 289-92
Spank Zine (Website) 223
Speculative fiction 293
Speeches 194

Spiders 157
Spider's Picks (Website) 5
Spirograph (Website) 6, 130-1
Splash Kids (Website) 6
Sports 20-2, 39, 171
Sports medicine 234
Star Child (Website) 289-90
Stars and Stripes 194
Star Trek 15
States, US 178
Statistics 129
Statistics, divorce 104
Stine, R.L. 210
Stone age 195
Stone Company (Website) 139
Stories 5
Stories, African 259
Stories, Online Children's (Website) 218
Storms 271
Storyhour Page (Website) 221
Storyweb (Website) 218
Stranger than Fiction (Website) 223
Stratosphere Ozone (Website) 140-1
String figures 17
Student art projects 119, 121
Students for the Exploration and Development of Space (Website) 289
Student home pages / websites 35-6
Student ezines (electronic magazines) 89
Student products, sample 3
Student project on conservation 274, 277
Student project on hurricane 270
Student project on jet aircraft 249
Student project on skycrapers 253
Student project on whales and dolphins 266
Student project on marine life 266
Student publications 90
Student science projects 133, 147
Students write about earthquake impact 270
Study, Research, & Writing Tools (Website) 84

Style Guide, MLA (Website) 84
Study Skills 92
Substance abuse 107-9
Subway Navigator (Website) 173, 248
Suess, Dr. (Websites) 207, 209
Sugar glider 172
Suicide 110
Susie's Place (Website) 227
Symbols, keyboard 30

Tales of Wonder (Website) 214, 218
Tampa Bay Aquarium 48
Teacher to teacher connections 28-9
Teachers, music 124
Teddy bears 14
Teen magazines online 223
Teen Page (Website) 223
Teen pregnancy 111-2
Teen resources 223
Teen Zine (Website) 223
Tele-garden (Website) 161
Telescopes (Website) 144
Telnet protocol 33
Tennessee 179
Tessa's Cool Links for Kids (see Cool Links for Kids)
Texas 34, 179, 253
Texas History Page (Website) 288
Texas River Project (Website) 147
Tobie Wan Kenobi 26
Theatre 128
Theme development / webbing 73-4
Theme parks 62
This Old House (Website) 255
Thomas Banchoff's Project List (Website) 130
Thomas Site (Website) 203
Thoreau, Henry D. 162, 264
Tibetan Mandala Archive 119
Timeline, Civil War 189
Time Tag (Website) 218
Tobacco 107-9
Tolkien, J.R.R. (Websites) 207

TOPEX/Poseidon Project (Website) 266
Topicing 69
Tossed Salad (Website) 229, 233
Toy Story (Website) 8
Traditions 195-6
Traffic Site (Website) 248
Transit Administration, Federal (FTA) 252
Transitional Maths Project (Website) 130
Translate into hieroglyphs 281
Transportation 248-50
Transportation & the Environment (Website) 249
Transportation Statistics, Bureau of (BTS) 252
Travel agencies 48
Travel & Leisure (Magazine website) 251
Travel and tourism 13, 184, 248-51
Trees (see also Forests) 171
Tree of Life (Website) 274
Tribal Voice (Website) 197
Tubman, Harriet 182
Twain, Mark (Websites) 207, 216
24 Hours of Democracy (Website) 228

Uncle Bob's Kid's Page (see Kid's Page)
Underwater World (Website) 266, 269
Unicycling 20
United Nations 167, 239, 242
University Council on Water Resources (Website) 147
USA Today Hydrology Page (Website) 149
USA Today Weather (Website) 150
US Census Bureau (Website) 204
US Coast Guard 252
US Courts (Website) 201, 203
US Dept of Transportation (Website) 249, 252
Useless Pages (Website) 5
US Fish and Wildlife (Website) 44
US Geological Survey (Website) 136, 138, 247
Using a Map and Compass (Website) 244
Using Search Engines (Website) 92

Utah 179

Vatican (Website) 191
Vegemite 171
Vermeer, Paintings of (Website) 119
Vermont 179
Vid Page (Website) 37
Vietnam 169
Views of the Solar System (Website) 144
Viking Center, Jorvic (Website) 279, 282
Vikings 191, 279
Viking History (Website) 279
Violence 94, 99-100
Virtual field trips 244
Virtual FlyLab (Website) 155
Virtual Garden (Website) 161, 163
Virtual Kitchen (Website) 229
Virtual Tourist (Website) 167
Virtual Tourist II 249
Virtual Zoo (Website) 51
Virus 154
Visions of Liberty (Website) 240
Visual human (Website) 153
Vocal Point (Website) 90
Voices on Adoption (Website) 111
Volcanoes 270-2
VolcanoesWorld (Website) 272
Volcano in Hawaii, Jason Project (Website) 270
Vote Smart Web (Website) 202

W's, the new eight (for information exploration) 64-8, 73, 77, 81 83, 85, 88, 91
Wacky Web Tales (Website) 11
Wangaratta, AU (Website) 172
Warhol, Andy (Website) 118
Warner Brothers (Website) 15
Warner Brothers Jazzspace (Website) 125
Washington Park Zoo, Metro (Website) 51
Washington (State) 179
'Watching' (Observe environment) 64-7
Waterlilies 161
Water 147-9

Water pollution 27
Water Travel (Website) 249
'Wave Rider' file 7
'Waving" (Publishing a project) 64-5, 88-90
Weather 13, 150-1, 251, 270-1
'Weaving' (Application and synthesis of information) 65-6, 81
'Webbing' (Locating information and connecting ideas) 65-6, 73
WebCrawler (Search engine) 72
Web Developer's Virtual Library (Website) 87
WebMuseum (Website) 119
Web page development 36, 87
Web page evaluation 77, 80
Web pubishing 88-90
Web66 (Website) 34, 238
Webtime Stories (Website) 221
Web Wonk: Tips for Web Writers 87
Welfare and Families (Website) 104
Welsh history 191, 279
West (US) 181-2, 184
West, Wild (Website) 284
Wetlands (Website) 274
Wetlands Project 265
Whales 48, 266
Whales Adoption Project (Website) 266
Whales Thematic Unit (Website) 266
"What Do Ya Think?" 26
'What Ifing' 81, 83
What's It Like Where You Live? (Website) 244
White blood cells 154
White House: First Family (Website) 256
Whitman, Walt (Website) 207, 215
'Wiggling' (search for clues, ideas, and perspectives) 64-5, 77
Wilder, Laura Ingalls (Website) 211
Wildflowers, Texas 161
Wildlife (see also animals) 44-53, 184, 262
Wildlife Art (Website) 119
Wild West (Website) 284
Winnie the Pooh 209

Wisconsin 179-80
'Wishing' (Reflect on the project) 64-5, 91-2
'Wondering' (Exploring ideas) 64-5, 68
Woodland Park Zoo (Website) 51
Wolves 45
Women's issues 113
Women's Net (Website) 113
Women Pioneers (Website) 113
Women Studies through Literature (Website) 113
Women Writers (Website) 113
Word games 227
World of Reading (Website) 222
World History 191-2
World Traveller Books and Maps (Website) 248
World War II 194
World Wide Web of Music (Website) 124
'Wrapping' (Packaging ideas, solutions, and communications) 64-5, 85
Wright Brothers 298
Wright, Frank Lloyd (Website) 255
"Write Me A Story" 26
Writers 206-13, 224
Writers, women 113
Writing Lab (Website) 226
Writing resources 84, 224-6
Writings of Ancient Egypt (Website) 191, 279
Writing styles 226
Writing Tools (Website) 84
Wyoming 179-80

Xerox PARC (Website) 247

Yahoo's Country List (Website) 167
Yahoo Clip Art (Website) 42
Yahoo Math Sites (Website) 130
Yahoo Zoo List (Website) 51
Yahooligans (Search engine) 72
Yahooligans (Website) 12, 37, 72, 167
Yahooligans Guide to Newspaper and Publications for Kids (Website) 89
Yahooligans-History 191
YesMag (Website) 89
Young Inventors 296
Young Inventor's Site, Canadian (Website) 296
Yo: Youth Outlook (Website) 223
Yucatan, Mexico 169

Zeen (Website) 89
Zia's Clip Art (Website) 42
Zoological Email Directory (Website) 51
ZooNet (Website) 44, 51-2
Zoos (see also Animals) 44, 51-2